Supernetworks

NEW DIMENSIONS IN NETWORKS

Series Editor: Anna Nagurney, *John F. Smith Memorial Professor, Isenberg School of Management, University of Massachusetts at Amherst, USA*

Networks provide a unifying framework for conceptualizing and studying problems and applications. They range from transportation and telecommunication networks and logistic networks to economic, social and financial networks. This series is designed to publish original manuscripts and edited volumes that push the development of theory and applications of networks to new dimensions. It is interdisciplinary and international in its coverage, and aims to connect existing areas, unveil new applications and extend existing conceptual frameworks as well as methodologies. An outstanding editorial advisory board made up of scholars from many fields and many countries assures the high quality and originality of all of the volumes in the series.

Supernetworks

Decision-Making for the Information Age

Anna Nagurney
University of Massachusetts at Amherst, USA

June Dong
SUNY Oswego, USA

NEW DIMENSIONS IN NETWORKS

Edward Elgar
Cheltenham, UK • Northampton, MA, USA

Published by
Edward Elgar Publishing Limited
Glensanda House
Montpellier Parade
Cheltenham
Glos GL50 1UA
UK

Edward Elgar Publishing, Inc.
136 West Street
Suite 202
Northampton
Massachusetts 01060
USA

Coventry University

A catalog record for this book
is available from the British Library

ISBN 1 84064 968 2

Printed and bound in Great Britain by MPG Books Ltd, Bodmin, Cornwall

Editorial Board

Janny Leung, Associate Professor, Department of Systems Engineering and Engineering Management, The Chinese University of Hong Kong, Hong Kong

Lars-Goran Mattsson, Professor and Chair, Division of Systems Analysis and Economics, Royal Institute of Technology (KTH), Stockholm, Sweden

Patricia L. Mokhtarian, Professor, Department of Civil and Environmental Engineering, University of California, Davis, USA

Panos Pardalos, University Professor, Department of Systems and Industrial Engineering, University of Florida, Gainesville, USA

Padma Ramanujam, Product Manager, i2 Technologies, Inc, Dallas, Texas, USA

Mauricio G. C. Resende, Technology Consultant, Algorithms and Optimization Research Department, AT&T Labs Research, Florham Park, New Jersey, USA

Berc Rustem, Professor, Department of Computing, Imperial College of Science, Technology & Medicine London, UK

Les Servi, Member of the Technical Staff, MIT Lincoln Laboratory, Lexington, Massachusetts, USA

Stavros Siokos, Managing Director and Head of Global Portfolio Trading Strategies, Schroder Salomon Smith Barney, London, UK

Katia Sycara, Principal Research Scientist and Professor, School of Computer Science and Director, Advanced Agent Technology Laboratory, Carnegie Mellon University, Pittsburgh, Pennsylvania, USA

Leigh Tesfatsion, Professor of Economics and Mathematics, Department of Economics, Iowa State University, Ames, USA

Andrew B. Whinston, Hugh Cullen Chaired Professor of Information Systems, Economics and Computer Science, Graduate School of Business, University of Texas, Austin, USA

Ding Zhang, Assistant Professor, Department of Management and Marketing, School of Business, State University of New York at Oswego, USA

Contents

List of Figures

List of Tables

Preface

Networks permeate our daily lives, underpinning our economies and societies and provide the infrastructure for business, science, technology, social systems, and education. Transportation networks give us the means to cross physical distance in order to see clients and conduct business, as well as to visit colleagues and friends and to explore new vistas and expand our horizons. They enable manufacturing processes through the supply of the necessary input components and the ultimate distribution of the finished products to the consumers.

Communication networks, in turn, allow us to access and to share data within our communities and across regions and national boundaries and to inform others as well as to be informed. Energy networks help to fuel not only transportation networks but in many settings also communication networks. They provide electricity to run the computers and to light our businesses, oil and gas to heat our homes and to power vehicles, and water for our very survival.

Financial networks supply businesses with the resources to expand, to innovate, and to satisfy the needs of consumers. They allow individuals to invest and to save for the future for themselves and for their children and for governments to provide for their citizens and to develop and enhance communities.

The advent of the Information Age with the increasing availability of new computer and communication technologies, along with the Internet, have transformed the ways in which individuals work, travel, and conduct their daily activities, with profound implications for existing and future networks. Moreover, the decision-making process itself has been altered due to the addition of alternatives and options which were not, heretofore, possible or even feasible. The boundaries for decision-making have been redrawn as individuals can now work from home or purchase products from work. Managers can now locate raw materials and other inputs from suppliers through information networks in order to maximize profits while simultaneously ensuring timely delivery of finished goods. Financing for their businesses can be obtained online. Individuals, in turn, can obtain information about products from their homes and make their purchasing decisions accordingly.

The reality of today's networks include: large-scale nature and complexity, increasing congestion, alternative behaviors of users of the networks, as well as interactions between the networks themselves, notably, between transportation and telecommunication networks. The decisions made by the users of the networks, in turn, affect not only the users themselves but others as well, in terms of profits and costs, timeliness of deliveries, the quality of the environment, etc.

In this book, we lay out the theory of *supernetworks* in order to formalize decision-making in the Information Age. "Super" networks are networks that are "above and beyond" existing networks, which consist of nodes, links, and flows, with nodes corresponding to locations in space, links to connections in the form of roads, cables, etc., and flows to vehicles, data, etc. Supernetworks are conceptual in scope, graphical in perspective, and, with the accompanying theory, predictive in nature.

In particular, we seek to capture, within a unifying framework, decision-making facing a variety of economic agents including consumers and producers as well as distinct intermediaries in the context of today's networked economy. The decision-making process may entail weighting trade-offs associated with the use of transportation versus telecommunication networks. The behavior of the individual agents is modeled as well as their interactions on the complex network systems with the goal of identifying the resulting equilibrium flows and prices.

This book provides the conceptual, analytical, and computational tools for the study of supernetworks. The approach is rigorous and of sufficient generality and detail to give added insight into the behavior and structure of large-scale, interacting and competitive network systems, consisting of numerous agents and alternatives.

This book consists of four parts, with a total of twelve chapters. The first part provides an introduction, discusses the origins of supernetworks, and lays the foundations for their study. Part II then focuses on multitiered supernetworks with applications to supply chain networks with electronic commerce and financial networks with intermediation. Dynamic versions of the models are studied using a multilevel network perspective. Part III turns to multicriteria network equilibrium models and addresses such relevant topics in the Information Age today as: telecommuting versus commuting decision-making, teleshopping versus shopping decision-making, as well as location and transportation decision-making. Part IV describes new directions for supernetworks by providing extensions and syntheses of some of the earlier material in this book.

The intended audience for this book includes students, researchers, and practitioners in economics and business, in computer science, in engineering, and in operations research and management science, who are interested in the formulation, qualitative analysis, application, and computation of complex network systems in the Information Age.

The writing of this book was made possible by the support of several National Science Foundation (NSF) grants. In particular, the authors acknowledge support under NSF Grant No.: IIS-0002647. The first author also acknowledges support under NSF Grant No.: CMS-0085720 and NSF Grant No.: INT-0000309. The authors would like to thank Dr. Suzi Iacono, Director, Computation and Social Systems Program at NSF, for support in this endeavor.

Anna Nagurney would also like to thank Dr. Mark Suskin, Program Manager, Western Europe Program, Division of International Programs, and Dr. Miriam Heller, Program Director, Information Technology for Infrastructure Systems at NSF for support. She also thanks Dr. Rick Adrion, Division Director of Experimental and Integrative Studies, Directorate for Computer and Information Science and Engineering at NSF and Professor of Computer Science at the University of Massachusetts at Amherst for encouragement and supportive conversations.

In addition, Nagurney would like to thank Mr. John F. Smith, Jr., the Chairman of the Board of General Motors, for his support through the John F. Smith Memorial Fund at the Isenberg School of Management at the University of Massachusetts at Amherst.

The writing of this book was initiated while Nagurney was visiting the Royal Institute of Technology (KTH) in Stockholm, Sweden, during the summer of 2001. The hospitality of the host institution and, in particular, the Division of Transport and Location Analysis and the Department of Infrastructure and Planning at KTH are warmly appreciated. The support of Swedish academic colleagues and collaborators, notably, Professors Lars-Goran Mattsson and Lars Lundqvist in this endeavor is recognized.

Dong thanks the Department of Management at the Hong Kong Polytechnic University for giving her the opportunity to visit. In particular, she would like to thank Professors Gerald Fryxell, Edwin Cheng, and Hong Yan for support.

The authors acknowledge the collaborations with Professor Ding Zhang of the State University of New York at Oswego and with Professor Patricia L. Mokhtarian of the University of California at Davis. The first author also thanks Professor Kitty Hancock of the Department of Civil and Environmental Engineering at the University of Massachusetts, Amherst and Dr. Frank Southworth of the Oak Ridge National Laboratory in Tennessee for their collaborations.

The authors acknowledge Professor Ladimer S. Nagurney of the University of Hartford for his technical assistance and Christopher Sullivan and Jose Cruz for their library and web-based research and for their reading of various parts of the manuscript.

The authors are grateful to their families for traveling with them in order to allow for the writing and completion of this book. Anna Nagurney thanks her husband, Ladimer, and daughter, Alexandra, for their support while in Sweden. She also acknowledges the outstanding housing arrangements in Stockholm provided by the Wenner Gren Centre Foundation, which enabled the establishment of new friendships and renewal of old ones with researchers and their families from around the world. June Dong thanks her husband, Ding Zhang, and their children, Alex and Alena, for their support while in China.

The authors are indebted to their home institutions, respectively, the Isenberg School of Management at the University of Massachusetts at Amherst and the School of Business at the State University of New York at Oswego for supportive work environments. The second author thanks SUNY at Oswego for granting her the sabbatical leave.

Finally, the authors acknowledge the contributions of the pioneers of the Internet, since without that network, the writing of this book would have been not only substantially more time-consuming but also not nearly as enjoyable.

Parts of Chapter 9 have appeared in "Urban Location and Transportation in the Information Age: A Multiclass, Multicriteria Network Equilibrium Perspective," A. Nagurney and J. Dong (2002), *Environment & Planning B* **29**, 53-74. Parts of Chapter 10 are forthcoming in "Spatial Economic Networks with Multicriteria Producers and Consumers: Statics and Dynamics," A. Nagurney, D. Zhang, and J. Dong (2002), *Annals of Regional Science*. Parts of Chapter 11 have appeared in "Bicriteria Decision Making and Financial Equilibrium: A Variational Inequality Perspective," J. Dong and A. Nagurney (2001), *Computational Economics* **17**, 29-42. Parts of Chapter 12 have appeared in "Paradoxes in Networks with Zero Emission Links: Implications for Telecommunications versus Transportation," A. Nagurney and J. Dong (2001b), *Transportation Research D* **6**, 283-296.

The authors acknowledge Pion Ltd., the publisher of *Environment & Planning B*, Springer Verlag, the publisher of *Annals of Regional Science*, Kluwer Academic Publishers, the publisher of *Computational Economics*, and Elsevier Science Ltd., the publisher of *Transportation Research D*, for the use of the above material in this book.

Part I Introduction and Foundations

1 Introduction and Overview

Throughout history, networks have served as the foundation for connecting humans to one another and their activities. Roads were laid, bridges built, and waterways crossed so that humans, be they on foot, on animal, or vehicle could traverse physical distance. The airways were conquered through flight. Communications, in turn, were conducted using the available means of the period, from smoke signals, drum beats, and pigeons, to the telegraph, telephone, and computer networks of today.

We live in an era in which the freedom to choose is weighted by the immensity of the number of choices and possibilities: Where should one live? Where should one work? And when? How should one travel? Or communicate? And with whom? Where should one shop? And how? Underlying the numerous choices available is the wealth of information that can be accessed through computer networks. How should businesses avail themselves of the new opportunities made possible through the Information Age? How can they effectively compete? How has the landscape changed for consumers as well?

In this book, we tackle the questions surrounding decision-making in the Information Age today. Our approach is conceptual, graphical, theoretical, and, ultimately, analytical. In particular, in this volume, we present a theory of supernetwork systems, that is, those that are "over and above" existing network systems, based on the visualization of decision-making in the Information Age as a network, oftentimes abstract, and consisting of nodes and links and the associated flows. Importantly, the depiction of decision-making as a network with the synthesis of the networks of interacting decision-makers to create a "supernetwork" adds a graphic dimension to the understanding of the fundamental underlying economic structure of complex network systems and their evolution over time.

Networks thread through our lives, and provide the fabric for our societies and economies and the infrastructure for commerce, science and technology, social systems, and education. Examples of networks which supply the basic foundation for economic and social activity are: transportation, communication, energy, and financial networks.

See Table 1.1, for some basic, classical networks and the associated nodes, links, and flows. By *classical* we mean that the nodes correspond to physical locations in space and the links to physical connections between the nodes.

Transportation networks give us the means to cross physical distance in order to conduct our daily activities. They provide us with access to food as well as to consumer products and come in a myriad of forms: road, air, rail, or waterway. According to the U.S. Department of Transportation, the significance of transportation in dollar value alone as spent by US consumers, businesses, and governments was $950 billion in 1998.

Communication networks, in turn, allow us to communicate with friends and colleagues and to conduct the necessary transactions of life. They, through such innovations as the Internet, have transformed the manner in which we live, work, and conduct business today. Communication networks allow the transmission of voice, data/information, and/or video and can involve telephones and computers, as well as satellites and microwaves. The trade publication *Purchasing* reports that corporate buyers alone spent $517.6 billion on telecommunications goods and services in 1999.

Energy networks, in addition, are essential to the very existence of the *Network Economy* and help to fuel not only transportation networks but in many settings also communication networks. They provide electricity to run the computers and to light our businesses, oil and gas to heat our homes and to power vehicles, and water for our very survival. In 1995, according to the U.S. Department of Commerce, the energy expenditures in the United States were $515.8 billion.

The topic of networks and the management thereof dates to ancient times with such classical examples including the publicly provided Roman road network and the "time of day" chariot policy, whereby chariots were banned from the ancient city of Rome at particular times of day.

The formal study of networks, consisting of nodes, links, and flows involves: how to model such applications (as well as numerous other ones) as mathematical entities, how to study the models qualitatively, and how to design algorithms to solve the resulting models effectively. The study of networks is necessarily interdisciplinary in nature due to their breadth of appearance and is based on scientific techniques from applied mathematics, computer science, and engineering with applications as varied as finance and even biology. Network models and tools are widely used by businesses and industries, as well as governments today (cf. Ahuja, Magnanti, and Orlin (1993), Nagurney (1999, 2000a), and the references therein).

Basic examples of network problems are: *the shortest path problem*, in which one seeks to determine the most efficient path from an origin node

Table 1.1. Examples of Classical Networks

Network System	Nodes	Links	Flows
Transportation			
Urban	Intersections, Homes, Places of Work	Roads	Autos
Air	Airports	Airline Routes	Planes
Rail	Railyards	Railroad Track	Trains
Manufacturing and Logistics	Distribution Points, Processing Points	Routes Assembly Line	Parts, Products
Communication	Computers Satellites Phone Exchanges	Cables Radio Cables, Microwaves	Messages Messages Voice, Video
Energy	Pumping Stations Plants	Pipelines Pipelines	Water Gas, Oil

to a destination node; *the maximum flow problem*, in which one wishes to determine the maximum flow that one can send from an origin node to a destination node, given that there are capacities on the links that cannot be exceeded, and *the minimum cost flow problem*, where there are both costs and capacities associated with the links and one must satisfy the demands at the destination nodes, given supplies at the origin nodes, at minimal total cost associated with shipping the flows, and subject to not exceeding the arc capacities. Applications of the shortest path problem are found in transportation and telecommunications, whereas the maximum flow problem arises in machine scheduling and network reliability settings, with applications of the minimum cost flow problem ranging from warehousing and distribution to vehicle fleet planning and scheduling.

Networks also appear in surprising and fascinating ways for problems, which initially may not appear to involve networks at all, such as a variety of financial problems and in knowledge production and dissemination. Hence, the study of networks is not limited only to physical networks where nodes coincide with locations in space but applies also to abstract networks. The ability to harness the power of a network formalism provides a competitive advantage since:

• many present-day problems are concerned with flows, be they material, human, capital, or informational over space and time and, hence, ideally suited as an application domain for network theory;

• one may avail oneself of a graphical or visual depiction of different problems;

• one may identify similarities and differences in distinct problems through their underlying network structure; and

• one may apply efficient network algorithms for problem solution.

Our framework for the study of decision-making in the Information Age focuses on supernetworks, which, in turn, may be comprised of such networks as transportation, telecommunication, logistical and financial networks, among others. Our approach depends crucially on the methodologies of finite-dimensional *variational inequality* theory (cf. Nagurney (1999)), which provides an extension of optimization theory, for the study of the equilibrium states and on *projected dynamical systems* theory (see Nagurney and Zhang (1996)) for the study of dynamics and disequilibrium behavior. At the same time, visualization and formulation of decision-making problems as network problems gives one the opportunity to apply network-based algorithms, coupled with the aforementioned methodologies, to solve such complex network problems.

In this book, the principal topic of concern is supernetworks as the embodiment of the individual decision-makers in conjunction with their particular behavior and their interactions over space and time. The supernetwork framework allows one to formalize the alternatives available to decision-makers, to model their individual behavior, typically, characterized by particular criteria which they wish to optimize, and ultimately to compute the flows on the supernetwork, which may consist of product shipments, travelers between origins and destinations, financial flows, as well as the associated "prices." Here we emphasize that in this book we are concerned with human decision-making and how the supernetwork concept can be utilized to crystallize and inform in this dimension.

This book is divided into four major parts, with each part consisting of three chapters. Part I provides the introductory and background material, and lays the foundations of the supernetwork concept. It unveils the origins of the term supernetwork in the transportation and computer science literatures and identifies also the use of the term in biology and genetics. Finally, it shows that the concept appears even earlier in the case of financial networks.

Part II focuses on "multitiered" supernetworks, that is, supernetworks, consisting of distinct tiers of decision-makers. It considers applications such as supply chain networks with electronic commerce and financial networks with intermediation and identifies the subnetworks of the various agents, be they manufacturers or suppliers, retailers, or intermediaries, or consumers located at the demand markets. Both static and dynamic models are presented with the latter models depicted graphically as "multilevel" supernetworks, which include not only logistical networks but information networks as well. The supernetwork structures of the respective applications reveal the similarities and differences between the supply chain and the financial applications. Each chapter in this part incorporates experiences from actual practice.

Part III, in turn, establishes the foundations for "multicriteria" supernetworks and formulates such decision-making problems as telecommuting versus commuting and teleshopping versus shopping.

These models explicitly recognize that distinct classes of decision-makers may weight the criteria they face, be they cost, time, risk, safety, etc., in an individual fashion. Additional applications concerning location and transportation decision-making in the Information Age are also formulated as multicriteria supernetworks. In this part of the book, practical experiences concerning the applications are illustrated through cases in the United States and contrasted with the European experience.

Part IV presents new directions for the formalism of supernetworks and develops models with a variety of extensions and syntheses of the work in the preceding chapters. In particular, it presents a supernetwork model with distinct tiers of decision-makers consisting of producers and consumers, who are now each multicriteria decision-makers and are faced with shipping alternatives. The model is further illustrated by discussions of the freight railroading industry in the United States and contrasted with the trucking industry. Part IV also develops, in the context of financial decision-making, an extension to multicriteria modeling in the form of variable, as opposed to fixed weights, in order to enhance the modeling of risk. Finally, in the concluding chapter, paradoxes regarding supernetworks are presented as regards environmental emissions, and then circumvented using policies and/or behavioral modification.

Each chapter in this book concludes with a Sources and Notes section. Three appendices are provided in order to establish the fundamental technical background and to serve as a convenient reference source.

The supernetwork framework developed here captures the essential components of decision-making in the Information Age in both a visual medium and mathematically and can be utilized for modeling, analysis, and computation purposes.

1.1   Sources and Notes

The origins of the theme of this book, as well as this chapter, come from the invited essay of Nagurney (2000a) in *OR/MS Today*. In that essay, she set out to capture the interrelationships among the foundational networks in our economies and societies today. The essay, in turn, was based on Nagurney's Distinguished Faculty Lecture given at the University of Massachusetts on April 5, 2000 (see Nagurney (2000b)). In Chapters 2 and 3 we further elaborate on the theme of supernetworks and discuss their foundations.

There are many books on networks, both methodological as well as historical. Here our interests focus on nonlinear, multidimensional, in the form of multiple tiers or multiple levels or multiple criteria, abstract networks in the form of supernetworks and this book is the first one on the topic.

2 Background

In this chapter, we highlight the major innovations that have led us to the Information Age. In Section 2.1, we provide a brief historical perspective which focuses on the importance of computer networks in its evolution. In Section 2.2, we then describe parallels between telecommunication and transportation networks which not only yield the critical infrastructure for the Information Age but serve as the basic components for the study of decision-making on supernetworks. We conclude with Section 2.3, in which we outline some of the specific challenges facing decision-makers in the Information Age.

2.1 A Historical Perspective of the Information Age

In 1946, the Electronic Numerical Integrator and Computer (ENIAC) was developed by J. Mauchly and W. Eckert and built at the University of Pennsylvania for the purpose of calculating firing tables for artillery weapons. That project, as well as several other crucial ones for the evolution of the Information Age, were funded by the United States government. Businesses were initially uncertain as to the use of computers and even Thomas J. Watson, former chairman of IBM, in a well-known quote, said: "I think there is a world market for maybe five computers." Just to further emphasize how far we have truly come, Hamilton (1949) in the magazine *Popular Mechanics*, page 258, predicted that: "Where a calculator like the ENIAC today is equipped with 18,000 vacuum tubes and weighs 30 tons, computers in the future may have only 1000 vacuum tubes and perhaps weigh only $1\frac{1}{2}$ tons."

According to Leiner, et al. (2000), the "first recorded description of the social interactions that could be enabled through networking was a series of memos written by J. C. R. Licklider at the Massachusetts Institute of Technology (MIT) in 1962 discussing his 'Galactic Network' concept." Licklider perceived of a network of globally interconnected computers which would permit access to computer programs and data from any of the sites. Hence, as noted by Leiner, et al., this concept was truly in spirit with the Internet of today.

One of the first major technological innovations for the ultimate realization of the Internet was a theoretical paper by L. Kleinrock published in 1961 with a book to follow in 1964 on *packet switching theory*. His work demonstrated that it was feasible, at least in theory, to have computers communicate with one another using packets rather than dedicated circuits, and, hence, this was a major step towards computer networking. Another principal step was made shortly thereafter when L. G. Roberts, in conjunction with T. Merrill, connected a computer in Massachusetts with one in California with a dial-up (low-speed) telephone line, yielding the first wide-area (two-node) computer network ever constructed (cf. Roberts and Merrill (1966), Roberts (1967)). This design project confirmed Kleinrock's push for the need for packet switching.

In 1966, Roberts went to the US Defense Department's Advanced Research Agency (DARPA) and put together a plan for the ARPANET, which was a computer network that was soon thereafter realized. In 1969 it permitted military scientists and engineers to share expensive computers and to do so on what was considered to be a secure computer network. The ARPANET had a decentralized structure and it was this structure that allowed it to eventually expand and to grow rapidly. Interestingly, researchers at both RAND and at NPL in the United Kingdom had been working in parallel and without knowledge of the work at MIT on packet network concepts. Kleinrock by that time had moved to the University of California at Los Angeles and his center there became one of the first nodes on the ARPANET. The original ARPANET, according to Leiner, et al. (2000) "grew into the Internet," with the ARPANET being the first packet switching network. In addition to wire links, it included satellite and radio links.

The Internet is characterized by the unique feature of being an open architecture network in that the selection of any specific network technology is not limited by a particular network architecture but, instead, can be selected by any provider and made to connect and work with other computer networks. The idea of an open networking architecture had been introduced by R. E. Kahn in 1972 at DARPA. He, along with V. Cerf, provided another major innovation for making the Internet realizable and that was to describe a protocol, called TCP, which formalized the transportation and forwarding services on computer networks (see Cerf and Kahn (1974)). This protocol later evolved into the protocol known as TCP/IP, which is the one used for the Internet today.

The TCP protocol was first implemented on large time-sharing computer systems but as the personal computers (PCs) became increasingly available, local area networks and workstations in the 1980s allowed the network to further evolve. The physical connectivity was made universal in 1973 by the development of the Ethernet by R. Metcalfe and others at Xerox PARC. This advance enabled computers of different manufacturers to seamlessly interconnect. The use of Ethernet for computer networking has become ubiquitous.

The usefulness of computer networking was also being investigated outside of DARPA, and by the mid 1970s, other computer networks were being constructed at the Department of Energy in the United States and at the National Aeronautical and Space and Administration Agency (NASA). In addition, academics, notably, R. Adrion, D. Farber, and L. Landweber established the CSNET for the academic and industrial computer science communities in a project funded by the National Science Foundation (NSF), a government agency in the United States. In 1981, R. Fuchs and G. Freeman (cf. Leiner, et al. (2000)) constructed BITNET, which connected academic mainframe computers and allowed for e-mail. AT&Ts active dissemination of the UNIX operating system, in turn, helped in the conception of USENET.

The National Science Foundation, in 1986, initiated the NSFNET, which expanded the ARPANET to connect researchers at US universities and the TCP/IP protocol was the protocol selected. That initiative led to the National Research and Education Network, or NREN, which was based on a report commissioned by NSF, and, entitled, "Towards a National Research Network." It was produced in 1988 by a National Research Council committee chaired by Kleinrock. This report was very influential with advocates such as Al Gore, who was a senator at that time. It helped to promote and realize, with funding, high speed networks, and the Internet.

It is important to note that, around the 1980s, computer networking grew to include not only the research communities but also the commercial sector. With such growth came the need for coordination and standardization bodies, which included the formation of the Internet Society in 1991.

In order to promote the retrieval of scientific information, T. Berners-Lee, while at CERN and now at MIT, developed in 1990 the hypertext transfer protocol, now known as http. This protocol allowed one to retrieve information from a computer without an account on that computer. Berners-Lee named the project the World Wide Web (WWW). Marc Andreesen, working at the National Center for Supercomputer Applications at the University of Illinois in Urbana/Champaign, developed a program, called MOSAIC, and known as a "browser," to view the hypertext information. It was considered to be the first web browser. MOSAIC was, subsequently, commercialized to be *NETSCAPE*.

In 1994, another report by the National Research Council committee, called NRenaissance, chaired by Kleinrock, entitled, "Realizing the Information Future: The Internet and Beyond," was published (NRC (1994)). This report is considered to be the seminal one in that, according to Leiner, et al. (2000), it "was the document in which the blueprint for the evolution of the information superhighway was articulated and which has had a lasting affect on the way to think about its evolution. It anticipated the critical issues of intellectual property rights, ethics, pricing, education, architecture and regulation for the Internet."

In 1995, the Federal Networking Council (cf. Leiner, et al. (2000)) passed a resolution defining the Internet as follows: "'Internet' refers to the global information system that:

(i) is logically linked together by a globally unique address space based on the Internet Protocol (IP) or its subsequent extensions/follow-ons;

(ii) is able to support communications using the Transmission Control Protocol/Internet Protocol (TCP/IP) suite or its subsequent extensions/follow-ons, and/or other IP-compatible protocols; and

(iii) provides, uses or makes accessible, either publicly or privately, high level services layered on the communications and related infrastructure described herein."

By the late 1990s, industry and government noted that due to the ease of information retrieval on the Web, it became essential to have a Web presence. With additions to the protocols that allowed transmission of data from the personal computer, electronic commerce and collaborative work on the Web became possible.

It is now well-recognized by governments, their citizens, businesses, as well as educational institutions and other enterprises that we are now in the midst of what is called the "Information Age." For example, according to an article in the *Scientific American* (cf. Wallich (1995)), by 1995, since the phrase "information superhighway" first appeared in 1992, there were already about 4,000 stories identified from magazines, newspapers, and broadcasts that had used that term. From the popular literature, there is the work of Alvin Toffler (1980), a historian, who refers to the transition the United States is undergoing as the "Third Wave," as opposed to the "First Wave" of change consisting of the agricultural revolution, and taking thousands of years, and the "Second Wave" of change, comprised of the rise of industrial civilization, with about three hundred years in duration.

Of course, Information Revolutions are not new, and, in particular, the invention of the printing press over 500 years ago by Gutenberg fueled an information revolution since his invention allowed for the mass distribution of information, including such scarce texts as the Bible. Moreover, as noted by Kelly (1994), the printing press revolutionized the way people interact and decreased the amount of information their minds needed to store. Today, massive amounts of information can be stored in computers and accessed directly and conveniently.

Other modes of communication also brought phenomenal changes and opportunities with notable inventions being the telegraph (cf. Standage (1999)), the telephone, the radio and television, including cable (cf. Jacobson (2000)), as well as fax machines. However, what is particularly novel and characteristic of the Information Age today, according to Dewar (1998), is the "networking" of computers, which is the first "many-to-many" communications medium. According to Dewar (1998), "Best estimates say there are 19.5 million computers connected to the Internet... and a respected estimate says in the United States 40.6 million people over 18 have used the Internet." According to Leiner, et al. (2000), there are presently over 50,000 operational networks on the Internet. Clearly, Licklider's vision of a "Galactic Network" had become a reality.

2.2 Parallels between Transportation and Telecommunication Networks

In this section, we focus on some of the relationships between transportation and telecommunication networks. As highlighted by Mokhtarian (1990), telecommunications "may be thought of as the transportation of information." Hence, *conceptually*, these two networks are similar, with terms derived from transportation such as: "superhighway," "traffic," "ports," and "pipelines," being used today in the context of telecommunication networks, and, in particular, for the Internet. Interestingly, the first use of the most prevalent telecommunications product, that is, the telephone, generated a "trip," when Alexander Graham Bell, uttering the first words into the telephone he had invented, said: "Watson, come here, I want you" (cf. De Sola Pool (1977)). Watson was located only several feet away.

In addition, as noted by Mokhtarian, there are *physical* parallels between these two types of networks, with telecommunication networks very often being superimposed over transportation networks. For example, she notes that the first uses of the telegraph included assisting in railroad network operations and, hence, early telegraph networks often followed railroad rights of way (see also Kieve (1973), Harlow (1936)). Even in this day, most fiber optic cables follow railroad networks. On the other hand, local telephone systems as well as cable television delivery systems typically follow city roads and streets. For an economic historical perspective on cable television, see Jacobson (2000). For example, U. S. Sprint, a telecommunications company, which was originally the telecommunications arm of the Southern Pacific Railroad, at first followed the railroad's right of way. For an overview of the growth of railroads and their role in the United States, see Friedlander (1995a). For background on telephones and telegraphs in the United States infrastructure to the middle of the last century, see Friedlander (1995b).

The economic parallels and relationships between telecommunication and transportation networks are many and multifaceted. Perhaps the best way to capture the relationships from an economic perspective is to discuss the impact of the supply of one on the demand for the other. For example, telecommunications has had an impact on the demand for transportation through such innovations as telecommuting, and teleshopping, among others. We provide greater background and citations to these subjects in Chapters 7 and 8 of this book.

Telecommunications can also have an effect on the supply of transportation through the more efficient use of transportation networks. We discuss some relationships to freight carriers in Chapter 10 of this book. Interestingly, Beniger (1986), according to Mokhtarian (1990), traces the origins of the "Information Revolution" to a "crisis of control" in the production, distribution, and consumption of goods and services in the middle of the nineteenth century. In Chapters 4 and 5 we discuss telecommunications and transportation alternatives in the context of supply chain networks in the Information Age.

There are also numerous innovations in terms of Intelligent Vehicle Transportation Systems from conceptual, modeling, and analytical perspectives (cf. Smith (1984, 1993), Kanafani and Parsons (1989), Mahmassani (1990), Papageorgiou (1990), Ben-Akiva, de Palma, and Kaysi (1991), Cascetta and Cantarella (1991), Janson (1991), Drissi-Kaitouni and Hameda-Benchekroun (1992), Mahmassani, et al. (1993), Dupuis and Nagurney (1993), Friesz, et al. (1994), Kobayashi (1994), Nijkamp, Pepping, and Banister (1996), Ran and Boyce (1996), Nagurney and Zhang (1996), Watling (1996), Slavin (1996), Zhang and Nagurney (1997), Wu, Chen, and Florian (1998), Zhang, Nagurney, and Wu (2001)). Intelligent Vehicle Transportation Systems apply telecommunications in order to enhance the operation of congested transportation systems including urban networks. In addition, air traffic control is another example of the effect of telecommunications on transportation (see Bertsimas and Odoni (1997)).

The impact of transportation on the demand for telecommunications will now be described. A clear example is the demand for a variety of mobile communications, including cellular phones. As noted by Mokhtarian (1990), page 234, "It is probably no coincidence that gridlocked Los Angeles is heralded as the largest cellular radio market in the world" (cf. Kim (1987)). In regard to the impact of transportation on the supply of telecommunications, we have addressed this aspect earlier in our discussions when we considered the use of transportation rights of way to construct fiber optic and other telecommunication networks.

Finally, there are clear analytical parallels between transportation and telecommunication networks, in that both systems are networks, consisting of nodes and links, with associated capacities and flows on them. In the case of telecommunication networks, the flows are "messages," whereas in the case of transportation networks, the flows are "vehicles." Moreover, as will be further emphasized in Chapter 3, these two classes of networks have similar characteristics today in terms of size, congestion, decentralized operations, and increasing competition, as well as paradoxical phenomena. Furthermore, as will also become increasingly apparent in this book, decision-making on such networks and, in particular, on supernetworks, consisting of these networks as subnetworks, can be handled in a unified manner using rigorous methodologies which are supported by theory.

2.3   Challenges Facing Decision-Makers

Al Gore, in a Vice Presidential address to students at the University of Pennsylvania, in 1996, as part of the fiftieth anniversary of the development of the ENIAC provided a new metaphor for the Information Revolution in the form of "distributed intelligence." He noted that the beginning of the computer era was symbolized and characterized by computers with central processing power and had since evolved to include new architectures such as massive parallelism whereby processing power and, hence, intelligence was distributed. Each processor could work on small pieces of the task with the results being periodically collated with the rest of the results. He emphasized that such an approach, he believed, was more effective in solving many problems. Moreover, he stated in his address that: "Distributed intelligence offers a pretty coherent explanation for why democracy triumphed over governments that depended on all-powerful central processing units. And it helps explain why American businesses are pushing power, responsibility, and information away from the center – and out to the salespeople, engineers, and suppliers who know the product best."

In the same address, Gore proceeded to ask the students in the audience the following questions: "How many of you, when you graduate, hope to climb the corporate ladder...rung after rung...same company for the next 40 years?...Or how many of you hope to maybe start your own business, move from project to project, or navigate whatever exciting webs of commerce present themselves?" His subsequent statement is especially appropriate to our supernetwork concept which seeks to capture the myriad possibilities and choices facing decision-makers today and we quote: "The ladder is a factory metaphor – one path, one destination, step by step. But the web is a distributed metaphor – innumerable paths, unimaginable destinations, any route you choose."

Clearly, if there is only one path, there is no decision that needs to be made except for, possibly, not to take the path at all, that is, to jump off the ladder entirely, which may or may not be feasible or advisable. On the other hand, with numerous paths, that is, choices, available, as well as associated destinations, one needs to make the best decision, that is, to select the "optimal" alternative. In this book, we provide a framework for making such decisions rationally, taking into consideration the interactions among the various decision-makers. Moreover, we explicitly focus on decentralized (as opposed to centralized) decision-making since that is clearly the reality in many organizations and application settings ranging from supply chain management to teleshopping and telecommuting in the Network Economy today. In the next chapter, we begin our discussion on decision-making concepts, which are then fully developed in a variety of applications throughout this book.

2.4   Sources and Notes

This chapter presented a brief historical overview of the Information Age in the context of networks, notably, the Internet, since the study of supernetworks, whose origins are outlined in Chapter 3, is the theme of this book. Section 2.1 relies on the information in the paper by Leiner, et al. (2000), which provides a (brief) but thorough history of the Internet and is co-authored by many of the computer networking pioneers. Section 2.2, in turn, draws from the paper by Mokhtarian (1990), which contains a typology of relationships between telecommunications and transportation. Section 2.3 discusses parallels between an address given by then Vice President Gore (1996) to an academic audience and some of the basic concepts in this book. For the reader interested in additional readings on computers and the Information Age and their relevance to both today and the future, see the books by Negroponte (1995), Gates, Myhrvold, and Rinearson (1995), and Dertouzos (1997). For a strategic perspective on the role of information in the Network Economy, see the book by Shapiro and Varian (1999). For those interested in a sociological perspective on the Information Age, and, in particular, on the transformation of work and employment and the rise of the network society, see the book by Castells (2000).

3 Foundations of Supernetworks

In this chapter, we present the foundations of supernetworks. We begin in Section 3.1 with a discussion of three foundational classes of networks: transportation, telecommunication, and economic and financial networks. Such networks have served not only as the basis for the origins of the term "supernetwork," but, also, they arise as critical subnetworks in the applications that are relevant to decision-making in the Information Age today and appear in various supernetwork models in subsequent parts of this book. We also include a discussion of the term "supernetworks" in genetics and biology since it holds not dissimilar connotations to our use of the term. Nevertheless, the focus in this book is on *human* decision-making in the context of supernetworks in the Information Age.

In Section 3.2, we describe the characteristics of supernetworks in order to delineate their scope. These include: typically, large-scale and, oftentimes, complex structure; increasing congestion, and interactions among the subnetworks comprising the supernetworks. In Section 3.3, we outline the decision-making concept that arises most frequently in the context of supernetworks, in particular, "user-optimization," in which there are numerous decision-makers, each seeking to determine his optimal decision and contrast it with "system-optimization," in which there is a single decision-maker, who controls the network, and optimizes accordingly.

3.1 Foundational Networks

In this section, we describe the foundational networks for supernetworks and trace the history of the term "supernetwork." We emphasize, as mentioned earlier, that "supernetwork" refers to networks that are above and beyond existing networks. Nevertheless, the foundations of supernetworks are built upon network systems that have not only been historically crucial to the development of economies and societies but that have also been subjected to rigorous analysis due to their practical importance.

3.1.1 Transportation Networks

Transportation networks are complex network systems in which the decisions of the individual travelers affect the efficiency and productivity of the entire network system. Transportation networks come in many forms: notably, urban networks, freight networks, and airline networks (see Table 1.1). The "supply" in such a network system is represented by the network topology and the underlying cost characteristics, whereas the "demand" is represented by the users of the network system, that is, the travelers.

The study of transportation networks and their efficient management dates to ancient times. Indeed, Romans imposed controls over chariot traffic during different times of the day in order to deal with the congestion (cf. Banister and Button (1993)).

In 1972, Dafermos demonstrated in a paper, through a formal model, how a *multiclass* traffic network could be cast into a single-class traffic network through the construction of an expanded (and *abstract*) network consisting of as many copies of the original network as there were classes. She clearly identified the origin/destination pairs, demands, link costs, and flows on the abstract network. The applications of such networks she stated on page 73 of that reference, "arise not only in street networks where vehicles of different types share the same roads (e.g., trucks and passenger cars) but also in other types of transportation networks (e. g., telephone networks)." Hence, she not only recognized that abstract networks could be used to handle multimodal transportation networks but also telecommunication networks! Moreover, she considered both user-optimizing and system-optimizing behavior, terms which she had coined with Sparrow in a paper in 1969, and which we further discuss in Sections 3.2 and 3.3.

In 1976, Dafermos proposed an integrated traffic network equilibrium model in which one could visualize and formalize the entire transportation planning process (consisting of origin selection, or destination selection, or both, in addition to route selection, in an optimal fashion) as path choices over an appropriately constructed *abstract* network. The genesis and formal treatment of decisions more complex than route choices as *path* choices on abstract networks, that is, supernetworks, were, hence, reported as early as 1972 and 1976.

The importance and wider relevance of such abstract networks in decision-making, with a focus on transportation planning were accentuated through the term "hypernetwork" used by Sheffi (1978), and Sheffi and Daganzo (1978, 1980), which was later retermed as "supernetwork" by Sheffi (1985).

For example, Sheffi and Daganzo (1978) described a framework for discussing many transportation supply-demand equilibrium problems, where (see page 113 therein), "the sequence of choices that the individual faces when he or she is about to make a travel (or not-to-travel) decision as a case choice of a route on an abstract network (hypernetwork)." They recognized the contribution of Dafermos (1976) and also considered probabilistic choice models. Thus, they explicitly considered that decision-making in a transportation context could be modeled as a "route" selection over an abstract network. The route, henceforth referred to as a "path" to emphasize the generality of the concept, would, thus, correspond to a choice and the links to parts and pieces of the complete decision.

The recognition and appropriate construction of *abstract* networks was pivotal in that it allowed for the incorporation of transportation-related decisions (where as noted by Dafermos (1972), transportation applied also to communication networks) which were not based solely on route selection in a classical sense, that is, what route should one take from one's origin, say, place of residence, to one's destination, say, place of employment. Hence, abstract networks, with origins and destinations corresponding to appropriately defined nodes, links connecting nodes having associated disutilities (that is, costs), and paths comprised of links (directed) connecting the origins and destinations, could capture such travel alternatives as not simply just a route but, also, the "mode" of travel, that is, for example, whether one chose to use private or public transportation. Furthermore, with the addition of not only added abstract links and paths, but abstract origin and destination nodes as well one could include the selection of such locational decisions as the origins and destinations themselves within the same decision-making framework.

For example, in order to fix ideas, in Figure 3.1, we present a supernetwork topology for an example of a simple mode/route choice problem. In this example, we recognize, at the outset, that the routes underlying the different modes may be distinct and, hence, rather than making copies of the network according to Dafermos (1972), we make the supernetwork construction with the path choices directly on the supernetwork itself.

In the network in Figure 3.1, travelers seek to determine their "best" paths (this is made definite in Section 3.3) from the origin node 1 to the destination node 4, where a path consists of both the selection of the mode of travel as well as the route of travel. The link from node 1 to node 4 corresponds to the use of public transit, and there is only one route choice using this mode of travel. On the other hand, if one selects private transportation (typically, the automobile), one could take either of two routes: with the first route consisting of the first link joining nodes 1 and 2 and then the link joining node 2 to node 4, and the second route consisting of the second link joining nodes 1 and 2 and then onto node 4. Finally, one could choose either of two pedestrian routes to travel from node 1 to node 4, with the pedestrian routes differing by their second component links.

We now provide another simple example, which illustrates simultaneous route and destination choice in a supernetwork framework, as conceived by Dafermos (1976), whose abstract network framework also captured other

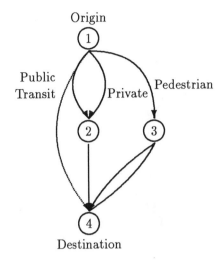

Origin

Public
Transit

Pedestrian

Private

Destination

Fig. 3.1. Example Mode and Route Choice Supernetwork Topology

transportation/location decisions. We refer the reader to the supernetwork depicted in Figure 3.2. Assume that there is a single origin, which corresponds to the place of residence and is denoted by node 1 in the figure. Assume that there are three places of (potential) employment, denoted, respectively, by nodes 2, 3, and 4. There are two available routes of travel from the origin to each employment node. Dafermos proposed, in this case, to construct a single abstract node, denoted by node 5 in Figure 3.2, which serves as the abstract destination, and to connect each of the nodes 2 through 4 with node 5. Hence, the paths connecting node 1 with node 5 represent both route and destination choices.

The behavioral principle utilized by Dafermos (1976) and by Sheffi and Daganzo (1978, 1980) (who also formulated stochastic models) was that decision-makers select the "cost-minimizing" routes among all their available choices. Dafermos (1972) considered both system-optimization as well as user-optimization. According to Sheffi and Daganzo (1978), the selection of cost-minimizing routes "this is consistent with the principle of utility maximization of choice theory." Moreover, they stated on page 116 of that reference that: "Although hypernetworks enable us to visualize choice problems in a unified way... their main advantage is that they enable us to perform supply-demand equilibrium analysis on a mathematically consistent basis with disaggregate demand models." We further elaborate on the behavioral principle known as user-optimization in Section 3.3.

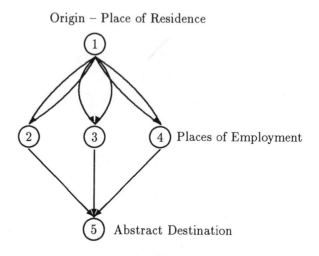

Origin – Place of Residence

Places of Employment

Abstract Destination

Fig. 3.2. Example Route and Destination Choice Supernetwork Topology

Sheffi and Daganzo (1978) (see page 115 therein) recognized that the idea of hypernetworks had "been latent in the literature for some time" (see also the references therein). In particular, Wilson (1973) had noted at the 1972 Williamsburg Conference, that "It is tempting as computer capacity expands to think of assigning on multimodal networks, in effect, possibly directly to routes on an abstract modal basis." Dafermos in 1972 published her multiclass traffic network paper and, shortly thereafter, developed her integrated traffic network equilibrium model with the addition of abstract nodes and links.

3.1.2   Telecommunication Networks

We now turn to a discussion of the use of the term "supernetworks" in the context of telecommunication networks. In the *American Scientist,* Denning (1985) continued his discussion of the internal structure of computer networks, which had appeared in a volume of the same journal earlier that year, and emphasized how (see page 127 therein) "protocol software can be built as a series of layers. Most of this structure is hidden from the users of the network." He then proceeded to ask the question, "What should the users see?" Denning, subsequently in the article, answered the question in the context of the then National Science Foundation's Advanced Scientific Computing Initiative to make national supercomputer centers accessible to the entire scientific community. He said that such a system would be a network of networks, that is, a "supernetwork," and a powerful tool for science.

Interestingly, he emphasized the importance of location-independent naming, so that if a physical location of a resource were to change, none of the supporting programs or files would need to be edited or recompiled. Hence, in a sense, his view of supernetworks is in concert with that of ours in that nodes do not need to correspond to locations in space and may have an abstract association.

Subsequently, Vogel (1990) (see page 2 therein) used the term in the context of knowledge representation as follows: "In the network approach to knowledge representation, concepts are represented as nodes in a network. Networks are compositional: a node in a network can be some other network, and the same subnetwork can be a subnetwork of several larger supernetworks..."

In 1997, the Illinois Bar Association considered the following to be an accepted definition of the Internet: "the Internet is a supernetwork of computers that links together individual computers and computer networks located at academic, commercial, government and military sites worldwide, generally by ordinary local telephone lines and long-distance transmission facilities. Communications between computers or individual networks on the Internet are achieved through the use of standard, nonproprietary protocols." The reference to the Internet as a supernetwork was also made by Fallows (1996) who stated in *The Atlantic Monthly* that "The Internet is the supernetwork that links computer networks around the world."

Mr. Vinton G. Cerf, the co-developer of the computer networking protocal, TCP/IP, used for the Internet, in his keynote address to the Internet/Telecom 95 Conference (see Telecom95 (1995)), noted that at that time there were an estimated 23 million users of the Internet, and that vast quantities of the US Internet traffic "pass through internet MCI's backbone." He then went on to say in the same source that "Just a few months back, MCI rolled out a supernetwork for the National Science Foundation known as the very broadband network service or VBNS...VBNS is being used as an experimental platform for developing new national networking applications."

In this book, we demonstrate how decision-making on transportation and telecommunication networks can be done simultaneously through the supernetwork concept. Specifically, Chapters 4 and 5 explore these issues in the context of supply chain networks with electronic commerce. Chapter 7, on the other hand, considers telecommuting versus commuting decision-making and teleshopping versus shopping decision-making. Chapter 9, in turn, expands upon the framework introduced by Dafermos (1976) to incorporate aspects of transportation/location decision-making in the Information Age. Indeed, as will be further revealed in Section 3.2, the characteristics of the two foundational network systems of the Information Age, transportation and telecommunication networks, are becoming increasingly alike.

3.1.3   Economic and Financial Networks

The concept of a network in economics was implicit as early as the classical work of Cournot (1838), who not only seems to have first explicitly stated that a competitive price is determined by the intersection of supply and demand curves, but had done so in the context of two spatially separated markets in which the cost of transporting the good between markets was considered.

Pigou (1920) also studied a network system in the setting of a transportation network consisting of two routes and noted that the "system-optimized" solution was distinct from the "user-optimized" solution.

Nevertheless, the first instance of an abstract network or supernetwork in the context of economic applications, was actually due to Quesnay (1758), who visualized the circular flow of funds in an economy as a network. Since that very early contribution there have been numerous economic and financial models that have been constructed over abstract networks. In particular, we note the work of Dafermos and Nagurney (1985) who identified the isomorphism between traffic network equilibrium problems and spatial price equilibrium problems, whose development had been originated by Samuelson (1952) (who, interestingly, focused on the bipartite network structure of the spatial price equilibrium problem) and Takayama and Judge (1971).

Zhao (1989) (see also Zhao and Dafermos (1991) and Zhao and Nagurney (1993)) identified the general economic equilibrium problem known as Walrasian price equilibrium as a network equilibrium problem over an abstract network with very simple structure. The structure consisted of a single origin/destination pair of nodes and single links joining the two nodes. This structure was then exploited for computational purposes. Nagurney (1989), in turn, proposed a migration equilibrium problem over an abstract network with an identical structure. A variety of abstract networks in economics were studied in the book by Nagurney (1999), which also contains extensive references to the subject. In this book, we further extend the abstract network concept under the umbrella of supernetworks to also capture the interactions between/among the underlying networks of economies and societies. In Chapter 6 and in Chapter 11, in particular, we consider financial networks as supernetworks, whereas in Chapter 5 we propose a multilevel supernetwork structure for the study of supply chain dynamics which includes financial networks as a level. As noted by Nagurney (2000a) on page 75: "The interactions among transportation networks, telecommunication networks, as well as financial networks is creating supernetworks ..." and in this book we make that visionary statement definite.

3.1.4   An Aside – Supernetworks in Genetics

Interestingly, our research into the foundations of supernetworks yielded a novel and, although dissimilar, potentially interesting and valuable context in biology, in particular in genetics. According to Noveen, Hartenstein, and

Chuong (1998), many interacting genes give rise to a gene network, with many interacting gene networks giving rise to a gene "supernetwork." They go on to further state: "The function of a gene supernetwork is more complicated than a gene network. A gene supernetwork, for example, may be involved in determining the development of an entire limb while a gene network, working within the supernetwork, may be involved in setting up one of the axes of the limb bud." According to the same source, a gene supernetwork is defined as "a collection of gene networks which participate with each other during the morphogenesis of a specific structure, for example an organ, a segment, or an appendage." The authors then go on to discuss duplication, divergence, and conservation of a gene supernetwork and note that, as with gene networks, gene supernetworks can be duplicated during evolution, "thus giving rise to new structures which are the same as or different from the original structure."

3.2   Characteristics of Supernetworks

Supernetworks are a conceptual and analytical formalism for the study of a variety of decision-making problems on networks. Hence, their characteristics include characteristics of the foundational networks. The characteristics of today's networks include: large-scale nature and complexity of network topology; congestion; alternative behavior of users of the network, which may lead to paradoxical phenomena; and the interactions among networks themselves such as in transportation versus telecommunications networks. Moreover, policies surrounding networks today may have a major impact not only economically but also socially.

Large-Scale Nature and Complexity

Many of today's networks are characterized by both a large-scale nature and complexity of the underlying network topology. For example, in Chicago's Regional Transportation Network, there are 12,982 nodes, 39,018 links, and 2,297,945 origin/destination (O/D) pairs (see Bar-Gera (1999)), whereas in the Southern California Association of Governments' model there are 3,217 origins and/or destinations, 25,428 nodes, and 99,240 links, plus 6 distinct classes of users (cf. Wu, Florian, and He (2000)).

In terms of the size of existing telecommunications networks, AT&T's domestic network has 100,000 origin/destination pairs (cf. Resende (2000)), whereas in their detail graph applications in which nodes are phone numbers and edges are calls, there are 300 million nodes and 4 billion edges (cf. Abello, Pardalos, and Resende (1999)).

Congestion

Congestion is playing an increasing role in not only transportation networks but also in telecommunication networks. For example, in the case of transportation networks in the United States alone, congestion results in $100 billion in lost productivity, whereas the figure in Europe is estimated to be

$150 billion. The number of cars is expected to increase by 50 percent by 2010 and to double by 2030 (see Nagurney (2000c)).

In terms of the Internet, with 275 million present users, the Federal Communications Commission reports that the volume of traffic is doubling every 100 days, which is remarkable given that telephone traffic has typically increased only by about 5 percent a year (cf. Labaton (2000)). As individuals increasingly access the Internet through wireless communication such as through handheld computers and cellular phones, experts fear that the heavy use of airwaves will create additional bottlenecks and congestion that could impede the further development of the technology.

System-Optimization versus User-Optimization

In many of today's networks, not only is congestion a characteristic feature leading to nonlinearities, but the behavior of the users of the networks themselves may be that of noncooperation. For example, in the case of urban transportation networks, travelers select their routes of travel from an origin to a destination so as to minimize their own travel cost or travel time, which although "optimal" from an individual's perspective (user-optimization) may not be optimal from a societal one (system-optimization) where one has control over the flows on the network and, in contrast, seeks to minimize the total cost in the network and, hence, the total loss of productivity. Consequently, in making any kind of policy decisions in such networks one must take into consideration the users of the particular network. Indeed, this point is vividly illustrated through a famous example known as Braess's paradox, in which it is assumed that the underlying behavioral principle is that of user-optimization. In the Braess (1968) network, the addition of a new road with no change in the travel demand results in all travelers in the network incurring a higher travel cost and, hence, being worse off.

The increase in travel cost on the paths is due, in part, to the fact that in this network two links are shared by distinct paths and these links incur an increase in flow and associated cost. Hence, Braess's paradox is related to the underlying topology of the networks. One may show, however, that the addition of a path connecting an O/D pair that shares no links with the original O/D pair will never result in Braess's paradox for that O/D pair.

Interestingly, as reported in the *New York Times* by Kolata (1990), this phenomenon has been observed in practice in the case of New York City when in 1990, 42nd Street was closed for Earth Day and the traffic flow actually improved. Just to show that it is not a purely New York or US phenomena concerning drivers and their behavior an analogous situation was observed in Stuttgart where a new road was added to the downtown but the traffic flow worsened and following complaints, the new road was torn down (see Bass (1992)).

This phenomenon is also relevant to telecommunications networks (see Korilis, Lazar, and Orda (1999)) and, in particular, to the Internet which is another example of a "noncooperative network" and, therefore, network tools have wide application in this setting as well, especially in terms of congestion management and network design (see also Cohen and Kelly (1990)).

Network Interactions

Clearly, one of the principal facets of the Network Economy is the interaction among the networks themselves. For example, the increasing use of e-commerce especially in business to business transactions is changing not only the utilization and structure of the underlying logistical networks but is also revolutionizing how business itself is transacted and the structure of firms and industries. Cellular phones are being using as vehicles move dynamically over transportation networks resulting in dynamic evolutions of the topologies themselves. This book explores the network interactions among such networks as transportation networks and telecommunication networks, as well as financial networks through the unifying concept of supernetworks.

3.3   Decision-Making Concepts

As the above discussion has revealed, networks in the Information Age are complex, typically large-scale systems and the study of their efficient operation, often through some outside intervention, has attracted much interest from economists, computer scientists and engineers, as well as transportation and urban planners and operations researchers.

As already noted, from an economic perspective, some of the earliest contributions to the subject date to Pigou (1920), who is also viewed as the forefather of road pricing. In particular, his idea of using road pricing to regulate traffic congestion on a simple two-node, two-link network has spawned additional research, discussion, and practical applications. Pigou (1920) (see also Knight (1924)) used the example of a congested road to illustrate the concepts of externality and optimal tolls as congestion charges. Specifically, Pigou argued that travelers should be charged according to their marginal external congestion costs. Note that an *externality* is present when the actions of some economic agents (such as travelers) affect the utility (typically travel time or cost in the case of transportation) or production set of another without that person's consent or compensation. An externality is seen as *negative* when the harm done to others is considered to be uncompensated. In the case of transportation networks, the harm may include, for example, increased travel time due to congestion, or increased pollution.

Vickrey (1960, 1963), in turn, emphasized that the cost of congestion was high, with the real economic cost of transportation infrastructure in the United States at that time being estimated to be approximately three times the total vehicular and gasoline taxes generated by car use on urban streets.

Engineers were also concerned about the operation of transportation networks. In particular, Wardrop (1952) explicitly recognized alternative possible behaviors of users of transportation networks and stated two principles, which are commonly named after him:

Table 3.1. Distinct Behavior on Transportation Networks

User-Optimization	System-Optimization
⇓	⇓
Equilibrium Principle: User travel costs on used paths for each O/D pair are equalized and minimal.	**Optimality Principle:** Marginals of the total travel cost on used paths for each O/D pair are equalized and minimal.

First Principle: The journey times of all routes actually used are equal, and less than those which would be experienced by a single vehicle on any unused route.

Second Principle: The average journey time is minimal.

The first principle corresponds to the behavioral principle in which travelers seek to (unilaterally) determine their minimal costs of travel whereas the second principle corresponds to the behavioral principle in which the total cost in the network is minimal.

Beckmann, McGuire, and Winsten (1956) were the first to rigorously formulate these conditions mathematically, as had Samuelson (1952) in the framework of spatial price equilibrium problems in which there were, however, no congestion effects. Specifically, Beckmann, McGuire, and Winsten (1956) established the equivalence between the *traffic network equilibrium* conditions, which state that all used paths connecting an origin/destination (O/D) pair will have equal and minimal travel times (or costs) (corresponding to Wardrop's first principle), and the Kuhn-Tucker (1951) conditions of an appropriately constructed optimization problem, under a symmetry assumption on the underlying functions (cf. Appendices A and B). Hence, in this case, the equilibrium link and path flows could be obtained as the solution of a mathematical programming problem. Their approach made the formulation, analysis, and subsequent computation of solutions to traffic network problems based on actual transportation networks realizable.

Dafermos and Sparrow (1969) coined the terms *user-optimized* (U-O) and *system-optimized* (S-O) transportation networks to distinguish between two distinct situations in which, respectively, users act unilaterally, in their own self-interest, in selecting their routes, and in which users select routes according to what is optimal from a societal point of view, in that the total cost in the system is minimized. In the latter problem, marginal costs rather than average costs are equilibrated. The former problem coincides with Wardrop's first principle, and the latter with Wardrop's second principle.

See Table 3.1 for the two distinct behavioral principles underlying transportation networks. The concept of "system-optimization" is also relevant to other types of "routing models" in transportation, as well as in communications (cf. Bertsekas and Gallager (1992)), including those concerned with the routing of freight and computer messages, respectively. Dafermos and Sparrow (1969) also provided explicit computational procedures, that is, *algorithms*, to compute the solutions to such network problems in the case where the user travel cost on a link was an increasing (in order to handle congestion) function of the flow on the particular link, and linear.

3.3.1 System-Optimization versus User-Optimization

In this section, the basic network models are first reviewed, under distinct assumptions of their operation and distinct behavior of the users of the network. The models are classical and were developed in the context of transportation. They are due to Beckmann, McGuire, and Winsten (1956) and Dafermos and Sparrow (1969). We later present more general models.

For definiteness, and for easy reference, we present the classical system-optimized network model in Section 3.3.1.1 and then the classical user-optimized network model in Section 3.3.1.2. Rather than couching these models in the context of transportation systems, we present them in the broader setting of, simply, network systems.

In Section 3.3.1.3, we then consider more general models, in which the user link cost functions are no longer separable and are also asymmetric. We provide the variational inequality formulations of the governing equilibrium conditions, since, in this case, the conditions can no longer be reformulated as the Kuhn-Tucker conditions of a convex optimization problem (see also Appendices A and B). Finally, we present the variational inequality formulations in the case of elastic demands.

3.3.1.1 The System-Optimized Problem

Consider a general network $\mathcal{G} = [\mathcal{N}, \mathcal{L}]$, where $\mathcal{N}$ denotes the set of nodes, and $\mathcal{L}$ the set of directed links. Let a denote a link of the network connecting a pair of nodes, and let p denote a path consisting of a sequence of links connecting an O/D pair. In transportation networks (see also Table 1.1), nodes correspond to origins and destinations, as well as to intersections. Links, on the other hand, correspond to roads/streets in the case of urban transportation networks and to railroad segments in the case of train networks. A path in its most basic setting, thus, is a sequence of "roads" which comprise a route from an origin to a destination. In the telecommunication context, however, nodes can correspond to switches or to computers and links to telephone lines, cables, microwave links, etc. In the supernetwork setting, a path is viewed more broadly and need not be limited to a route-type decision.

Let P_ω denote the set of paths connecting the origin/destination (O/D) pair of nodes ω. Let P denote the set of all paths in the network and assume that there are J origin/destination pairs of nodes in the set Ω. Let x_p

represent the flow on path p and let f_a denote the flow on link a. The path flows on the network are grouped into the column vector $x \in R_+^{n_P}$, where n_P denotes the number of paths in the network. The link flows, in turn, are grouped into the column vector $f \in R_+^n$, where n denotes the number of links in the network.

The following conservation of flow equation must hold:

$$f_a = \sum_{p \in P} x_p \delta_{ap}, \quad \forall a \in \mathcal{L}, \tag{3.1}$$

where $\delta_{ap} = 1$, if link a is contained in path p, and 0, otherwise. Expression (3.1) states that the flow on a link a is equal to the sum of all the path flows on paths p that contain (traverse) link a.

Moreover, if one lets d_ω denote the demand associated with O/D pair ω, then one must have that

$$d_\omega = \sum_{p \in P_\omega} x_p, \quad \forall \omega \in \Omega, \tag{3.2}$$

where $x_p \geq 0$, $\forall p \in P$; that is, the sum of all the path flows between an origin/destination pair ω must be equal to the given demand d_ω.

Let c_a denote the user link cost associated with traversing link a, and let C_p denote the user cost associated with traversing the path p.

Assume that the user link cost function is given by the *separable* function

$$c_a = c_a(f_a), \quad \forall a \in \mathcal{L}, \tag{3.3}$$

where c_a is assumed to be an increasing function of the link flow f_a in order to model the effect of the link flow on the cost.

The total cost on link a, denoted by $\hat{c}_a(f_a)$, hence, is given by:

$$\hat{c}_a(f_a) = c_a(f_a) \times f_a, \quad \forall a \in \mathcal{L}, \tag{3.4}$$

that is, the total cost on a link is equal to the user link cost on the link times the flow on the link. Here the cost is interpreted in a general sense. From a transportation engineering perspective, however, the cost on a link is assumed to coincide with the travel time on a link. In Part III of this book, we consider generalized cost functions of the links which are constructed using weights and different criteria.

In the system-optimized problem, there exists a central controller who seeks to minimize the total cost in the network system, where the total cost is expressed as

$$\sum_{a \in \mathcal{L}} \hat{c}_a(f_a), \tag{3.5}$$

where the total cost on a link is given by expression (3.4).

The system-optimization problem is, thus, given by:

$$\text{Minimize} \quad \sum_{a \in \mathcal{L}} \hat{c}_a(f_a) \tag{3.6}$$

subject to:

$$\sum_{p \in P_\omega} x_p = d_\omega, \quad \forall \omega \in \Omega, \tag{3.7}$$

$$f_a = \sum_{p \in P} x_p, \quad \forall a \in \mathcal{L}, \tag{3.8}$$

$$x_p \geq 0, \quad \forall p \in P. \tag{3.9}$$

The constraints (3.7) and (3.8), along with (3.9), are commonly referred to in network terminology as *conservation of flow equations*. In particular, they guarantee that the flow in the network, that is, the users (whether these are travelers or computer messages, for example) do not "get lost."

The total cost on a path, denoted by $\hat{C}_p$, is the user cost on a path times the flow on a path, that is,

$$\hat{C}_p = C_p x_p, \quad \forall p \in P, \tag{3.10}$$

where the user cost on a path, C_p, is given by the sum of the user costs on the links that comprise the path, that is,

$$C_p = \sum_{a \in \mathcal{L}} c_a(f_a)\delta_{ap}, \quad \forall a \in \mathcal{L}. \tag{3.11}$$

In view of (3.8), one may express the cost on a path p as a function of the path flow variables and, hence, an alternative version of the above system-optimization problem can be stated in path flow variables only, where one has now the problem:

$$\text{Minimize} \quad \sum_{p \in P} C_p(x)x_p \tag{3.12}$$

subject to constraints (3.7) and (3.9).

System-Optimality Conditions
Under the assumption of increasing user link cost functions, the objective function in the S-O problem is convex, and the feasible set consisting of the linear constraints is also convex. Therefore, the optimality conditions, that is, the Kuhn-Tucker conditions (see Appendix A) are: For each O/D pair $\omega \in \Omega$, and each path $p \in P_\omega$, the flow pattern x (and link flow pattern f), satisfying (3.7)–(3.9) must satisfy:

$$\hat{C}'_p \begin{cases} = \mu_\omega, & \text{if } x_p > 0 \\ \geq \mu_\omega, & \text{if } x_p = 0, \end{cases} \tag{3.13}$$

where $\hat{C}_p'$ denotes the marginal of the total cost on path p, given by:

$$\hat{C}_p' = \sum_{a \in \mathcal{L}} \frac{\partial \hat{c}_a(f_a)}{\partial f_a} \delta_{ap}, \qquad (3.14)$$

and in (3.13) it is evaluated at the solution.

Note that in the S-O problem, according to the optimality conditions (3.13), it is the marginal of the total cost on each used path connecting an O/D pair which is equalized and minimal. Indeed, conditions (3.13) state that a system-optimized flow pattern is such that for each origin/destination pair the incurred marginals of the total cost on all used paths are equal and minimal (see also Table 3.1).

3.3.1.2   The User-Optimized Problem

We now describe the user-optimized network problem, also commonly referred to in the transportation literature as the *traffic assignment* problem or the *traffic network equilibrium* problem. Again, as in the system-optimized problem of Section 3.3.1.1, the network $\mathcal{G} = [\mathcal{N}, \mathcal{L}]$, the demands associated with the origin/destination pairs, as well as the user link cost functions are assumed as given. Recall that user-optimization follows Wardrop's first principle.

Network Equilibrium Conditions

Now, however, one seeks to determine the path flow pattern x^* (and link flow pattern f^*) which satisfies the conservation of flow equations (3.7), (3.8), and the nonnegativity assumption on the path flows (3.9), and which also satisfies the network equilibrium conditions given by the following statement.

For each O/D pair $\omega \in \Omega$ and each path $p \in P_\omega$:

$$C_p \begin{cases} = \lambda_\omega, & \text{if } x_p^* > 0 \\ \geq \lambda_\omega, & \text{if } x_p^* = 0. \end{cases} \qquad (3.15)$$

Hence, in the user-optimization problem there is no explicit optimization concept, since now users of the network system act independently, in a noncooperative manner, until they cannot improve on their situations unilaterally and, thus, an equilibrium is achieved, governed by the above equilibrium conditions. Indeed, conditions (3.15) are simply a restatement of Wardrop's (1952) first principle mathematically and mean that only those paths connecting an O/D pair will be used which have equal and minimal user costs. Otherwise, a user of the network could improve upon his situation by switching to a path with lower cost. User-optimization represents decentralized decision-making, whereas system-optimization represents centralized decision-making. See also Table 3.1.

In order to obtain a solution to the above problem, Beckmann, McGuire, and Winsten (1956) established that the solution to the equilibrium problem, in the case of user link cost functions (cf. (3.3)) in which the cost on a link only depends on the flow on that link could be obtained by solving the following optimization problem:

$$\text{Minimize} \quad \sum_{a \in \mathcal{L}} \int_0^{f_a} c_a(y) dy \qquad (3.16)$$

subject to:

$$\sum_{p \in P_\omega} x_p = d_\omega, \quad \forall \omega \in \Omega, \qquad (3.17)$$

$$f_a = \sum_{p \in P} x_p \delta_{ap}, \quad \forall a \in \mathcal{L}, \qquad (3.18)$$

$$x_p \geq 0, \quad \forall p \in P. \qquad (3.19)$$

Note that the conservation of flow equations are identical in both the user-optimized network problem (see (3.17)–(3.19)) and the system-optimized problem (see (3.7)–(3.9)). The behavior of the individual decision-makers termed "users," however, is different. Users of the network system, which generate the flow on the network now act independently, and are not controlled by a centralized controller.

The objective function given by (3.16) is simply a device constructed to obtain a solution using general purpose convex programming algorithms. It does not possess the economic meaning of the objective function encountered in the system-optimization problem given by (3.6), equivalently, by (3.12).

3.3.1.3 Models with Asymmetric Link Costs

There has been much dynamic research activity in the past several decades in both the modeling and the development of methodologies to enable the formulation and computation of more general network equilibrium models, with a focus on traffic networks. Examples of general models include those that allow for multiple modes of transportation or multiple classes of users, who perceive cost on a link in an individual way. We now consider network models in which the user cost on a link is no longer dependent solely on the flow on that link. Other network models, including dynamic traffic models, can be found in Mahmassani et al. (1993), and in the books by Ran and Boyce (1996) and Nagurney and Zhang (1996), and the references therein. Additional citations were given earlier in Section 2.2.

We now consider user link cost functions which are of a general form, that is, in which the cost on a link may depend not only on the flow on the link but on other link flows on the network, that is,

$$c_a = c_a(f), \quad \forall a \in \mathcal{L}. \qquad (3.20)$$

In the case where the symmetry assumption exists, that is, $\frac{\partial c_a(f)}{\partial f_b} = \frac{\partial c_b(f)}{\partial f_a}$, for all links $a, b \in \mathcal{L}$, one can still reformulate the solution to the network equilibrium problem satisfying equilibrium conditions (3.15) as the solution to an optimization problem (cf. Dafermos (1972), Appendices A and B, and the references therein), albeit, again, with an objective function that is artificial and simply a mathematical device. However, when the symmetry assumption is no longer satisfied, such an optimization reformulation no longer exists and one must appeal to *variational inequality theory* (see Appendix B).

Indeed, it was in the domain of traffic network equilibrium problems that the theory of finite-dimensional variational inequalities realized its earliest success, beginning with the contributions of Smith (1979) and Dafermos (1980). For an introduction to the subject, as well as applications ranging from traffic network equilibrium problems to financial equilibrium problems, see the book by Nagurney (1999). The methodology of finite-dimensional variational inequalities is utilized in this book in order to develop a spectrum of supernetwork models. A basic introduction to the subject can be found in Appendix B.

The system-optimization problem, in turn, in the case of nonseparable (cf. (3.20)) user link cost functions becomes (see also (3.6)–(3.9)):

$$\text{Minimize} \quad \sum_{a \in \mathcal{L}} \hat{c}_a(f), \tag{3.21}$$

subject to (3.7)–(3.9), where $\hat{c}_a(f) = c_a(f) \times f_a, \forall a \in \mathcal{L}$.

The system-optimality conditions remain as in (3.13), but now the marginal of the total cost on a path becomes, in this more general case:

$$\hat{C}'_p = \sum_{a,b \in \mathcal{L}} \frac{\partial \hat{c}_b(f)}{\partial f_a} \delta_{ap}, \quad \forall p \in P. \tag{3.22}$$

Variational Inequality Formulations of Fixed Demand Problems

As mentioned earlier, in the case where the user link cost functions are no longer symmetric, one cannot compute the solution to the U-O, that is, to the network equilibrium, problem using standard optimization algorithms. Such cost functions are very important from an application standpoint since they allow for asymmetric interactions on the network. For example, allowing for asymmetric cost functions permits one to handle the situation when the flow on a particular link affects the cost on another link in a different way than the cost on the particular link is affected by the flow on the other link.

Since in this book equilibrium is such a fundamental concept in terms of supernetworks and since variational inequality theory is one of the basic ways in which to study such problems we now, for completeness, also give variational inequality formulations of the network equilibrium conditions (3.15).

These formulations are presented without proof (for derivations, see Smith (1979) and Dafermos (1980), as well as Florian and Hearn (1995) and the book by Nagurney (1999)). Moreover, appropriate variational inequalities for the specific models are derived later in this book.

First, the definition of a variational inequality problem is recalled (see also Appendix B). We then give both the variational inequality formulation in path flows as well as in link flows of the network equilibrium conditions. In Chapter 7, we extend these concepts to multicriteria, multiclass network equilibrium problems.

Specifically, the variational inequality problem (finite-dimensional) is defined as follows:

Definition 3.1: Variational Inequality Problem
The finite-dimensional variational inequality problem, VI(F, K), is to determine a vector $X^* \in K$ such that

$$\langle F(X^*), X - X^* \rangle \geq 0, \quad \forall X \in K, \tag{3.23}$$

where F is a given continuous function from K to R^N, K is a given closed convex set, and $\langle \cdot, \cdot \rangle$ denotes the inner product in R^N.

Variational inequality (3.23) is referred to as being in *standard form*. Hence, for a given problem, typically an *equilibrium* problem, one must determine the function F that enters the variational inequality problem, the vector of variables X, as well as the feasible set K.

The variational inequality problem contains, as special cases, such well-known problems as systems of equations, optimization problems (see Appendices A and B), and complementarity problems. Thus, it is a powerful unifying methodology for equilibrium analysis and computation.

Theorem 3.1: Variational Inequality Formulation of Network Equilibrium with Fixed Demands – Path Flow Version
A vector $x^* \in K^1$ is a network equilibrium path flow pattern, that is, it satisfies equilibrium conditions (3.15) if and only if it satisfies the variational inequality problem:

$$\sum_{\omega \in \Omega} \sum_{p \in P_\omega} C_p(x^*) \times (x - x^*) \geq 0, \quad \forall x \in K^1, \tag{3.24}$$

or, in vector form:

$$\langle C(x^*), x - x^* \rangle \geq 0, \quad \forall x \in K^1, \tag{3.25}$$

where C is the n_P-dimensional column vector of path user costs and K^1 is defined as: $K^1 \equiv \{x \geq 0, \text{ such that } (3.17) \text{ holds}\}$.

Theorem 3.2: Variational Inequality Formulation of Network Equilibrium with Fixed Demands – Link Flow Version

A vector $f^* \in K^2$ is a network equilibrium link flow pattern if and only if it satisfies the variational inequality problem:

$$\sum_{a \in \mathcal{L}} c_a(f^*) \times (f_a - f_a^*) \geq 0, \quad \forall f \in K^2, \tag{3.26}$$

or, in vector form:

$$\langle c(f^*), f - f^* \rangle \geq 0, \quad \forall f \in K^2, \tag{3.27}$$

where c is the n-dimensional column vector of link user costs and K^2 is defined as: $K^2 \equiv \{f \mid there\ exists\ an\ x \geq 0\ and\ satisfying\ (3.17)\ and\ (3.18)\}$.

Note that one may put variational inequality (3.25) in standard form (3.23) by letting $F \equiv C$, $X \equiv x$, and $\mathcal{K} \equiv K^1$. Also, one may put variational inequality (3.27) in standard form where now $F \equiv c$, $X \equiv f$, and $\mathcal{K} \equiv K^2$.

Alternative variational inequality formulations of a problem are useful in devising other models, including dynamic versions, as well as for purposes of computation using different algorithms.

Variational Inequality Formulations of Elastic Demand Problems

We now describe the general network equilibrium model with elastic demands due to Dafermos (1982). Specifically, it is assumed that now one has associated with each O/D pair ω in the network a disutility λ_ω, where here the general case is considered in which the disutility may depend upon the entire vector of demands, which are no longer fixed, but are now variables, that is,

$$\lambda_\omega = \lambda_\omega(d), \quad \forall \omega \in \Omega, \tag{3.28}$$

where d is the J-dimensional column vector of the demands.

The notation, otherwise, is as described earlier, except that here we also consider user link cost functions which are general, that is, of the form (3.20). The conservation of flow equations (see also (3.1) and (3.2)), in turn, are given by

$$f_a = \sum_{p \in P} x_p \delta_{ap}, \quad \forall a \in \mathcal{L}, \tag{3.29}$$

$$d_\omega = \sum_{p \in P_\omega} x_p, \quad \forall \omega \in \Omega, \tag{3.30}$$

$$x_p \geq 0, \quad \forall p \in P. \tag{3.31}$$

Hence, in the elastic demand case, the demands in expression (3.30) are now variables and no longer given, as was the case for the fixed demand expression in (3.2).

Network Equilibrium Conditions in the Case of Elastic Demand

The network equilibrium conditions (see also (3.15)) now take on in the elastic demand case the following form: For every O/D pair $\omega \in \Omega$, and each path $p \in P_\omega$, a vector of path flows and demands (x^*, d^*) satisfying (3.30)–(3.31) (which induces a link flow pattern f^* through (3.29)) is a network equilibrium pattern if it satisfies:

$$C_p(x^*) \begin{cases} = \lambda_\omega(d^*), & \text{if } x_p^* > 0 \\ \geq \lambda_\omega(d^*), & \text{if } x_p^* = 0. \end{cases} \tag{3.32}$$

Equilibrium conditions (3.32) state that the costs on used paths for each O/D pair are equal and minimal and equal to the disutility associated with that O/D pair. Costs on unutilized paths can exceed the disutility.

In the next two theorems, both the path flow version and the link flow version of the variational inequality formulations of the network equilibrium conditions (3.32) are presented. These are analogues of the formulations (3.24) and (3.25), and (3.26) and (3.27), respectively, for the fixed demand model. Extensions of such models are given in Chapter 7 and applied to telecommuting versus commuting decision-making and teleshopping versus shopping decision-making.

Theorem 3.3: Variational Inequality Formulation of Network Equilibrium with Elastic Demands – Path Flow Version

A vector $(x^*, d^*) \in K^3$ is a network equilibrium path flow pattern, that is, it satisfies equilibrium conditions (3.32) if and only if it satisfies the variational inequality problem:

$$\sum_{\omega \in \Omega} \sum_{p \in P_\omega} C_p(x^*) \times (x - x^*) - \sum_{\omega \in \Omega} \lambda_\omega(d^*) \times (d_\omega - d_\omega^*) \geq 0, \quad \forall (x, d) \in K^3,$$

$$\tag{3.33}$$

or, in vector form:

$$\langle C(x^*), x - x^* \rangle - \langle \lambda(d^*), d - d^* \rangle \geq 0, \quad \forall (x, d) \in K^3, \tag{3.34}$$

where λ is the J-dimensional vector of disutilities and K^3 is defined as: $K^3 \equiv \{x \geq 0, \text{ such that } (3.30) \text{ holds}\}$.

Theorem 3.4: Variational Inequality Formulation of Network Equilibrium with Elastic Demands – Link Flow Version

A vector $(f^*, d^*) \in K^4$ is a network equilibrium link flow pattern if and only if it satisfies the variational inequality problem:

$$\sum_{a \in \mathcal{L}} c_a(f^*) \times (f_a - f_a^*) - \sum_{\omega \in \Omega} \lambda_\omega(d^*) \times (d_\omega - d_\omega^*) \geq 0, \quad \forall (f, d) \in K^4, \tag{3.35}$$

or, in vector form:

$$\langle c(f^*), f - f^* \rangle - \langle \lambda(d^*), d - d^* \rangle \geq 0, \quad \forall (f, d) \in K^4, \tag{3.36}$$

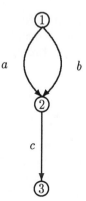

Fig. 3.3. An Elastic Demand Example

where $K^4 \equiv \{(f, d)$, such that there exists an $x \geq 0$ satisfying (3.29), (3.31)\}

Note that, under the symmetry assumption on the disutility functions, that is, if $\frac{\partial \lambda_w}{\partial d_\omega} = \frac{\partial \lambda_\omega}{\partial d_w}$, for all w, ω, in addition to such an assumption on the user link cost functions (see following (3.20)), one can obtain (see Beckmann, McGuire, and Winsten (1956) and Appendix B) an optimization reformulation of the network equilibrium conditions (3.32), which in the case of separable user link cost functions and disutility functions is given by:

$$\text{Minimize} \quad \sum_{a \in \mathcal{L}} \int_0^{f_a} c_a(y)dy - \sum_{w \in \Omega} \int_0^{d_\omega} \lambda_\omega(z)dz \qquad (3.37)$$

subject to: (3.29)–(3.31).

We now present an example of a simple elastic demand network equilibrium problem.

Example 3.1

Consider the network depicted in Figure 3.3 in which there are three nodes: 1, 2, 3; three links: a, b, c; and a single O/D pair $\omega_1 = (1, 3)$. Let path $p_1 = (a, c)$ and path $p_2 = (b, c)$.

Assume that the user link cost functions are:

$$c_a(f) = 5f_a + 2f_b + 10, \quad c_b(f) = 7f_b + f_a + 10, \quad c_c(f) = 3f_c + f_a + f_b + 12,$$

and the disutility (or inverse demand) function is given by:

$$\lambda_{\omega_1}(d_{\omega_1}) = -2d_{\omega_1} + 109.$$

Observe that in this example, the user link cost functions are non-separable and asymmetric and, hence, the equilibrium conditions (3.32) cannot be reformulated as the solution to an optimization problem, but, rather, as the solution to the variational inequalities (3.33) (or (3.34)), or (3.35) (or (3.36)).

The U-O flow and demand pattern that satisfies equilibrium conditions (3.32) is: $x^*_{p_1} = 5$, $x^*_{p_2} = 4$, and $d^*_{\omega_1} = 9$, with associated link flow pattern: $f^*_a = 5$, $f^*_b = 4$, $f^*_c = 9$.

The incurred user costs on the paths are: $C_{p_1} = C_{p_2} = 91$, which is precisely the value of the disutility λ_{ω_1}. Hence, this flow and demand pattern satisfies equilibrium conditions (3.32). Indeed, both paths p_1 and p_2 are utilized and their user paths costs are equal to each other. In addition, these costs are equal to the disutility associated with the origin/destination pair that the two paths connect.

The concept of system-optimization has been presented here for clarity and exposition purposes. User-optimization, on the other hand, is a particularly relevant concept for decision-making on supernetworks and will be the basic concept utilized in Part III of this book where we present a variety of multicriteria, multiclass network equilibrium models and applications. In Part II of this book, in which the focus is on multitiered supernetworks, we describe an alternative decision-making concept, also dealing with noncooperative behavior, and referred to as Nash (1950) equilibrium.

3.4   Sources and Notes

In this chapter, we have presented the foundations of the theory and concept of supernetworks. We identified the uses of the term in the literature that are in concert with the perspective in this book. In particular, we identified the early formal treatments of abstract networks for decision-making purposes in transportation in an equilibrium context, which as noted by Dafermos (1972) are also relevant to telecommunication networks. We recognized that abstract networks have been developed for transportation decision-making for mode selection, as well as in location-related decision-making.

Abstract networks have also had wide application since the work of Dial (1967) in the study of a particular class of transportation network problem known as the transit assignment problem. For a thorough survey on this topic, see Bouzaiene-Ayari, Gendreau, and Nguyen (1998). Moreover, it is important to note that abstract networks have also been used to transform elastic demand networks to fixed demand networks through the appropriate addition of links and definitions of associated costs on them (see, for example, Gartner (1980a,b) and the references therein).

The topics of such foundational networks as transportation and telecommunications are huge and we have focused on citations that are directly related to the subjects and themes of this book. Additional sources of material for this chapter are from Nagurney (1999, 2000a, b, c).

Part II Multitiered Networks

4 Supply Chain Networks and Electronic Commerce

This chapter begins the second part of this book, which is devoted to multitiered supernetworks, that is, supernetworks, which consist of distinct tiers of decision-makers, whose behavior, in turn, affects the variables on the networks in the form of flows as well as prices. Chapters 4 and 5 focus on supply chain networks. Chapter 6, subsequently, through the use of the multitiered (and, also, multilevel) supernetwork concept, explores another application area – that of financial networks with intermediation.

The study of supply chain networks here is in the context of the Information Age with the innovations brought about by electronic commerce. As is well recognized, electronic commerce (e-commerce), with the advent of the Information Age, has had an enormous effect on the manner in which businesses as well as consumers order goods and have them transported. Electronic commerce is defined as a "trade" that takes place over the Internet usually through a buyer visiting a seller's website and making a transaction there. The major portion of e-commerce transactions is in the form of business-to-business (B2B) with estimates ranging from approximately $1 billion to $1 trillion in 1998 and with forecasts reaching as high as $4.8 trillion in 2003 in the United States (see Federal Highway Administration (2000), Southworth (2000)). The business-to-consumer (B2C) component, on the other hand, has seen tremendous growth in recent years but its impact on the US retail activity is still relatively small. Nevertheless, this segment should grow to $80 billion per year (Southworth (2000)).

As noted by Handfield and Nichols (1999) and by the National Research Council (2000), the principal effect of B2B commerce, estimated to be 90 percent of all e-commerce by value and volume, is in the creation of new and more profitable *supply chain networks*. A supply chain is a chain of relationships which synthesizes and integrates the movement of goods between suppliers, manufacturers, distributors, retailers, and consumers.

The topic of supply chain analysis is multidisciplinary by nature since it involves aspects of manufacturing, transportation and logistics, retailing/marketing, as well as economics. It has been the subject of a growing body of literature with researchers focusing both on the conceptualization of the underlying problems (see, e.g., Andersson, et al. (1993), Poirier (1996, 1999), Bovet (2000), Mentzer (2001)), due to the complexity of the problem and the numerous agents, such as manufacturers, retailers, or consumers involved in the transactions, as well as on the analytics (cf. Federgruen (1993), Graves, Rinooy Kan, and Zipkin (1993), Slats, et al. (1995), Bramel and Simchi-Levi (1997), Stadtler and Kilger (2000), Miller (2001), Hensher, Button, and Brewer (2001), and the references therein).

The introduction of e-commerce has unveiled new opportunities in terms of research and practice in supply chain analysis and management (see, e.g., Kuglin and Rosenbaum (2001)). Indeed, the primary benefit of the Internet for business is its open access to potential suppliers and customers both within a particular country and beyond national boundaries. Consumers, on the other hand, may obtain goods which they physically could not locate otherwise.

In this chapter, a supernetwork framework is constructed for the study of supply chains with electronic commerce in the form of B2C and B2B transactions. The framework is sufficiently general to allow for the modeling, analysis, and computation of solutions to such problems. Here the focus is on the network interactions of the underlying agents and on the underlying competitive processes. Moreover, the emphasis is placed on the equilibrium aspects of the problems rather than, simply, the optimization ones. Of course, it is assumed that the agents in the supply chain behave in some optimal fashion. An equilibrium approach is necessary and valuable since it provides a benchmark against which one can evaluate both prices and product flows. Moreover, it captures the independent behavior of the various decision-makers as well as the effect of their interactions. Finally, it provides for the development of dynamic models, with possible disequilibrium behavior, which is the topic of Chapter 5, to enable the study of the evolution of supply chains.

In this chapter, manufacturers are considered who are involved in the production of a homogeneous commodity, referred to also as the product, which can then be shipped to the retailers or to the consumers directly or to both. The manufacturers obtain a price for the product (which is endogenous) and seek to determine their optimal production and shipment quantities, given the production costs as well as the *transaction* costs associated with conducting business with the different retailers and demand markets. Here a transaction cost is considered to be sufficiently general, for example, to include the transportation/shipping cost. On the other hand, in the case of an e-commerce link, the transaction costs can include the cost associated with the use of such a link, the lack of productivity due to congestion, an associated risk, etc.

The retailers, in turn, must agree with the manufacturers as to the volume of shipments, either ordered physically or through the Internet, since they are faced with the handling cost associated with having the product in their retail outlet. In addition, they seek to maximize their profits with the price that the consumers are willing to pay for the product being endogenous.

Finally, in this supply chain, the consumers provide the "pull" in that, given the demand functions at the various demand markets, they determine their optimal consumption levels from the various retailers (transacted either physically or through the Internet) and from the manufacturers (transacted through the Internet), subject both to the prices charged for the product as well as the cost of conducting the transaction (which, of course, may include the cost of transportation associated with obtaining the product from the manufacturer or the retailer). Thus, the demand for the product is a central part of the supply chain framework.

In this chapter, it is shown that, in equilibrium, the structure of the supply chain network is that of a three-tiered network, with links connecting the top tier (the manufacturers) with the bottom tier (the demand markets) to represent e-commerce links and additional links from the top tier to the middle tier (the retailers) and from the middle tier to the bottom tier nodes to also represent the e-commerce links. The variational inequality formulation of the governing equilibrium conditions is then utilized in order to obtain both qualitative properties as well as an algorithm for the computation of the equilibrium flows and prices.

The chapter is organized as follows. In Section 4.1, the supply chain network model with electronic commerce is presented, the optimality conditions for each set of network agents or decision-makers derived, and the governing equilibrium conditions given. The finite-dimensional variational inequality formulation of the equilibrium conditions is also established. We then discuss two applications of the model to an online grocery and to an online bookseller, respectively. In Section 4.2, some qualitative properties of the equilibrium pattern are obtained as well as the necessary properties for proving convergence of a computational procedure. In Section 4.3, the computational procedure is described, which, in the context of the supply chain application, resolves the supernetwork problem into subproblems, each of which can be solved exactly and in closed form. In Section 4.4, the algorithm is applied to numerical examples to determine the equilibrium flows and prices.

4.1 The Supply Chain Network Model with Electronic Commerce

In this section, the supply chain network model is developed. It consists of manufacturers, retailers, and consumers. The manufacturers can sell directly

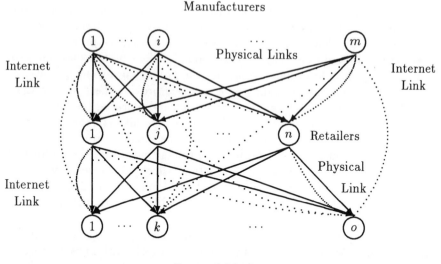

Fig. 4.1. The Multitiered Supernetwork Structure of the Supply Chain Network with E-Commerce at Equilibrium

to the consumers at the demand markets through the Internet and can also conduct their business transactions with the retailers through the Internet. The consumers, in turn, can also purchase the product from the retailers either "physically" or electronically, that is, "on-line," through the Internet. Figure 4.1 depicts the multitiered supernetwork structure of the supply chain network, at equilibrium, which is established in this section.

Specifically, consider m manufacturers involved in the production of a homogeneous product which can then be purchased by n retailers and/or directly by the consumers located at the o demand markets. Denote a typical manufacturer by i, a typical retailer by j, and a typical demand market by k. Note that the manufacturers are located at the top tier of nodes of the network, the retailers at the middle tier, and the demand markets at the third or bottom tier of nodes.

The links in the supply chain supernetwork in Figure 4.1 include classical physical links as well as Internet links to allow for e-commerce. The introduction of e-commerce allows for "connections" that were, heretofore, not possible, such as enabling consumers, for example, to purchase a product directly from the manufacturers. In order to conceptualize this B2C type of transaction, a direct link has been constructed from each top tier node to each bottom tier node. In addition, since manufacturers can transact not only with the consumers directly but also with the retailers through the Internet, an additional link is added (to represent such a possible B2B transaction) between each top tier node and each middle tier node. Hence, a manufacturer may transact with a retailer through either a physical link or through an Internet link, or through both. Finally, consumers can transact with retailers either via a physical link, or through an Internet link, or through both.

The behavior of the various economic network agents represented by the three tiers of nodes in Figure 4.1 is now described. We first focus on the manufacturers. We then turn to the retailers and, subsequently, to the consumers.

The Behavior of the Manufacturers and their Optimality Conditions

Let q_i denote the nonnegative production output of manufacturer i. Group the production outputs of all manufacturers into the column vector $q \in R_+^m$. Here it is assumed that each manufacturer i is faced with a production cost function f_i, which can depend, in general, on the entire vector of production outputs, that is,

$$f_i = f_i(q), \quad \forall i. \tag{4.1}$$

Hence, the production cost of a particular manufacturer can depend not only on his production output but also on those of the other manufacturers. This allows one to model competition.

Figure 4.2 depicts the allowable transactions of a typical manufacturer i with the consumers at the demand markets and with the retailers. Note that a manufacturer may transact with a retailer via a physical link, and/or via an Internet link.

The transaction cost associated with manufacturer i transacting with retailer j via link (also referred to as *mode*) l, where $l = 1$ denotes a physical link and $l = 2$ denotes an Internet link, is denoted by c_{ijl}. The product shipment associated with manufacturer i, retailer j, and mode of transaction l is denoted by q_{ijl}, and these product shipments into the column vector $Q^1 \in R_+^{2mn}$. In addition, a manufacturer i may transact directly with consumers located at a demand market k with this transaction cost associated with the Internet transaction denoted by c_{ik} and the associated product shipment from manufacturer i to demand market k by q_{ik}. Group these product shipments into the column vector $Q^2 \in R_+^{mo}$.

The transaction cost between a manufacturer and retail pair and the transaction cost between a manufacturer and consumers at a demand market may depend upon the volume of transactions between each such pair, and are given, respectively, by:

$$c_{ijl} = c_{ijl}(q_{ijl}), \quad \forall i, j, l, \tag{4.2a}$$

and

$$c_{ik} = c_{ik}(q_{ik}), \quad \forall i, k. \tag{4.2b}$$

Manufacturer

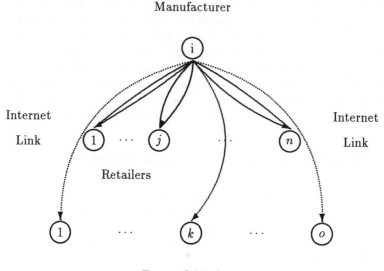

Fig. 4.2. Network Structure of Manufacturer i's Transactions

The quantity produced by manufacturer i must satisfy the following conservation of flow equation:

$$q_i = \sum_{j=1}^{n}\sum_{l=1}^{2} q_{ijl} + \sum_{k=1}^{o} q_{ik}, \qquad (4.3)$$

which states that the quantity produced by manufacturer i is equal to the sum of the quantities shipped from the manufacturer to all retailers and to all demand markets.

The total costs incurred by a manufacturer i, thus, are equal to the sum of the manufacturer's production cost plus the total transaction costs. His revenue, in turn, is equal to the price that the manufacturer charges for the product (and the consumers are willing to pay) times the total quantity obtained/purchased of the product from the manufacturer by all the retail outlets and consumers at all demand markets. Let ρ^*_{1ijl} denote the price charged for the product by manufacturer i to retailer j who has transacted using mode l, and let ρ^*_{1ik} denote the price charged by manufacturer i for the product to consumers at demand market k. Hence, manufacturers can price according to their location, as to whether the product is sold to the retailers or to the consumers directly, and according to whether the transaction was conducted via the Internet or not. How these prices are arrived at is discussed later in this section.

Noting the conservation of flow equations (4.3) and the production cost functions (4.1), one can express the criterion of profit maximization for manufacturer i as:

$$\text{Maximize} \sum_{j=1}^{n}\sum_{l=1}^{2} \rho_{1ijl}^{*} q_{ijl} - f_i(Q^1, Q^2) - \sum_{j=1}^{n}\sum_{l=1}^{2} c_{ijl}(q_{ijl}) - \sum_{k=1}^{o} c_{ik}(q_{ik})$$

$$+ \sum_{k=1}^{o} \rho_{1ik}^{*} q_{ik}, \tag{4.4}$$

subject to $q_{ijl} \geq 0$, for all j, l, and $q_{ik} \geq 0$, for all k.

The manufacturers are assumed to compete in a noncooperative fashion. Also, it is assumed that the production cost functions and the transaction cost functions for each manufacturer are continuous and convex (see Appendix A). The governing optimization/equilibrium concept underlying noncooperative behavior is that of Nash (1950, 1951), which states, in this context, that each manufacturer will determine his optimal production quantity and shipments, given the optimal ones of the competitors. Hence, the optimality conditions for all manufacturers *simultaneously* can be expressed as the following inequality (see also Gabay and Moulin (1980), Dafermos and Nagurney (1987), Bazaraa, Sherali, and Shetty (1993), and Nagurney (1999)): determine the solution (Q^{1*}, Q^{2*}), which satisfies:

$$\sum_{i=1}^{m}\sum_{j=1}^{n}\sum_{l=1}^{2} \left[\frac{\partial f_i(Q^{1*}, Q^{2*})}{\partial q_{ijl}} + \frac{\partial c_{ijl}(q_{ijl}^{*})}{\partial q_{ijl}} - \rho_{1ijl}^{*} \right] \times \left[q_{ijl} - q_{ijl}^{*} \right]$$

$$+ \sum_{i=1}^{m}\sum_{k=1}^{o} \left[\frac{\partial f_i(Q^{1*}, Q^{2*})}{\partial q_{ik}} + \frac{\partial c_{ik}(q_{ik}^{*})}{\partial q_{ik}} - \rho_{1ik}^{*} \right] \times \left[q_{ik} - q_{ik}^{*} \right] \geq 0, \tag{4.5}$$

$$\forall Q^1 \in R_{+}^{2mn}, \forall Q^2 \in R_{+}^{mo}.$$

The inequality (4.5), which is a *variational inequality* (see also Appendix B) has a nice economic interpretation. In particular, from the first term one can infer that, if there is a positive shipment of the product transacted either in a classical manner or via the Internet from a manufacturer to a retailer, then the marginal cost of production plus the marginal cost of transacting must be equal to the price that the retailer is willing to pay for the product. If the marginal cost of production plus the marginal cost of transacting exceeds that price, then there will be zero volume of flow of the product on that link. The second term in (4.5) has a similar interpretation; in particular, there will be a positive volume of flow of the product from a manufacturer to a demand market if the marginal cost of production of the manufacturer plus the marginal cost of transacting with the consumers at a demand market via the Internet is equal to the price the consumers are willing to pay for the product at the demand market.

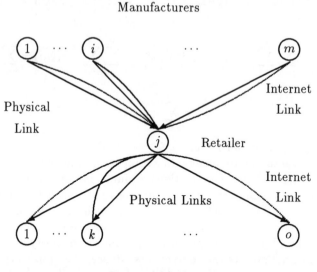

Fig. 4.3. Network Structure of Retailer j's Transactions

The Behavior of the Retailers and their Optimality Conditions

The retailers, in turn, are involved in transactions both with the manufacturers since they wish to obtain the product for their retail outlets, as well as with the consumers, who are the ultimate purchasers of the product. Thus, a retailer conducts transactions both with the manufacturers as well as with the consumers. See Figure 4.3 for a graphical depiction.

A retailer j is faced with what is termed a *handling* cost, which may include, for example, the display and storage cost associated with the product. Denote this cost by c_j and, in the simplest case, one would have that c_j is a function of $\sum_{i=1}^{m} \sum_{l=1}^{2} q_{ijl}$, that is, the holding cost of a retailer is a function of how much of the product he has obtained from the various manufacturers via the two different modes of transacting. However, for the sake of generality, and to enhance the modeling of competition, allow the function to, in general, depend also on the amounts of the product held by other retailers and, therefore, one may write:

$$c_j = c_j(Q^1), \quad \forall j. \tag{4.6}$$

The retailers, in turn, also have associated transaction costs in regard to transacting with the manufacturers via either modal alternative. Denote the transaction cost associated with retailer j transacting with manufacturer i using mode l by $\hat{c}_{ijl}$ and assume that the function can depend upon the product shipment q_{ijl}, that is,

$$\hat{c}_{ijl} = \hat{c}_{ijl}(q_{ijl}), \quad \forall i, j, l. \tag{4.7}$$

Let q_{jkl} denote the amount of the product purchased/consumed by consumers located at demand market k from retailer j, using transaction mode l, where, as in the case of the manufacturer/retailer transactions discussed above, $l = 1$ denotes a physical mode (and corresponding link) of transaction, whereas $l = 2$ denotes an electronic mode of transaction (through an Internet link). Group these consumption quantities into the column vector $Q^3 \in R_+^{2no}$.

The retailers associate a price with the product at their retail outlet, which is denoted by γ_j^*, for retailer j. This price, as will be shown, will also be endogenously determined in the model and will be, given a positive volume of flow between a retailer and any demand market, equal to a clearing-type price. Assuming, as mentioned earlier in this chapter, that the retailers are also profit-maximizers, the optimization problem of a retailer j is given by:

$$\text{Maximize} \quad \gamma_j^* \sum_{k=1}^{o} \sum_{l=1}^{2} q_{jkl} - c_j(Q^1) - \sum_{i=1}^{m} \sum_{l=1}^{2} \hat{c}_{ijl}(q_{ijl}) - \sum_{i=1}^{m} \sum_{l=1}^{2} \rho_{1ijl}^* q_{ijl} \tag{4.8}$$

subject to:

$$\sum_{k=1}^{o} \sum_{l=1}^{2} q_{jkl} \leq \sum_{i=1}^{m} \sum_{l=1}^{2} q_{ijl}, \tag{4.9}$$

and the nonnegativity constraints: $q_{ijl} \geq 0$, and $q_{jkl} \geq 0$, for all i, l, and k. Objective function (4.8) expresses that the difference between the revenues and the handling cost plus the transaction costs and the payout to the manufacturers should be maximized. Constraint (4.9) simply expresses that consumers cannot purchase more from a retailer than is held in stock.

The optimality conditions of the retailers are now obtained, assuming that each retailer is faced with the optimization problem (4.8), subject to (4.9), and the nonnegativity assumption on the variables. Here it is also assumed that the retailers compete in a noncooperative manner so that each maximizes his profits, given the actions of the other retailers. Note that, at this point, we consider that retailers seek to determine not only the optimal amounts purchased by the consumers from their specific retail outlet but, also, the amount that they wish to obtain from the manufacturers. In equilibrium, all the shipments between the tiers of network agents will have to coincide.

Assuming that the handling cost for each retailer is continuous and convex as are the transaction costs, the optimal $(Q^{1^*}, Q^{3^*}, \rho_2^*)$ satisfy the optimality conditions for all the retailers (cf. Appendix B) or, equivalently, the variational inequality:

$$\sum_{i=1}^{m} \sum_{j=1}^{n} \sum_{l=1}^{2} \left[\frac{\partial c_j(Q^{1^*})}{\partial q_{ijl}} + \rho_{1ijl}^* + \frac{\partial \hat{c}_{ijl}(q_{ijl}^*)}{\partial q_{ijl}} - \rho_{2j}^* \right] \times [q_{ijl} - q_{ijl}^*]$$

$$+ \sum_{j=1}^{n} \sum_{k=1}^{o} \sum_{l=1}^{2} \left[-\gamma_j^* + \rho_{2j}^* \right] \times \left[q_{jkl} - q_{jkl}^* \right]$$

$$+ \sum_{j=1}^{n} \left[\sum_{i=1}^{m} \sum_{l=1}^{2} q_{ijl}^* - \sum_{k=1}^{o} \sum_{l=1}^{2} q_{jkl}^* \right] \times \left[\rho_{2j} - \rho_{2j}^* \right] \geq 0, \qquad (4.10)$$

$$\forall Q^1 \in R_+^{2mn}, \forall Q^3 \in R_+^{2no}, \forall \rho_2 \in R_+^n,$$

where ρ_{2j} is the Lagrange multiplier associated with constraint (4.9) for manufacturer j and ρ_2 is the column vector of all the manufacturers' multipliers. For further background on such a derivation, see Bertsekas and Tsitsiklis (1989) and Appendix B. In this derivation, as in the derivation of inequality (4.5), the prices charged were not variables. We let γ^* be the column vector of endogenous equilibrium retailer prices with components $(\gamma_1^*, \ldots, \gamma_n^*)$.

The economic interpretation of the retailers' optimality conditions is now highlighted. From the second term in inequality (4.10), one has that, if consumers at demand market k purchase the product from a particular retailer j using mode l, that is, if the q_{jkl}^* is positive, then the price charged by retailer j, γ_j^*, is precisely equal to ρ_{2j}^*, which, from the third term in the inequality, serves as the price to clear the market from retailer j. Also, note that, from the second term, one sees that if no product is sold by a particular retailer, then the price associated with holding the product can exceed the price charged to the consumers. Furthermore, from the first term in inequality (4.10), one can infer that, if a manufacturer transacts with a retailer via a particular mode resulting in a positive flow of the product between the two, then the price ρ_{2j}^* is precisely equal to the retailer j's payment to the manufacturer, ρ_{1ijl}^*, plus his marginal cost of handling the product plus the retailer's marginal cost of transaction associated with transacting with the particular manufacturer.

The Consumers at the Demand Markets and the Equilibrium Conditions

We now describe the consumers located at the demand markets. The consumers take into account in making their consumption decisions not only the price charged for the product by the retailers and the manufacturers but also their transaction costs associated with obtaining the product. The consumers at the demand markets can transact either directly with the producing manufacturers through the Internet or physically with the retailers. In Figure 4.4, a depiction of consumers transacting at a typical demand market k is given.

Let $\hat{c}_{jkl}$ denote the unit transaction cost associated with obtaining the product by consumers at demand market k from retailer j via mode l and recall that q_{jkl} is the amount of the product puchased (or flowing) between retailer j and consumers at demand market k on the connecting link l. Assume that the transaction cost is continuous and can, in general, depend

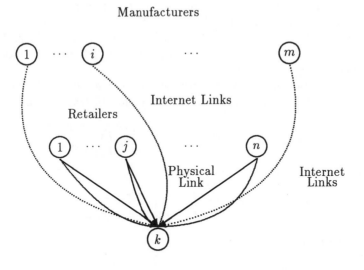

Fig. 4.4. Network Structure of Consumers' Transactions at Demand Market k

upon all the product shipments to all the demand markets, that is:

$$\hat{c}_{jkl} = \hat{c}_{jkl}(Q^2, Q^3), \quad \forall j, k, l. \tag{4.11}$$

Also, let $\hat{c}_{ik}$ denote the unit transaction cost, from the perspective of the consumers at demand market k, associated with manufacturer i. Assume that

$$\hat{c}_{ik} = \hat{c}_{ik}(Q^2, Q^3), \quad \forall i, k. \tag{4.12}$$

Hence, the cost of conducting a transaction with a manufacturer via the Internet can depend, in general, upon the volumes of the product transacted via all the Internet links as well as those transacted from all the retailers.

Let now ρ_{3k} denote the demand price of the product at demand market k. Further, denote the demand for the product at demand market k by d_k and assume, as given, the continuous demand functions:

$$d_k = d_k(\rho_3), \quad \forall k, \tag{4.13}$$

where ρ_3 is the o-dimensional column vector of demand market prices. Thus, according to (4.13), the demand of consumers for the product at a demand market depends, in general, not only on the price of the product at that demand market but also on the prices of the product at the other demand markets. Consequently, consumers at a demand market, in a sense, also compete with consumers at other demand markets.

The consumers take the price charged by the retailers for the product, which was denoted by γ_j^* for retailer j, plus the transaction cost associated with obtaining the product, in making their consumption decisions. In addition, they take the price charged by a producer, ρ_{1ik}^*, plus that associated transaction cost into consideration.

The equilibrium conditions for consumers at demand market k, thus, take the form: for all retailers: $j; j = 1, \ldots, n$, and for all transaction modes l; $l = 1, 2$:

$$\gamma_j^* + \hat{c}_{jkl}(Q^{2*}, Q^{3*}) \begin{cases} = \rho_{3k}^*, & \text{if} \quad q_{jkl}^* > 0 \\ \geq \rho_{3k}^*, & \text{if} \quad q_{jkl}^* = 0, \end{cases} \tag{4.14}$$

for all manufacturers $i; i = 1, \ldots, m$:

$$\rho_{1ik}^* + \hat{c}_{ik}(Q^{2*}, Q^{3*}) \begin{cases} = \rho_{3k}^*, & \text{if} \quad q_{ik}^* > 0 \\ \geq \rho_{3k}^*, & \text{if} \quad q_{ik}^* = 0, \end{cases} \tag{4.15}$$

and for demand market k:

$$d_k(\rho_3^*) \begin{cases} = \displaystyle\sum_{j=1}^{n}\sum_{l=1}^{2} q_{jkl}^* + \sum_{i=1}^{m} q_{ik}^*, & \text{if} \quad \rho_{3k}^* > 0 \\ \leq \displaystyle\sum_{j=1}^{n}\sum_{l=1}^{2} q_{jkl}^* + \sum_{i=1}^{m} q_{ik}^*, & \text{if} \quad \rho_{3k}^* = 0. \end{cases} \tag{4.16}$$

Conditions (4.14) state that consumers at demand market k will purchase the product from retailer j, transacted via mode l, if the price charged by the retailer for the product plus the transaction cost (from the perspective of the consumers) does not exceed the price that the consumers are willing to pay for the product. Conditions (4.15), in turn, state the analogue for the manufacturers and demand market. Conditions (4.16), on the other hand, reflect that, if the price the consumers are willing to pay for the product at a demand market is positive, then the quantity consumed by the consumers at the demand market is precisely equal to the demand. These conditions correspond to the well-known spatial price equilibrium conditions (cf. Samuelson (1952), Takayama and Judge (1971), and Nagurney (1999) and the references therein).

In equilibrium, conditions (4.14), (4.15), and (4.16) will have to hold for all demand markets k, and these, in turn, can also be expressed as a variational inequality problem akin to (4.5) and (4.10) and given by: determine $(Q^{2*}, Q^{3*}, \rho_3^*) \in R^{mo+2no+n}$, such that

$$\sum_{j=1}^{n}\sum_{k=1}^{o}\sum_{l=1}^{2} \left[\gamma_j^* + \hat{c}_{jkl}(Q^{2*}, Q^{3*}) - \rho_{3k}^*\right] \times \left[q_{jkl} - q_{jkl}^*\right]$$

$$+ \sum_{i=1}^{m}\sum_{k=1}^{n} \left[\rho_{1ik}^* + \hat{c}_{ik}(Q^{2*}, Q^{3*}) - \rho_{3k}^*\right] \times \left[q_{ik} - q_{ik}^*\right]$$

$$+ \sum_{k=1}^{o} \left[\sum_{j=1}^{n} \sum_{l=1}^{2} q_{jkl}^* + \sum_{i=1}^{m} q_{ik}^* - d_k(\rho_3^*) \right] \times [\rho_{3k} - \rho_{3k}^*] \geq 0, \qquad (4.17)$$

$$\forall (Q^2, Q^3, \rho_3) \in R_+^{mo+2no+n}.$$

Note that, in the context of the consumption decisions, demand functions, rather than utility functions, have been utilized, in contrast to the manufacturers and the retailers, who were assumed to be faced with profit functions, which correspond to utility functions. Of course, demand functions can be derived from utility functions (cf. Arrow and Intrilligator (1982)). One can expect the number of consumers to be much greater than that of the manufacturers and retailers and, hence, the above formulation is the more natural and tractable one.

The Equilibrium Conditions of the Supply Chain

In equilibrium, the shipments of the product that the manufacturers ship to the retailers must be equal to the shipments that the retailers accept from the manufacturers. In addition, the amounts of the product purchased by the consumers must be equal to the amounts sold by the retailers and directly to the consumers by the manufacturers. Furthermore, the equilibrium shipment and price pattern in the supernetwork must satisfy the sum of the inequalities (4.5), (4.10), and (4.17) in order to formalize the agreements between the tiers. This is now stated formally in the following definition.

Definition 4.1: Supply Chain Network Equilibrium
The equilibrium state of the supernetwork consisting of the supply chain with electronic commerce is one where the flows between the tiers of the supernetworks coincide and the product shipments and prices satisfy the sum of the optimality conditions (4.5), (4.10), and the conditions (4.17).

The variational inequality formulation of the governing equilibrium conditions is now derived. It is used as the basis for obtaining qualitative properties of the equilibrium shipment and price pattern as well as an algorithm for its computation. We also utilize it to provide an alternative but equivalent interpretation of the equilibrium state as defined above.

Theorem 4.1: Variational Inequality Formulation
A product shipment and price pattern $(Q^{1*}, Q^{2*}, Q^{3*}, \rho_2^*, \rho_3^*) \in \mathcal{K}$ is an equilibrium pattern of the supply chain model with electronic commerce according to Definition 4.1 if and only if it satisfies the variational inequality problem:

$$\sum_{i=1}^{m} \sum_{j=1}^{n} \sum_{l=1}^{2} \left[\frac{\partial f_i(Q^{1*}, Q^{2*})}{\partial q_{ijl}} + \frac{\partial c_{ijl}(q_{ijl}^*)}{\partial q_{ijl}} + \frac{\partial c_j(Q^{1*})}{\partial q_{ijl}} + \frac{\partial \hat{c}_{ijl}(q_{ijl}^*)}{\partial q_{ijl}} - \rho_{2j}^* \right]$$

$$\times \left[q_{ijl} - q_{ijl}^* \right]$$

$$+\sum_{i=1}^{m}\sum_{k=1}^{o}\left[\frac{\partial f_i(Q^{1*},Q^{2*})}{\partial q_{ik}}+\frac{\partial c_{ik}(q_{ik}^*)}{\partial q_{ik}}+\hat{c}_{ik}(Q^{2*},Q^{3*})-\rho_{3k}^*\right]\times[q_{ik}-q_{ik}^*]$$

$$+\sum_{j=1}^{n}\sum_{k=1}^{o}\sum_{l=1}^{2}\left[\rho_{2j}^*+\hat{c}_{jkl}(Q^{2*},Q^{3*})-\rho_{3k}^*\right]\times[q_{jkl}-q_{jkl}^*]$$

$$+\sum_{j=1}^{n}\left[\sum_{i=1}^{m}\sum_{l=1}^{2}q_{ijl}^*-\sum_{k=1}^{o}\sum_{l=1}^{2}q_{jkl}^*\right]\times[\rho_{2j}-\rho_{2j}^*]$$

$$+\sum_{k=1}^{o}\left[\sum_{j=1}^{n}\sum_{l=1}^{2}q_{jkl}^*+\sum_{i=1}^{m}q_{ik}^*-d_k(\rho_3^*)\right]\times[\rho_{3k}-\rho_{3k}^*]\geq 0,\qquad(4.18)$$

$$\forall(Q^1,Q^2,Q^3,\rho_2,\rho_3)\in\mathcal{K},$$

where $\mathcal{K}\equiv\{(Q^1,Q^2,Q^3,\rho_2,\rho_3)|(Q^1,Q^2,Q^3,\rho_2,\rho_3)\in R_+^{2mn+mo+2no+n+o}\}.$

Proof: It is first established that the equilibrium conditions imply variational inequality (4.18). Summing up inequalities (4.5), (4.10), and (4.17) yields, after algebraic simplification, variational inequality (4.18).

We now establish the converse, that is, that a solution to variational inequality (4.18) satisfies the sum of inequalities (4.5), (4.10), and (4.17), and is, hence, an equilibrium according to Definition 4.1.

To inequality (4.18), add the term $-\rho_{1ijl}^*+\rho_{1ijl}^*$ to the term in the first set of brackets preceding the multiplication sign. Similarly, add the term $-\rho_{1ik}^*+\rho_{1ik}^*$ to the term preceding the second multiplication sign, and, finally, add the term $-\gamma_j^*+\gamma_j^*$ to the term preceding the third multiplication sign. Such "terms" do not change the value of the inequality since they are identically equal to zero, with the resulting inequality of the form:

$$\sum_{i=1}^{m}\sum_{j=1}^{n}\sum_{l=1}^{2}\left[\frac{\partial f_i(Q^{1*},Q^{2*})}{\partial q_{ijl}}+\frac{\partial c_{ijl}(q_{ijl}^*)}{\partial q_{ijl}}+\frac{\partial c_j(Q^{1*})}{\partial q_{ijl}}+\frac{\partial\hat{c}_{ijl}(q_{ijl}^*)}{\partial q_{ijl}}-\rho_{2j}^*\right.$$

$$\left.-\rho_{1ijl}^*+\rho_{1ijl}^*\right]\times[q_{ijl}-q_{ijl}^*]$$

$$+\sum_{i=1}^{m}\sum_{k=1}^{o}\left[\frac{\partial f_i(Q^{1*},Q^{2*})}{\partial q_{ik}}+\frac{\partial c_{ik}(q_{ik})}{\partial q_{ik}}+\hat{c}_{ik}(Q^{2*},Q^{3*})-\rho_{3k}^*-\rho_{1ik}^*+\rho_{1ik}^*\right]$$

$$\times[q_{ik}-q_{ik}^*]$$

$$+\sum_{j=1}^{n}\sum_{k=1}^{o}\sum_{l=1}^{2}\left[\rho_{2j}^*+\hat{c}_{jk}(Q^{2*},Q^{3*})-\rho_{3k}^*-\gamma_j^*+\gamma_j^*\right]\times[q_{jkl}-q_{jkl}^*]$$

$$+\sum_{j=1}^{n}\left[\sum_{i=1}^{m}\sum_{l=1}^{2}q_{ijl}^*-\sum_{k=1}^{o}\sum_{l=1}^{2}q_{jkl}^*\right]\times[\rho_{2j}-\rho_{2j}^*]$$

$$\sum_{k=1}^{o} \left[\sum_{j=1}^{n} \sum_{l=1}^{2} q_{jkl}^* + \sum_{i=1}^{m} q_{ik}^* - d_k(\rho_3^*) \right] \times [\rho_{3k} - \rho_{3k}^*] \geq 0, \qquad (4.19)$$

$$\forall (Q^1, Q^2, Q^3, \rho_2, \rho_3) \in \mathcal{K},$$

which, in turn, can be rewritten as:

$$\sum_{i=1}^{m} \sum_{j=1}^{n} \sum_{l=1}^{2} \left[\frac{\partial f_i(Q^{1*}, Q^{2*})}{\partial q_{ijl}} + \frac{\partial c_{ijl}(q_{ijl}^*)}{\partial q_{ijl}} - \rho_{1ijl}^* \right] \times [q_{ijl} - q_{ijl}^*]$$

$$+ \sum_{i=1}^{m} \sum_{k=1}^{o} \left[\frac{\partial f_i(Q^{1*}, Q^{2*})}{\partial q_{ik}} + \frac{\partial c_{ik}(q_{ik}^*)}{\partial q_{ik}} - \rho_{1ik}^* \right] \times [q_{ik} - q_{ik}^*]$$

$$+ \sum_{i=1}^{m} \sum_{j=1}^{n} \sum_{l=1}^{2} \left[\frac{\partial c_j(Q^{1*})}{\partial q_{ijl}} + \rho_{1ijl}^* + \frac{\partial \hat{c}_{ijl}(q_{ijl}^*)}{\partial q_{ijl}} - \rho_{2j}^* \right] \times [q_{ijl} - q_{ijl}^*]$$

$$+ \sum_{j=1}^{n} \sum_{k=1}^{o} \sum_{l=1}^{2} \left[-\gamma_j^* + \rho_{2j}^* \right] \times [q_{jkl} - q_{jkl}^*]$$

$$+ \sum_{j=1}^{n} \left[\sum_{i=1}^{m} \sum_{l=1}^{2} q_{ijl}^* - \sum_{k=1}^{o} \sum_{l=1}^{2} q_{jkl}^* \right] \times [\rho_{2j} - \rho_{2j}^*]$$

$$+ \sum_{j=1}^{n} \sum_{k=1}^{o} \sum_{l=1}^{2} \left[\gamma_j^* + \hat{c}_{jkl}(Q^{2*}, Q^{3*}) - \rho_{3k}^* \right] \times [q_{jkl} - q_{jkl}^*]$$

$$+ \sum_{i=1}^{m} \sum_{k=1}^{o} \left[\rho_{1ik}^* + \hat{c}_{ik}(Q^{2*}, Q^{3*}) - \rho_{3k}^* \right] \times [q_{ik} - q_{ik}^*]$$

$$\sum_{k=1}^{o} \left[\sum_{j=1}^{n} \sum_{l=1}^{2} q_{jkl}^* + \sum_{i=1}^{m} q_{ik}^* - d_k(\rho_3^*) \right] \times [\rho_{3k} - \rho_{3k}^*] \geq 0, \qquad (4.20)$$

$$\forall (Q^1, Q^2, Q^3, \rho_2, \rho_3) \in \mathcal{K}.$$

But inequality (4.20) is equivalent to the price and shipment pattern satisfying the sum of conditions (4.5), (4.10), and (4.17). The proof is complete. □

We now utilize variational inequality (4.18) to derive alternative but equivalent equilibrium conditions to those in Definition 4.1 which highlight the consistency of the supernetwork framework and the integration of the preceding conditions for the distinct networks tiers.

In particular, we note that if we let $(Q^2, Q^3, \rho_2, \rho_3) = (Q^{2*}, Q^{3*}, \rho_2^*, \rho_3^*)$ and substitute into (4.18), the resulting inequality is equivalent to the statement that: For all i, j, l, in equilibrium, we must have that:

$$\frac{\partial f_i(Q^{1*}, Q^{2*})}{\partial q_{ijl}} + \frac{\partial c_{ijl}(q_{ijl}^*)}{\partial q_{ijl}} + \frac{\partial c_j(Q^{1*})}{\partial q_{ijl}} + \frac{\partial \hat{c}_{ijl}(q_{ijl}^*)}{\partial q_{ijl}} \begin{cases} = \rho_{2j}^*, & \text{if} \quad q_{ijl}^* > 0 \\ \geq \rho_{2j}^*, & \text{if} \quad q_{ijl}^* = 0. \end{cases} \quad (4.21)$$

Similarly, if we set $(Q^1, Q^3, \rho_2, \rho_3) = (Q^{1*}, Q^{3*}, \rho_2^*, \rho_3^*)$ and substitute the resultant into inequality (4.18), we obtain an inequality which is equivalent to the statement that, in equilibrium, we must have that, for all i, k:

$$\frac{\partial f_i(Q^{1*}, Q^{2*})}{\partial q_{ik}} + \frac{\partial c_{ik}(q_{ik}^*)}{\partial q_{ik}} + \hat{c}_{ik}(Q^{2*}, Q^{3*}) \begin{cases} = \rho_{3k}^*, & \text{if} \quad q_{ik}^* > 0 \\ \geq \rho_{3k}^*, & \text{if} \quad q_{ik}^* = 0. \end{cases} \quad (4.22)$$

If we now make the substitution $(Q^1, Q^2, \rho_2, \rho_3) = (Q^{1*}, Q^{2*}, \rho_2^*, \rho_3^*)$ in (4.18) we obtain the inequality which is equivalent to the statement that, for all j, k, l:

$$\rho_{2j}^* + \hat{c}_{jkl}(Q^{2*}, Q^{3*}) \begin{cases} = \rho_{3k}^*, & \text{if} \quad q_{jkl}^* > 0 \\ \geq \rho_{3k}^*, & \text{if} \quad q_{jkl}^* = 0. \end{cases} \quad (4.23)$$

Similarly, if we now let $(Q^1, Q^2, Q^3, \rho_3) = (Q^{1*}, Q^{2*}, Q^{3*}, \rho_3^*)$ and substitute into (4.18), the resulting inequality is equivalent to the statement that, for all j, we must have that:

$$\sum_{j=1}^n \left[\sum_{i=1}^m \sum_{l=1}^2 q_{ijl}^* - \sum_{k=1}^o \sum_{l=1}^2 q_{jkl}^* \right] \begin{cases} = 0, & \text{if} \quad \rho_{2j}^* > 0 \\ \geq 0, & \text{if} \quad \rho_{2j}^* = 0. \end{cases} \quad (4.24)$$

Analogously, if we let $(Q^1, Q^2, Q^2, \rho_2) = (Q^{1*}, Q^{2*}, Q^{3*}, \rho_2^*)$ and make this substitution into (4.18), we obtain precisely the inequality representing conditions (4.16).

We now provide an economic interpretation for the equilibrium conditions (4.21) , (4.22), and (4.24). The economic interpretation of (4.16) was given earlier, whereas that for (4.23) coincides with that for (4.14).

Specifically, we have that, according to (4.21), if the product shipment transacted via a mode is positive between a manufacturer and retailer, then the marginal production cost plus the marginal transaction costs and marginal handling cost is equal to the price of the product associated at the retailer. If the sum of all those marginal costs exceeds the price, then there will be a zero amount of the product transacted via that mode and between that manufacturer and retailer pair.

Similarly, according to (4.22), we have that if there is a positive amount of the product shipped between a manufacturer and demand market in equilibrium, then the marginal production cost of the manufacturer plus the associated marginal transaction cost plus the unit transaction cost from the consumers' perspective must be equal to the demand price at the demand market. The product shipment will be zero between the manufacturer and demand market pair if the sum of the above described marginal and unit costs exceeds the demand market price.

According to (4.24), in turn, we have that if the price associated with a retailer is positive in equilibrium, then the product shipments into that retailer must be equal to the product shipments out (that is, to the consumers). If the product shipments to a retailer exceed the product shipments out, then the associated price of the product at the retailer will be zero in equilibrium.

Standard Variational Inequality Formulation

For easy reference in the subsequent sections, variational inequality problem (4.18) can be rewritten in standard variational inequality form (cf. Definition 3.1 and Appendix B) as follows:

$$\langle F(X^*), X - X^* \rangle \geq 0, \quad \forall X \in \mathcal{K}, \tag{4.25}$$

where $X \equiv (Q^1, Q^2, Q^3, \rho_2, \rho_3)$, $F(X) \equiv (F_{ijl}, F_{ik}, F_{jkl}, F_j, F_k)$ for $\{i = 1, ..., m; j = 1, ..., n; l = 1, 2; k = 1, ..., o\}$, with the specific components of F given by the functional terms preceding the multiplication signs in (4.18), respectively. The feasible set $\mathcal{K}$ was defined previously following (4.18). The term $\langle \cdot, \cdot \rangle$ denotes the inner product in N-dimensional Euclidean space.

We now discuss how to recover the prices ρ^*_{1ijl}, for all i, j, l, and γ^*_j, for all j, from the solution of variational inequality (4.18). (In Section 4.3 we describe an algorithm for computing the solution.) Recall that, in the preceding discussions, it was noted that if $q^*_{jkl} > 0$, for some k, j, and l, then γ^*_j is precisely equal to ρ^*_{2j}, which can be obtained from the solution of (4.18). The prices ρ^*_{1ijl}, in turn (cf. also (4.20)), can be obtained by finding a $q^*_{ijl} > 0$, and then setting $\rho^*_{1ijl} = \left[\frac{\partial f(Q^{1*}, Q^{2*})}{\partial q_{ijl}} + \frac{\partial c_{ijl}(q^*_{ijl})}{\partial q_{ijl}} \right]$, or, equivalently, to $\left[\rho^*_{2j} - \frac{\partial c_j(Q^{1*})}{\partial q_{ijl}} - \frac{\partial \hat{c}_{ijl}(q^*_{ijl})}{\partial q_{ijl}} \right]$, for all such i, j, l. The prices ρ^*_{1ik} can be obtained by finding a $q^*_{ik} > 0$ and setting $\rho^*_{1ik} = \left[\frac{\partial f_i(Q^{1*}, Q^{2*})}{\partial q_{ik}} + \frac{\partial c_{ik}(q^*_{ik})}{\partial q_{ik}} \right]$, or, equivalently, to $\left[\rho^*_{3k} - \hat{c}_{ik}(Q^{2*}, Q^{3*}) \right]$, for all such i, k.

The supernetwork representing the supply chain network in equilibrium (cf. Figure 4.1) is now constructed, using, as building blocks, the previously drawn networks in Figures 4.2 through 4.4 corresponding, respectively, to the transactions of the manufacturers, the retailers, and the consumers. First, however, one needs to establish the result that, in equilibrium, the sum of the product shipments to each retailer is equal to the sum of the product shipments out. Hence, the corresponding ρ^*_{2j}s will all be positive. This means that each retailer, assuming profit-maximization, only purchases from the manufacturers the amount of the product that is actually consumed by the consumers. In order to establish this result, variational inequality (4.18) is utilized. Clearly, one knows that, if $\rho^*_{2j} > 0$, then the "market clears" for that retailer, that is, $\sum_{i=1}^{m} \sum_{l=1}^{2} q^*_{ijl} = \sum_{k=1}^{o} \sum_{l=1}^{2} q^*_{jkl}$. Let us now consider the case where $\rho_{2j}^* = 0$ for some retailer j. From the first term in inequality (4.18), since the production cost functions, and the transaction cost functions and handling cost functions have been assumed to be convex, and, assuming further, which is not unreasonable, that either the marginal cost of production or the marginal transaction costs or the marginal holding cost for each manufacturer/mode/retailer combination is strictly positive at equilibrium, then one knows that $\frac{\partial f_i(Q^{1*}, Q^{2*})}{\partial q_{ijl}} + \frac{\partial c_{ijl}(q_{ijl}^*)}{\partial q_{ijl}} + \frac{\partial c_j(Q^{1*})}{\partial q_{ijl}} + \frac{\partial \hat{c}_{ijl}(q_{ijl}^*)}{\partial q_{ijl}} > 0$, which implies that $q_{ijl}^* = 0$, and this holds for all i, l. It follows then from the fourth term in (4.18), that $\sum_{k=1}^o \sum_{l=1}^2 q_{jkl}^* = 0$, and, hence, the market clears also in this case since the flow into a retailer is equal to the flow out and equal to zero. The following result has, thus, been established:

Corollary 4.1: The Market Clears for the Retailers
The market for the product clears for each retailer in the supply chain network with e-commerce at equilibrium.

In Figure 4.1, the supernetwork structure of the supply chain network in equilibrium, is depicted. It consists of all the manufacturers, all the retailers, and all the demand markets. In order to construct the supernetwork in Figure 4.1, Figure 4.2 has been replicated for all the manufacturers; Figure 4.3 has been replicated for all the retailers, and Figure 4.4 for all the demand markets. The supernetwork represents the possible transactions of all the economic agents. In addition, since there must be agreement between/among the transactors at equilibrium, the analogous links (and equilibrium flows on them) must coincide, yielding the network structure given in Figure 4.1. The vectors of prices ρ_1^*, γ^* and ρ_2^*, and ρ_3^* are associated, respectively, with the top tier, the middle tier, and the bottom tier of nodes in the Figure 4.1 network. The components of the vector of equilibrium product shipments Q^{1*} correspond to the flows on the links joining the manufacturing (top tier) nodes with the retailer (middle tier) nodes. The components of the vector of equilibrium product shipments Q^{2*} correspond to the flows on the Internet links joining the manufacturer nodes with the demand market nodes, whereas the components of the vector of equilibrium product shipments Q^{3*} correspond to the flow on the links (physical or Internet) joining the retailer nodes with the demand market nodes.

Clearly, the special cases of our model in which there is only B2B commerce or only B2C commerce can be studied in this framework, as well, with a suitable reduction of the links and associated transaction costs and product shipments (and prices). In particular, in the absence of electronic commerce the supernetwork depicted in Figure 4.1 reduces to the network drawn in Figure 4.5.

Note that in the network in Figure 4.5 there are no Internet links and, thus, there are no Q^2 variables. Moreover, since there is only one mode of transacting between the manufacturers and the retailers, and one mode between the retailers and the demand markets, one can drop the subscript

Manufacturers

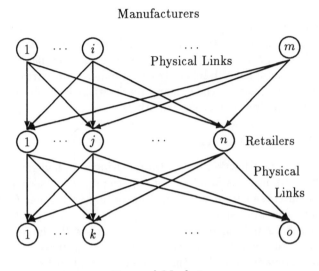

Demand Markets

Fig. 4.5. The Multitiered Supernetwork Structure of the Supply Chain Network without E-Commerce

l from those cost and flow terms and one has immediately the variational inequality formulation of the governing equilibrium conditions for this special case model:

Corollary 4.2: Variational Inequality Formulation of Supply Chain Network Equilibrium without E-Commerce
The variational inequality formulation of the supply chain network without Internet links is given by: determine $(Q^{1*}, Q^{3*}, \rho_2^*, \rho_3^*) \in \mathcal{K}^1$ *satisfying:*

$$\sum_{i=1}^{m}\sum_{j=1}^{n}\left[\frac{\partial f_i(Q^{1*})}{\partial q_{ij}} + \frac{\partial c_{ij}(q_{ij}^*)}{\partial q_{ij}} + \frac{\partial c_j(Q^{1*})}{\partial q_{ij}} + \frac{\partial \hat{c}_{ij}(q_{ij}^*)}{\partial q_{ij}} - \rho_{2j}^*\right] \times \left[q_{ij} - q_{ij}^*\right]$$

$$+\sum_{j=1}^{n}\sum_{k=1}^{o}\left[\rho_{2j}^* + \hat{c}_{jk}(Q^{3*}) - \rho_{3k}^*\right] \times \left[q_{jk} - q_{jk}^*\right]$$

$$+\sum_{j=1}^{n}\left[\sum_{i=1}^{m}q_{ij}^* - \sum_{k=1}^{o}q_{jk}^*\right] \times \left[\rho_{2j} - \rho_{2j}^*\right]$$

$$+\sum_{k=1}^{o}\left[\sum_{j=1}^{n}q_{jk}^* - d_k(\rho_3^*)\right] \times \left[\rho_{3k} - \rho_{3k}^*\right] \geq 0, \quad \forall(Q^1, Q^3, \rho_2, \rho_3) \in \mathcal{K}^1, \quad (4.26)$$

where $\mathcal{K}^1 \equiv \{(Q^1, Q^3, \rho_2, \rho_3) | (Q^1, Q^3, \rho_2, \rho_3) \in R_+^{mn+no+n+o}\}.$

4.1.1   Applications

We now consider two applications of the above supernetwork framework for supply chain analysis. In Section 4.1.1.1, we describe an online grocer, whereas in Section 4.1.1.2, we discuss an online book retailer. Both of these businesses are examples of B2C electronic commerce (in particular, between a retailer and consumers at the demand markets) with the online grocer also consisting of brick and mortar supermarkets.

4.1.1.1   An Online Grocer – Tesco

Tesco, a supermarket located in the United Kingdom, had revenues in 2000 of $30 billion. It uses its hundreds of supermarkets as bases for deliveries of products purchased from it online. According to Kapner (2001), Tesco invested only $56 million in its online grocery initiative, a business that presently has $422 million in sales annually, and is the largest of its type of business in the world. Last year, according to analysts (cf. Kapner (2001)), the company earned in the range of $7 million from its online service. Hence, as reflected in Figure 4.1, Tesco is a retailer (in the form of an online grocer) who sells to consumers at a variety of demand markets either physically or electronically. Of course, it also competes with other supermarkets and grocery outlets and can obtain its products from different producers/manufacturers. Interestingly, for its online service it has opted not to use any warehouses, but has its outlets serve, in effect, as distribution centers. Moreover, according to Kapner (2001), Tesco charges a fee of $7 per online transaction, which can also be handled by the above model through the concept of transaction cost. Fascinatingly, the company, well-aware of congestion and its effect on timely deliveries, has also devised, in a sense, "optimal" routes for product acquisition within its outlets, as well as planned routes of delivery in London, which should not exceed 25 minutes for delivery. Clearly, this enterprise reflects a strategic integration of logistics, transportation, and telecommunication networks.

Of course, in this as in any application, one may have to modify the supply chain network to reflect the particularities of the specific scenario. For example, in the case of multiple retail outlets controlled by the same firm, one may wish to optimize across the retail outlets, being aware that these, in turn, have to compete with other retailers providing the same or similar products. In addition, if certain links are absent (or if additional ones are present) one would have to revise the supernetwork in Figure 4.1 accordingly. Nevertheless, the above framework is valuable for both conceptualization and theoretical purposes.

4.1.1.2   An Online Book Retailer – Amazon.com

No discussion of electronic commerce and supply chain issues would be complete without the inclusion of information about Amazon.com, a leader of the "dot.comers." Established in July, 1995 by Jeff Bezos, with a goal of changing book buying into the most convenient and easiest shopping experience, its web site (cf. Amazon.com (2001)) states that "29 million people in more than 160 countries have made us the leading online shopping site," with its selection of products vastly expanded from its original business of online book selling. Although in business six years, however, it has yet to make a pro forma profit (see *The Economist* (2001b)). Nevertheless, its size is huge with nearly $3 billion of sales a year and it is believed to be close to realizing profits.

Amazon.com obtains books from manufacturers/publishers and, in the case of a particular book, the supply chain (cf. Figure 4.1) would correspond to a single node in the top tier, with links connecting it to the second tier nodes, that is, the book retailers, who could be exclusively online, as is Amazon.com, or be both physical and online, or only physical. Amazon.com, hence, competes for consumers with other book retailers. Interestingly, as the above model reflects, each retailer prices the product identically, irregardless of whether the transaction is online or physical with the consumers. Indeed, as reported in *The Economist* (2001b), Amazon.com discovered that customers strongly dislike the idea of price discrimination, which the company attempted to achieve by charging different customers different prices for the same book.

In addition, the above model explicitly incorporates handling costs and, as reported in *The Economist* (2001b), Amazon.com has relatively fixed handling costs and this is viewed as one of its advantages, especially in regards to brick- and mortar- type of competitors. However, as also reported therein (cf. page 71), Amazon's business model depends on its supply chain efficiency, which is "held hostage by the pace at which its partners, from suppliers to transportation companies upgrade their own systems to complement Amazon's." Our supply chain framework explicitly allows for decentralized decision-making through a variety of network agents and, thus, allows one to capture and study such complex behavior and relationships.

4.1.2   An Extension

The above discussions focused on a 3-tiered network. It is now shown that the multitiered network concept can also be used to handle even more complex supply chain situations. In particular, suppliers are now explicitly considered. For example, in Figure 4.6, a 4-tiered supply chain is depicted where now suppliers represent the top tier of network agents and the remainder of the supernetwork is as drawn in Figure 4.1. There are two possible types of B2B e-commerce transactions: the B2B transactions via the Internet between manufacturers and the retailers and those between the suppliers and the manufacturers. Depending on the product, the suppliers may supply the same or different inputs to the manufacturers' production processes.

We emphasize that physical links of the supply chain models described

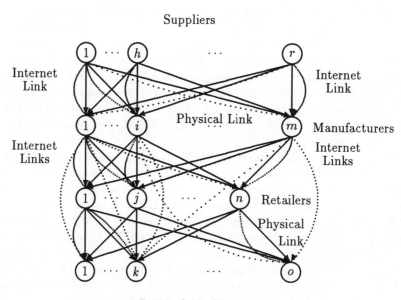

Fig. 4.6. The 4-Tiered Supernetwork Structure of the Supply Chain Network with Suppliers, Manufacturers, Retailers, and Demand Markets

in this and the next chapter are, in actuality, aggregations of transportation networks with associated origins, destinations, and routes. On these transportation networks, additional agents, in the form of shippers/carriers, interact in moving the freight (see Friesz, Gottfried, and Morlok (1986)). The freight consists of product inputs from suppliers to the manufacturers, and of products from manufacturers to retailers and/or to consumers. On the other hand, consumers in obtaining the product from the retailers must also cross physical distance to obtain the product and, hence, they interact on a transportation network as well. They, as the carriers of the freight, need to determine their optimal routes of transportation but in support of their retail activities. We discuss decision-making on transportation networks in a variety of contexts in Part III of this book.

Furthermore, the e-commerce links joining the manufacturers to the retailers and to the consumers, the suppliers to manufacturers, and the retailers to the consumers actually consist of telecommunication networks over which such transactions take place. E-commerce transactions, hence, trigger flows over the telecommunication networks, which, in turn, can trigger flows over transportation networks.

The above discussion points to further interrelationships among a variety of networks in regards to supply chains. We discuss such multilevel supernetworks in Chapter 5.

4.2   Qualitative Properties

In this section, some qualitative properties of the solution to variational inequality (4.18) are provided, notably, existence and uniqueness results. Properties of the function F (cf. (4.25)) that enters the variational inequality are also investigated. Existence of a solution is important to determine because without knowing that a solution exists, a model is vacuous.

Since the feasible set is not compact (that is, closed and bounded) one cannot derive existence of a solution, according to basic variational inequality theory, simply from the assumption of continuity of the functions (see also Appendix B). Nevertheless, one can impose a rather weak condition to guarantee existence of a solution pattern. Let

$$\mathcal{K}_b = \{(Q^1, Q^2, Q^3, \rho_2, \rho_3)|$$

$$0 \le Q^1 \le b_1; \ 0 \le Q^2 \le b_2; 0 \le Q^3 \le b_3; \ 0 \le \rho_2 \le b_4; \ 0 \le \rho_3 \le b_5\}, \quad (4.27)$$

where $b = (b_1, b_2, b_3, b_4, b_5) \ge 0$ and $Q^1 \le b_1; Q^2 \le b_2; Q^3 \le b_3; \rho_2 \le b_4; \rho_3 \le b_5$ means that $q_{ijl} \le b_1; \ q_{ik} \le b_2; \ q_{jkl} \le b_3; \ \rho_{2j} \le b_4;$ and $\rho_{3k} \le b_5$ for all i, j, l, k. Then $\mathcal{K}_b$ is a bounded closed convex subset of $R^{2mn+mo+2no+n+o}$. Thus, the following variational inequality

$$\langle F(X^b), X - X^b \rangle \ge 0, \quad \forall X^b \in \mathcal{K}_b, \quad (4.28)$$

admits at least one solution $X^b \in \mathcal{K}_b$, from the standard theory of variational inequalities, since $\mathcal{K}_b$ is compact and F is continuous. Following Kinderlehrer and Stampacchia (1980) (see also Theorem B.3 in Appendix B), one then has:

Theorem 4.2
Variational inequality (4.18) admits a solution if and only if there exists a $b > 0$, such that variational inequality (4.28) admits a solution in $\mathcal{K}_b$ with

$$Q^{1b} < b_1, \quad Q^{2b} < b_2, \quad Q^{3b} < b_3, \quad \rho_2^b < b_4, \quad \rho_3^b < b_5. \tag{4.29}$$

Theorem 4.3: Existence
Suppose that there exist positive constants M, N, R with $R > 0$, such that:

$$\frac{\partial f_i(Q^1, Q^2)}{\partial q_{ijl}} + \frac{\partial c_{ijl}(q_{ijl})}{\partial q_{ijl}} + \frac{\partial c_j(Q^1)}{\partial q_{ijl}} + \frac{\partial \hat{c}_{ijl}(q_{ijl})}{\partial q_{ijl}} \geq M, \quad \forall Q^1 \text{ with } q_{ijl} \geq N,$$

$$\forall i, j, l, \tag{4.30}$$

$$\frac{\partial f_i(Q^1, Q^2)}{\partial q_{ik}} + \frac{\partial c_{ik}(q_{ik})}{\partial q_{ik}} + \hat{c}_{ik}(Q^2, Q^3) \geq M, \quad \forall Q^2 \text{ with } q_{ik} \geq N, \quad \forall i, k,$$

$$\hat{c}_{jkl}(Q^2, Q^3) \geq M, \quad \forall Q^3 \text{ with } q_{jkl} \geq N, \quad \forall j, k, l,$$

$$d_k(\rho_3^*) \leq N, \quad \forall \rho \text{ with } \rho_{3k} > R, \quad \forall k. \tag{4.31}$$

Then variational inequality (4.18); equivalently, variational inequality (4.25), admits at least one solution.

Proof: Under the conditions (4.30) and (4.31) it is possible to construct a $b > 0$ such that (4.29) holds and existence, hence, follows. See also Nagurney and Zhao (1993) and Nagurney, Dong, and Zhang (2000). $\square$

Assumptions (4.30) and (4.31) are reasonable from an economics perspective, since when the product shipment between a manufacturer and demand market pair or a manufacturer and retailer is large, one can expect the corresponding marginal cost of production and/or the marginal cost of transaction from either the manufacturer's or the retailer's/consumers' perspectives to be bounded from below by positive constants. Moreover, in the case where the demand price of the product as perceived by a demand market is high, one can expect that the demand for the product will be low at that market.

We now recall the definition of an additive production cost introduced in Zhang and Nagurney (1996) for establishing some qualitative properties in dynamic network oligopoly problems, which will be utilized as an assumption for establishing additional qualitative properties of the supply chain network model.

Definition 4.2: Additive Production Cost

Suppose that for each manufacturer i, the production cost f_i is additive, that is,

$$f_i(q) = f_i^1(q_i) + f_i^2(\bar{q}_i), \tag{4.32}$$

where $f_i^1(q_i)$ is the internal production cost that depends solely on the manufacturer's own output level q_i, which may include the cost of production operation and facility maintenance, etc., and $f_i^2(\bar{q}_i)$ is the interdependent part of the production cost that is a function of all the other manufacturers' output levels $\bar{q}_i = (q_1, \cdots, q_{i-1}, q_{i+1}, \cdots, q_m)$ and reflects the impact of the other manufacturers' production patterns on manufacturer i's cost. This interdependent part of the production cost may describe the competition for the resources, consumption of the homogeneous raw materials, etc.

The properties of monotonicity and Lipschitz continuity of F (see also Appendix B) are now established and these properties will be utilized in the subsequent section for proving convergence of the algorithmic scheme. Furthermore, these properties will be utilized to obtain a variety of results for the dynamic version of this model in Chapter 5. Hence, proofs are provided here for completeness and easy reference.

Theorem 4.4: Monotonicity

Suppose that the production cost functions f_i; $i = 1, ..., m$, are additive, as defined in Definition 4.2, and f_i^1; $i = 1, ..., m$, are convex functions. If the c_{ijl}, c_j, and $\hat{c}_{ijl}$, and c_{ik} functions are convex; the $\hat{c}_{jkl}$ and the $\hat{c}_{ik}$ functions are monotone increasing, and the d_k functions are monotone decreasing functions of the demand prices, for all i, l, j, k, then the vector function F that enters the variational inequality (4.25) is monotone, that is,

$$\langle F(X') - F(X''), X' - X'' \rangle \geq 0, \quad \forall X', X'' \in \mathcal{K}. \tag{4.33}$$

Proof: Let $X' = (Q^{1'}, Q^{2'}, Q^{3'}, \rho_2', \rho_3')$, $X'' = (Q^{1''}, Q^{2''}, Q^{3''}, \rho_2'', \rho_3'')$. Then,

$$\langle F(X') - F(X''), X' - X'' \rangle$$

$$= \sum_{i=1}^{m} \sum_{j=1}^{n} \sum_{l=1}^{2} \left[\frac{\partial f_i(Q^{1'}, Q^{2'})}{\partial q_{ijl}} - \frac{\partial f_i(Q^{1''}, Q^{2''})}{\partial q_{ijl}} \right] \times \left[q'_{ijl} - q''_{ijl} \right]$$

$$+ \sum_{i=1}^{m} \sum_{j=1}^{n} \sum_{l=1}^{2} \left[\frac{\partial c_{ijl}(q'_{ijl})}{\partial q_{ijl}} - \frac{\partial c_{ijl}(q''_{ijl})}{\partial q_{ijl}} \right] \times \left[q'_{ijl} - q''_{ijl} \right]$$

$$+ \sum_{i=1}^{m} \sum_{j=1}^{n} \sum_{l=1}^{2} \left[\frac{\partial c_j(Q^{1'})}{\partial q_{ijl}} - \frac{\partial c_j(Q^{1''})}{\partial q_{ijl}} \right] \times \left[q'_{ijl} - q''_{ijl} \right]$$

$$+\sum_{i=1}^{m}\sum_{j=1}^{n}\sum_{l=1}^{2}\left[\frac{\partial\hat{c}_{ijl}(q'_{ijl})}{\partial q_{ijl}}-\frac{\partial\hat{c}_{ijl}(q''_{ijl})}{\partial q_{ijl}}\right]\times[q'_{ijl}-q''_{ijl}]$$

$$+\sum_{i=1}^{m}\sum_{k=1}^{o}\left[\frac{\partial f_{i}(Q^{1'},Q^{2'})}{\partial q_{ik}}-\frac{\partial f_{i}(Q^{1''},Q^{2''})}{\partial q_{ik}}\right]\times[q'_{ik}-q''_{ik}]$$

$$+\sum_{i=1}^{m}\sum_{k=1}^{o}\left[\frac{\partial c_{ik}(q'_{ik})}{\partial q_{ik}}-\frac{\partial c_{ik}(q''_{ik})}{\partial q_{ik}}\right]\times[q'_{ik}-q''_{ik}]$$

$$+\sum_{i=1}^{m}\sum_{k=1}^{o}\left[\hat{c}_{ik}(Q^{2'},Q^{3'})-\hat{c}_{ik}(Q^{2''},Q^{3''})\right]\times[q'_{ik}-q''_{ik}]$$

$$+\sum_{j=1}^{n}\sum_{k=1}^{o}\sum_{l=1}^{2}\left[\hat{c}_{jkl}(Q^{2'},Q^{3'})-\hat{c}_{jkl}(Q^{2''},Q^{3''})\right]\times[q'_{jkl}-q''_{jkl}]$$

$$+\sum_{k=1}^{o}[-d_{k}(\rho'_{3})+d_{k}(\rho''_{3})]\times[\rho'_{3k}-\rho''_{3k}]$$

$$= (I)+(II)+(III)+(IV)+(V)+(VI)+(VII)+(VIII)+(IX). \quad (4.34)$$

Since the f_i; $i = 1,...,m$, are assumed to be additive, and the f_i^1; $i = 1,...,m$, are convex functions, one has

$$(I)+(V)=\sum_{i=1}^{m}\sum_{j=1}^{n}\sum_{l=1}^{2}\left[\frac{\partial f_{i}^{1}(Q^{1'},Q^{2'})}{\partial q_{ijl}}-\frac{\partial f_{i}^{1}(Q^{1''},Q^{2''})}{\partial q_{ijl}}\right]\times[q'_{ijl}-q''_{ijl}]$$

$$+\sum_{i=1}^{m}\sum_{k=1}^{o}\left[\frac{\partial f_{i}^{1}(Q^{1'},Q^{2'})}{\partial q_{ik}}-\frac{\partial f_{i}^{1}(Q^{1''},Q^{2''})}{\partial q_{ik}}\right]\times[q'_{ik}-q''_{ik}]\geq 0. \quad (4.35)$$

The convexity of the transaction and handling cost functions: c_{ijl}, c_j, $\hat{c}_{ijl}$, and of c_{ik}, $\forall i, j, k, l$, gives, respectively:

$$(II)=\sum_{i=1}^{m}\sum_{j=1}^{n}\sum_{l=1}^{2}\left[\frac{\partial c_{ijl}(q'_{ijl})}{\partial q_{ijl}}-\frac{\partial c_{ijl}(q''_{ijl})}{\partial q_{ijl}}\right]\times[q'_{ijl}-q''_{ijl}]\geq 0, \quad (4.36)$$

$$(III)=\sum_{i=1}^{m}\sum_{j=1}^{n}\sum_{l=1}^{2}\left[\frac{\partial c_{j}(Q^{1'})}{\partial q_{ijl}}-\frac{\partial c_{j}(Q^{1''})}{\partial q_{ijl}}\right]\times[q'_{ijl}-q''_{ijl}]\geq 0, \quad (4.37)$$

$$(IV)=\sum_{i=1}^{m}\sum_{j=1}^{n}\sum_{l=1}^{2}\left[\frac{\partial\hat{c}_{ijl}(q'_{ijl})}{\partial q_{ijl}}-\frac{\partial\hat{c}_{ijl}(q''_{ijl})}{\partial q_{ijl}}\right]\times[q'_{ijl}-q''_{ijl}]\geq 0, \quad (4.38)$$

$$(VI)=\sum_{i=1}^{m}\sum_{k=1}^{o}\left[\frac{\partial c_{ik}(q'_{ik})}{\partial q_{ik}}-\frac{\partial c_{ik}(q''_{ik})}{\partial q_{ik}}\right]\times[q'_{ik}-q''_{ik}]\geq 0. \quad (4.39)$$

Since the transaction cost functions $\hat{c}_{ik}$, $\forall i, k$, and $\hat{c}_{jkl}$, $\forall j, k, l$, in turn, are assumed to be monotone increasing, and the demand functions d_k, $\forall k$, are assumed to be monotone decreasing, one has

$$(VII) = \sum_{i=1}^{m} \sum_{k=1}^{o} \left[\hat{c}_{ik}(Q^{2\prime}, Q^{3\prime}) - \hat{c}_{ik}(Q^{2\prime\prime}, Q^{3\prime\prime}) \right] \times [q'_{ik} - q''_{ik}] \geq 0, \quad (4.40)$$

$$(VIII) = \sum_{j=1}^{n} \sum_{k=1}^{o} \sum_{l=1}^{2} \left[\hat{c}_{jkl}(Q^{2\prime}, Q^{3\prime}) - \hat{c}_{jkl}(Q^{2\prime\prime}, Q^{3\prime\prime}) \right] \times [q'_{jkl} - q''_{jkl}] \geq 0,$$
$$(4.41)$$

and

$$(IX) = \sum_{k=1}^{o} [-d_k(\rho'_3) + d_k(\rho''_3)] \times [\rho'_{3k} - \rho''_{3k}] \geq 0. \quad (4.42)$$

Bringing (4.35)–(4.42) into the right-hand side of (4.34), the conclusion follows. □

Theorem 4.5: Strict Monotonicity

Assume all the conditions of Theorem 4.4. In addition, suppose that one of the five families of convex functions $f_i^1; i = 1, ..., m$; $c_{ijl}; i = 1, ..., m$; $j = 1, ..., n$; $l = 1, 2$; c_j; $j = 1, ..., n$; $\hat{c}_{ijl}; i = 1, ..., m$; $j = 1, ..., n$; $l = 1, 2$; and c_{ik}; $i = 1, ..., m$; $k = 1, ..., o$, is a family of strictly convex functions. Suppose that $\hat{c}_{ik}$; $i = 1, ..., m$; $k = 1, ..., o$; $\hat{c}_{jkl}$; $j = 1, ..., n$; $k = 1, ..., o$; $l = 1, 2$, and $-d_k$; $k = 1, ..., o$, are strictly monotone. Then, the vector function F that enters the variational inequality (4.25) is strictly monotone, with respect to (Q^1, Q^2, Q^3, ρ_3), that is, for any two X', X'' with $(Q^{1\prime}, Q^{2\prime}, Q^{3\prime}, \rho'_3) \neq (Q^{1\prime\prime}, Q^{2\prime\prime}, Q^{3\prime\prime}, \rho''_3)$

$$\langle F(X') - F(X''), X' - X'' \rangle > 0. \quad (4.43)$$

Proof: For any two distinct $(Q^{1\prime}, Q^{2\prime}, Q^{3\prime}\rho'_3)$, $(Q^{1\prime\prime}, Q^{2\prime\prime}, Q^{3\prime\prime}, \rho''_3)$, one must have at least one of the following four cases:

(i) $Q^{1\prime} \neq Q^{1\prime\prime}$,

(ii) $Q^{2\prime} \neq Q^{2\prime\prime}$,

(iii) $Q^{3\prime} \neq Q^{3\prime\prime}$,

(iv) $\rho'_3 \neq \rho''_3$.

Under the condition of the theorem, if (i) holds true, then, on the right-hand side of (4.34), at least one of (I), (II), (III), or (IV) is positive. If (ii) is true, then (V), (VI), or (VII) is positive. In the case of (iii), (VIII) is positive. In the case of (iv), (IX) is positive. Hence, one can conclude that the right-hand side of (4.34) is greater than zero. The proof is complete. □

Theorem 4.5 has an important implication for the uniqueness of the manufacturer shipments, Q^1, the retailer shipments, Q^2, and the prices at the demand markets, ρ_3, at the equilibrium as is now established. Note also that no guarantee of a unique ρ_{2j}; $j = 1, ..., n$, can generally be expected at the equilibrium.

Theorem 4.6: Uniqueness
Under the conditions of Theorem 4.5, there must be a unique shipment pattern (Q^{1*}, Q^{2*}, Q^{3*}), *and a unique demand price vector* ρ_3^* *satisfying the equilibrium conditions of the supply chain. In other words, if the variational inequality (4.25) admits a solution, then that is the only solution in* (Q^1, Q^2, Q^3, ρ_3).

Proof: Under the strict monotonicity result of Theorem 4.5, uniqueness follows from the standard variational inequality theory (cf. Theorem B.4 in Appendix B). □

Theorem 4.7: Lipschitz Continuity
The function that enters the variational inequality problem (4.25) is Lipschitz continuous, that is,

$$\|F(X') - F(X'')\| \leq L\|X' - X''\|, \quad \forall X', X'' \in \mathcal{K}, \qquad (4.44)$$

under the following conditions:
(i) Each f_i; $i = 1, ..., m$, is additive and has a bounded second-order derivative;
(ii) c_{ijl}, c_j, $\hat{c}_{ijl}$ and c_{ik} have bounded second-order derivatives, for all i, j, l, k;
(iii) $\hat{c}_{ik}$, $\hat{c}_{jkl}$, and d_k have bounded first-order derivatives for all i, j, k, l.

Proof: The result is direct by applying a mid-value theorem from calculus to the vector function F that enters the variational inequality problem (4.25). □

4.3   The Algorithm

In this section, we consider the computation of solutions to variational inequality (4.18). The algorithm that will be used is the modified projection method of Korpelevich (1977), which is guaranteed to solve any variational inequality problem in standard form (see (4.25)) provided that the function F that enters the variational inequality is monotone and Lipschitz continuous (and that a solution exists). The statement of the algorithm in its general form is given in Appendix C. Below is its realization for the solution of variational inequality problem (4.18) representing the equilibrium for the supply chain network model with electronic commerce. In the next section, the algorithm is applied to several numerical examples. An iteration counter is denoted by $\mathcal{T}$.

Modified Projection Method for the Solution of Variational Inequality (4.18)

Step 0: Initialization

Set $(Q^{1^0}, Q^{2^0}, Q^{3^0}, \rho_2^0, \rho_3^0) \in \mathcal{K}$. Let $\mathcal{T} = 1$ and set α such that $0 < \alpha \le \frac{1}{L}$, where L is the Lipschitz constant for the problem (cf. (4.44)).

Step 1: Computation

Compute $(\bar{Q}^{1^{\mathcal{T}}}, \bar{Q}^{2^{\mathcal{T}}}, \bar{Q}^{3^{\mathcal{T}}}, \bar{\rho}_2^{\mathcal{T}}, \bar{\rho}_3^{\mathcal{T}}) \in \mathcal{K}$ by solving the variational inequality subproblem:

$$
\sum_{i=1}^{m}\sum_{j=1}^{n}\sum_{l=1}^{2}\left[\bar{q}_{ijl}^{\mathcal{T}} + \alpha\left(\frac{\partial f_i(Q^{1^{\mathcal{T}-1}}, Q^{2^{\mathcal{T}-1}})}{\partial q_{ijl}} + \frac{\partial c_{ijl}(q_{ijl}^{\mathcal{T}-1})}{\partial q_{ijl}} + \frac{\partial c_j(Q^{1^{\mathcal{T}-1}})}{\partial q_{ijl}} \right. \right.
$$

$$
\left. \left. +\frac{\partial \hat{c}_{ijl}(q_{ijl}^{\mathcal{T}-1})}{\partial q_{ijl}} - \rho_{2j}^{\mathcal{T}-1}\right) - q_{ijl}^{\mathcal{T}-1}\right] \times \left[q_{ijl} - \bar{q}_{ijl}^{\mathcal{T}}\right]
$$

$$
+\sum_{i=1}^{m}\sum_{k=1}^{o}\sum_{l=1}^{2}\left[\bar{q}_{ik}^{\mathcal{T}} + \alpha\left(\frac{\partial f_i(Q^{1^{\mathcal{T}-1}}, Q^{2^{\mathcal{T}-1}})}{\partial q_{ik}} + \frac{\partial c_{ik}(q_{ik}^{\mathcal{T}-1})}{\partial q_{ik}} \right. \right.
$$

$$
\left. \left. +\hat{c}_{ik}(Q^{2^{\mathcal{T}-1}}, Q^{3^{\mathcal{T}-1}}) - \rho_{3k}^{\mathcal{T}-1}\right) - q_{ik}^{\mathcal{T}-1}\right] \times \left[q_{ik} - \bar{q}_{ik}^{\mathcal{T}}\right]
$$

$$
+\sum_{j=1}^{n}\sum_{k=1}^{o}\sum_{l=1}^{2}\left[\bar{q}_{jkl}^{\mathcal{T}} + \alpha(\rho_{2j}^{\mathcal{T}-1} + \hat{c}_{jkl}(Q^{2^{\mathcal{T}-1}}, Q^{3^{\mathcal{T}-1}}) - \rho_{3k}^{\mathcal{T}-1}) - q_{jkl}^{\mathcal{T}-1}\right]
$$

$$
\times \left[q_{jkl} - \bar{q}_{jkl}^{\mathcal{T}}\right]
$$

$$
+\sum_{j=1}^{n}\left[\bar{\rho}_{2j}^{\mathcal{T}} + \alpha(\sum_{i=1}^{m}\sum_{l=1}^{2}q_{ijl}^{\mathcal{T}-1} - \sum_{k=1}^{o}\sum_{l=1}^{2}q_{jk}^{\mathcal{T}-1}) - \rho_{2j}^{\mathcal{T}-1}\right] \times \left[\rho_{2j} - \bar{\rho}_{2j}^{\mathcal{T}}\right]
$$

$$
+\sum_{k=1}^{o}\left[\bar{\rho}_{3k}^{\mathcal{T}} + \alpha(\sum_{j=1}^{n}\sum_{l=1}^{2}q_{jkl}^{\mathcal{T}-1} + \sum_{i=1}^{m}q_{ik}^{\mathcal{T}-1} - d_k(\rho_3^{\mathcal{T}-1})) - \rho_{3k}^{\mathcal{T}-1}\right]
$$

$$
\times \left[\rho_{3k} - \bar{\rho}_{3k}^{\mathcal{T}}\right] \ge 0, \qquad \forall(Q^1, Q^2, Q^3, \rho_2, \rho_3) \in \mathcal{K}. \tag{4.45}
$$

Step 2: Adaptation

Compute $(Q^{1^{\mathcal{T}}}, Q^{2^{\mathcal{T}}}, Q^{3^{\mathcal{T}}}, \rho_2^{\mathcal{T}}, \rho_3^{\mathcal{T}}) \in \mathcal{K}$ by solving the variational inequality subproblem:

$$
\sum_{i=1}^{m}\sum_{j=1}^{n}\sum_{l=1}^{2}\left[q_{ijl}^{\mathcal{T}} + \alpha\left(\frac{\partial f_i(\bar{Q}^{1^{\mathcal{T}}}, \bar{Q}^{2^{\mathcal{T}}})}{\partial q_{ijl}} + \frac{\partial c_{ijl}(\bar{q}_{ijl}^{\mathcal{T}})}{\partial q_{ijl}} + \frac{\partial c_j(\bar{Q}^{1^{\mathcal{T}}})}{\partial q_{ijl}} \right. \right.
$$

$$
\left. \left. +\frac{\partial \hat{c}_{ijl}(\bar{q}_{ijl}^{\mathcal{T}})}{\partial q_{ijl}} - \bar{\rho}_{2j}^{\mathcal{T}}\right) - q_{ijl}^{\mathcal{T}-1}\right] \times \left[q_{ijl} - q_{ijl}^{\mathcal{T}}\right]
$$

$$+\sum_{i=1}^{m}\sum_{k=1}^{o}\sum_{l=1}^{2}\left[q_{ik}^{T}+\alpha(\frac{\partial f_i(\bar{Q}^{1T},\bar{Q}^{2T})}{\partial q_{ik}}+\frac{\partial c_{ik}(\bar{q}_{ijk}^{T})}{\partial q_{ik}}+\hat{c}_{ik}(\bar{Q}^{2T},\bar{Q}^{3T})\right.$$

$$\left.-\bar{\rho}_{3k}^{T})-q_{ik}^{T-1}\right]\times\left[q_{ik}-q_{ik}^{T}\right]$$

$$+\sum_{j=1}^{n}\sum_{k=1}^{o}\sum_{l=1}^{2}\left[q_{jkl}^{T}+\alpha(\bar{\rho}_{2j}^{T}+\hat{c}_{jkl}(\bar{Q}^{2T},\bar{Q}^{3T})-\bar{\rho}_{3k}^{T})-q_{jkl}^{T-1}\right]\times\left[q_{jkl}-q_{jkl}^{T}\right]$$

$$+\sum_{j=1}^{n}\left[\rho_{2j}^{T}+\alpha(\sum_{i=1}^{m}\sum_{l=1}^{2}\bar{q}_{ijl}^{T}-\sum_{k=1}^{o}\sum_{l=1}^{2}\bar{q}_{jkl}^{T})-\rho_{2j}^{T-1}\right]\times\left[\rho_{2j}-\rho_{2j}^{T}\right]$$

$$+\sum_{k=1}^{o}\left[\rho_{3k}^{T}+\alpha(\sum_{j=1}^{n}\sum_{l=1}^{2}\bar{q}_{jkl}^{T}+\sum_{i=1}^{m}\bar{q}_{ik}^{T}-d_k(\bar{\rho}_3^{T}))-\rho_{3k}^{T-1}\right]\times\left[\rho_{3k}-\rho_{3k}^{T}\right]\geq0,$$

$$\forall(Q^1,Q^2,Q^3,\rho_2,\rho_3)\in\mathcal{K}.\qquad(4.46)$$

Step 3: Convergence Verification

If $|q_{ijl}^{T}-q_{ijl}^{T-1}|\leq\epsilon$, $|q_{ik}^{T}-q_{ik}^{T-1}|\leq\epsilon$, $|q_{jkl}^{T}-q_{jkl}^{T-1}|\leq\epsilon$, $|\rho_{2j}^{T}-\rho_{2j}^{T-1}|\leq\epsilon$, $|\rho_{3k}^{T}-\rho_{3k}^{T-1}|\leq\epsilon$, for all $i=1,\cdots,m$; $j=1,\cdots,n$; $l=1,2$; $k=1,\cdots,o$, with $\epsilon>0$, a pre-specified tolerance, then stop; otherwise, set $T:=T+1$, and go to Step 1.

Although the solution of Steps 1 and 2 as stated by (4.45) and (4.46), at first glance, may appear ominous, the variational inequality subproblems (4.45) and (4.46) can be solved explicitly and in closed form since the feasible set is that of the nonnegative orthant. Indeed, they yield subproblems in the q_{ijl}, q_{ik}, q_{jkl}, ρ_{2j}, and ρ_{3k} variables $\forall i,j,l,k$. Hence, the computation of solutions to subproblems (4.45) and (4.46) is actually remarkably simple.

Specifically, subproblem (4.45) can be solved *exactly* and in *closed form* as follows.

Computation of the Product Shipments

At iteration T, compute the $\bar{q}_{ijl}^{T}$s, $\forall i,j,l$, according to:

$$\bar{q}_{ijl}^{T}=\max\left\{0,q_{ijl}^{T-1}-\alpha(\frac{\partial f_i(Q^{1T-1},Q^{2T-1})}{\partial q_{ijl}}+\frac{\partial c_{ijl}(q_{ijl}^{T-1})}{\partial q_{ijl}}+\frac{\partial c_j(Q^{1T-1})}{\partial q_{ijl}}\right.$$

$$\left.+\frac{\partial\hat{c}_{ijl}(q_{ijl}^{T-1})}{\partial q_{ijl}}-\rho_{2j}^{T-1})\right\}.\qquad(4.47)$$

In addition, at iteration T, compute the $\bar{q}_{ik}^{T}$s, $\forall i,k$, according to:

$$\bar{q}_{ik}^{T}=\max\left\{0,q_{ik}^{T-1}-\alpha(\frac{\partial f_i(Q^{1T-1},Q^{2T-1})}{\partial q_{ik}}+\frac{\partial c_{ik}(q_{ik}^{T-1})}{\partial q_{ik}}\right.$$

$$+\hat{c}_{ik}(Q^{2^{T-1}}, Q^{3^{T-1}}) - \rho_{3k}^{T-1})\}. \tag{4.48}$$

Also, at iteration T compute the $\bar{q}_{jkl}^{T}$s according to:

$$\bar{q}_{jkl}^{T} = \max\{0, q_{jkl}^{T-1} - \alpha(\rho_{2j}^{T-1} + \hat{c}_{jkl}(Q^{2^{T-1}}, Q^{3^{T-1}}) - \rho_{3k}^{T-1})\}, \quad \forall j, k, l. \tag{4.49}$$

Computation of the Prices

The prices, $\bar{\rho}_{2j}^{T}$, in turn, are computed at iteration T explicitly according to:

$$\bar{\rho}_{2j}^{T} = \max\{0, \rho_{2j}^{T-1} - \alpha(\sum_{i=1}^{m}\sum_{l=1}^{2} q_{ijl}^{T-1} - \sum_{k=1}^{o}\sum_{l=1}^{2} q_{jkl}^{T-1})\}, \quad \forall j, \tag{4.50}$$

whereas the prices, $\bar{\rho}_{3k}^{T}$, are computed according to:

$$\bar{\rho}_{3k}^{T} = \max\{0, \rho_{3k}^{T-1} - \alpha(\sum_{j=1}^{n}\sum_{l=1}^{2} q_{jkl}^{T-1} + \sum_{i=1}^{m} q_{ik}^{T-1} - d_{k}(\rho_{3}^{T-1}))\}, \quad \forall k. \tag{4.51}$$

The solution to subproblem (4.46) can be obtained in analogous fashion. Hence, although the solution of (4.45) and (4.46) may, at first, appear challenging, the resulting computations can be accomplished exactly and in closed form as described above.

An Adjustment Process Interpretation

The solution of (4.45) and (4.46), with the former being solved according to (4.47) through (4.51), has an elegant interpretation as an adjustment process. Note that, according to (4.47), the product shipments between the manufacturers and the retailers are determined from iteration to iteration (which may also be interpreted as a time period) independently and simultaneously using only the shipments from the manufacturers from the preceding iteration and the retailers' prices. The shipments from the manufacturers to the demand markets, in turn, are determined at a given iteration according to (4.48) using only the demand market prices from the preceding iteration as well as the shipments. Finally, the shipments from the retailers to the demand markets at a particular iteration are computed according to (4.49) using the retailers' prices and the demand market prices from the preceding iteration and the product shipments to the demand markets.

The computation of the retail prices according to (4.50) at an iteration requires the price of the particular retailer at the preceding iteration as well as the product shipments to and from the retailer. Finally, the demand market prices, according to (4.51), can be computed using the prices at the demand markets at the preceding iteration and the product shipments to the particular demand market

The solution of subproblem (4.46), which is an adaptation step, has a similar interpretation as given above, but now the information in terms of the product flows and prices computed as the solution to (4.45) are used as inputs along with the original flows and prices at the beginning of the iteration. Hence, the nomenclature of "Adaptation" for this step.

The convergence result for the modified projection method for this model is now given.

Theorem 4.8: Convergence

Assume that the function that enters the variational inequality (4.18) (or (4.25)) satisfies the conditions in Theorems 4.3, 4.4, and in Theorem 4.7. Then the modified projection method described above converges to the solution of the variational inequality (4.18) or (4.25).

Proof: According to Korpelevich (1977), the modified projection method converges to the solution of the variational inequality problem of the form (4.25), provided that the function F that enters the variational inequality is monotone and Lipschitz continuous and that a solution exists. Existence of a solution follows from Theorem 4.3. Monotonicity follows Theorem 4.4. Lipschitz continuity, in turn, follows from Theorem 4.7. $\square$

It is worth noting that the algorithm may, nevertheless, converge even if the above conditions are not satisfied and, if it converges, it converges to a solution of the variational inequality problem; equivalently, it determines an equilibrium flow and price pattern.

4.4   Numerical Examples

In this section, the modified projection method is applied to several numerical examples. The algorithm was implemented in FORTRAN and the computer system used was a DEC Alpha system located at the University of Massachusetts at Amherst. The convergence criterion utilized was that the absolute value of the product flows and prices between two successive iterations differed by no more than 10^{-4}. For the examples, α was set to .01 in the algorithm. The numerical examples had the network structure depicted in Figure 4.7 and consisted of two manufacturers, two retailers, and two demand markets, with both B2B and B2C transactions permitted, with the B2C transactions being between the manufacturers and the demand markets, for simplicity.

Example 4.1

The data for the first example were constructed for easy interpretation purposes. The production cost functions for the manufacturers were given by:

$$f_1(q) = 2.5q_1^2 + q_1q_2 + 2q_1, \quad f_2(q) = 2.5q_2^2 + q_1q_2 + 2q_2.$$

The transaction cost functions faced by the manufacturers and associated with transacting with the retailers using the physical link, that is, mode 1,

Manufacturers

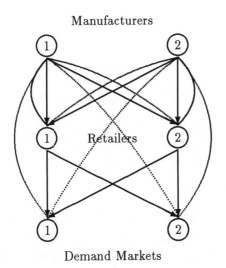

Demand Markets

Fig. 4.7. Supply Chain Network Structure for the Numerical Examples

were given by:

$$c_{111}(q_{111}) = .5q_{111}^2 + 3.5q_{111}, \quad c_{121}(q_{121}) = .5q_{121}^2 + 3.5q_{121},$$

$$c_{211}(q_{211}) = .5q_{211}^2 + 3.5q_{211}, \quad c_{221}(q_{221}) = .5q_{221}^2 + 3.5q_{221},$$

whereas the analogous transaction costs, but for mode 2, were given by:

$$c_{112}(q_{112}) = 1.5q_{112}^2 + 3q_{112}, \quad c_{122}(q_{122}) = 1.5q_{122}^2 + 3q_{122},$$

$$c_{212}(q_{212}) = 1.5q_{212}^2 + 3q_{212}, \quad c_{222}(q_{222}) = 1.5q_{222}^2 + 3q_{222},$$

The transaction costs of the manufacturers associated with dealing with the consumers at the demand markets via the Internet were given by:

$$c_{11}(q_{11}) = q_{11}^2 + 2q_{11}, \quad c_{12}(q_{12}) = q_{12}^2 + 2q_{12},$$

$$c_{21}(q_{21}) = q_{21}^2 + 2q_{21}, \quad c_{22}(q_{22}) = q_{22}^2 + 2q_{22}.$$

The handling costs of the retailers, in turn, were given by:

$$c_1(Q^1) = .5(\sum_{i=1}^{2}\sum_{l=1}^{2} q_{i1l})^2, \quad c_2(Q^1) = .5(\sum_{i=1}^{2}\sum_{l=1}^{2} q_{i2l})^2.$$

The transaction costs of the retailers associated with transacting with the manufacturers via mode 1 and mode 2 were, respectively, given by:

$$\hat{c}_{111}(q_{111}) = 1.5q_{111}^2 + 3q_{111}, \quad \hat{c}_{121}(q_{121}) = 1.5q_{121}^2 + 3q_{121},$$

$$\hat{c}_{211}(q_{211}) = 1.5q_{211}^2 + 3q_{211}, \quad \hat{c}_{221}(q_{221}) = 1.5q_{221}^2 + 3q_{221},$$
$$\hat{c}_{112}(q_{112}) = 1.5q_{112}^2 + 3q_{112}, \quad \hat{c}_{122}(q_{122}) = 1.5q_{122}^2 + 3q_{122},$$
$$\hat{c}_{212}(q_{212}) = 1.5q_{212}^2 + 3q_{212}, \quad \hat{c}_{222}(q_{222}) = 1.5q_{222}^2 + 3q_{222}.$$

The demand functions at the demand markets were:

$$d_1(\rho_3) = -2\rho_{31} - 1.5\rho_{32} + 1000, \quad d_2(\rho_3) = -2\rho_{32} - 1.5\rho_{31} + 1000,$$

and the transaction costs between the retailers and the consumers at the demand markets (denoted for a typical pair by $\hat{c}_{jkl}$ with the associated shipment by q_{jkl} with $l = 1$) were given by:

$$\hat{c}_{111}(Q^2, Q^3) = q_{111} + 5, \quad \hat{c}_{121}(Q^2, Q^3) = q_{121} + 5,$$
$$\hat{c}_{211}(Q^2, Q^3) = q_{211} + 5, \quad \hat{c}_{221}(Q^2, Q^3) = q_{221} + 5,$$

whereas the transaction costs associated with transacting with the manufacturers via the Internet for the consumers at the demand markets (denoted for a typical such pair by $\hat{c}_{ik}$ with the associated shipment of q_{ik}) were given by:

$$\hat{c}_{11}(Q^2, Q^3) = q_{11} + 1, \quad \hat{c}_{12}(Q^2, Q^3) = q_{12} + 1,$$
$$\hat{c}_{21}(Q^2, Q^3) = q_{21} + 1, \quad \hat{c}_{22}(Q^2, Q^3) = q_{22} + 1.$$

The modified projection method converged in 1055 iterations and yielded the following equilibrium pattern: the product shipments between the two manufacturers and the two retailers associated with the physical links, and with the Internet links, respectively, that is, with transacting via mode 1 and mode 2 were:

$$Q^{1*} : q_{111}^* = q_{121}^* = q_{211}^* = q_{221}^* = 3.4611,$$
$$q_{112}^* = q_{122}^* = q_{212}^* = q_{222}^* = 2.3907.$$

The product shipments between the two manufacturers and the two demand markets with transactions conducted through the Internet were:

$$Q^{2*} : q_{11}^* = q_{12}^* = q_{21}^* = q_{22}^* = 13.3033.$$

The product shipments (consumption volumes) between the two retailers and the two demand markets were:

$$Q^{3*} : q_{111}^* = q_{121}^* = q_{211}^* = q_{221}^* = 5.8513.$$

The vector ρ_2^*, which was equal to the prices charged by the retailers γ^*, had components:

$$\rho_{21}^* = \rho_{22}^* = 263.9088,$$

and the demand prices at the demand markets were:

$$\rho_{31}^* = \rho_{32}^* = 274.7701.$$

It is easy to verify that the optimality/equilibrium conditions were satisfied with good accuracy.

The prices charged by the manufacturers were as follows and were recovered according to the discussion following variational inequality (4.25). The ρ^*_{1ijl}s were for $l = 1$ and for $l = 2$, respectively: all ρ^*_{1ij1}s$=$ 238.8218 and all ρ^*_{1ij2}s$=$ 242.0329. All the ρ^*_{1ik}s were equal to 260.4673. These values were obtained in both ways as discussed following (4.25) and each manner yielded the same value for the corresponding price. Note that the price charged by the manufacturers to the consumers at the demand markets, approximately 260, was higher than the price charged to the retailers, regardless of the mode of transacting. The price charged to the retailers for the product transacted via the Internet, in turn, exceeded that charged using the classical physical manner.

Example 4.2

Example 4.1 was then modified as follows: The production cost function for manufacturer 1 was now given by:

$$f_1(q) = 2.5q_1^2 + q_1q_2 + 12q_1,$$

whereas the transaction costs for manufacturer 1 were now given by:

$$c_{11}(Q^1) = q_{11}^2 + 3.5q_{11}, \quad c_{12}(Q^1) = q_{12}^2 + 3.5q_{12}.$$

The remainder of the data was as in Example 4.1. Hence, both the production costs and the transaction costs increased for manufacturer 1.

The modified projection method converged in 1056 iterations and yielded the following equilibrium pattern: the product shipments between the two manufacturers and the two retailers associated with the physical links, and with the Internet links, respectively, that is, with transacting via mode 1 and mode 2 were:

$$Q^{1^*} : q^*_{111} = q^*_{121} = 3.3265, \quad q^*_{211} = q^*_{221} = 3.5408,$$

$$q^*_{112} = q^*_{122} = 2.3010, \quad q^*_{212} = q^*_{222} = 2.4438.$$

The product shipments between the two manufacturers and the two demand markets with transactions conducted through the Internet were:

$$Q^{2^*} : q^*_{11} = q^*_{12} = 12.5781, \quad q^*_{21} = q^*_{22} = 13.3638.$$

The product shipments (consumption volumes) between the two retailers and the two demand markets were:

$$Q^{3^*} : q^*_{11} = q^*_{12} = q^*_{21} = q^*_{22} = 5.8056.$$

The vector ρ^*_2 had components:

$$\rho^*_{21} = \rho^*_{22} = 264.1706,$$

and the demand prices at the demand markets were:

$$\rho_{31}^* = \rho_{32}^* = 274.9861.$$

The optimality/equilibrium conditions were, again, satisfied at the desired accuracy.

The ρ_{1ijl}^*s were as follows for $l = 1$ and for $l = 2$, respectively: The ρ_{11j1}^*s= 239.5789 for both j and the ρ_{11j2}^*s= 242.6553 for both j. For manufacturer 2, on the other hand, $\rho_{12j1}^* = 238.9360$ for both j, whereas $\rho_{12j2}^* = 242.268$ for both j. The ρ_{11k}^*s were equal to 261.4085, for both k, whereas the ρ_{12k}^*s were equal to 260.6223 for both k. Note that these values were obtained in both ways as discussed following (4.25) and each manner yielded the same value for the corresponding price. Note that, again, the prices charged by the manufacturers to the consumers at the demand markets were higher than the prices charged to the retailers. Of course, the demand price was, nevertheless, equal for all consumers at a given demand market. In fact, both in this and in the preceding example the equilibrium demand prices were the same for each demand market.

Hence, manufacturer 1 now produced less than it did in Example 4.1, whereas manufacturer 2 increased its production output. The prices charged by the retailers to the consumers increased, as did the prices at the demand markets, with a decrease in the incurred demand.

Example 4.3

Example 4.3 was constructed by changing Example 4.2 as follows. The data were identical to that in Example 4.2 except that the demand function for demand market 1 was now:

$$d_1(\rho_3) = -2\rho_{31} - 1.5\rho_{32} + 2000.$$

The modified projection method converged in 1466 iterations and yielded the following equilibrium pattern: the product shipments between the two manufacturers and the two retailers associated with the physical links, and with the Internet links, respectively, that is, with transacting via mode 1 and mode 2 were:

$$Q^{1^*} : q_{111}^* = q_{121}^* = 16.1444, \quad q_{211}^* = q_{221}^* = 16.4974,$$

$$q_{112}^* = q_{122}^* = 10.8463, \quad q_{212}^* = q_{222}^* = 11.0816.$$

The product shipments between the two manufacturers and the two demand markets with transactions conducted through the Internet were:

$$Q^{2^*} : q_{11}^* = 60.2397, \quad q_{12}^* = 0.0000, \quad q_{21}^* = 61.2103, \quad q_{22}^* = 0.0000.$$

The product shipments (consumption volumes) between the two retailers and the two demand markets were:

$$Q^{3^*} : q_{111}^* = 54.5788, \quad q_{121}^* = 0.0000, \quad q_{211}^* = 54.5788, \quad q_{221}^* = 0.0000,$$

the vector ρ_2^*, which was equal to the prices charged by the retailers γ^*, had components:

$$\rho_{21}^* = \rho_{22}^* = 825.1216,$$

and the demand prices at the demand markets were:

$$\rho_{31}^* = 884.694, \quad \rho_{32}^* = 0.0000.$$

It is easy to verify that the optimality/equilibrium conditions were satisfied with good accuracy.

The prices charged by the manufacturers were as follows and were, again, recovered according to the discussion following variational inequality (4.25). The ρ_{1ijl}^*s were as follows for $l = 1$ and for $l = 2$, respectively: $\rho_{1111}^* = 719.1185 = \rho_{1121}^*$; $\rho_{1211}^* = 718.0597 = \rho_{1221}^*$; $\rho_{1112}^* = \rho_{1122}^* = 735.019$, and $\rho_{1212}^* = \rho_{1222}^* = 734.3071$. The ρ_{111}^*s was equal to 823.4536, whereas the ρ_{121}^* was equal to 822.4830. In this example, only the consumers at demand market 1 consume a positive amount. Indeed, there is no consumption of the product by consumers located at demand market 2.

4.5   Sources and Notes

Nagurney, Dong, and Zhang (2001) introduced the supply chain network model without electronic commerce and formulated it as a variational inequality problem akin to the one given in (4.26). Later, Nagurney, Loo, Dong, and Zhang (2001) extended that framework which focused on decentralized decision-making in supply chains to include electronic commerce. This chapter extends the model in the latter paper to include B2C electronic commerce between retailers and consumers, as well. This chapter provides complete proofs of the results, and includes new ideas, topical applications, and extensions. In addition, the work is now framed in a supernetwork context. The numerical examples in Section 4.4 are from Nagurney, Loo, Dong, and Zhang (2001).

This chapter has provided the foundations for supply chain networks with decentralized decision-makers in a multitiered context. It considered both models with electronic commerce as well as one without. Given the complexity of interactions among the network agents, the formalism provided here is both conceptual in nature, since it abstracts the problem as a supernetwork, as well as theoretically rigorous. Moreover, the theoretical foundations serve as the basis for the development and analysis of other supply chain network structures. For background reading on the economics of electronic commerce, see Whinston, Stahl, and Choi (1997).

5 A Multilevel Perspective for Supply Chain Dynamics

In this chapter, a supernetwork framework is developed for the conceptualization of the dynamics underlying supply chains. The supernetwork is a multilevel network consisting of: the logistical network, the information network, and the financial network. Such a perspective allows one to visualize and to identify the interrelationships between the individual networks. For example, in the case of e-commerce, orders over the Internet trigger shipments over logistical and transportation networks, and financial payments, in turn, over a financial network.

The novelty of the proposed multilevel network framework allows one to capture distinct flows, in particular, logistical, information, and financial within the same network system. Moreover, since both the logistical and financial networks are multitiered in structure, one is able to observe, through a discrete-time process, how the prices as well as the product shipments are adjusted from iteration to iteration (time period to time period), until the equilibrium state is reached. Although the focus here is on a supply chain consisting of competing manufacturers, retailers, and consumers, the framework is sufficiently general to include other levels of decision-makers in the network such as suppliers and/or owners of distribution centers, for example.

The chapter is organized as follows. In Section 5.1, the multilevel network representing the supply chain system and consisting of the logistical, the information, and the financial networks is presented. The disequilibrium dynamics underlying the supply chain problem are described, and the projected dynamical system, which formulates the dynamic model given. We also provide an extension of the supernetwork to include suppliers and present applications to B2B exchanges. In Section 5.2, some qualitative properties of the dynamic trajectories, along with stability analysis results are given. A discrete-time adjustment process is outlined in Section 5.3. The adjustment process is a time discretization of the continuous adjustment process given in Section 5.1. In Section 5.4, the discrete-time adjustment process is implemented and applied to several numerical examples. In Section 5.5, the multilevel network concept for supply chains is extended to include transportation and telecommunication networks.

5.1   The Dynamic Supply Chain Model

In this section, the dynamic supply chain model with electronic commerce is developed using a multilevel network perspective. The model is a dynamic version of the static model described in Chapter 4 and consists of manufacturers, retailers, and consumers located at the demand markets. The multilevel network consists of a logistical network, an information network, and a financial network. The multilevel network structure of the problem is first identified along with the corresponding flows and prices. The underlying functions and the behavior of the various networks agents, that is, the manufacturers, the retailers, and the consumers located at the demand markets are then described.

The notation utilized in this chapter is as was outlined in Chapter 4. Hence, consider m manufacturers involved in the production of a homogeneous commodity, also referred to as "the product," which can then be sold and shipped to n retailers or to the consumers directly who are located at o demand markets. Recall that a typical manufacturer is denoted by i, a typical retailer by j, and a typical demand market by k.

The logistical network (cf. Figure 5.1) is the bottom network of the multilevel network for the supply chain model. Specifically, the logistical network represents the commodity production outputs and the shipments between the network agents, that is, between the manufacturers and the retailers, between the manufacturers and the consumers at the demand markets who have transacted directly through e-commerce, and the shipments from the retailers to the demand markets. As depicted in Figure 5.1, the top tier of nodes of the logistical network consists of the manufacturers; the middle tier consists of nodes of the retailers, and the bottom tier, of the demand markets. The links joining different tiers of nodes correspond to transactions between the nodes in the supply chain that take place. Each pair of manufacturer/retailer nodes is connected by two links, one depicting a physical link and the other an Internet link to represent B2B transactions. In addition, each manufacturer/demand market pair is connected with a link depicting an Internet link to allow for direct manufacturer/consumer transactions in the form of B2C business. Finally, each retailer/demand market pair is connected by two links, the first being a physical link and the second the Internet link to reflect this type of B2C electronic transaction. Observe that the lo-

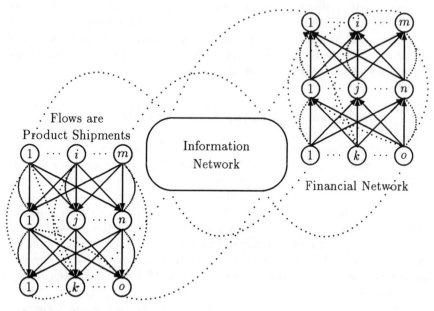

Fig. 5.1. Multilevel Network Structure of the Supply Chain System with Electronic Commerce

gistical network in Figure 5.1 is precisely the network depicted in Figure 4.1 to represent the supply chain network model in the preceding section, which was, however, static in scope. In this chapter, we go further in the use of the supernetwork concept through the introduction of dynamics as well as the explicit identification of other networks essential to the realization of effective and integrated supply chains.

The flows on the links in the logistical network correspond to the product shipments with the flow on a link (i, j, l) joining a node i in the top tier with node j via link l in the middle tier given by q_{ijl}. Here, as in Chapter 4, let $l = 1$ denote a physical link and let $l = 2$ denote an Internet link. The flow on link (i, k) joining manufacturer node i with demand market node k is denoted by q_{ik}. The flow on a link (j, k, l) joining node j at the middle tier with node k at the bottom tier via the link l, is, as before, denoted by q_{jkl}.

The financial network, in turn, is the top network in the multilevel framework shown in Figure 5.1 and its flows are the prices associated with the product. This financial network also has a three-tiered nodal structure as does the logistical network with the nodes corresponding to network agents as before. However, the links in the financial network go in the opposite direction from those in the logistical network. This reflects both the "bottom up" approach of our model, in that the consumers provide the "pull" through the prices they are willing to pay for the product, as well as representing the payments for the product, which move in an upward direction. Note that Internet payments are made electronically whereas the physical payments are made physically.

Recall that ρ_{1ijl} denotes the price of the product of manufacturer i (located at tier 1 of the financial network) associated with retailer j and transaction mode l. We refer now to the price of the product associated with retailer j, located at tier 2, by ρ_{2j} and recall that ρ_{3k} denotes the demand price of the product at demand market k (at the third tier of nodes)

Central to the multilevel network perspective of the supply chain model is the Information Network depicted between the Logistical and Financial Networks in Figure 5.1. Observe that the links in the Information Network are bidirectional since the information network, as shall subsequently be described, stores and provides the product shipment and price information over time, which allows for the recomputation of the new product shipments and prices, until, ultimately, the equilibrium pattern is attained.

The Dynamics

We now turn to describing the dynamics by which the manufacturers adjust their product shipments over time, the consumers adjust their consumption amounts based on the prices of the product at the demand markets, and the retailers operate between the two. We also describe the dynamics by which the prices adjust over time. The product flows evolve over time on the logistical network, whereas the prices do so over the financial network. The information network stores and provides the product shipment and price information so that the new product shipments and prices between tiers of network agents can be computed. The dynamics are derived from the bottom tier of nodes on up since, as mentioned previously, it is the demand for the product (and the corresponding prices) that actually drives the supply chain dynamics.

The Demand Market Price Dynamics

We begin by describing the dynamics underlying the prices of the product associated with the demand markets (see the bottom-tiered nodes in the financial network). Assume, as given, a demand function d_k, which can depend, in general, upon the entire vector of prices ρ_3, as described by the function in (4.13).

Assume that the rate of change of the price ρ_{3k}, denoted by $\dot{\rho}_{3k}$, is equal to the difference between the demand at the demand market k, as a function of the demand market prices, and the amount available from the retailers and the manufacturers at the demand market. Hence, if the demand for the product at the demand market (at an instant in time) exceeds the amount available, the price at that demand market will increase; if the amount available exceeds the demand at the price, then the price at the demand market will decrease. Furthermore, it is guaranteed that the prices do not become negative. Consequently, the dynamics of the price ρ_{3k} associated with the product at demand market k can be expressed as:

$$\dot{\rho}_{3k} = \begin{cases} d_k(\rho_3) - \sum_{j=1}^n \sum_{l=1}^2 q_{jkl} - \sum_{i=1}^m q_{ik}, & \text{if} \quad \rho_{3k} > 0 \\ \max\{0, d_k(\rho_3) - \sum_{j=1}^n \sum_{l=1}^2 q_{jkl} - \sum_{i=1}^m q_{ik}\}, & \text{if} \quad \rho_{3k} = 0. \end{cases}$$
$$(5.1)$$

The Dynamics of the Product Shipments between the Retailers and the Demand Markets

The dynamics of the product shipments in the logistical network taking place over the links joining the retailers to the demand markets are now described. Recall that there is a unit transaction cost $\hat{c}_{jkl}$ associated with transacting between retailer j and the consumers at demand market k, via mode l, where $\hat{c}_{jkl}$ is given by (4.11) and can depend upon, in general, all the product shipments to all the demand markets. The rate of change of the product shipment q_{jkl} is assumed to be equal to the difference between the price the consumers are willing to pay for the product at demand market k minus the unit transaction cost and the price charged for the product at the retail outlet. Of course, one also must guarantee that these product shipments do not become negative. Hence, one may write:

$$\dot{q}_{jkl} = \begin{cases} \rho_{3k} - \hat{c}_{jkl}(Q^2, Q^3) - \rho_{2j}, & \text{if} \quad q_{jkl} > 0 \\ \max\{0, \rho_{3k} - \hat{c}_{jkl}(Q^2, Q^3) - \rho_{2j}\}, & \text{if} \quad q_{jkl} = 0, \end{cases} \qquad (5.2)$$

where $\dot{q}_{jkl}$ denotes the rate of change of the product shipment q_{jkl}.

Thus, according to (5.2), if the price the consumers are willing to pay for the product at a demand market exceeds the price the retailers charge for the product at the outlet plus the unit transaction cost (at an instant in time), then the volume of the product between that retail and demand market pair will increase; if the price charged by the retailer plus the transaction cost exceeds the price the consumers are willing to pay, then the volume of flow of the product between that pair will decrease.

The Dynamics of the Product Shipments between the Manufacturers and the Demand Markets

As in Chapter 4, it is assumed that each manufacturer i is faced with a production cost f_i, which can depend, in general, upon all the product shipments from all the manufacturers to the retailers and demand markets, that is,

$$f_i = f_i(Q^1, Q^2), \quad \forall i. \qquad (5.3)$$

In addition, recall that c_{ik} is the transaction cost associated with manufacturer i transacting with demand market k, with the function being given by (4.2b). The consumers at the demand markets, in turn, are also faced with a transaction cost associated with transacting with a manufacturer directly. For manufacturer/demand market pair (i, k), this function is denoted by $\hat{c}_{ik}$ and, as in Chapter 4 expression (4.12), can depend, in general, upon all the product shipments to all the demand markets from all the manufacturers or retailers.

Since each manufacturer is assumed to be a profit-maximizer according to (4.4), a fair price to charge the consumers at a demand market who have transacted directly via a manufacturer through an Internet link is to charge the manufacturer's marginal production cost plus its marginal transaction cost, which for a pair (i, k) would be equal to: $\frac{\partial f_i(Q^1, Q^2)}{\partial q_{ik}} + \frac{\partial c_{ik}(q_{ik})}{\partial q_{ik}}$. The consumers at demand market k also incur a unit transaction cost associated with transacting with manufacturer i. Thus, the following rate of change for the product shipments between the top tier of nodes and the bottom tier of nodes in the logistical network is proposed:

$$
\dot{q}_{ik} = \begin{cases} \rho_{3k} - \frac{\partial f_i(Q^1, Q^2)}{\partial q_{ik}} - \frac{\partial c_{ik}(q_{ik})}{\partial q_{ik}} - \hat{c}_{ik}(Q^2, Q^3), & \text{if} \quad q_{ik} > 0 \\ \max\{0, \rho_{3k} - \frac{\partial f_i(Q^1, Q^2)}{\partial q_{ik}} - \frac{\partial c_{ik}(q_{ik})}{\partial q_{ik}} - \hat{c}_{ik}(Q^2, Q^3)\}, & \text{if} \quad q_{ik} = 0, \end{cases}
$$
(5.4)

where $\dot{q}_{ik}$ denotes the rate of change of the product shipment q_{ik}.

Thus, according to (5.4), if the demand price at a demand market exceeds the marginal production cost plus the marginal transaction cost of the manufacturer associated with transacting via the Internet directly with the consumers and the consumers' transaction cost, then the volume of the product transacted via the Internet between the manufacturer/demand market pair will increase; if the demand price at the demand market is less than the above described marginal and unit costs, then the volume of product shipment between the pair will decrease.

The Dynamics of the Prices at the Retail Outlets

The prices for the product at the retail outlets, in turn, must reflect supply and demand conditions as well (and as shall be shown shortly also reflect profit-maximizing behavior on the part of the retailers who seek to determine how much of the product they obtain from the different manufacturers for their outlet). In particular, assume that the price for the product associated with retail outlet j, ρ_{2j}, and computed at node j lying in the second tier of nodes of the financial network, evolves over time according to:

$$
\dot{\rho}_{2j} = \begin{cases} \sum_{k=1}^{o} \sum_{l=1}^{2} q_{jkl} - \sum_{i=1}^{m} \sum_{l=1}^{2} q_{ijl}, & \text{if} \quad \rho_{2j} > 0 \\ \max\{0, \sum_{k=1}^{o} \sum_{l=1}^{2} q_{jkl} - \sum_{i=1}^{m} \sum_{l=1}^{2} q_{ijl}\}, & \text{if} \quad \rho_{2j} = 0, \end{cases}
$$
(5.5)

where $\dot{\rho}_{2j}$ denotes the rate of change of the retail price ρ_{2j}. Hence, if the amount of the product desired to be transacted by the consumers (at an instant in time) exceeds that available at the retail outlet, then the price at the retail outlet will increase; if the amount available is greater than that desired by the consumers, then the price at the retail outlet will decrease.

The Dynamics of Product Shipments between Manufacturers and Retailers

The dynamics underlying the product shipments between the manufacturers and the retailers are now described. As already noted, each manufacturer is faced with a production cost and transaction costs. Recall that the transaction cost associated with manufacturer i and retailer j transacting via mode l is denoted by c_{ijl} and is of the form (4.2a).

As noted in Chapter 4, the total costs incurred by a manufacturer i, thus, are equal to the sum of the manufacturer's production cost plus the total transaction costs. His revenue, in turn, with regard to the transactions associated with the retailers, is equal to the price that the manufacturer charges for the product to the retailers (and the retailers are willing to pay) times the quantity of the product obtained/purchased from the manufacturer by the retail outlets and by the consumers directly. Hence, a fair price for the product associated with a given manufacturer/retailer pair and transacted via a mode is equal to the manufacturer's corresponding marginal costs of production and transacting, that is to: $\frac{\partial f_i(Q^1, Q^2)}{\partial q_{ijl}} + \frac{\partial c_{ijl}(q_{ijl})}{\partial q_{ijl}}$.

Recall that a retailer j, in turn, is faced with a handling cost given by (4.6). A retailer j, on the other hand, ideally, would accept a product shipment from manufacturer i at a price that is equal to the price charged at the retail outlet for the product (and that the consumers are willing to pay) minus its marginal cost associated with handling the product. Now, since the product shipments sent from the manufacturers must be accepted by the retailers in order for the transactions to take place in the supply chain, we propose the following rate of change for the product shipments between the top tier of nodes and the middle tier in the logistical network:

$$
\dot{q}_{ijl} = \begin{cases} \rho_{2j} - \frac{\partial f_i(Q^1, Q^2)}{\partial q_{ijl}} - \frac{\partial c_{ijl}(q_{ijl})}{\partial q_{ijl}} - \frac{\partial c_j(Q^1)}{\partial q_{ijl}} - \frac{\partial \hat{c}_{ijl}(q_{ijl})}{\partial q_{ijl}}, \text{ if } q_{ijl} > 0 \\ \max\{0, \\ \rho_{2j} - \frac{\partial f_i(Q^1, Q^2)}{\partial q_{ijl}} - \frac{\partial c_{ijl}(q_{ijl})}{\partial q_{ijl}} - \frac{\partial c_j(Q^1)}{\partial q_{ijl}} - \frac{\partial \hat{c}_{ijl}(q_{ijl})}{\partial q_{ijl}}\}, \text{ if } q_{ijl} = 0, \end{cases}
$$
(5.6)

where $\dot{q}_{ijl}$ denote the rate of change of the product shipment between manufacturer i and retailer j transacted via mode l.

Following the above discussion, (5.6) states that the product shipment between a manufacturer/retailer pair via a transaction mode evolves according to the difference between the price charged for the product by the retailer and its marginal costs, and the price charged by the manufacturer (which, recall, assuming profit-maximizing behavior, was set to the marginal cost of production plus its marginal cost of transacting with the retailer via the mode). Here it is also guaranteed that the product shipments do not become negative as they evolve over time.

The Projected Dynamical System

Consider now the dynamic model in which the demand prices evolve according to (5.1) for all demand market prices k, the retail/demand market product shipments evolve according to (5.2) for all retailers/demand markets/modes j, k, l, and the product shipments between the manufacturers and the demand markets evolve according to (5.4). The retail prices, in turn, evolve according to (5.5) for all retailers j, and the product shipments between the manufacturers and retailers evolve over time according to (5.6) for all manufacturer/retailer/mode combinations i, j, l.

Let X and $-F(X)$ be defined as: $X \equiv (Q^1, Q^2, Q^3, \rho_2, \rho_3)$, $F(X) \equiv (F_{ijl}, F_{ik}, F_{jkl}, F_j, F_k)$ for $\{i = 1, ..., m; j = 1, ..., n; l = 1, 2; k = 1, ..., o\}$, where the specific components of $-F$ are given by the functional terms preceding the first "if" term in (5.6), (5.4), (5.2), (5.5), and (5.1), respectively. Here $\mathcal{K} \equiv \{(Q^1, Q^2, Q^3, \rho_2, \rho_3)|(Q^1, Q^2, Q^3, \rho_2, \rho_3) \in R_+^{2mn+mo+2no+n+o}\}$.

Then the dynamic model described by (5.6), (5.4), (5.2), (5.5), and (5.1) for all k, i, j, l can be rewritten as the projected dynamical system (PDS) (cf. Definition B.7 in Appendix B) defined by the following initial value problem:

$$\dot{X} = \Pi_{\mathcal{K}}(X, -F(X)), \quad X(0) = X_0, \qquad (5.7)$$

where $\Pi_{\mathcal{K}}$ is the projection operator of $-F(X)$ onto $\mathcal{K}$ at X and $X_0 = (Q^{1^0}, Q^{2^0}, Q^{3^0}, \rho_2^0, \rho_3^0)$ is the initial point corresponding to the initial product shipments between the manufacturers and the retailers and the demand markets; the initial product shipments between the retailers and the demand markets; and the initial retailers' prices and the demand prices. Since the feasible set $\mathcal{K}$ underlying the dynamic supply chain is simply the nonnegative orthant, the projection operation is very simple. Indeed, it simply guarantees, through the use of the "max" term (cf. (5.1)–(5.6)), that the dynamic trajectory never yields negative values for the product flows and prices.

The trajectory of (5.7) describes the dynamic evolution of and the dynamic interactions among the product flows between the tiers of the logistical network and the prices on the financial network. The information network, in turn, stores and provides the product shipment and price information over time as needed for the dynamic evolution of the supply chain transactions. The dynamical system (5.7) is non-classical in that the right-hand side is discontinuous in order to guarantee that the constraints, which in the context of the above model are nonnegativity constraints on the variables, are not violated. Such dynamical systems were introduced by Dupuis and Nagurney (1993) and to date have been used to model a variety of applications ranging from dynamic traffic network problems (cf. Nagurney and Zhang (1997)) and oligopoly problems (see Nagurney, Dupuis, and Zhang (1994)) and spatial price equilibrium problems (cf. Nagurney, Takayama, and Zhang (1995a,b)). See Appendix B for a greater discussion and additional references.

Stationary/Equilibrium Points

The following theorem states that the projected dynamical system evolves until it reaches a stationary point, that is, $\dot{X} = 0$, in which there is no change in the product shipments and prices, and that the stationary point coincides with the equilibrium point of the supply chain network model according to Definition 4.1. The notation "*" is utilized here to denote an equilibrium point, as was also done in Chapter 4, as well as a stationary point, since these are shown to be equivalent in Theorem 5.1 below.

Theorem 5.1: Set of Stationary Points Coincides with Set of Equilibrium Points

The set of stationary points of the projected dynamical system (5.7) coincides with the set of equilibrium points defined by Definition 4.1.

Proof: According to Theorem B.6, the necessary and sufficient condition for X^* to be a stationary point of the PDS (5.7), that is, to satisfy:

$$\dot{X} = 0 = \Pi_{\mathcal{K}}(X^*, -F(X^*)),$$

is that $X^* \in \mathcal{K}$ solves the variational inequality problem:

$$\langle F(X^*), X - X^* \rangle \geq 0, \quad \forall X \in \mathcal{K}, \tag{5.8}$$

where, in our problem, $F(X)$, X, and $\mathcal{K}$ are as defined preceding (5.7). Writing out (5.8) explicitly, we have that

$$\sum_{i=1}^{m}\sum_{j=1}^{n}\sum_{l=1}^{2}\left[\frac{\partial f_i(Q^{1^*}, Q^{2^*})}{\partial q_{ijl}} + \frac{\partial c_{ijl}(q_{ijl}^*)}{\partial q_{ijl}} + \frac{\partial c_j(Q^{1^*})}{\partial q_{ijl}} + \frac{\partial \hat{c}_{ijl}(q_{ijl}^*)}{\partial q_{ijl}} - \rho_{2j}^*\right]$$

$$\times \left[q_{ijl} - q_{ijl}^*\right]$$

$$+\sum_{i=1}^{m}\sum_{k=1}^{o}\left[\frac{\partial f_i(Q^{1^*}, Q^{2^*})}{\partial q_{ik}} + \frac{\partial c_{ik}(q_{ik}^*)}{\partial q_{ik}} + \hat{c}_{ik}(Q^{2^*}, Q^{3^*}) - \rho_{3k}^*\right] \times \left[q_{ik} - q_{ik}^*\right]$$

$$+\sum_{j=1}^{n}\sum_{k=1}^{o}\sum_{l=1}^{2}\left[\rho_{2j}^* + \hat{c}_{jkl}(Q^{2^*}, Q^{3^*}) - \rho_{3k}^*\right] \times \left[q_{jkl} - q_{jkl}^*\right]$$

$$+\sum_{j=1}^{n}\left[\sum_{i=1}^{m}\sum_{l=1}^{2}q_{ijl}^* - \sum_{k=1}^{o}\sum_{l=1}^{2}q_{jkl}^*\right] \times \left[\rho_{2j} - \rho_{2j}^*\right]$$

$$+\sum_{k=1}^{o}\left[\sum_{j=1}^{n}\sum_{l=1}^{2}q_{jkl}^* + \sum_{i=1}^{m}q_{ik}^* - d_k(\rho_3^*)\right] \times \left[\rho_{3k} - \rho_{3k}^*\right] \geq 0, \tag{5.9}$$

$$\forall(Q^1, Q^2, Q^3, \rho_2, \rho_3) \in \mathcal{K}.$$

But variational inequality (5.9) is precisely the variational inequality (4.18) (and their corresponding $F(\cdot)$s, Xs, and Ks are one and the same), which, in turn, according to Theorem 4.1 coincides with $(Q^{1*}, Q^{2*}, Q^{3*}, \rho_2^*, \rho_3^*)$ being an equilibrium pattern according to Definition 4.1. The proof is complete. □

Hence, Theorem 5.1 establishes the linkage between the solution to the variational inequality problem (4.18), governing the static supply chain network model with e-commerce presented in Chapter 4, and the stationary points of the dynamic supply chain model described by the projected dynamical system (5.7). Indeed, it shows that they are one and the same. Thus, once a stationary point of the dynamic supply chain model has been achieved, that point satisfies the equilibrium conditions (4.21)–(4.24) and (4.16), at which the manufacturers, retailers, and consumers have formalized their agreements and the shipments between the tiers coincide.

5.1.1   An Extension

We now present an extension to the supernetwork depicting the supply chain in Figure 5.1. Specifically, as was done in Section 4.1.2, we now allow for another tier of nodes (cf. Figure 5.2) corresponding to decision-makers, in the form of suppliers (cf. Figure 4.6). These suppliers, in turn, are connected to the second tier of nodes, that is, the manufacturers, through both physical and Internet links. In a multilevel network setting, akin to the one in Figure 5.1, the multilevel structure would still consist of the logistical network, the information network, and the financial network, but the structure of the logistical and the financial networks would now each include an additional tier of nodes as given in Figure 5.2.

Hence, in this supernetwork, both in the logistical and the financial networks, there are now 4 tiers of decision-makers.

5.1.1.1   An Application to a B2B Exchange – Covisint

We now illustrate some of the above concepts with a discussion of a specific application, that of a B2B Exchange, still under development, and known as *Covisint*. Covisint is an independent company, which was founded by major decision-makers in the automotive industry. According to its website (cf. Covisint (2001)), it expects to become one of the world's leading B2B Internet exchanges with joint ownership by General Motors, Ford, Daimler Chrysler, Renault/Nissan, Commerce One, and Oracle. The exchange will provide supply chain, procurement as well as product development functions. The name itself, according to the same source, is a synthesis of "Co," "Vis," and "Int," with "Co" denoting "connectivity, collaboration, and communication;" with "Vis" representing "the visibility that the Internet provides, and the vision of future supply chain management;" and with "Int" representing "the integrated solutions the venture will provide as well as the international scope of the exchange."

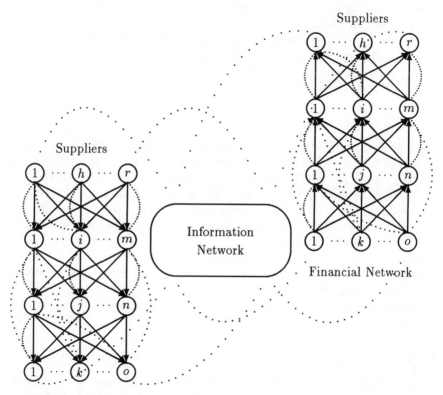

Fig. 5.2. Multilevel Network Structure of the Supply Chain System with a Tier of Suppliers

Still in its development, it is expected to offer an online marketplace for automotive parts and supplies as well as related products. Hence, the structure of the interactions is similar to that depicted in Figure 5.2 with suppliers, interacting with manufacturers, and, ultimately, retailers, and consumers.

According to Covisint's website, the service will "allow individual organizations to 'see' the current and future status of their respective supply chains' material flows, inventory levels, and capacity constraints." Hence, there is a particular emphasis given to the information network as depicted in Figure 5.2. In particular, it is stated therein that "Everyone will be able to communicate information in real-time." Moreover, with the value of supply chain inventories in the automotive industry being approximately 10–15 percent, according to industry and financial analysts and as reported on the website, it is very important for timely and cost-effective production to reduce the inventories. Note that, as established in Chapter 4, at the equilibrium of the 3-tiered supply chain, at which the decision-makers have achieved their optimal decisions, the retail outlets "import" as much of a product as they "export" in that the flow in of the product is equal to the flow out for each retailer node, and, hence, in a sense, the inventory at that level of nodes is minimized. This clearly has both strategic and financial implications in this expanded supply chain network as well.

Interestingly, as also appears on the company's website, Covisint is expected to add additional value services including financial services and payment services, which is also reflected in the supernetwork drawn in Figure 5.2.

In Section 5.3, we describe a discrete-time process which provides an evolution of the major variables underlying the supply chain network over time through the perspective of the multilevel network framework. It is a time-discretization of the continuous time dynamical system (5.7) and provides a dynamic "story" of how the product shipments and prices are adjusted over time, along with the information requirements, so that the decision-makers optimize their decisions, even in the presence of competition.

5.1.1.2   B2B Electronic Commerce and General Electric

Jack Welch, while CEO of General Electric, one of the largest and best-managed companies in the world, said in 1999 and we quote: "The Internet makes old, young. Makes big, small. Makes slow, fast...It just doesn't get much better than this" (see General Electric (2001)). Since then General Electric (GE) has been working hard to develop its Internet strategy. Its electronic sales (see Tedeschi (2001)) reached 10 percent of its total revenues of $130 billion in 2000.

For example, GE's appliances division now yields $6 billion of the company's total sales and almost 100 percent of its sales come over the Internet. According to Tedeschi (2001), "the cost difference between a phone order and a web-based order is $5 versus 20 cents," or, in our parlance, the transaction costs associated with different modes of transacting can vary greatly and this aspect is handled by our models.

General Electric's Global eXchange (GXS) (see PR Newswire (2000)) operates one of the largest B2B e-commerce networks in the world, with more than 100,000 trading partners. It now has a presence in 58 countries and its 1 billion annual transactions account for $1 trillion in services and goods. Its goal is to provide e-commerce solutions that help businesses remove costs from their supply chains. Of particular emphasis is the sharing of information, which is also central to the model developed in this chapter. For example, on August 22, 2000 (see Balluck (2000)), GXS announced that it had that day "enabled partners in the US and Canada for the first time to share standardized product information through a centralized, Web-based catalog." It is expected that the "cross-border sharing of coded product information will save supply chain costs for retail trading partners..." The information available can be highly detailed and about diverse items.

5.2   Qualitative Properties

In this section, some qualitative properties of the dynamic supply chain model with electronic commerce are given. In particular, a fundamental property of the projected dynamical system – that of the existence of a unique solution to the initial value problem (5.7) is revealed in the following theorem. Note that this result is not identical to Theorems 4.3 and 4.6 since Theorem 4.3 is concerned with the existence of a solution to the variational inequality problem and here existence is in the context of a dynamic trajectory; moreover, Theorem 4.6 established uniqueness, under reasonable conditions, for an equilibrium or solution pattern of (4.18) (equivalently (5.9)) and not of the dynamic trajectory. Theorem 5.2 below is important since it states that if one begins with an initial product shipment and price pattern, then one can trace out a unique (one and only one) trajectory of the dynamics over time.

Theorem 5.2: Existence and Uniqueness
Assume the conditions of Theorem 4.7. Then, for any $X_0 \in \mathcal{K}$, there exists a unique solution $X_0(t)$ to the initial value problem (5.7).

Proof: Lipschitz continuity of the function F is sufficient for the conclusion based on Theorem 2.5 in Nagurney and Zhang (1996) (see also Theorem B.7 in Appendix B).

Hence, according to Theorem 5.2, the disequilibrium dynamics of the supply chain network model are well defined. It is worth emphasizing that the PDS (5.7) provides the dynamics of the supply chain network model with e-commerce until the stationary point is reached; equivalently, the equilibrium point is attained. The equilibrium point, in turn, satisfies the variational inequality (4.18) (and (5.9)).

We now turn to addressing the stability (see also Zhang and Nagurney (1995), Nagurney and Zhang (2001), and Appendix B) of the supply chain network system through the initial value problem (5.7). First, we recall the following:

Definition 5.2: Stability of the System
The system defined by (5.7) is stable if, for every X_0 and every equilibrium point X^*, the Euclidean distance $\|X^* - X_0(t)\|$ is a monotone nonincreasing function of time t.

A *global* stability result is stated in the next theorem.

Theorem 5.3: Stability of the Dynamic Supply Chain Network System
Assume the conditions of Theorem 4.4. Then the dynamical system (5.7) underlying the supply chain is stable.

Proof: Under the assumptions of Theorem 4.4, $F(X)$ is monotone and, hence, the conclusion follows directly from Theorem 4.1 of Zhang and Nagurney (1995) (see also Theorem B.8). □

The stability of the supply chain network system demonstrates the validity of the equilibrium concept. In particular, stability of the system says that for any initial product shipment and price pattern, an equilibrium product shipment and price pattern is eventually attained.

5.3   The Discrete-Time Adjustment Process

Note that the projected dynamical system (5.7) is a continuous time adjustment process. However, in order to further fix ideas and to provide a means of "tracking" the trajectory, a discrete-time adjustment process is proposed. The discrete-time adjustment process is a special case of the general iterative scheme of Dupuis and Nagurney (1993) and is, in fact, an Euler method (cf. Appendix C). Specifically, the complete statement of this method in the context of the model with electronic commerce takes the following form where τ is now used to denote an iteration to distinguish the iteration from $\mathcal{T}$ as used for the modified projection method in Section 4.3:

Step 0: Initialization Step
Set $(Q^{10}, Q^{20}, Q^{30}, \rho_2^0, \rho_3^0) \in \mathcal{K}$. Let $\tau = 1$ and set the sequence $\{\alpha_\tau\}$ so that $\sum_{\tau=1}^{\infty} a_\tau = \infty$, $a_\tau > 0$, $a_\tau \to 0$, as $\tau \to \infty$.

Step 1: Computation
Compute $(Q^{1^\tau}, Q^{2^\tau}, Q^{3^\tau}, \rho_2^\tau, \rho_3^\tau) \in \mathcal{K}$ by solving the variational inequality subproblem:

$$\sum_{i=1}^{m} \sum_{j=1}^{n} \sum_{l=1}^{2} \left[q_{ijl}^\tau + \alpha_\tau \left(\frac{\partial f_i(Q^{1^{\tau-1}}, Q^{2^{\tau-1}})}{\partial q_{ijl}} + \frac{\partial c_{ijl}(q_{ijl}^{\tau-1})}{\partial q_{ijl}} + \frac{\partial c_j(Q^{1^{\tau-1}})}{\partial q_{ijl}} \right. \right.$$

$$+\frac{\partial \hat{c}_{ijl}(q_{ijl}^{\tau-1})}{\partial q_{ijl}} - \rho_{2j}^{\tau-1}) - q_{ijl}^{\tau-1}\bigg] \times \big[q_{ijl} - q_{ijl}^{\tau}\big]$$

$$+\sum_{i=1}^{m}\sum_{k=1}^{o}\sum_{l=1}^{2}\bigg[q_{ik}^{\tau} + \alpha_{\tau}(\frac{\partial f_i(Q^{1^{\tau-1}}, Q^{2^{\tau-1}})}{\partial q_{ik}} + \frac{\partial c_{ik}(q_{ik}^{\tau-1})}{\partial q_{ik}}$$

$$+\hat{c}_{ik}(Q^{2^{\tau-1}}, Q^{3^{\tau-1}}) - \rho_{3k}^{\tau-1}) - q_{ik}^{\tau-1}\bigg] \times \big[q_{ik} - q_{ik}^{\tau}\big]$$

$$+\sum_{j=1}^{n}\sum_{k=1}^{o}\sum_{l=1}^{2}\bigg[q_{jkl}^{\tau} + \alpha_{\tau}(\rho_{2j}^{\tau-1} + \hat{c}_{jkl}(Q^{2^{\tau-1}}, Q^{3^{\tau-1}}) - \rho_{3k}^{\tau-1}) - q_{jkl}^{\tau-1}\bigg]$$

$$\times \big[q_{jkl} - q_{jkl}^{\tau}\big]$$

$$+\sum_{j=1}^{n}\bigg[\rho_{2j}^{\tau} + \alpha_{\tau}(\sum_{i=1}^{m}\sum_{l=1}^{2}q_{ijl}^{\tau-1} - \sum_{k=1}^{o}\sum_{l=1}^{2}q_{jkl}^{\tau-1}) - \rho_{2j}^{\tau-1}\bigg] \times \big[\rho_{2j} - \rho_{2j}^{\tau}\big]$$

$$+\sum_{k=1}^{o}\bigg[\rho_{3k}^{\tau} + \alpha_{\tau}(\sum_{j=1}^{n}\sum_{l=1}^{2}q_{jkl}^{\tau-1} + \sum_{i=1}^{m}q_{ik}^{\tau-1} - d_k(\rho_3^{\tau-1})) - \rho_{3k}^{\tau-1}\bigg]$$

$$\times \big[\rho_{3k} - \rho_{3k}^{\tau}\big] \geq 0, \quad \forall(Q^1, Q^2, Q^3, \rho_2, \rho_3) \in \mathcal{K}. \tag{5.10}$$

Step 2: Convergence Verification

If $|q_{ijl}^{\tau} - q_{ijl}^{\tau-1}| \leq \epsilon$, $|q_{ik}^{\tau} - q_{ik}^{\tau-1}| \leq \epsilon$, $|q_{jkl}^{\tau} - q_{jkl}^{\tau-1}| \leq \epsilon$, $|\rho_{2j}^{\tau} - \rho_{2j}^{\tau-1}| \leq \epsilon$, $|\rho_{3k}^{\tau} - \rho_{3k}^{\tau-1}| \leq \epsilon$, for all $i = 1, \cdots, m$; $j = 1, \cdots, n$; $l = 1, 2$; $k = 1, \cdots, o$, with $\epsilon > 0$, a pre-specified tolerance, then stop; otherwise, set $\tau := \tau + 1$, and go to Step 1.

Since $\mathcal{K}$ is the nonnegative orthant the solution of (5.10) is accomplished exactly and in closed form. Indeed, note the similarity of variational inequality (5.10) to variational inequality (4.45) encountered at the Computation Step of the modified projection method. In the Euler method, there is a varying α, which has to satisfy the conditions in the Initialization Step, whereas in the modified projection method the α term was fixed from iteration to iteration. The sequence $\{\alpha_{\tau}\}$, has an interpretation that "learning" is taking place from time period to time period in that, at first, the value is larger, and then as time proceeds, it gets smaller and smaller. Note also, that the Euler method does not require an Adaptation Step as did the modified projection method. Nevertheless, both algorithms are projection-type methods (see also Appendix C), with one being a "modified" one and the other a projection method with a varying parameter α.

Hence, the implementation of the Euler method is identical to the Computation Step of the modified projection method with the parameter α varying according to the series $\{\alpha_{\tau}\}$. Thus, the computation of the product shipments can be done explicitly and in closed form according to the expressions

(4.47), (4.48), and (4.49), and the prices according to the expressions (4.50) and (4.51), with the substitutions: τ for iteration T and α_τ for α.

For completeness and easy reference, we show how problem (5.10) can be solved exactly and in closed form below:

Computation of the Product Shipments

At iteration τ compute the q_{ijl}^τs according to:

$$q_{ijl}^\tau = \max \left\{ 0, q_{ijl}^{\tau-1} - \alpha_\tau \left(\frac{\partial f_i(Q^{1^{\tau-1}}, Q^{2^{\tau-1}})}{\partial q_{ijl}} + \frac{\partial c_{ijl}(q_{ijl}^{\tau-1})}{\partial q_{ijl}} + \frac{\partial c_j(Q^{1^{\tau-1}})}{\partial q_{ijl}} \right. \right.$$

$$\left. \left. + \frac{\partial \hat{c}_{ijl}(q_{ijl}^{\tau-1})}{\partial q_{ijl}} - \rho_{2j}^{\tau-1} \right) \right\}, \quad \forall i, j, l. \tag{5.11}$$

In addition, at iteration τ, compute the q_{ik}^τs according to:

$$q_{ik}^\tau = \max \left\{ 0, q_{ik}^{\tau-1} - \alpha_\tau \left(\frac{\partial f_i(Q^{1^{\tau-1}}, Q^{2^{\tau-1}})}{\partial q_{ik}} + \frac{\partial c_{ik}(q_{ik}^{\tau-1})}{\partial q_{ik}} \right. \right.$$

$$\left. \left. + \hat{c}_{ik}(Q^{2^{\tau-1}}, Q^{3^{\tau-1}}) - \rho_{3k}^{\tau-1} \right) \right\}, \quad \forall i, k. \tag{5.12}$$

Also, at iteration τ compute the q_{jkl}^τs according to:

$$q_{jkl}^\tau = \max\{0, q_{jkl}^{\tau-1} - \alpha_\tau(\rho_{2j}^{\tau-1} + \hat{c}_{jkl}(Q^{2^{\tau-1}}, Q^{3^{\tau-1}}) - \rho_{3k}^{\tau-1})\}, \quad \forall j, k, l. \tag{5.13}$$

Computation of the Prices

The prices, ρ_{2j}^τ, in turn, are computed at iteration τ explicitly according to:

$$\rho_{2j}^\tau = \max\{0, \rho_{2j}^{\tau-1} - \alpha_\tau(\sum_{i=1}^{m}\sum_{l=1}^{2} q_{ijl}^{\tau-1} - \sum_{k=1}^{o}\sum_{l=1}^{2} q_{jkl}^{\tau-1})\}, \quad \forall j, \tag{5.14}$$

whereas the prices, ρ_{3k}, are computed according to:

$$\rho_{3k}^\tau = \max\{0, \rho_{3k}^{\tau-1} - \alpha_\tau(\sum_{j=1}^{n}\sum_{l=1}^{2} q_{jkl}^{\tau-1} + \sum_{i=1}^{m} q_{ik}^{\tau-1} - d_k(\rho_3^{\tau-1}))\}, \quad \forall k. \tag{5.15}$$

We now discuss the above discrete-time adjustment process in the context of the multilevel network in Figure 5.1. The computation of the product flows takes place on the logistical network, whereas the computation of the prices at the tiers takes place on the financial network.

Note that, in order to compute the new product shipment between a manufacturer/retailer pair transacted via a mode, according to (5.11), the logistical network requires, from the information network, the price at the particular retailer from the preceding iteration as well as all the product shipments from the manufacturers at the preceding iteration. This type of computation can be done simultaneously for all combinations of manufacturers/retailers/modes. In addition, in order to determine the new product shipments transacted between manufacturers and demand markets according to (5.12) at a given iteration or time period, the logistical network requires the demand market price at the preceding iteration at the demand market along with the product shipments at the preceding iteration or time period. Similarly, according to (5.13), in order to compute the new product shipment between a retailer and demand market pair, the logistical network requires from the information network the price at the particular retail outlet from the preceding iteration, and also the demand market price, as well as the product shipments to the demand markets from the preceding iteration.

The financial network requires from the information network, at a given iteration (or time period) for the computation of the retail prices (cf. (5.14)), the product shipments to and from the particular retailer at the preceding iteration, as well as the retail price at the retail outlet from the preceding iteration.

Finally, for the computation of the demand market price at a given iteration according to (5.15), the financial network requires from the information network the demand prices for the products at the demand markets from the preceding iteration that the demand function depends upon and the product flows at the preceding iteration from the retailers to the particular demand market. The computation of the demand market prices at all the demand markets are accomplished in a similar manner.

Hence, according to the discrete-time adjustment process described above, the process is initialized with a vector of product shipments and prices. Of course, the vector components can all be set to zero, which signifies that "at the beginning" there is no production and shipment and zero prices for the product. The system will then evolve, simulated, in a sense, by the discrete-time adjustment process (5.11) through (5.15) until a stationary/equilibrium point is achieved. The information network stores the price and product shipment information at each iteration and then the logistical network and the financial network simultaneously compute the new product flows between tiers of nodes and the new prices at the nodes, respectively. This information is then fed back to the information network and transferred to the logistical and financial networks at the next iteration as needed. This process continues until convergence is reached, that is, until the absolute difference of the product shipments between two successive iterations and that of the prices between two successive iterations lies within an acceptable tolerance. Clearly, it is easy to see from (5.11)–(5.15) that once the convergence tolerance has been reached (and, hence, these differences are approximately zero) then the equilibrium conditions (4.21), (4.22), (4.23), (4.24), and (4.16) are satisfied; equivalently, a stationary point of the projected dynamical system (5.7) is attained, and also a solution to variational inequality (4.18) (or (5.9)).

The equilibrium prices ρ_2^* (cf. Figure 5.1) are associated with the second tier of nodes in the financial network, whereas the equilibrium demand market prices are associated with the bottom tier of nodes in the financial network. Although the equilibrium prices ρ_1^* associated with the top tier of nodes (and representing the manufacturer nodes) are not explicitly computed through the discrete-time algorithm, they can, nevertheless, be recovered from the equilibrium solution as described in Section 4.1, since profit-maximization behavior for both the producing manufacturers and the retailers has been assumed.

The equilibrium product shipments Q^{1*}, in turn, are associated with the links in the logistical network joining the top tier of nodes to the middle tier of nodes. The equilibrium shipments Q^{2*}, in turn, are associated with the links joining the top tier with the bottom tier of nodes in the logistical network, and, finally, the equilibrium shipments Q^{3*} are associated with the links joining the middle tier (retailer) nodes with the bottom tier (demand market) nodes in the logistical network.

Convergence conditions for this method can be found in Dupuis and Nagurney (1993) and have been studied in a variety of application contexts in Nagurney and Zhang (1996). See also Theorem C.1 in Appendix C.

Clearly, in view of Corollary 4.2, one can also apply the Euler method to compute the solution to variational inequality (4.26) governing the supply chain model without e-commerce. In this context, the Euler method also has an interpretation of a discrete-time adjustment process which tracks the corresponding dynamic trajectory of the product flows and prices but now there are no shipments transacted through the Internet. The realization of the Euler method (with a corresponding simplification in notation) for the supply chain network model without electronic commerce is given below.

Computation of the Product Shipments

At iteration τ compute the q_{ij}^τs according to:

$$q_{ij}^\tau = \max\{0, q_{ij}^{\tau-1} - \alpha_\tau(\frac{\partial f_i(Q^{1^{\tau-1}})}{\partial q_{ij}} + \frac{\partial c_{ij}(q_{ij}^{\tau-1})}{\partial q_{ij}} + \frac{\partial c_j(Q^{1^{\tau-1}})}{\partial q_{ij}} + \frac{\partial \hat{c}_{ij}(q_{ij}^{\tau-1})}{\partial q_{ij}}$$

$$-\rho_{2j}^{\tau-1})\}, \quad \forall i, j. \tag{5.16}$$

Also, at iteration τ compute the q_{jk}^τs according to:

$$q_{jk}^\tau = \max\{0, q_{jk}^{\tau-1} - \alpha_\tau(\rho_{2j}^{\tau-1} + \hat{c}_{jk}(Q^{2^{\tau-1}}) - \rho_{3k}^{\tau-1})\}, \quad \forall j, k. \tag{5.17}$$

Computation of the Prices

The retail prices, ρ_{2j}^τ, in turn, are computed at iteration τ explicitly according to:

$$\rho_{2j}^\tau = \max\{0, \rho_{2j}^{\tau-1} - \alpha_\tau(\sum_{i=1}^m q_{ij}^{\tau-1} - \sum_{k=1}^o q_{jk}^{\tau-1})\}, \quad \forall j, \tag{5.18}$$

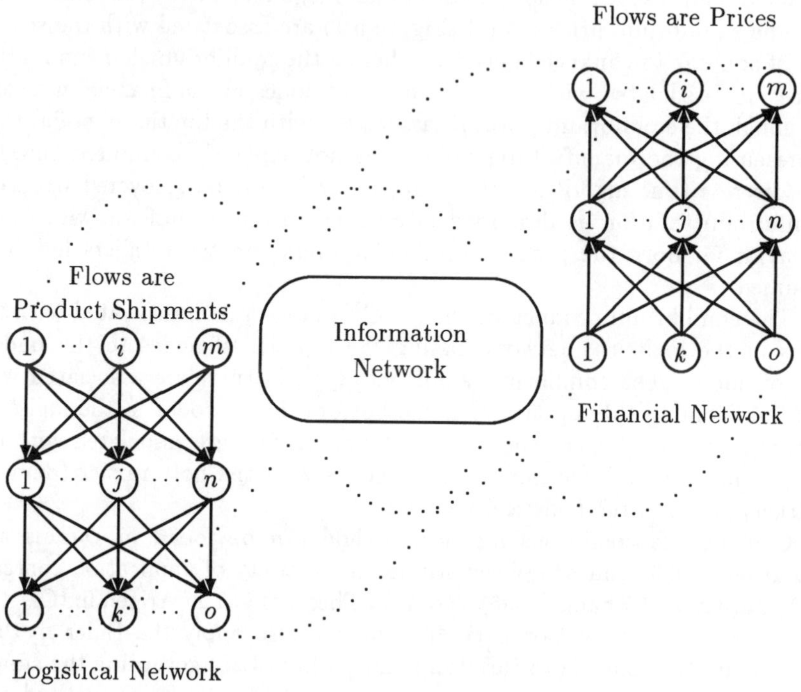

Flows are Prices

. Flows are
Product Shipments

Information
Network

Financial Network

Logistical Network

Fig. 5.3. Multilevel Network Structure of the Supply Chain System without Electronic Commerce

whereas the demand market prices, ρ_{3k}, are computed according to:

$$\rho_{3k}^\tau = \max\{0, \rho_{3k}^{\tau-1} - \alpha_\tau(\sum_{j=1}^n q_{jk}^{\tau-1} - d_k(\rho_3^{\tau-1}))\}, \quad \forall k. \tag{5.19}$$

For completeness, the multilevel network structure of the supply chain network model without e-commerce is given in Figure 5.3. Note that it has a structure similar to the supernetwork in Figure 5.1, but now there are no Internet links.

5.4   Numerical Examples

In this section, the discrete-time adjustment process (the Euler method) is applied to several dynamic numerical supply chain examples. Two sets of examples were solved, consisting of three examples each. The first set of numerical examples consisted of supply chain network problems with e-commerce and these were solved via a FORTRAN implementation of (5.11)–(5.15). The

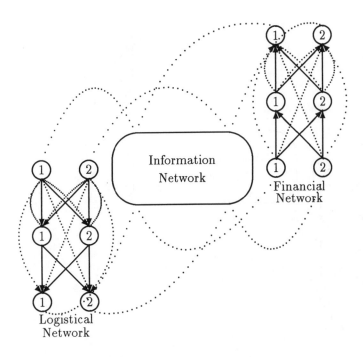

Fig. 5.4. Multilevel Network for Examples 5.1, 5.2, and 5.3

second set of numerical examples consisted of supply chain network problems without e-commerce and these were solved via a FORTRAN implementation of (5.16)–(5.19). The computer system used was a DEC Alpha system located at the University of Massachusetts at Amherst. The convergence criterion was that the absolute value of the flows and prices between two successive iterations differed by no more than 10^{-4}. The sequence $\{a_\tau\}$ was set to $\{1, \frac{1}{2}, \frac{1}{2}, \frac{1}{3}, \frac{1}{3}, \frac{1}{3}, \ldots\}$ for all the examples. The initial product shipments and prices were all set to zero for each example.

Examples 5.1, 5.2, and 5.3

The first three numerical examples had the multilevel network structure depicted in Figure 5.4 and consisted of two manufacturers, two retailers, and two demand markets with electronic commerce between manufacturers and retailers and manufacturers and the demand markets only. The data for the three examples were as given, respectively, in numerical examples 4.1, 4.2, and 4.3 in the preceding chapter.

The Euler method converged for each of these three examples and yielded equilibrium product and price patterns which were almost equal (to two decimal places to the right of the decimal point) to those reported in Section 4.4

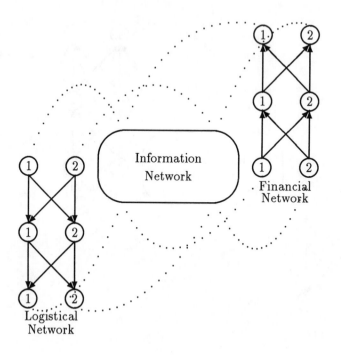

Fig. 5.5. Multilevel Network for Example 5.4

and obtained by the modified projection method. For the first two examples, the Euler method required 256 iterations for convergence, whereas for the third example, it required 304 iterations. Thus, as supported by theory, the Euler method is not only a discrete-time approximation to the continuous time adjustment process or dynamic model (5.7) of the supply chain network system with electronic commerce, but it also computes the stationary point of the system (5.7); equivalently, an equilibrium point, that is, a solution to variational inequality (4.18).

In the next three examples, supply chain network problems with no e-commerce were solved via the Euler method using (5.16)–(5.19).

Example 5.4

The first example in the second set consisted of two manufacturers, two retailers, and two demand markets, and its multilevel network structure was, hence, as depicted in Figure 5.5. There was no e-commerce in this and the next two examples.

The production cost functions for the manufacturers were given by:

$$f_1(q) = 2.5q_1^2 + q_1q_2 + 10q_1, \quad f_2(q) = 2.5q_2^2 + q_1q_2 + 2q_2.$$

The transaction cost functions faced by the manufacturers and associated with transacting with the retailers were given by:

$$c_{11}(q_{11}) = q_{11}^2 + 3.5q_{11}, \quad c_{12}(q_{12}) = .5q_{12}^2 + 3.5q_{12},$$

$$c_{21}(q_{21}) = .5q_{21}^2 + 3.5q_{21}, \quad c_{22}(q_{22}) = .5q_{22}^2 + 3q_{22}.$$

The handling costs of the retailers, in turn, were given by:

$$c_1(Q^1) = .5(\sum_{i=1}^{2} q_{i1})^2, \quad c_2(Q^1) = .75(\sum_{i=1}^{2} q_{i2})^2.$$

The demand functions at the demand markets were:

$$d_1(\rho_3) = -2\rho_{31} - 1.5\rho_{32} + 1200, \quad d_2(\rho_3) = -2.5\rho_{32} - 1\rho_{31} + 1000,$$

and the transaction costs between the retailers and the consumers at the demand markets were given by:

$$\hat{c}_{11}(Q^3) = q_{11}+5, \quad \hat{c}_{12}(Q^3) = q_{12}+5, \quad \hat{c}_{21}(Q^3) = 3q_{21}+5, \quad \hat{c}_{22}(Q^3) = q_{22}+5.$$

All other functions were set to zero.

The Euler method converged in 196 iterations and yielded the following equilibrium pattern. The product shipments between the two manufacturers and the two retailers were:

$$Q^{1*} : q_{11}^* = 19.002, \quad q_{12}^* = 16.920, \quad q_{21}^* = 30.225, \quad q_{22}^* = 9.6402,$$

the product shipments (consumption volumes) between the two retailers and the two demand markets were:

$$Q^{3*} : q_{11}^* = 49.228, \quad q_{12}^* = 0.000, \quad q_{21}^* = 26.564, \quad q_{22}^* = 0.000,$$

the vector ρ_2^* had components:

$$\rho_{21}^* = 320.2058, \quad \rho_{22}^* = 289.7407,$$

and the demand prices at the demand markets were:

$$\rho_{31}^* = 374.433, \quad \rho_{32}^* = 250.227.$$

Note that there were zero shipments of the product from both retailers to demand market 2, where the demand for the product was zero.

Example 5.5

The second supply chain problem in this set of numerical examples consisted of two manufacturers, three retailers, and two demand markets. Its multilevel network structure is given in Figure 5.6.

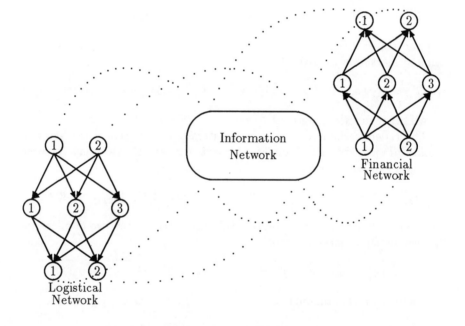

Fig. 5.6. Multilevel Network for Example 5.5

The production cost functions for the manufacturers were given by:

$$f_1(q) = 2.5q_1^2 + q_1q_2 + 2q_1, \quad f_2(q) = 2.5q_2^2 + q_1q_2 + 12q_2.$$

The transaction cost functions faced by the two manufacturers and associated with transacting with the three retailers were:

$$c_{11}(q_{11}) = q_{11}^2 + 3.5q_{11}, \quad c_{12}(q_{12}) = q_{12}^2 + 3.5q_{12}, \quad c_{13}(q_{13}) = .5q_{13}^2 + 5q_{13},$$

$$c_{21}(q_{21}) = .5q_{21}^2 + 3.5q_{21}, \quad c_{22}(q_{22}) = .5q_{22}^2 + 3.5q_{22}, \quad c_{23}(q_{23}) = .5q_{23}^2 + 5q_{23}.$$

The handling costs of the retailers, in turn, were:

$$c_1(Q^1) = .5(\sum_{i=1}^{2} q_{i1})^2, \quad c_2(Q^1) = .5(\sum_{i=1}^{2} q_{i2})^2, \quad c_3(Q^1) = .5(\sum_{i=1}^{2} q_{i3})^2.$$

The demand functions at the demand markets were:

$$d_1(\rho_3) = -2\rho_{31} - 1.5\rho_{32} + 1000, \quad d_2(\rho_3) = -2\rho_{32} - 1.5\rho_{31} + 1000,$$

and the transaction costs between the retailers and the consumers at the demand markets were given by:

$$\hat{c}_{11}(Q^3) = q_{11} + 5, \quad \hat{c}_{12}(Q^3) = q_{12} + 5,$$

$$\hat{c}_{21}(Q^3) = q_{21} + 5, \quad \hat{c}_{22}(Q^3) = q_{22} + 5,$$

$$\hat{c}_{31}(Q^3) = q_{31} + 5, \quad \hat{c}_{32}(Q^3) = q_{32} + 5.$$

All other functions were assumed to be zero.

The Euler method converged in 215 iterations and yielded the following equilibrium pattern. The product shipments between the two manufacturers and the three retailers were:

$$Q^{1*} : q_{11}^* = q_{12}^* = 9.243, \quad q_{13}^* = 14.645, \quad q_{21}^* = q_{22}^* = 13.567, \quad q_{23}^* = 9.726,$$

the product shipments between the three retailers and the two demand markets were:

$$Q^{3*} : q_{11}^* = q_{12}^* = q_{21}^* = q_{22}^* = 11.404, \quad q_{31}^* = q_{32}^* = 12.184.$$

The vector of retail prices ρ_2^* had components:

$$\rho_{21}^* = \rho_{22}^* = 259.310, \quad \rho_{23}^* = 258.530,$$

and the prices at the demand markets were:

$$\rho_{31}^* = \rho_{32}^* = 275.717.$$

Example 5.6

The third numerical example in this set of examples without e-commerce consisted of three manufacturers, two retailers, and three demand markets. The multilevel network structure for this supply chain problem is given in Figure 5.7.

The production cost functions for the manufacturers were given by:

$$f_1(q) = 2.5q_1^2 + q_1q_2 + 2q_1, \quad f_2(q) = 2.5q_2^2 + q_1q_2 + 2q_2, \quad f_3(q) = .5q_3^2 + .5q_1q_3 + 2q_3.$$

The transaction cost functions faced by the manufacturers and associated with transacting with the retailers were given by:

$$c_{11}(q_{11}) = .5q_{11}^2 + 3.5q_{11}, \quad c_{12}(q_{12}) = .5q_{12}^2 + 3.5q_{12},$$

$$c_{21}(q_{21}) = .5q_{21}^2 + 3.5q_{21}, \quad c_{22}(q_{22}) = .5q_{22}^2 + 3.5q_{22},$$

$$c_{31}(q_{31}) = .5q_{31}^2 + 2q_{31}, \quad c_{32}(q_{32}) = .5q_{32}^2 + 2q_{32}.$$

The handling costs of the retailers, in turn, were given by:

$$c_1(Q^1) = .5\left(\sum_{i=1}^{2} q_{i1}\right)^2, \quad c_2(Q^1) = .5\left(\sum_{i=1}^{2} q_{i2}\right)^2.$$

The demand functions at the demand markets were:

$$d_1(\rho_3) = -2\rho_{31} - 1.5\rho_{32} + 1000, \quad d_2(\rho_3) = -2\rho_{32} - 1.5\rho_{31} + 1000,$$

$$d_3(\rho_3) = -2\rho_{33} - 1.5\rho_{31} + 1000,$$

and the transaction costs between the retailers and the consumers at the demand markets were given by:

$$\hat{c}_{11}(Q^3) = q_{11} + 5, \quad \hat{c}_{12}(Q^3) = q_{12} + 5,$$

$$\hat{c}_{13}(Q^3) = q_{13} + 5, \quad \hat{c}_{21}(Q^3) = q_{21} + 5,$$

$$\hat{c}_{22}(Q^3) = q_{22} + 5, \quad \hat{c}_{23}(Q^3) = q_{23} + 5.$$

All other functions were set to zero.

The Euler method converged in 175 iterations and yielded the following equilibrium pattern. The product shipments between the three manufacturers and the two retailers were:

$$Q^{1*} : q_{11}^* = q_{12}^* = q_{21}^* = q_{22}^* = 12.395, \quad q_{31}^* = q_{32}^* = 50.078.$$

The product shipments (consumption levels) between the two retailers and the three demand markets were computed as:

$$Q^{3*} : q_{11}^* = q_{12}^* = q_{13}^* = q_{21}^* = q_{22}^* = q_{23}^* = 24.956,$$

whereas the retail prices were now equal to:

$$\rho_{21}^* = \rho_{22}^* = 241.496,$$

and the demand prices at the three demand markets were:

$$\rho_{31}^* = \rho_{32}^* = \rho_{33}^* = 271.454.$$

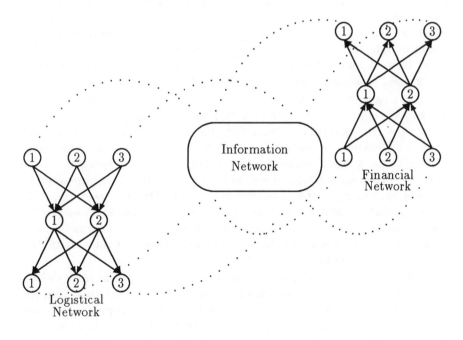

Fig. 5.7. Multilevel Network for Example 5.6

5.5   Transportation and Telecommunication Network Level

In order to fix ideas and for the sake of tractability, this chapter has focused on dynamic supply chain problems from a multilevel perspective in which the component networks consist of the logistical, the information, and the financial networks. Here, in order to further emphasize the multilevel network structure as being a primary structure of many supernetworks, we now elaborate further on the specific physical and Internet links.

In Figure 5.8, the physical links comprising the logistical network in Figure 5.1 are disaggregated to form transportation networks which comprise another level network. In the case of a physical link between a manufacturer i and retailer j, the product would be shipped on a transportation network, which is a freight network. Different paths in such a network may correspond to different freight alternatives such as truck, air freight, etc., as well as to different routes that a distinct freight carrier can take. For additional background on freight networks, see Crainic (1999).

In the case of a physical link between a retailer j and a demand market k (see Figure 5.8), the link may be further disaggregated to reflect the consumers' transportation network from the retailer to the demand market. In such a passenger transportation network, distinct paths from the retailer (origin) to the demand market (destination) (or vice versa) reflect the routes that the consumers can take as well as the modes of travel that are available to them, such as public transportation in the form of buses, subways, etc. Of course, pedestrian movement is also a form of transportation. Nodes on the transportation networks can correspond, besides origins and destinations, to intersections, for example, and links, depending on the type of transportation flow, to vehicles, trains, trucks, planes, etc.

In Figure 5.9, the Internet links have been disaggregated in order to focus on the telecommunication links underlying them. In order for a manufacturer i to be able to transact with retailer j via the Internet, appropriate service providers, switches, etc., are needed and these would be associated with the nodes. The links, in turn, correspond to cables, microwave links, etc., over which the telecommunication messages flow. Of course, each manufacturer and retailer node may also have underlying them an intranet over which communication within the organization can take place. For additional background on telecommunication networks, see Berstekas and Gallager (1992).

For a manufacturer to be able to transact with consumers at a demand market (and vice versa), each Internet link connecting manufacturer i with demand market k must also have the appropriate telecommunication network infrastructure. The same holds for an Internet transaction between a retailer and a demand market. Clearly, as in B2B electronic commerce, B2C electronic commerce requires that the origins and destinations of the messages have the necessary computers and the required Internet hookups and service.

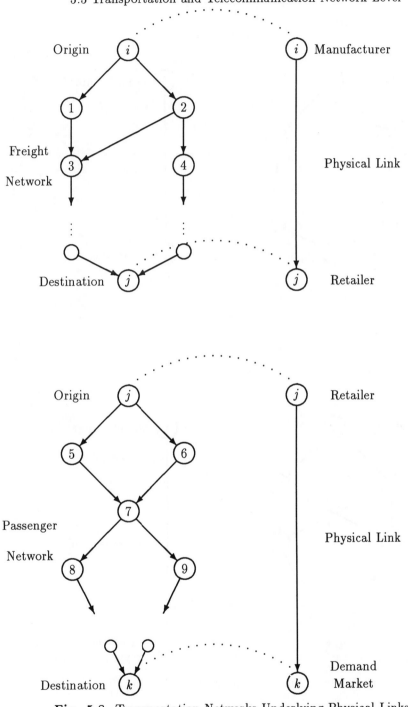

Fig. 5.8. Transportation Networks Underlying Physical Links

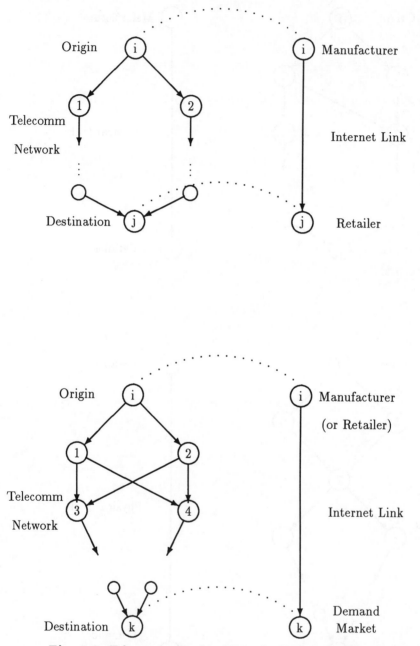

Fig. 5.9. Telecommunication Networks Underlying Virtual Links

Otherwise, the transaction costs will be so high as to preclude such transactions. It is imperative to emphasize that transactions over the Internet trigger shipments over transportation networks (recalling that in the case of electronic dissemination, the "transportation" would take place over telecommunication networks), and, hence, underlying a telecommunication network (in a multilevel representation) would also be a transportation network over which the goods get shipped and delivered to either the other businesses, that is, retailers here, or to the consumers at the demand markets.

In the next chapter, we address another multilevel network application – that of financial networks with intermediation, the structure of which is closely related to that of supply chain networks. Through the identification of the supernetwork structure of distinct problems one can then discover and exploit similarities as well as differences among applications.

5.6   Sources and Notes

This chapter developed a new dynamic supply chain network model with electronic commerce. The presentation and construction of the model were done using a supernetwork perspective in the form of a multilevel network consisting of the logistical, information, and the financial networks. Both the logistical and the financial networks, in turn, were multitiered networks. This chapter also presented an extension of the model in graphical format to include an added tier of decision-makers in the form of suppliers and then described applications to two B2B exchanges. The idea of multilevel networks for the study of supply chains, in particular, dynamic supply chains, is due to Nagurney, Ke, Cruz, Hancock, and Southworth (2001), where Figure 5.3 was introduced. The model, therein, however, did not consider electronic commerce. The numerical examples 5.4 through 5.6 are taken from that paper.

6 Dynamic Financial Networks with Intermediation

In this chapter, we explore the multilevel network concept developed in Chapter 5, for a new area of application – that of dynamic financial networks with intermediation. This enables the further evolution of the supernetwork concept and it ties supply chain networks and financial networks with intermediation rigorously together. A connection between logistical networks and financial networks with intermediation was suggested in a book on the latter topic by Thore (1980). Here, we utilize the supernetwork framework to connect both the structure and the behavior of the economic agents in these two applications.

The conceptualization of financial systems as networks dates to Quesnay (1758) who depicted the circular flow of funds in an economy as a network. His basic idea was subsequently applied to the construction of flow of funds accounts, which are a statistical description of the flows of money and credit in an economy (cf. Board of Governors (1980), Cohen (1987), Nagurney and Hughes (1992)). However, since the flow of funds accounts are in matrix form, and, hence, two-dimensional, they fail to capture the dynamic behavior on a micro level of the various financial agents/sectors in an economy, such as banks, households, insurance companies, etc. Moreover, as noted by the Board of Governors (1980) on page 6 of that publication, "the generality of the matrix tends to obscure certain structural aspects of the financial system that are of continuing interest in analysis," with the structural concepts of concern including financial intermediation.

Thore (1980) recognized some of the shortcomings of financial flow of funds accounts and developed, instead, network models of linked portfolios with financial intermediation, using decentralization/decomposition theory. Note that intermediation is typically associated with financial businesses, including banks, savings institutions, investment and insurance companies, etc., and the term implies borrowing for the purpose of lending, rather than for nonfinancial purposes. Thore also constructed some basic intertemporal models. However, the intertemporal models were not fully developed and the computational techniques at that time were not sufficiently advanced for computational purposes.

In this chapter, we address the dynamics of the financial economy which explicitly includes financial intermediaries along with the "sources" and "uses" of financial funds. The perspective is a supernetwork one in an equilibrium context since the equilibrium state serves as a valuable benchmark. Tools are provided for studying the disequilibrium dynamics as well as the equilibrium state. Also, transaction costs are considered as they were in the supply chain models of Chapters 4 and 5, since they bring a greater degree of realism to the study of financial intermediation. Transaction costs have been studied to date in multi-sector, multi-instrument financial equilibrium models by Nagurney and Dong (1995, 1996 a,b) but without considering the more general dynamic intermediation setting.

This chapter is organized as follows. In Section 6.1, the dynamic financial model is developed with three distinct types of agents, the multilevel network structure of the problem is identified, and the disequilibrium dynamics are proposed. Transaction costs are introduced and associated with transactions conducted between agents located at distinct tiers of the networks. The problem is formulated as a projected dynamical system and a discussion of the stationary/equilibrium point is given. We also present an application to an online brokerage in the United States and discuss online broking elsewhere. In Section 6.2, some qualitative properties of the dynamic trajectories are provided, along with stability analysis results. In Section 6.3, a discrete-time algorithm is proposed, which is a time discretization of the continuous adjustment process given in Section 6.1. The algorithm resolves the network problem into subproblems, each of which can be solved exactly and in closed form. In Section 6.4, the discrete-time adjustment process is implemented and applied to several numerical examples to determine the equilibrium flows and prices.

6.1   The Dynamic Financial Network Model with Intermediation

In this section, the dynamic financial network model is developed. The model consists of agents with sources of funds, agents who are intermediaries, as well as agents who are consumers located at the demand markets. Specifically, consider m agents with sources of financial funds, such as households and businesses, involved in the allocation of their financial resources among a portfolio of financial instruments which can be obtained by transacting with distinct n financial intermediaries, such as banks, insurance and investment

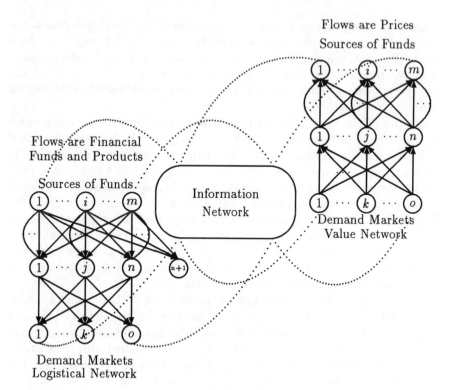

Fig. 6.1. Multilevel Network Structure of the Financial System with Intermediation

companies, etc. The financial intermediaries, in turn, in addition to transacting with the source agents, also determine how to allocate the incoming financial resources among distinct uses, as represented by o demand markets with a demand market corresponding to, for example, the market for real estate loans, household loans, or business loans, etc.

The multilevel financial network is now described and depicted graphically in Figure 6.1. The multilevel network consists of the logistical network, the information network, and what is termed a *value* network to distinguish the network from the basic financial network application. The top network is the value network, the middle one the information network, and the bottom one, the logistical network.

The logistical network is concerned with the flow of financial funds from the source of funds to the intermediaries and their conversion to the products demanded by the consumers at the demand markets. Hence, the financial intermediaries are truly involved in a logistics operation. The top tier of nodes in the logistical and the value networks in Figure 6.1 consist of the agents with sources of funds, with a typical source agent denoted by i and associated with node i. The middle tiers of nodes in the top and bottom networks in Figure 6.1 consist of the intermediaries, with a typical intermediary denoted by j and associated with node j in the networks. The bottom tiers of nodes in the value network and the logistical network consist of the demand markets, with a typical demand market denoted by k and corresponding to the node k in each such network.

For simplicity of notation, assume that there are L financial instruments associated with each intermediary. Hence, from each source of funds node in the logistical network, there are L links connecting such a node with an intermediary node with the l-th such link corresponding to the l-th financial instrument available from the intermediary. In addition, the option of non-investment in the available financial instruments is allowed and to denote this option, construct an additional link from each source node in the logistical network to the middle tier node $n+1$, which represents non-investment. Note that, in the logistical network (cf. Figure 5.1) for the supply chain application there were only two links connecting each top tier node with each middle tier node to reflect two distinct modes of transaction. In the financial application, however, there are as many links connecting each top tier node with each intermediary node as needed to reflect the number of financial instruments available. Also, note that in the logistical network in Figure 6.1, there is an additional abstract node $n+1$ with a link connecting each source node to it, which, as shall shortly be shown, will be used to "collect" the financial funds which are not invested. Such a node did not appear in the logistical network underlying supply chains (cf. Figure 5.1) since there was no fixed supply of product for each manufacturer. In the financial application, it will be assumed that each source agent has a fixed amount of financial funds.

From each intermediary node, then construct o links, one to each "use" node or demand market in the bottom tier of nodes in the logistical network to denote the transaction between the intermediary and the consumers at the demand market. Note that in the logistical network in Figure 6.1, in contrast to the logistical network in Figure 5.1, there are no direct links between sources of funds and uses of funds. Such links could, nevertheless, be added to reflect transactions between use and source agents without any intermediation.

Let x_{ijl} denote the nonnegative amount of the funds that source i "invests" in financial instrument l obtained from intermediary j. Group the financial flows associated with source agent i, which are associated with the links emanating from the top tier node i to the intermediary nodes in the logistical network, into the column vector $x_i \in R_+^{nL}$. Assume that each source has, at his disposal, an amount of funds S_i and denote the unallocated portion of this amount (and flowing on the link joining node i with node $n+1$) by s_i. Group then the x_is of all the source agents into the column vector $x \in R_+^{mnL}$.

Associate a distinct financial product k with each demand market, bottom-tiered node k and let y_{jk} denote the amount of the financial product obtained by consumers at demand market k from intermediary j. Group these "consumption" quantities into the column vector $y \in R_+^{no}$. The intermediaries convert the incoming financial flows x into the outgoing financial flows y.

Note that the value network in Figure 6.1 has a structure similar to that of the logistical network and with similar nodal interpretations. However, here, as in the multilevel supply chain network in Figure 5.1, the arrows in the value network point in the opposite direction from those in the logistical network to represent the upward flow of prices, that is, "the value" of the product/transaction, and the payments. Moreover, the value network, in contrast to the logistical network, does not contain a non-investment node, since such transactions are not priced.

The notation for the prices is now given. It is similar to that used for the dynamic supply chain model in Chapter 5, without any loss of generality. Note that there will be prices associated with each of the tiers of nodes in the value network. Let ρ_{1ijl} denote the price associated with instrument l as quoted by intermediary j to source agent i and group the first tier prices into the column vector $\rho_1 \in R_+^{mnL}$. Also, let ρ_{2j} denote the price charged by intermediary j and group all such prices into the column vector $\rho_2 \in R_+^n$. Finally, let ρ_{3k} denote the price of the financial product at the third or bottom-tiered node k in the value network, and group all such prices into the column vector $\rho_3 \in R_+^o$.

We now turn to describing the dynamics by which the source agents adjust the amounts they allocate to the various financial instruments over time, the dynamics by which the intermediaries adjust their transactions, and those by which the consumers obtain the financial products at the demand markets. In addition, we describe the dynamics by which the prices adjust over time. The dynamics are derived from the bottom tier of nodes of the financial network on up since, as mentioned previously, it is assumed that it is the demand for the financial products (and the corresponding prices) that actually drives the economic dynamics. We first present the price dynamics and then the dynamics underlying the financial flows.

The Demand Market Price Dynamics

We begin by describing the dynamics underlying the prices of the financial products associated with the demand markets (see the bottom-tiered nodes in the value network). Assume, as given, a demand function d_k, which can depend, in general, upon the entire vector of prices ρ_3, that is,

$$d_k = d_k(\rho_3), \quad \forall k. \tag{6.1}$$

Moreover, assume that the rate of change of the price ρ_{3k}, denoted by $\dot{\rho}_{3k}$, is equal to the difference between the demand at the demand market k, as a function of the demand market prices, and the amount available from the intermediaries at the demand market. Hence, if the demand for the product at the demand market (at an instant in time) exceeds the amount available, the price of the financial product at that demand market will increase; if the amount available exceeds the demand at the price, then the price at the demand market will decrease. Furthermore, it is guaranteed that the prices do not become negative. Thus, the dynamics of the price ρ_{3k} associated with the product at demand market k can be expressed as:

$$\dot{\rho}_{3k} = \begin{cases} d_k(\rho_3) - \sum_{j=1}^n y_{jk}, & \text{if} \quad \rho_{3k} > 0 \\ \max\{0, d_k(\rho_3) - \sum_{j=1}^n y_{jk}\}, & \text{if} \quad \rho_{3k} = 0. \end{cases} \qquad (6.2)$$

The Dynamics of the Prices at the Intermediaries

The prices charged for the financial funds at the intermediaries, in turn, must reflect supply and demand conditions as well (and as shall be shown shortly also reflect profit-maximizing behavior on the part of the intermediaries who seek to determine how much of the financial flows they obtain from the different sources of funds). In particular, assume that the price associated with intermediary j, ρ_{2j}, and computed at node j lying in the second tier of nodes of the value network, evolves over time according to:

$$\dot{\rho}_{2j} = \begin{cases} \sum_{k=1}^o y_{jk} - \sum_{i=1}^m \sum_{l=1}^L x_{ijl}, & \text{if} \quad \rho_{2j} > 0 \\ \max\{0, \sum_{k=1}^o y_{jk} - \sum_{i=1}^m \sum_{l=1}^L x_{ijl}\}, & \text{if} \quad \rho_{2j} = 0, \end{cases} \qquad (6.3)$$

where $\dot{\rho}_{2j}$ denotes the rate of change of the j-th intermediary's price. Hence, if the amount of the financial funds desired to be transacted by the consumers (at an instant in time) exceeds that available at the intermediary, then the price charged at the intermediary will increase; if the amount available is greater than that desired by the consumers, then the price charged at the intermediary will decrease. As in the case of the demand market prices, it is guaranteed that the prices charged by the intermediaries remain nonnegative.

Precursors to the Dynamics of the Financial Flows

We first introduce some preliminaries that will allow us to develop the dynamics of the financial flows over the links of the logistical network in the multilevel network depiction of the financial application. In particular, the utility-maximizing behavior of the source agents and that of the intermediaries is now discussed.

Assume that each such source agent's and each intermediary agent's utility can be defined as a function of the expected future portfolio value, where the expected value of the future portfolio is described by two characteristics: the expected mean value and the uncertainty surrounding the expected mean. Here, the expected mean portfolio value is assumed to be equal to the market value of the current portfolio. Each agent's uncertainty, or assessment of risk, in turn, is based on a variance-covariance matrix denoting the agent's assessment of the standard deviation of the prices for each instrument/product. The variance-covariance matrix associated with source agent i's assets is denoted by Q^i and is of dimension $nL \times nL$, and is associated with vector x_i, whereas intermediary agent j's variance-covariance matrix is denoted by Q^j, is of dimension $o \times o$, and is associated with the vector y_j. For further discussion of such assumptions, see the books by Nagurney and Siokos (1997) and Markowitz (1959) and the references therein.

Optimizing Behavior of the Source Agents

Denote the total transaction cost associated with source agent i transacting with intermediary j to obtain financial instrument l by c_{ijl} and assume that:

$$c_{ijl} = c_{ijl}(x_{ijl}), \quad \forall i, j, l. \tag{6.4}$$

Note that this transaction cost can also reflect the *mode* of transaction, that is, whether physical or electronic, with the transaction cost associated with the latter type of transaction expected to be lower than that associated with the former.

The total transaction costs incurred by source agent i, thus, are equal to the sum of all the agent's transaction costs. His revenue, in turn, is equal to the sum of the price (rate of return) that the the agent can obtain for the financial instrument times the total quantity obtained/purchased of that instrument. Recall that ρ_{1ijl} denotes the price associated with agent i/intermediary j/instrument l.

Assume that each such source agent seeks to maximize net return while, simultaneously, minimizing the risk, with source agent i's utility function denoted by U^i. Moreover, assume that the variance-covariance matrix Q^i is positive semidefinite and that the transaction cost functions are continuously differentiable and convex (refer to Appendix A). Hence, one can express the optimization problem facing source agent i as:

$$\text{Maximize} \quad U_i(x_i) = \sum_{j=1}^{n} \sum_{l=1}^{L} \rho_{1ijl} x_{ijl} - \sum_{j=1}^{n} \sum_{l=1}^{L} c_{ijl}(x_{ijl}) - x_i^T Q^i x_i, \tag{6.5}$$

subject to $x_{ijl} \geq 0$, for all j, l, and to the constraint:

$$\sum_{j=1}^{n} \sum_{l=1}^{L} x_{ijl} \leq S^i, \tag{6.6}$$

that is, the allocations of source agent i's funds among the financial instruments made available by the different intermediaries cannot exceed his holdings. Note that the utility function given in (6.5) is concave for each source agent i. Note that (6.6) allows a source agent to not invest in any of the instrument. Indeed, as shall be illustrated through numerical examples in Section 6.5, this constraint has important financial implications.

Clearly, in the case of *unconstrained* utility maximization, the gradient of source agent i's utility function with respect to the vector of variables x_i

and denoted by $\nabla_{x_i} U_i$, where $\nabla_{x_i} U_i = (\frac{\partial U_i}{\partial x_{i11}}, \ldots, \frac{\partial U_i}{\partial x_{inL}})$, represents agent i's idealized direction, with the jl-component of $\nabla_{x_i} U_i$ given by:

$$(\rho_{1ijl} - 2Q^i_{z_{jl}} \cdot x_i - \frac{\partial c_{ijl}(x_{ijl})}{\partial x_{ijl}}), \tag{6.7}$$

where $Q^i_{z_{jl}}$ denotes the z_{jl}-th row of Q^i, and z_{jl} is the indicator defined as: $z_{jl} = (l - 1)n + j$. We return later to describe how the constraints are explicitly incorporated into the dynamics.

Optimizing Behavior of the Intermediaries

The intermediaries (cf. Figure 6.1), in turn, are involved in transactions both with the source agents, as well as with the users of the funds, that is, with the ultimate consumers associated with the markets for the distinct types of loans/products at the bottom tier of the logistical and the value networks. Thus, an intermediary conducts transactions both with the "source" agents as well as with the consumers at the demand markets.

An intermediary j is faced with what is termed a *handling/conversion* cost, which may include, for example, the cost of converting the incoming financial flows into the financial loans/products associated with the demand markets. Denote this cost by c_j and, in the simplest case, one would have that c_j is a function of $\sum_{i=1}^m \sum_{l=1}^L x_{ijl}$, that is, the holding/conversion cost of an intermediary is a function of how much he has obtained from the various source agents. For the sake of generality, however, allow the function to, in general, depend also on the amounts held by other intermediaries and, therefore, one may write:

$$c_j = c_j(x), \quad \forall j. \tag{6.8}$$

The intermediaries also have associated transaction costs in regard to transacting with the source agents, which are assumed to be dependent on the type of instrument and, these, as discussed in the context of the transaction costs (6.4), can also be associated with whether the transaction was electronic or not. Denote the transaction cost associated with intermediary j transacting with source agent i associated with instrument l by $\hat{c}_{ijl}$ and assume that it is of the form

$$\hat{c}_{ijl} = \hat{c}_{ijl}(x_{ijl}), \quad \forall i, j, l. \tag{6.9}$$

Recall that the intermediaries convert the incoming financial flows x into the outgoing financial flows y. Assume that an intermediary j incurs a transaction cost c_{jk} associated with transacting with demand market k, where

$$c_{jk} = c_{jk}(y_{jk}), \quad \forall j, k. \tag{6.10}$$

The intermediaries associate a price with the financial funds, which is denoted by ρ_{2j}, for intermediary j. Assuming that the intermediaries are also utility maximizers with the utility functions for each being comprised of net revenue maximization as well as risk minimization, then the utility maximization problem for intermediary agent j with his utility function denoted by U^j, can be expressed as:

$$\text{Maximize} \quad U_j(x_j, y_j)$$

$$= \sum_{i=1}^{m} \sum_{l=1}^{L} \rho_{2j} x_{ijl} - c_j(x) - \sum_{i=1}^{m} \sum_{l=1}^{L} \hat{c}_{ijl}(x_{ijl}) - \sum_{k=1}^{o} c_{jk}(y_{jk})$$

$$- \sum_{i=1}^{m} \sum_{l=1}^{L} \rho_{1ijl} x_{ijl} - y_j^T Q^j y_j, \tag{6.11}$$

subject to the nonnegativity constraints: $x_{ijl} \geq 0$, and $y_{jk} \geq 0$, for all i, l, and k. Here, for convenience, we have let $x_j = (x_{1j1}, \ldots, x_{mjL})$. Objective function (6.11) expresses that the difference between the revenues minus the handling cost and the transaction costs and the payout to the source agents should be maximized, whereas the risk should be minimized. Assume now that the variance-covariance matrix Q^j is positive semidefinite and that the transaction cost functions are continuously differentiable and convex. Hence, the utility function given in (6.11) is concave for each intermediary j.

The gradient $\nabla_{x_j} U_j = (\frac{\partial U_j}{\partial x_{1j1}}, \ldots, \frac{\partial U_j}{\partial x_{mjL}})$ represents agent j's idealized direction in terms of x_j, ignoring the constraints, for the time being, whereas the gradient $\nabla_{y_j} U_j = (\frac{\partial U_j}{\partial y_{j1}}, \ldots, \frac{\partial U_j}{\partial y_{jo}})$ represents his idealized direction in terms of y_j. Note that the il-th component of $\nabla_{x_j} U_j$ is given by:

$$(\rho_{2j} - \rho_{1ijl} - \frac{\partial c_j(x)}{\partial x_{ijl}} - \frac{\partial \hat{c}_{ijl}(x_{ijl})}{\partial x_{ijl}}), \tag{6.12}$$

whereas the jk-th component of $\nabla_{y_j} U_j$ is given by:

$$(-\frac{\partial c_{jk}(y_{jk})}{\partial y_{jk}} - 2Q_k^j \cdot y_j). \tag{6.13}$$

However, since both source agent i and intermediary j must agree in terms of the x_{ijl}s, the direction (6.7) must coincide with that in (6.12), so adding both gives us a "combined force," which, after algebraic simplification, yields:

$$(\rho_{2j} - 2Q_{z_{jl}}^i \cdot x_i - \frac{\partial c_{ijl}(x_{ijl})}{\partial x_{ijl}} - \frac{\partial c_j(x)}{\partial x_{ijl}} - \frac{\partial \hat{c}_{ijl}(x_{ijl})}{\partial x_{ijl}}). \tag{6.14}$$

The Dynamics of the Financial Flows between the Source Agents and the Intermediaries

We are now ready to express the dynamics of the financial flows between the source agents and the intermediaries. In particular, define the feasible set $K_i \equiv \{x_i | x_{ijl} \geq 0, \forall i, j, l, \text{ and } (6.6) \text{ holds}\}$. Let also K be the Cartesian product given by $K \equiv \Pi_{i=1}^{m} K_i$ and define F_{ijl}^1 as minus the term in (6.14) with $F_i^1 = (F_{i11}^1, \ldots, F_{inL}^1)$. Then the *best realizable* direction for the vector of financial instruments x_i can be mathematically expressed as:

$$\dot{x}_i = \Pi_{K_i}(x_i, -F_i^1), \tag{6.15}$$

where $\Pi_K(X, v)$ is defined as (see also (B.15) in Appendix B):

$$\Pi_K(X, v) = \lim_{\delta \to 0} \frac{P_K(X + \delta v) - X}{\delta}, \tag{6.16}$$

and P_K is the norm projection (see also (B.14)) defined by

$$P_K(X) = \mathrm{argmin}_{X' \in K} \|X' - X\|. \tag{6.17}$$

The Dynamics of the Financial Flows between the Intermediaries and the Demand Markets

In terms of the financial flows between the intermediaries and the demand markets, both the intermediaries and the consumers must be in agreement as to the financial flows y. The consumers take into account in making their consumption decisions not only the price charged for the financial product by the intermediaries but also their transaction costs associated with obtaining the product.

Let $\hat{c}_{jk}$ denote the transaction cost associated with obtaining the product at demand market k from intermediary j. Assume that this unit transaction cost is continuous and of the general form:

$$\hat{c}_{jk} = \hat{c}_{jk}(y), \quad \forall j, k. \tag{6.18}$$

The consumers take the price charged by the intermediaries, which was denoted by ρ_{2j} for intermediary j, plus the unit transaction cost, in making their consumption decisions. From the perspective of the consumers at the demand markets, one can expect that an idealized direction in terms of the evolution of the financial flow of a product between an intermediary/demand market pair would be:

$$(\rho_{3k} - \hat{c}_{jk}(y) - \rho_{2j}). \tag{6.19}$$

On the other hand, as already derived above, one can expect that the intermediaries would adjust the volume of the product to a demand market according to (6.13). Combining now (6.13) and (6.19), and guaranteeing that the financial products do not assume negative quantities, yields the following dynamics:

$$\dot{y}_{jk} = \begin{cases} \rho_{3k} - \hat{c}_{jk}(y) - \rho_{2j} - \frac{\partial c_{jk}(y_{jk})}{\partial y_{jk}} - 2Q_k^j \cdot y_j, & \text{if } y_{jk} > 0 \\ \max\{0, \rho_{3k} - \hat{c}_{jk}(y) - \rho_{2j} - \frac{\partial c_{jk}(y_{jk})}{\partial y_{jk}} - 2Q_k^j \cdot y_j\}, & \text{if } y_{jk} = 0. \end{cases} \tag{6.20}$$

The Projected Dynamical System

Consider now the dynamic model in which the demand prices evolve according to (6.2) for all demand markets k, the prices at the intermediaries evolve according to (6.3) for all intermediaries j; the financial flows between the source agents and the intermediaries evolve according to (6.15) for all source agents i, and the financial products between the intermediaries and the demand markets evolve according to (6.20) for all intermediary/demand market pairs j, k.

Let now X denote the aggregate column vector (x, y, ρ_2, ρ_3) in the feasible set $\mathcal{K} \equiv K \times R_+^{no+n+o}$. Define the column vector $F(X) \equiv (F^1, F^2, F^3, F^4)$, where F^1 is as has been defined previously; $F^2 = (F_{11}^2, \ldots, F_{no}^2)$, with component $F_{jk}^2 \equiv (2Q_k^j \cdot y_j + \frac{\partial c_{jk}(y_{jk})}{\partial y_{jk}} + \hat{c}_{jk}(y) + \rho_{2j} - \rho_{3k}), \forall j, k;$ $F^3 = (F_1^3, \ldots, F_n^3)$, where $F_j^3 \equiv (\sum_{i=1}^m \sum_{l=1}^L x_{ijl} - \sum_{k=1}^o y_{jk})$, and $F^4 = (F_1^4, \ldots, F_o^4)$, with $F_k^4 \equiv (\sum_{j=1}^n y_{jk} - d_k(\rho_3))$.

Then the dynamic model described by (6.2), (6.3), (6.15), and (6.20) for all k, j, i, l can be rewritten as the *projected dynamical system* (see Definition B.7 in Appendix B) defined by the following initial value problem:

$$\dot{X} = \Pi_{\mathcal{K}}(X, -F(X)), \quad X(0) = X_0, \tag{6.21}$$

where, as defined in (B.15), $\Pi_{\mathcal{K}}$ is the projection operator of $-F(X)$ onto $\mathcal{K}$ at X and $X_0 = (x^0, y^0, \rho_2^0, \rho_3^0)$ is the initial point corresponding to the initial financial flows and the initial prices. The trajectory of (6.21) describes the dynamic evolution of and the dynamic interactions among the prices and the financial flows.

As noted in Chapter 5, the dynamical system (6.21) is non-classical in that the right-hand side is discontinuous in order to guarantee that the constraints in the context of the above model are not only nonnegativity constraints on the variables, but also a form of budget constraints. Here this methodology is applied to study financial systems in the presence of intermediation. A variety of dynamic financial models, but without intermediation, formulated as projected dynamical systems can be found in the book by Nagurney and Siokos (1997).

Indeed, in the dynamic supply chain model with the projected dynamical systems formulation given by (5.7), the feasible set $\mathcal{K}$ was simply the nonnegative orthant, that is, the only constraints imposed on the product shipment and price variables were that they must all be nonnegative. In the financial network with intermediation application, in contrast, the feasible set $\mathcal{K}$ now also includes the source agent budget constraints (6.6), in addition to the nonnegativity constraints on all the flow and price variables. Hence, the projected dynamical system (6.21) now also guarantees (with the F, X, and $\mathcal{K}$ redefined accordingly) that the budget constraints will not be violated. Referring now back to Figure 6.1, we see that the budget constraint (6.6) is modeled on the logistical network so that what is not invested by each agent flows on the corresponding link to the non-investment node $n + 1$.

A Stationary/Equilibrium Point

We now discuss the stationary point of the projected dynamical system (6.21). Recall that a stationary point is that point when $\dot{X} = 0$ and, hence, in the context of the dynamic financial model with intermediation, when there is no change in the financial flows in the financial network and no change in the prices. Moreover, as established in Dupuis and Nagurney (1993) (see also Theorem B.6 in Appendix B), since the feasible set $\mathcal{K}$ is a polyhedron and convex, the set of stationary points of the projected dynamical system of the form given in (6.21) coincides with the set of solutions to the variational inequality problem given by: determine $X^* \in \mathcal{K}$, such that

$$\langle F(X^*), X - X^* \rangle \geq 0, \quad \forall X \in \mathcal{K}, \tag{6.22}$$

where in the model $F(X)$ and X are as defined above and recall that $\langle \cdot, \cdot \rangle$ denotes the inner product in N-dimensional Euclidean space where here $N = mnL + no + n + o$.

Variational Inequality Formulation of Financial Equilibrium with Intermediation

In particular, variational inequality (6.22) here takes the form: determine $(x^*, y^*, \rho_2^*, \rho_3^*) \in \mathcal{K}$, satisfying:

$$\sum_{i=1}^{m} \sum_{j=1}^{n} \sum_{l=1}^{L} \left[2Q_{z_{jl}}^i \cdot x_i^* + \frac{\partial c_{ijl}(x_{ijl}^*)}{\partial x_{ijl}} + \frac{\partial c_j(x^*)}{\partial x_{ijl}} + \frac{\partial \hat{c}_{ijl}(x_{ijl}^*)}{\partial x_{ijl}} - \rho_{2j}^* \right]$$

$$\times \left[x_{ijl} - x_{ijl}^* \right]$$

$$+ \sum_{j=1}^{n} \sum_{k=1}^{o} \left[2Q_k^j \cdot y_j^* + \frac{\partial c_{jk}(y_{jk}^*)}{\partial y_{jk}} + \hat{c}_{jk}(y^*) + \rho_{2j}^* - \rho_{3k}^* \right] \times \left[y_{jk} - y_{jk}^* \right]$$

$$+ \sum_{j=1}^{n} \left[\sum_{i=1}^{m} \sum_{l=1}^{L} x_{ijl}^* - \sum_{k=1}^{o} y_{jk}^* \right] \times \left[\rho_{2j} - \rho_{2j}^* \right]$$

$$+ \sum_{k=1}^{o} \left[\sum_{j=1}^{n} y_{jk}^* - d_k(\rho_3^*) \right] \times \left[\rho_{3k} - \rho_{3k}^* \right] \geq 0, \quad \forall(x, y, \rho_2, \rho_3) \in \mathcal{K}, \tag{6.23}$$

where $\mathcal{K} \equiv \{K \times R_+^{no+n+o}\}$ and $Q_{z_{jl}}^i$ is as was defined following (6.7).

We now discuss the equilibrium conditions. First, note that if the rate of change of the demand price $\dot{\rho}_{3k} = 0$, then from (6.2) one can conclude that:

$$d_k(\rho_3^*) \begin{cases} = \sum_{j=1}^{n} y_{jk}^*, & \text{if} \quad \rho_{3k}^* > 0 \\ \leq \sum_{j=1}^{n} y_{jk}^*, & \text{if} \quad \rho_{3k}^* = 0. \end{cases} \tag{6.24}$$

Condition (6.24) states that, if the price the consumers are willing to pay for the financial product at a demand market is positive, then the quantity consumed by the consumers at the demand market is precisely equal to the demand. If the demand is less than the amount of the product available, then the price for that product is zero. This condition holds for all demand market prices in equilibrium.

Note that condition (6.24) also follows directly from variational inequality (6.23) if one sets $x = x^*$, $y = y^*$, and $\rho_2 = \rho_2^*$, and make the substitution into (6.23) and note that the demand prices must be nonnegative.

Observe now that if the rate of change of a price charged by an intermediary is zero, that is, $\dot{\rho}_{2j} = 0$, then (6.3) implies that

$$\sum_{i=1}^{m}\sum_{l=1}^{L} x_{ijl}^* - \sum_{k=1}^{o} y_{jk}^* \begin{cases} = 0, & \text{if} \quad \rho_{2j}^* > 0 \\ \geq 0, & \text{if} \quad \rho_{2j}^* = 0. \end{cases} \tag{6.25}$$

In other words, if the price for the financial funds at an intermediary is positive, then the market for the funds "clears" at the intermediary, that is, the supply of funds, as given by $\sum_{i=1}^{m}\sum_{l=1}^{L} x_{ijl}^*$ is equal to the demand of funds, $\sum_{k=1}^{o} y_{jk}^*$ at the intermediary. If the supply exceeds the demand, then the price at the intermediary will be zero. These are well-known economic equilibrium conditions as are those given in (6.24). Of course, condition (6.25) could also be recovered from variational inequality (6.23) by setting $x = x^*$, $y = y^*$, and $\rho_3 = \rho_3^*$, and making the substitution into (6.23) and noting that these prices must be nonnegative. In equilibrium, condition (6.25) holds for all intermediary prices.

On the other hand, if one sets $\dot{x}_i = 0$ (cf. (6.15) and (6.21)), for all i and $\dot{y}_{jk} = 0$ for all j, k (cf. (6.20) and (6.21)), one obtains the equilibrium conditions, which correspond, equivalently, to the first two summands in inequality (6.23) being greater than equal to zero. Expressed in another manner, we must have that the sum of the inequalities (6.26), (6.27), and (6.28b) below must be satisfied.

Optimality Conditions for all Source Agents

Indeed, note that the optimality conditions for all source agents i, since each K_i is closed and convex, and the objective function (6.5) is concave, can be expressed as (assuming a given ρ_{1jl}^*, for all i, j, l, which we return to later; see also Appendices A and B):

$$\sum_{i=1}^{m}\sum_{j=1}^{n}\sum_{l=1}^{L}\left[2Q_{z_{jl}}^i \cdot x_i^* + \frac{\partial c_{ijl}(x_{ijl}^*)}{\partial x_{ijl}} - \rho_{1ijl}^*\right] \times \left[x_{ijl} - x_{ijl}^*\right] \geq 0, \quad \forall x \in K. \tag{6.26}$$

Optimality Conditions for all Intermediary Agents

The optimality conditions for all the intermediaries j, with objective functions of the form (6.11), which are concave, and, given ρ_1^* and ρ_2^*, can, in turn, be expressed as:

$$\sum_{i=1}^{m}\sum_{j=1}^{n}\sum_{l=1}^{L}\left[\frac{\partial c_j(x^*)}{\partial x_{ijl}}+\rho^*_{1ijl}+\frac{\partial \hat{c}_{ijl}(x^*_{ijl})}{\partial x_{ijl}}-\rho^*_{2j}\right]\times\left[x_{ijl}-x^*_{ijl}\right]$$

$$+\sum_{j=1}^{n}\sum_{k=1}^{o}\left[2Q^j_k\cdot y_j+\frac{\partial c_{jk}(y^*_{jk})}{\partial y_{jk}}\right]\times\left[y_{jk}-y^*_{jk}\right]\geq 0, \forall x\in R^{mnL}_+, \forall y\in R^{no}_+.$$

$$(6.27)$$

Note that (6.27) provides a means for recovering the top-tiered prices, ρ^*_1. Indeed, for each $x^*_{ijl}>0$ one can set $\rho^*_{1ijl}=\rho^*_{2j}-\frac{\partial c_j(x^*)}{\partial x_{ijl}}-\frac{\partial \hat{c}_{ijl}(x^*_{ijl})}{\partial x_{ijl}}$. This is precisely done in Section 6.5, when numerical examples are presented.

Equilibrium Conditions for Consumers at the Demand Markets

Also, the equilibrium conditions for consumers at demand market k, thus, take the form: for all intermediaries: $j; j=1,\ldots,n$:

$$\rho^*_{2j}+\hat{c}_{jk}(y^*)\begin{cases} =\rho^*_{3k}, & \text{if } y^*_{jk}>0 \\ \geq \rho^*_{3k}, & \text{if } y^*_{jk}=0, \end{cases} \qquad (6.28a)$$

with (6.28a) holding for all demand markets k, which is equivalent to $y^*\in R^{no}_+$ satisfying:

$$\sum_{j=1}^{n}\sum_{k=1}^{o}(\rho^*_{2j}+\hat{c}_{jk}(y^*)-\rho^*_{3k}))\times(y_{jk}-y^*_{jk})\geq 0, \quad \forall y\in R^{no}_+. \qquad (6.28b)$$

Conditions (6.28a) simply state that consumers at demand market k will purchase the product from intermediary j, if the price charged by the intermediary for the product plus the transaction cost (from the perspective of the consumers) does not exceed the price that the consumers are willing to pay for the product, that is, ρ^*_{3k}.

Note the similarity between these conditions and those corresponding to the supernetwork supply chain network model of Chapter 4. Equilibrium conditions (6.24) are similar to conditions (4.16); equilibrium conditions (6.25), in turn, are analogous to conditions (4.24), whereas equilibrium conditions (6.28a,b) correspond to (4.23). The equilibrium conditions represented by the sum of (6.26) and (6.27), on the other hand, are analogous to the equilibrium pattern satisfying the sum of the optimality conditions for the top two tiers of network agents (see also (4.21)–(4.23)) in the supply chain network.

In Nagurney and Ke (2001a) a variational inequality of the form (6.23) was derived in a manner entirely different from that given above for a static financial network model with intermediation, but with a slightly different feasible set where it was assumed that the constraints (6.6) had to be tight, that is, to hold as an equality. In that paper, a different notation was also utilized for the prices at the intermediary nodes.

6.1.1   Charles Schwab & Co., Inc. – An Online Brokerage

Charles Schwab, the Chairman and the Co-CEO of Charles Schwab & Co., Inc., according to its website (see AboutSchwab.com (2001)), founded the company in 1975 in order to "serve the investment needs of the ordinary investor." Presently, the company has 6.5 million individual investor accounts in every state in the United States and is considered to be the largest online financial brokerage. As noted in *The Economist* (2000b), financial brokerages, as reported by the Boston Consulting Group, represented the third largest segment of US online transactions with the 1999 forecast being just under $6 billion.

Mr. Schwab, in his testimony to the US Senate Committee of Banking, Housing, and Urban Affairs (AboutSchwab.com (2001)), states that: "competition may not be perfect or elegant, but a competitive market reponds quickly to address inefficiencies." In the above financial network system model we explicitly allow for competition among the various financial agents. Moreover, Mr. Schwab argues for the importance of information and that "regulators should be eliminating regulation that impedes competition among markets" and that "prevents transparencies of critical market information and information about issuers." He emphasizes in his testimony also "dynamic, competitive markets," and our model is precisely of that ilk, with the information network being central to the multilevel supernetwork structure.

Furthermore, in his testimony, Mr. Schwab argues for decentralization in that "centralized structures are also antithetical to the architectures the U.S. and the rest of the world are adopting in terms of computer protocols and networks." Furthermore, "all other industries in this country, from utilities to telephony, are deregulating and moving away from centralized structures." Our model is based on decentralized decision-making and can capture the complexities of a variety of agent interactions with the ultimate result in terms of the equilibrium financial flows and prices.

6.1.2   Experiences with Online Investing outside the United States

Online stockbroking is considered one of the Internet's greatest success stories and, hence, it is illuminating to highlight and to contrast the experiences of this segment of e-commerce outside the United States. According to *The Economist* (2000c), although online investing started later outside the US it is, nevertheless, experiencing spectacular growth in other countries. For example, in parts of Europe, it is growing faster than in the US, although far fewer Europeans own shares. For example, Datamonitor, a research firm, quoted in the same article, estimated that in January 2000, an average of 466 new online accounts were being opened in Sweden every day, 685 in England, and 1,178 in Germany. The expectation is that in the year 2002, the number of online brokerage accounts in Europe will reach 10.5 million.

As the participation grows, so will the competition, with US brokers moving in, with Charles Schwab &Co., Inc., having entered this market already.

Interestingly, according to *The Economist* (2000c), the largest potential for growth in online broking may actually lie in Japan, although it presently lags behind its neighbors of South Korea and Taiwan. The Japanese quickly adopt new technologies and mobile telephones linked to the Internet may enhance online investing. Moreover, the Japanese have an enormous amount of personal savings, estimated to be $12 trillion, with the majority of this amount in the postal savings system, with relatively low yields. Nevertheless, the Japanese, according to the same source, have "an acute aversion to risk." We note that our model allows for individual sources of funds (as well as the intermediaries) to have their own perceptions of risk and, thus, the model helps to reflect what is actually happening in reality.

6.2   Qualitative Properties

In this section, some qualitative properties of the dynamical financial network model with intermediation developed in Section 6.2 are provided. In particular, conditions for establishing the existence of a unique trajectory to the initial value problem (6.21) are given along with a global stability analysis result.

Two properties of the function F describing the financial model are now established, in particular, monotonicity and Lipschitz continuity. These properties were also established in the context of the supply chain network model in Chapter 4 and then utilized to obtain additional qualitative properties of the dynamic version of the model in Chapter 5.

Theorem 6.1: Monotonicity
If the c_{ijl}, c_j, and $\hat{c}_{ijl}$, and c_{jk} functions are convex, the $\hat{c}_{jk}$ functions are monotone increasing, the d_k functions are monotone decreasing functions, for all i, l, j, k, and the variance-covariance matrices Q^i are positive semidefinite for all i, as are the matrices Q^k for all k, then the vector function F that enters the variational inequality (6.22) (and (6.23)) is monotone, that is,

$$\langle F(X') - F(X''), X' - X'' \rangle \geq 0, \quad \forall X', X'' \in \mathcal{K}. \tag{6.29}$$

Proof: The expression $\langle F(X') - F(X''), X' - X'' \rangle$ is equal to the expression (after some algebraic simplifications):

$$\sum_{i=1}^{m} \sum_{j=1}^{n} \sum_{l=1}^{L} \left[\left[2Q^i_{z_{jl}} \cdot x'_i + \frac{\partial c_{ijl}(x'_{ijl})}{\partial x_{ijl}} + \frac{\partial c_j(x')}{\partial x_{ijl}} + \frac{\partial \hat{c}_{ijl}(x'_{ijl})}{\partial x_{ijl}} \right] \right.$$
$$\left. - \left[2Q^i_{z_{jl}} \cdot x''_i + \frac{\partial c_{ijl}(x''_{ijl})}{\partial x_{ijl}} + \frac{\partial c_j(x'')}{\partial x_{ijl}} + \frac{\partial \hat{c}_{ijl}(x''_{ijl})}{\partial x_{ijl}} \right] \right] \times [x'_{ijl} - x''_{ijl}]$$

$$+ \sum_{i=1}^{m} \sum_{k=1}^{o} \left[\left[2Q_k^i \cdot y_j' + \frac{\partial c_{jk}(y_{jk}')}{\partial y_{jk}} + \hat{c}_{jk}(y') \right] \right.$$

$$\left. - \left[2Q_k^i \cdot y_j'' + \frac{\partial c_{jk}(y_{jk}'')}{\partial y_{jk}} + \hat{c}_{jk}(y'') \right] \right] \times [y_{jk}' - y_{jk}'']$$

$$+ \sum_{k=1}^{o} \left[-d_k(\rho_3') + d_k(\rho_3'') \right] \times [\rho_{3k}' - \rho_{3k}''] . \tag{6.30}$$

But (6.30) must be greater than or equal to zero, under the above assumptions, and, hence, $F(X)$ as defined following (6.22) is monotone. $\square$

Theorem 6.2: Strict Monotonicity

Assume all the conditions of Theorem 6.1. In addition, suppose that one of the four families of convex functions $c_{ijl}; i = 1, ..., m; j = 1, ..., n; l = 1, ..., L; c_j; j = 1, ..., n; \hat{c}_{ijl}; i = 1, ..., m; j = 1, ..., n; l = 1, ..., L; and c_{jk}; i = 1, ..., n; k = 1, ..., o, is a family of strictly convex functions. Suppose that $\hat{c}_{jk}; j = 1, ..., n; k = 1, ..., o$ and $-d_k; k = 1, ..., o$, are strictly monotone and that the variance-covariance matrices Q^i and Q^k are positive definite, respectively, for all i and k. Then, the function F that enters the variational inequality (6.22) is strictly monotone, with respect to (x, y, ρ_3), that is, for any two X^1, X^2 with $(x', y', \rho_3') \neq (x'', y'', \rho_3'')$:

$$\langle F(X') - F(X''), X' - X'' \rangle > 0. \tag{6.31}$$

Proof: Note that the term $\langle F(X') - F(X''), X' - X'' \rangle$ has already been constructed in the proof of Theorem 6.1 and is given by (6.30) but now, under the assumptions of Theorem 6.2 one has that this term must be strictly greater than zero and, hence, $F(X)$ is, therefore, strictly monotone. $\square$

Theorem 6.3: Uniqueness

Assuming the condition of Theorem 6.2, there must be a unique equilibrium pattern in financial flows x^*, y^*, and a unique demand price vector ρ_3^* satisfying the equilibrium conditions of the financial problem with intermediation. In other words, if the variational inequality (6.22) (or (6.23)) admits a solution, then that is the only solution in $x, y,$ and ρ_3.

Proof: Under the strict monotonicity result of Theorem 6.2, uniqueness follows from the standard variational inequality theory (cf. Kinderlehrer and Stampacchia (1980) and Theorem B.4 in Appendix B) $\square$

Theorem 6.4: Lipschitz Continuity

The function that enters the variational inequality problem (6.22) is Lipschitz continuous, that is,

$$\| F(X') - F(X'') \| \leq L \| X' - X'' \|, \quad \forall X', X'' \in \mathcal{K}, \tag{6.32}$$

under the following conditions:
(i) c_{ijl}, c_j, $\hat{c}_{ijl}$, and c_{jk} have bounded second-order derivatives, for all i, j, l, k;
(ii) $\hat{c}_{jk}$ and d_k have bounded first-order derivatives.

Proof: The result is direct by applying a mid-value theorem from calculus to the function F that enters the variational inequality problem (6.22). □

We now turn to addressing the stability of the financial network system through the initial value problem (6.21). We first recall the following, which was also used in Chapter 5:

Definition 6.1: Stability of the System
The system defined by (6.21) is stable if, for every X_0 and every equilibrium point X^*, the Euclidean distance $\|X^* - X_0(t)\|$ is a monotone nonincreasing function of time t.

We state a global stability result in the next theorem.

Theorem 6.5: Stability of the Financial System
Assume the conditions of Theorem 6.1. Then the dynamical system (6.21) underlying the financial network system with intermediation is stable.

Proof: Under the assumptions of Theorem 6.1, $F(X)$ is monotone and, hence, the conclusion follows directly from Theorem 4.1 of Zhang and Nagurney (1995) (see also Theorem B.8 in Appendix B). □

From the above results, one sees that the dynamic financial network model with intermediation as given by (6.21) is well defined and, moreover, the financial network system with intermediation is stable.

6.3   The Discrete-Time Adjustment Process

Note that the projected dynamical system (6.21) is a continuous time adjustment process. However, in order to further fix ideas and to provide a means of "tracking" the trajectory, we propose a discrete-time adjustment process. The discrete-time adjustment process (the Euler method) was also applied to track the dynamic trajectory for the supply chain network model in Sections 5.3 and 5.4. The statement of this method in the context of the dynamic financial model takes the form:

Step 0: Initialization Step
Set $(x^0, y^0, \rho_2^0, \rho_3^0) \in \mathcal{K}$. Let $\tau = 1$, where τ is the iteration counter, and set the sequence $\{\alpha_\tau\}$ so that $\sum_{\tau=1}^{\infty} \alpha_\tau = \infty$, $\alpha_\tau > 0$, $\alpha_\tau \to 0$, as $\tau \to \infty$.

Step 1: Computation Step
Compute $(x^\tau, y^\tau, \rho_2^\tau, \rho_3^\tau) \in \mathcal{K}$ by solving the variational inequality subproblem:

$$\sum_{i=1}^{m} \sum_{j=1}^{n} \sum_{l=1}^{L} \left[x_{ijl}^\tau + \alpha_\tau \left(2Q_{zjl}^i \cdot x_i^{\tau-1} + \frac{\partial c_{ijl}(x_{ijl}^{\tau-1})}{\partial x_{ijl}} + \frac{\partial c_j(x^{\tau-1})}{\partial x_{ijl}} \right.\right.$$

$$+ \frac{\partial \hat{c}_{ijl}(x_{ijl}^{\tau-1})}{\partial x_{ijl}} - \rho_{2j}^{\tau-1}) - x_{ijl}^{\tau-1}\right] \times [x_{ijl} - x_{ijl}^{\tau}]$$

$$+ \sum_{j=1}^{n} \sum_{k=1}^{o} \left[y_{jk}^{\tau} + \alpha_{\tau}(2Q_k^i \cdot y_j^{\tau-1} + \hat{c}_{jk}(y^{\tau-1}) + \frac{\partial c_{jk}(y_{jk}^{\tau-1})}{\partial y_{jk}} \right.$$

$$\left. + \rho_{2j}^{\tau-1} - \rho_{3k}^{\tau-1}) - y_{jk}^{\tau-1} \right] \times [y_{jk} - y_{jk}^{\tau}]$$

$$+ \sum_{j=1}^{n} \left[\rho_{2j}^{\tau} + \alpha_{\tau}(\sum_{i=1}^{m} \sum_{l=1}^{L} x_{ijl}^{\tau-1} - \sum_{k=1}^{o} y_{jk}^{\tau-1}) - \rho_{2j}^{\tau-1} \right] \times [\rho_{2j} - \rho_{2j}^{\tau}]$$

$$+ \sum_{k=1}^{o} \left[\rho_{3k}^{\tau} + \alpha_{\tau}(\sum_{j=1}^{n} y_{jk}^{\tau-1} - d_k(\rho_3^{\tau-1})) - \rho_{3k}^{\tau-1} \right] \times [\rho_{3k} - \rho_{3k}^{\tau}] \geq 0, \quad (6.33)$$

$$\forall (x, y, \rho_2, \rho_3) \in \mathcal{K}.$$

Step 2: Convergence Verification

If $|x_{ijl}^{\tau} - x_{ijl}^{\tau-1}| \leq \epsilon$, $|y_{jk}^{\tau} - y_{jk}^{\tau-1}| \leq \epsilon$, $|\rho_{2j}^{\tau} - \rho_{2j}^{\tau-1}| \leq \epsilon$, $|\rho_{3k}^{\tau} - \rho_{3k}^{\tau-1}| \leq \epsilon$, for all $i = 1, \cdots, m$; $j = 1, \cdots, n$; $l = 1, \ldots, L$; $k = 1, \cdots, o$, with $\epsilon > 0$, a pre-specified tolerance, then stop; otherwise, set $\tau := \tau + 1$, and go to Step 1.

Note that the variational inequality subproblem (6.33) encountered at each iteration of the discrete-time algorithm can be solved explicitly and in closed form since it is actually a quadratic programming problem and the feasible set is a Cartesian product consisting of the product of K, which has a simple network structure, and the nonnegative orthants, R_+^{no}, R_+^n, and R_+^o, corresponding to the variables x, y, ρ_2, and ρ_3, respectively.

Computation of Financial Flows and Products

In fact, the subproblem in (6.33) in the x variables can be solved using exact equilibration (cf. Dafermos and Sparrow (1969), Nagurney (1999), and Appendix C), whereas the remainder of the variables in (6.33) can be obtained by explicit formulae, which are provided below for convenience. In particular, compute, at iteration τ, the y_{jk}^{τ}s, according to:

$$y_{jk}^{\tau} = \max\{0, y_{jk}^{\tau-1} - \alpha_{\tau}(2Q_k^i \cdot y_j^{\tau-1} + \hat{c}_{jk}(y^{\tau-1}) + \frac{\partial c_{jk}(y_{jk}^{\tau-1})}{\partial y_{jk}} + \rho_{2j}^{\tau-1} - \rho_{3k}^{\tau-1})\},$$

$$\forall j, k. \quad (6.34)$$

Computation of the Prices

At iteration τ, compute the ρ_{2j}^{τ}s according to:

$$\rho_{2j}^{\tau} = \max\{0, \rho_{2j}^{\tau-1} - \alpha_{\tau}(\sum_{i=1}^{m} \sum_{l=1}^{L} x_{ijl}^{\tau-1} - \sum_{k=1}^{o} y_{jk}^{\tau-1})\}, \quad \forall j, \quad (6.35)$$

whereas the ρ_{3k}^τs are computed explicitly and in closed form according to:

$$\rho_{3k}^\tau = \max\{0, \rho_{3k}^{\tau-1} - \alpha_\tau(\sum_{j=1}^n y_{jk}^{\tau-1} - d_k(\rho_3^{\tau-1}))\}, \quad \forall k. \qquad (6.36)$$

Note that in the discrete-time adjustment process, the financial flows, the products, and the prices are updated simultaneously at each iteration, with the computation of the financial flows and products taking place on the logistical network (cf. Figure 6.1) and that of the prices on the value network. The information network, in turn, stores the flows and prices from iteration to iteration. Convergence results can be found in Appendix C.

6.4   Numerical Examples

In this section, the discrete-time algorithm is applied to several numerical examples. The algorithm was implemented in FORTRAN and the computer system used was, again, a DEC Alpha system located at the University of Massachusetts at Amherst. For the solution of the induced network subproblems in x, we utilized the exact equilibration algorithm described in Appendix C.

The convergence criterion used was that the absolute value of the flows and prices between two successive iterations differed by no more than 10^{-4}. For the examples, the sequence $\{\alpha_\tau\} = .1\{1, \frac{1}{2}, \frac{1}{2}, \frac{1}{3}, \frac{1}{3}, \frac{1}{3}, \ldots\}$, which is of the form given in the intialization step of the algorithm in the preceding section. The numerical examples had the network structure depicted in Figure 6.2 and consisted of two source agents, two intermediaries, and two demand markets, with a single financial instrument handled by each intermediary.

We initialized the algorithm as follows: since there was a single financial instrument associated with each of the intermediaries, we set $x_{ij1} = \frac{S^i}{n}$ for each source agent i. All the other variables, that is, the initial vectors y, ρ_2, and ρ_3 were set to zero.

Example 6.1

The data for the first example were constructed for easy interpretation purposes. The supplies of the two source agents were: $S^1 = 10$ and $S^2 = 10$. The variance-covariance matrices Q^i and Q^j were equal to the identity matrices for all source agents i and all intermediaries j.

The transaction cost functions faced by the source agents associated with transacting with the intermediaries were given by:

$$c_{111}(x_{111}) = .5x_{111}^2 + 3.5x_{111}, \quad c_{121}(x_{121}) = .5x_{121}^2 + 3.5x_{121},$$

$$c_{211}(x_{211}) = .5x_{211}^2 + 3.5x_{211}, \quad c_{221}(x_{221}) = .5x_{221}^2 + 3.5x_{221}.$$

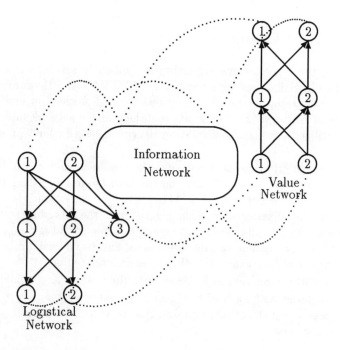

Fig. 6.2. Multilevel Network Structure of the Numerical Examples

The handling costs of the intermediaries, in turn, were given by:

$$c_1(x) = .5(\sum_{i=1}^{2} .5x_{i11})^2, \quad c_2(x) = .5(\sum_{i=1}^{2} x_{i21})^2.$$

The transaction costs of the intermediaries associated with transacting with the source agents were, respectively, given by:

$$\hat{c}_{111}(x_{111}) = 1.5x_{111}^2 + 3x_{111}, \quad \hat{c}_{121}(x_{121}) = 1.5x_{121}^2 + 3x_{121},$$

$$\hat{c}_{211}(x_{211}) = 1.5x_{211}^2 + 3x_{211}, \quad \hat{c}_{221}(x_{221}) = 1.5x_{221}^2 + 3x_{221}.$$

The demand functions at the demand markets were:

$$d_1(\rho_3) = -2\rho_{31} - 1.5\rho_{32} + 1000, \quad d_2(\rho_3) = -2\rho_{32} - 1.5\rho_{31} + 1000,$$

and the transaction costs between the intermediaries and the consumers at the demand markets were given by:

$$\hat{c}_{11}(y) = y_{11} + 5, \quad \hat{c}_{12}(y) = y_{12} + 5, \quad \hat{c}_{21}(y) = y_{21} + 5, \quad \hat{c}_{22}(y) = y_{22} + 5.$$

We assumed for this and the subsequent examples that the transaction costs as perceived by the intermediaries and associated with transacting with the demand markets were all zero, that is, $c_{jk}(y_{jk}) = 0$, for all j, k.

The discrete-time algorithm converged and yielded the following equilibrium pattern:

$$x_{111}^* = x_{121}^* = x_{211}^* = x_{221}^* = 5.000,$$

$$y_{11}^* = y_{12}^* = y_{21}^* = y_{22}^* = 5.000.$$

The vector ρ_2^* had components: $\rho_{21}^* = \rho_{22}^* = 262.6664$, and the computed demand prices at the demand markets were: $\rho_{31}^* = \rho_{32}^* = 282.8106$.

It is easy to verify that the optimality/equilibrium conditions were satisfied with good accuracy. Note that in this example, constraint (6.6) was tight for both source agents, that is, $s_1^* = s_2^* = 0$, where $s_i^* = S^i - \sum_{j=1}^{n} \sum_{l=1}^{L} x_{ijl}^*$, and, hence, there was zero flow on the links connecting node 3 with top tier nodes 1 and 2. Thus, it was optimal for both source agents to invest their entire financial holdings in each instrument made available by each of the two intermediaries.

The top-tiered equilibrium prices in the logistical and value networks were recovered according to the discussion following (6.27) and were as follows: All ρ_{1ij1}^*s= 234.6664.

Example 6.2

We then constructed the following variant of Example 6.1. The data were identical to that in Example 6.1 except that the supply for each source sector was increased so that $S^1 = S^2 = 50$.

The discrete-time algorithm converged and yielded the following new equilibrium pattern:

$$x_{111}^* = x_{121}^* = x_{211}^* = x_{221}^* = 23.6832,$$

$$y_{11}^* = y_{12}^* = y_{21}^* = y_{22}^* = 23.7247.$$

The vector ρ_2^* had components: $\rho_{21}^* = \rho_{22}^* = 196.0174$, and the demand prices at the demand markets were: $\rho_{31}^* = \rho_{32}^* = 272.1509$.

It is easy to verify that the optimality/equilibrium conditions, again, were satisfied with good accuracy. Note, however, that unlike the solution for Example 6.1, both source agent 1 and source agent 2 did not invest their entire financial holdings. Indeed, each opted to not invest the amount 23.7209 and this was the volume of flow on each of the two links ending in node 3 in Figure 6.2.

All the ρ_{1ij1}^*s= 74.6013. Since the supply of financial funds increased, the price for the instruments charged by the intermediaries decreased from 262.6664 to 196.1074. The demand prices at the demand markets also decreased, from 282.8106 to 272.1509.

Example 6.3

Example 6.2 was then modified as follows: the data were identical to that in Example 6.2 except that we modified the first diagonal term in the variance-covariance matrix Q^1 from 1 to 2.

The discrete-time algorithm converged, yielding the following new equilibrium pattern:

$$x_{111}^* = 18.8676, \quad x_{121}^* = 23.7285, \quad x_{211}^* = 25.1543, \quad x_{221}^* = 23.7267,$$

$$y_{11}^* = y_{12}^* = 22.0501, \quad y_{21}^* = y_{22}^* = 23.7592.$$

The vector ρ_2^* had components: $\rho_{21}^* = 201.4985$, $\rho_{22}^* = 196.3633$, and the demand prices at the demand markets were: $\rho_{31}^* = \rho_{32}^* = 272.6178$.

The prices ρ_{1ijl}^*, $\forall i, j, l$, at equilibrium were, respectively: $\rho_{1111}^* = 97.8737$, $\rho_{1121}^* = 74.7227$, $\rho_{1211}^* = 79.0138$, and $\rho_{1221}^* = 74.7281$.

Example 6.4

The fourth example was constructed from Example 6.3. In particular, a single change was made to the second demand function by modifying the fixed term 1000 to 1200. Thus, in effect, the demand for the second financial product was increased.

The discrete-time algorithm yielded the following equilibrium pattern:

$$x_{111}^* = 22.3404, \quad x_{121}^* = 27.6596, \quad x_{211}^* = 26.0638, \quad x_{221}^* = 23.9362,$$

$$y_{11}^* = 0.0000, \quad y_{12}^* = 48.6257, \quad y_{21}^* = 0.0000, \quad y_{22}^* = 51.8172.$$

The vector ρ_2^* had components: $\rho_{21}^* = 248.4244$, $\rho_{22}^* = 238.8500$, and the demand prices at the demand markets were: $\rho_{31}^* = 200.6086$, $\rho_{32}^* = 399.2637$.

Hence, the constraints (6.6) were tight for each source agent and the flows on the links ending in node 3 in Figure 6.2 were equal to zero.

The top-tiered prices at equilibrium were as follows: $\rho^*_{1111} = 129.9989$, $\rho^*_{1121} = 101.2755$, $\rho^*_{1211} = 118.887$, and $\rho^*_{1221} = 112.4457$.

Note that since now the demand for financial product 1 is identically equal to zero, there are zero flows on links joining intermediary nodes 1 and 2 to the bottom tier node 1.

6.5   Concluding Remarks

This chapter concludes Part II of this book, which focused on multitiered networks. The applications explored included supply chain networks and financial networks with intermediation. For both these applications, dynamic models were also presented and visualized as multilevel networks. Through the multitiered, multilevel representations of these supernetworks, we were able to identify both the similarities as well as the differences between the supply chain and financial network applications. This work is, by no means, the end to the story. In fact, here we simply lay down the foundations and hope that they will stimulate further research on the topic and will unveil new applications with related structures. For example, in the context of the financial network with intermediation, electronic links can be introduced between the source agent nodes and the demand market nodes to model the transformation/transaction of the financial funds electronically (without any intermediation) and, hence, additional types of electronic funds transfers. The supernetwork concept is sufficiently general to do this, as has been demonstrated, in the context of supply chains.

Interestingly, as reported in *The Economist* (2001b), in terms of the economics of the "web," the most obvious gains come from cutting "shopfront costs and intermediaries, and from cheaper distribution," which we model here as "transaction costs." However, also in that source, it is noted that the Internet is as often "changing the role and function of intermediaries, not eliminating them." The same article goes on to reference the work of Evans and Wurster (1999) who discuss "navigators" who will appear to represent customers to assist them in extracting the positives out of the web and the work of Hagel and Singer (1999) who are given credit for coining the term "infomediary," whose role is to ensure individuals' privacy or payment security. All these terms emphasize that the inclusion of intermediaries is important in the Information Age and the modeling of such agents has been the focus of this chapter, in the context of financial systems.

Moreover, although we have not addressed policy interventions here, a variety of additional constraints can be added to the financial network model with intermediation and the underlying feasible set redefined accordingly. We hope that this work also stimulates research in this direction.

6.6   Sources and Notes

Copeland, in his 1952 book, recognized the idea of conceptualizing the inter-relationships of financial funds as a network, raised the question, "Does money flow like water or electricity?" and devoted a section to this topic. Furthermore, he provided a "wiring diagram for the main money circuit." Such analogue computational devices, however, were soon to be superseded by digital computers, and accompanied by parallel developments in rigorous computational methodologies.

Thore, as early as 1969, had introduced networks, along with the mathe-matics, for the study of financial systems of linked portfolios (see also Charnes and Cooper (1967)) in the context of credit networks and made use of linear programming. Storoy, Thore, and Boyer (1975), in turn, presented a net-work model of the interconnection of capital markets and demonstrated how decomposition theory of mathematical programming could be exploited for the computation of equilibrium. The utility functions facing a sector were no longer restricted to being linear functions.

Network models have also been proposed for financial problems charac-terized by a single objective function to be optimized such as in portfolio optimization and asset allocation problems, currency translation, and risk management problems, among others. This literature is based on the funda-mental work of Markowitz (1952, 1959), whose mean-variance minimization problem was, in fact, a network optimization problem with a nonlinear ob-jective function (cf. Mulvey (1987)). Of course, more general multi-sector, multi-instrument financial equilibrium models have utilized such a theory as a building block. For an extensive set of references of networks in finance, see the book by Nagurney and Siokos (1997).

In particular, Nagurney, Dong, and Hughes (1992) developed a multi-sector, multi-instrument financial equilibrium model and recognized the net-work structure underlying the subproblems encountered in their proposed decomposition scheme, which was based on finite-dimensional variational in-equality theory. Nagurney and Ke (2001a), in turn, presented a general but, static, model of financial intermediation. This chapter builds upon that work as well as the contribution of Dong, Zhang, and Nagurney (1996). These au-thors were the first to develop a dynamic model of general financial equilib-rium with multiple sectors and multiple financial instruments, in which both the prices and the flows were endogenous. They formulated the model as a projected dynamical system and then established stability analysis results. This work was later extended to the international domain by Nagurney and Siokos (1997).

This chapter, although based on the paper of Nagurney and Ke (2001b), from which the numerical examples are taken, nevertheless, goes further than that work in introducing the supernetwork, multilevel network interpretation of the dynamic model. This chapter also describes a practical example to an online brokerage and, in addition, it contains proofs of the theoretical results.

Part III Multicriteria Networks

7 Multicriteria Network Equilibrium Modeling

This chapter begins the third part of this book, the focus of which is supernetworks with multicriteria decision-makers. Specifically, the concept of multicriteria supernetwork is utilized to address decision-making in the Information Age with applications ranging from telecommuting and teleshopping to financial decision-making. The term "multicriteria" captures the multiplicity of criteria that decision-makers are often faced with in making their choices, be they regarding consumption, production, transportation, location, or investment. Criteria which are considered as part of the decision-making process in this and the next part of the book include: cost minimization, time minimization, opportunity cost minimization, profit maximization, as well as risk minimization, among others.

Indeed, the Information Age, with the increasing availability of new computer and communication technologies, along with the Internet, has transformed the ways in which many individuals work, travel, and conduct their daily activities today. Moreover, the decision-making process itself has been altered through the addition of alternatives which were not, heretofore, possible or even feasible. As stated in a recent issue of *The Economist* (2000a), on page 9, "The boundaries for employees are redrawn... as people work from home and shop from work."

This chapter takes on the challenge of developing the foundations of a multicriteria network equilibrium framework for decision-making in the Information Age. The modeling approach captures choices made possible through transportation and telecommunication mode alternatives. Moreover, it allows for the prediction of the volumes of flow in terms of decision-makers' selections and the effects of their choices on such possible criteria as time, cost, and/or risk.

It is our belief that a network equilibrium framework is natural since not only are many of the relevant decisions now taking place on networks but also the concept of a supernetwork – as shall be demonstrated in this chapter – is sufficiently general in an abstract and mathematical setting to capture many of the salient features comprising decision-making today. Further applications, as well as extensions and variations to the work set forth in this chapter, are presented in the remainder of this book. In particular, in Chapter 8, the supernetwork concept is utilized to construct a space-time network for telecommuting versus commuting decision-making over a finite-time horizon. In Chapter 9, supernetworks are constructed to address location and transportation decision-making simultaneously.

The second part of this book, in contrast, focused on decentralized decision-making supernetwork models in which the agents (on multitiered networks) were characterized by single criterion objective functions which they wished to optimize. However, Chapter 6 did include, albeit implicitly, multiple criteria in that the source and the intermediary agents sought to minimize risk, while, simultaneously, maximizing net returns.

The first publications in the area of multicriteria decision-making on networks focused on transportation networks, and were by Schneider (1968) and Quandt (1967). However, they assumed fixed travel times and travel costs. Here, in contrast, these functions (as well as any other appropriate criteria functions) are flow-dependent. The first flow-dependent such model was by Dafermos (1981), who considered an infinite number of decision-makers, rather than a finite number as is done here. Furthermore, she assumed two criteria, whereas we consider a finite number, where the number can be as large as necessary. Moreover, the modeling framework set out in this chapter can also handle elastic demands. The first general elastic demand multicriteria network equilibrium model was developed by Nagurney and Dong (2000), who considered two criteria and fixed weights and allowed the weights to be class- and link-dependent. The models in this chapter, in contrast, allow for as many finite criteria as are relevant to the particular application and retain the flexible feature of permitting the weights associated with the criteria to be both class- and link-dependent.

Table 7.1 contains a list of additional references. All the citations in Table 7.1 consider two criteria only, typically, time and cost, which are of particular relevance to route selection on transportation networks, when the behavior of the travelers is that of user-optimization. In particular, Table 7.1 describes, briefly, the type of multicriteria traffic network models that are studied in the specific citation. It notes whether separable functions, that is, functions that depend only on the flow on the particular link are used, or whether general ones are treated in the formulations. The citations are distinguished as to the type of formulation used, that is, whether the model is an infinite (inf.) or finite-dimensional (fin.) variational inequality (VI) one or an optimization one. It also notes whether an algorithm is included in the paper.

Table 7.1. Some Multicriteria Traffic Network Equilibrium Contributions Post 1968

Citation	Flow Dependence	Type of Demand	Formulation	Algorithm
Dial (1979)	No	fixed	optimization	Yes
Dafermos (1981)	Yes	fixed; class-dependent	inf.-dim. VI	Yes; for network of special structure
Leurent (1993a)	time only	elastic; separable, not class-dependent	optimization	Yes
Leurent (1993b)	time only; general functions	elastic; separable, not class-dependent	fin.-dim. VI	Yes
Marcotte, Nguyen, and Tanguay (1996); see also Marcotte and Zhu (1994)	Yes; general functions	fixed; class-dependent	inf.-dim. VI	Yes
Leurent (1996)	time only; general functions	elastic; not class-dependent	fin.-dim. VI	Yes; optimization case only
Dial (1996)	Yes; separable functions	fixed; class-dependent	optimization; inf.- and fin.-dim. VI	Yes; for special case
Marcotte and Zhu (1997)	Yes; general functions	fixed; class-dependent	inf.-dim VI	Yes
Marcotte (1998)	Yes; general functions	fixed; class-dependent	inf.-dim. VI; fin.-dim. VI	Yes
Dial (1999)	Yes; separable functions	fixed; class-dependent	optimization; inf.- and fin.-dim. VI	No
Nagurney (2000d)	Yes; general functions	fixed; class-dependent	fin.-dim. VI	Yes

This chapter is organized as follows. In Section 7.1, the multiclass, multicriteria network equilibrium models with elastic demand and with fixed demand, respectively, are developed. Each class of decision-maker is allowed to have weights associated with the criteria which are also permitted to be link-dependent for modeling flexibility purposes. In Section 7.1, the governing equilibrium conditions along with the variational inequality formulations are presented. Section 7.2 provides some qualitative properties of the equilibrium patterns, notably, existence and uniqueness. In addition, certain properties of the functions that enter the variational inequality problems which are needed for establishing convergence of the algorithmic scheme in Section 7.4 are included.

The usefulness of the multicriteria, multiclass network equilibrium framework is then illustrated in Section 7.3 by applying it to two distinct areas: telecommuting versus commuting decision-making and teleshopping versus shopping decision-making. In Section 7.4, a computational procedure is outlined, along with convergence results. In Section 7.5, the algorithm is then applied to numerical examples drawn from the applications proposed in Section 7.3.

7.1   The Multiclass, Multicriteria Network Equilibrium Models

In this section, the multiclass, multicriteria network equilibrium models are developed. The elastic demand model is presented first and then the fixed demand model. The equilibrium conditions are, subsequently, shown to satisfy finite-dimensional variational inequality problems.

Consider a general network $G = [\mathcal{N}, \mathcal{L}]$, where $\mathcal{N}$ denotes the set of nodes in the network and $\mathcal{L}$ the set of directed links. Let a denote a link of the network connecting a pair of nodes and let p denote a path, assumed to be acyclic, consisting of a sequence of links connecting an origin/destination (O/D) pair of nodes. There are n links in the network and n_P paths. Let Ω denote the set of J O/D pairs. The set of paths connecting the O/D pair ω is denoted by P_ω and the entire set of paths in the network by P.

Note that in the supernetwork framework a link may correspond to an actual physical link of transportation or to an abstract or virtual link corresponding to telecommunications, as was also done in the supernetwork models in Chapters 4 and 5. Furthermore, the supernetwork representing the problem under study can be as general as necessary and a path may consist also of a set of links corresponding to a combination of physical and virtual choices. A path, hence, as was also discussed in Chapter 3, abstracts a decision as a sequence of links or possible choices from an origin node, which represents the beginning of the decision, to the destination node, which represents its completion.

Assume that there are k classes of decision-makers in the network with a typical class denoted by i. Let f_a^i denote the flow of class i on link a and let x_p^i denote the nonnegative flow of class i on path p. The relationship between the link flows by class and the path flows is:

$$f_a^i = \sum_{p \in P} x_p^i \delta_{ap}, \quad \forall i, \quad \forall a \in \mathcal{L}, \qquad (7.1)$$

where $\delta_{ap} = 1$, if link a is contained in path p, and 0, otherwise. Hence, the flow of a class of decision-maker on a link is equal to the sum of the flows of the class on the paths that contain that link.

In addition, let f_a denote the total flow on link a, where

$$f_a = \sum_{i=1}^{k} f_a^i, \quad \forall a \in \mathcal{L}. \qquad (7.2)$$

Thus, the total flow on a link is equal to the sum of the flows of all classes on that link. Group the class link flows into the kn-dimensional column vector $\tilde{f}$ with components $\{f_1^1, \ldots, f_n^1, \ldots, f_1^k, \ldots, f_n^k\}$ and the total link flows $\{f_1, \ldots, f_n\}$ into the n-dimensional column vector f. Also, group the class path flows into the kn_P-dimensional column vector $\tilde{x}$ with components $\{x_{p_1}^1, \ldots, x_{p_{n_P}}^k\}$. The demand associated with origin/destination (O/D) pair ω and class i will be denoted by d_ω^i. Group the demands into a column vector $d \in R^{kJ}$. Clearly, the demands must satisfy the following conservation of flow equations:

$$d_\omega^i = \sum_{p \in P_\omega} x_p^i, \quad \forall i, \forall \omega, \qquad (7.3)$$

that is, the demand for an O/D pair for each class is equal to the sum of the path flows of that class on the paths that join the O/D pair.

The functions associated with the links are now described. In particular, assume that there are H criteria which the decision-makers may utilize in their decision-making with a typical criterion denoted by h. Assume that C_{ha} denotes criterion h associated with link a, where

$$C_{ha} = C_{ha}(f), \quad \forall a \in \mathcal{L}, \qquad (7.4)$$

where C_{ha} is assumed to be a continuous function.

For example, criterion 1 may be time, in which case we would have

$$C_{1a} = C_{1a}(f) = t_a(f), \quad \forall a \in \mathcal{L}, \qquad (7.5)$$

where $t_a(f)$ denotes the time associated with traversing link a. In the case of a transportation link, one would expect the function to be higher than for a telecommunications link. Another relevant criterion may be cost, that is,

$$C_{2a} = C_{2a}(f) = c_a(f), \quad \forall a \in \mathcal{L}, \qquad (7.6)$$

which might reflect (depending on the link a) an access cost in the case of a telecommunications link, or a transportation or shipment cost in the case of a transportation link. One can expect both time and cost to be relevant criteria in decision-making in the Information Age especially since telecommunications is at times a substitute for transportation and it is typically associated with higher speed and lower cost (cf. Mokhtarian (1990)).

In addition, another relevant criterion in evaluating decision-making in the Information Age is opportunity cost since one may expect that this cost would be high in the case of teleshopping, for example (since one cannot physically experience and evaluate the product), and lower in the case of shopping. Furthermore, in the case of telecommuting, there may be perceived to be a higher associated opportunity cost by some classes of decision-makers who may miss the socialization provided by face-to-face interactions with coworkers and colleagues. Hence, a third possible criterion may be opportunity cost, where

$$C_{3a} = C_{3a}(f) = o_a(f), \quad \forall a \in \mathcal{L}, \tag{7.7}$$

with $o_a(f)$ denoting the opportunity cost associated with link a. Finally, a decision-maker may wish to associate a safety cost in which case the fourth criterion may be

$$C_{4a} = C_{4a}(f) = s_a(f), \quad \forall a \in \mathcal{L}, \tag{7.8}$$

where $s_a(f)$ denotes a security or safety cost measure associated with link a. In the case of teleshopping, for example, decision-makers may be concerned with revealing personal or credit information, whereas in the case of transportation, commuters may view certain neighborhood roads as being dangerous.

We assume that each class of decision-maker has a potentially different perception of the trade-offs among the criteria, which are represented by the nonnegative weights: $w_{1a}^i, \ldots, w_{Ha}^i$. Hence, w_{1a}^i denotes the weight on link a associated with criterion 1 for class i, w_{2a}^i denotes the weight associated with criterion 2 for class i, and so on. Observe that the weights are link-dependent and can incorporate specific link-dependent factors which could include for a particular class factors such as convenience and sociability. A typical weight associated with class i, link a, and criterion h is denoted by w_{ha}^i.

Nagurney and Dong (2000) were the first to model link-dependent weights but only considered two criteria. Nagurney, Dong, and Mokhtarian (2000), in turn, used link-dependent weights but assumed only three criteria, in particular, travel time, travel cost, and opportunity cost in their integrated multicriteria network equilibrium models for telecommuting versus commuting.

Here, a generalized cost function is proposed and defined as follows.

Definition 7.1: Generalized Link Cost Function

A generalized link cost of class i associated with link a and denoted by C_a^i is *given by:*

$$C_a^i = \sum_{h=1}^{H} w_{ha}^i C_{ha}, \quad \forall i, \quad \forall a \in \mathcal{L}. \tag{7.9}$$

For example, (7.9) states that each class of decision-maker i when faced by H distinct criteria on each link a assigns his own weights $\{w_{ha}^i\}$ to the links and criteria.

In lieu of (7.2)–(7.9), one can write

$$C_a^i = C_a^i(\tilde{f}), \quad \forall i, \quad \forall a \in \mathcal{L}, \tag{7.10}$$

and group the generalized link costs into the kn-dimensional column vector C with components: $\{C_1^1, \ldots, C_n^1, \ldots, C_1^k, \ldots, C_n^k\}$.

For example, if there are four criteria associated with decision-making and they are given by (7.5) through (7.8), then the generalized cost function on a link a as perceived by class i would have the form:

$$C_a^i = w_{1a}^i C_{1a}(\tilde{f}) + w_{2a}^i C_{2a}(\tilde{f}) + w_{3a}^i C_{3a}(\tilde{f}) + w_{4a}^i C_{4a}(\tilde{f}). \tag{7.11}$$

Let now C_p^i denote the generalized cost of class i associated with path p in the network where

$$C_p^i = \sum_{a \in \mathcal{L}} C_a^i(\tilde{f})\delta_{ap}, \quad \forall i, \quad \forall p. \tag{7.12}$$

Hence, the generalized cost associated with a class and a path is that class's weighted combination of the various criteria on the links that comprise the path.

Note from the structure of the criteria on the links as expressed by (7.4) and the generalized cost structure assumed for the different classes on the links according to (7.9) and (7.10), that it is explicitly being assumed that the relevant criteria are functions of the total flows on the links, where the total flows (see (7.2)) correspond to the total number of decision-makers of all classes that selects a particular link. This is not unreasonable since one can expect that the greater the number of decision-makers that select a particular link (which comprises a part of a path), the greater the congestion on that link and, hence, one can expect the time of traversing the link as well as the cost to increase.

In the case of the elastic demand model, assume, as given, the inverse demand functions λ_ω^i for all classes i and all O/D pairs ω, where:

$$\lambda_\omega^i = \lambda_\omega^i(d), \quad \forall i, \forall \omega, \tag{7.13}$$

where these functions are assumed to be smooth and continuous. Group the inverse demand functions into a column vector $\lambda \in R^{kJ}$.

The Behavioral Assumption

Assume that the decision-making involved in the problem is repetitive in nature such as, for example, in the case of commuting versus telecommuting, or shopping versus teleshopping. The behavioral assumption that is proposed, hence, is that decision-makers select their paths so that their generalized costs are minimized.

Specifically, the behavioral assumption utilized is similar to that underlying traffic network assignment models (cf. (3.15) and (3.32)) (see, e.g., Beckmann, McGuire, and Winsten (1956), Dafermos and Sparrow (1969), and Dafermos (1982)) in that it is assumed that each class of decision-maker in the network selects a path so as to minimize the generalized cost on the path, given that all other decision-makers have made their choices. Such an idea has also been used in the context of multiclass, multicriteria traffic networks, as noted in Table 7.1. The generalized path costs in our model (cf. (7.9) and (7.12)), however, are more general than those in the models featured in Table 7.1.

In particular, the following are the network equilibrium conditions for the problem outlined above:

Multiclass, Multicriteria Network Equilibrium Conditions for the Elastic Demand Case

For each class i, for all O/D pairs $\omega \in \Omega$, and for all paths $p \in P_\omega$, the flow pattern $\tilde{x}^*$ is said to be *in equilibrium* if the following conditions hold:

$$C_p^i(\tilde{f}^*) \begin{cases} = \lambda_\omega^i(d^*), & \text{if} \quad x_p^{i*} > 0 \\ \geq \lambda_\omega^i(d^*), & \text{if} \quad x_p^{i*} = 0. \end{cases} \tag{7.14}$$

In other words, all utilized paths by a class connecting an O/D pair have equal and minimal generalized costs and the generalized cost on a used path by a class is equal to the inverse demand/disutility for that class and the O/D pair that the path connects.

In the case of the fixed demand model, in which the demands in (7.3) are now assumed known and fixed, the multicriteria network equilibrium conditions now take the following form.

Multiclass, Multicriteria Network Equilibrium Conditions for the Fixed Demand Case

For each class i, for all O/D pairs $\omega \in \Omega$, and for all paths $p \in P_\omega$, the flow pattern $\tilde{x}^*$ is said to be *in equilibrium* if the following conditions hold:

$$C_p^i(\tilde{f}^*) \begin{cases} = \lambda_\omega^i, & \text{if} \quad x_p^{i*} > 0 \\ \geq \lambda_\omega^i, & \text{if} \quad x_p^{i*} = 0, \end{cases} \tag{7.15}$$

where now the λ_ω^i denotes simply an indicator representing the minimal incurred generalized path cost for class i and O/D pair ω. Equilibrium conditions (7.15) state that all used paths by a class connecting an O/D pair have equal and minimal generalized costs.

We now present the variational inequality formulations of the equilibrium conditions governing the elastic demand and the fixed demand problems, respectively, given by (7.14) and (7.15). In Section 7.2, some qualitative properties of the solutions to the variational inequality problems are presented.

Theorem 7.1: Variational Inequality Formulation of the Elastic Demand Model

The variational inequality formulation of the multicriteria network model with elastic demand satisfying equilibrium conditions (7.14) is given by: determine $(\tilde{f}^*, d^*) \in \mathcal{K}^1$, *satisfying*

$$\sum_{i=1}^{k} \sum_{a \in \mathcal{L}} C_a^i(\tilde{f}^*) \times (f_a^i - f_a^{i*}) - \sum_{i=1}^{k} \sum_{\omega \in \Omega} \lambda_\omega^i(d^*) \times (d_\omega^i - d_\omega^{i*}) \geq 0, \quad \forall (\tilde{f}, d) \in \mathcal{K}^1,$$

(7.16a)

where $\mathcal{K}^1 \equiv \{(\tilde{f}, d) | \tilde{x} \geq 0,$ *and (7.1), (7.2), and (7.3) hold*$\}$; *equivalently, in standard variational inequality form:*

$$\langle F(X^*), X - X^* \rangle \geq 0, \quad \forall X \in \mathcal{K},$$

(7.16b)

where $F \equiv (C, \lambda)$, $X \equiv (\tilde{f}, d)$, *and* $\mathcal{K} \equiv \mathcal{K}^1$.

Proof: We first establish that an equilibrium pattern $(\tilde{f}^*, d^*) \in \mathcal{K}^1$ satisfying equilibrium conditions (7.14) satisfies variational inequality (7.16a). We then prove the converse. From (7.14), we have, for a class i, O/D pair ω, and a path $p \in P_\omega$, that:

$$(C_p^i(\tilde{f}^*) - \lambda_\omega^i(d^*)) \times (x_p^i - x_p^{i*}) \geq 0, \quad \forall x_p^i \geq 0.$$

(7.17)

Indeed, if $x_p^{i*} > 0$, then, according to (7.14) the generalized cost on that path for that class is equal to the disutility for that class associated with that pair, so the left term in (7.17) is zero, and, thus, the inequality in (7.17) holds true. On the other hand, if $x_p^{i*} = 0$, then, according to (7.14) the generalized cost on that path for that class is greater than or equal to the disutility associated with that O/D pair and class and, hence, the first term in (7.17) is greater than or equal to zero. The second term in (7.17) is also greater than or equal to zero in this case since $x_p^i \geq 0$ (path flows must be nonnegative) and, hence, since $x_p^{i*} = 0$, the second term in (7.17) is also nonnegative. Since the product of two nonnegative terms is also nonnegative, inequality (7.17) holds true. Summing now (7.17) over all classes i, all O/D pairs ω, and all paths connecting O/D pair ω yields:

$$\sum_{i=1}^{k} \sum_{\omega \in \Omega} \sum_{p \in P_\omega} (C_p^i(\tilde{f}^*) - \lambda_\omega^i(d^*)) \times (x_p^i - x_p^{i*}) \geq 0.$$

(7.18)

But (7.18) can be rewritten, using the conservation of flow equations (7.3), as:

$$\sum_{i=1}^{k} \sum_{\omega \in \Omega} \sum_{p \in P_\omega} C_p^i(\tilde{f}^*) \times (x_p^i - x_p^{i*}) - \sum_{i=1}^{k} \sum_{\omega \in \Omega} \lambda_\omega^i(d^*) \times (d_\omega^i - d_\omega^{i*}) \geq 0. \quad (7.19)$$

Using now the relationship between the generalized cost on a path and the generalized costs on the links that comprise the path given by (7.12) and also the conservation of flow equations (7.1) for the relationship between the class link flows and path flows, (7.19) can be expressed as:

$$\sum_{i=1}^{k} \sum_{a \in \mathcal{L}} C_a^i(\tilde{f}^*) \times (f_a^i - f_a^{i*}) - \sum_{i=1}^{k} \sum_{\omega \in \Omega} \lambda_\omega^i(d^*) \times (d_\omega^i - d_\omega^{i*}) \geq 0,$$

$$\forall (\tilde{f}, d) \in \mathcal{K}^1. \quad (7.20)$$

But, (7.20) is precisely variational inequality (7.16a), which, in standard form, is as given by (7.16b).

We now show that a solution to variational inequality (7.16a) also satisfies equilibrium conditions (7.14). Using (7.1), (7.3), and (7.12), variational inequality (7.16a) can be expressed as:

$$\sum_{i=1}^{k} \sum_{\omega \in \Omega} \sum_{p \in P_\omega} (C_p^i(\tilde{f}^*) - \lambda_\omega^i(d^*)) \times (x_p^i - x_p^{i*}) \geq 0. \quad (7.21)$$

Let now $x_p^i = x_p^{i*}$ for all p, $p \in P_\omega$, for all ω and i, except for a particular $q \neq p \in P_w$. Making this substitution into (7.21) yields:

$$(C_q^i(\tilde{f}^*) - \lambda_w^i(d^*)) \times (x_q^i - x_q^{i*}) \geq 0. \quad (7.22)$$

From (7.22) it is now easy to infer equilibrium conditions (7.14). Indeed, if $x_q^{i*} = 0$, then since $(x_q^i - x_q^{i*}) \geq 0$, for (7.22) to hold, its first term must also be nonnegative, which implies the second part of the equilibrium conditions (7.14) (since q and w could be any path and O/D pair, respectively). On the other hand, if $x_q^{i*} > 0$, then since the second term in (7.22) can now be positive, negative, or zero, for (7.22) to hold, the first term must be equal to zero, which is the first part of (7.14) (for any q and w and i). The proof is complete □.

Hence, a flow and demand pattern satisfies equilibrium conditions (7.14) if and only if it also satisfies the variational inequality problem (7.16a) or (7.16b). The variational inequality formulation of equilibrium conditions (7.15) can be established using similar arguments as in the proof of Theorem 7.1, by also making note that, in the fixed demand case, where (cf. (7.3)) the demands for the O/D pairs and classes are assumed known and given, the term $\sum_{i=1}^{k} \sum_{\omega \in \Omega} \lambda_\omega^i(d^*) \times (d_\omega^i - d_\omega^{i*})$ in (7.16a) regarding the demands, thus, drops out. Therefore, we have the following:

Theorem 7.2: Variational Inequality Formulation of the Fixed Demand Model
The variational inequality formulation of the fixed demand multiciteria network equilibrium model satisfying equilibrium conditions (7.15) is given by: determine $\tilde{f} \in \mathcal{K}^2$, satisfying

$$\sum_{i=1}^{k} \sum_{a \in \mathcal{L}} C_a^i(\tilde{f}^*) \times (f_a^i - f_a^{i*}) \geq 0, \qquad \forall \tilde{f} \in \mathcal{K}^2, \qquad (7.23a)$$

where $\mathcal{K}^2 \equiv \{\tilde{f} | \exists \tilde{x} \geq 0, and\ satisfying\ (7.1),\ (7.2),\ and\ (7.3),\ with\ d\ known\}$; equivalently, in standard variational inequality form:

$$\langle F(X^*), X - X^* \rangle \geq 0, \quad \forall X \in \mathcal{K}, \qquad (7.23b)$$

where $F \equiv C$, $X \equiv \tilde{f}$, and $\mathcal{K} \equiv \mathcal{K}^2$.

Consequently, a flow pattern satisfies equilibrium conditions (7.15) if and only if it satisfies variational inequality (7.23a) or (7.23b).

Note that both (7.16) and (7.23) are finite-dimensional variational inequality problems. Finite-dimensional variational inequality formulations were also obtained by Nagurney (2000d) for her bicriteria fixed demand traffic network equilibrium model in which the weights were fixed and only class-dependent. Nagurney and Dong (2000), in turn, formulated an elastic demand traffic network problem as a finite-dimensional variational inequality problem with two criteria and weights which were fixed but class- and link-dependent. The first use of a finite-dimensional variational inequality formulation of a multicriteria network equilibrium problem is due to Leurent (1993b), who, however, only allowed one of the two criteria to be flow-dependent. Moreover, although his model was an elastic demand model, the demand functions were separable and not class-dependent as are ours.

7.2   Qualitative Properties

We now derive some qualitative properties of the solutions to variational inequalities (7.16) and (7.23), in particular, existence and uniqueness results. We first present the existence results and then the uniqueness results. Subsequently, some of the properties of the functions that enter the variational inequality problems (7.16b) and (7.23b) are presented, which will be needed to establish convergence of the algorithmic scheme in Section 7.4.

We first consider the variational inequality (7.23) governing the fixed demand model. Noting that the feasible set $\mathcal{K}^2$ is compact and that the function C is assumed to be continuous, one has, immediately, from the standard theory of variational inequalities (see Theorem B.2 in Appendix B), the following existence result.

Theorem 7.3 Existence of an Equilibrium in the Case of the Fixed Demand Model

Let C_{ha} be given continuous functions as in (7.4), for all links $a \in \mathcal{L}$ and for all criteria h. Also, let the weights w_{ha}^i and the generalized link cost functions be as defined in Definition 7.1 for all a, h, and i. Then, variational inequality (7.23a) (equivalently, (7.23b)) has at least one solution.

In the case of the elastic demand model, however, the feasible set $\mathcal{K}^1$ is no longer compact (that is, closed and bounded) as $\mathcal{K}^2$ is in the case of the fixed demand model. Nevertheless, one can impose the following conditions, under which the existence of a solution to variational inequality (7.16a) will be guaranteed. The conditions are generalizations of those used by Dafermos (1986) and Nagurney and Dong (2000) to establish existence in their elastic demand models. See also Theorem B.3.

In particular, let C_{ha} be given continuous criterion functions for all h and a with the following properties: There exist positive numbers $\hat{C}$ and k_2, such that

$$C_{ha}(f) \geq \hat{C}, \quad \forall a, h, \quad \forall f \in \mathcal{K}^1, \tag{7.24}$$

$$\lambda_\omega^i(d) < k_1, \quad \forall i, \forall \omega, \quad \text{with} \quad d_\omega^i \geq k_2, \tag{7.25}$$

where $k_1 = \min_{h,i,a} w_{ha}^i \hat{C} \geq 0$.
Thus, one has that

$$C_a^i(\tilde{f}) \geq k_1, \quad \forall a, \forall \omega, \forall i, \quad \forall f \in \mathcal{K}^1. \tag{7.26}$$

Condition (7.24) assumes only that the fixed parts of the criterion functions are not zero. Condition (7.25), in turn, assumes that the inverse demands would not be too large.

Referring now to Nagurney (1999) and to Dafermos (1986) (see also Nagurney and Dong (2000)), and the references therein, the following result can be immediately presented.

Theorem 7.4: Existence of an Equilibrium for the Model with Elastic Demand

Let C_{ha}, for all links a and for all criteria h, and λ be given continuous functions satisfying conditions (7.24) through (7.26). Then, variational inequality (7.16a) (equivalently (7.16b)) has at least one solution.

We now turn to examining uniqueness for both models. Although one cannot expect uniqueness of an equilibrium multiclass link flow pattern to hold, in general, one can, nevertheless, show, in a special case of the above model(s), uniqueness not of the vector of class link flows $\tilde{f}^*$ but, rather, of the total link flows f^*. Indeed, one of the challenges posed by the qualitative analysis of multicriteria network equilibrium problems is that if certain conditions (such as monotonicity or strict monotonicity) are imposed on the criteria functions (7.4), that does not ensure that the generalized link cost functions, which are of the form (7.9) and (7.10), retain such properties.

Specifically, consider now a generalized link cost function for each class i and each link a of the special form:

$$C_a^i = w_{1a}^i C_{1a} + w_{2a}^i C_{2a} + \ldots + w_{H-1}^i C_{(H-1)a} + (1 - \sum_{h=1}^{H-1} w_{ha}^i) C_{Ha}, \quad \forall a, \forall i,$$

(7.27)

where $w_{ha}^i > 0$, for each h, a, i. Assume that each criterion function, in turn, is of the form:

$$C_{ha} = g_a(f) + g_{ha}, \quad \forall a \in \mathcal{L}, \forall h.$$

(7.28)

Note that (7.28) implies that criteria differ from one another by their fixed terms, whereas (7.27) states that the weights for a given link and class associated with the criteria sum up to one.

Assume now that the column vector of g_a functions, denoted by g, is strictly monotone, that is,

$$\langle g(f^1) - g(f^2), f^1 - f^2 \rangle > 0, \quad \forall f^1, f^2 \in \mathcal{K}^1, \quad f^1 \neq f^2.$$

(7.29)

Also, assume that the inverse demand function λ is strictly monotone decreasing, that is,

$$-\langle \lambda(d^1) - \lambda(d^2), d^1 - d^2 \rangle > 0, \quad \forall d^1, d^2 \in \mathcal{K}^1, \quad d^1 \neq d^2.$$

(7.30)

Thus, we have the following:

Theorem 7.5: Uniqueness of the Equilibrium Total Link Flow and Demand Pattern for the Elastic Demand Model in a Special Case
The total link flow pattern f^* induced by a solution $\tilde{f}^*$ to variational inequality (7.16a) in the case of generalized link cost functions C of the form (7.27) and (7.28), and the demand pattern d^* are guaranteed to be unique if g satisfies condition (7.29) and λ satisfies condition (7.30), $\forall i, a,$ and ω.

Proof: Assume that there are two solutions to variational inequality (7.16a) given by $(\tilde{f}', d')$ and $(\tilde{f}'', d'')$. Denote the total link flow patterns induced by these class patterns through (7.2) by f' and f'', respectively. Then, since $(\tilde{f}', d')$ is assumed to be a solution, one must have that

$$\sum_{i=1}^{k} \sum_{a \in \mathcal{L}} [w_{1a}^i(g_a(f') + c_{1a}) + w_{2a}^i(g_a(f') + c_{2a}) + \ldots$$

$$+ (1 - \sum_{h=1}^{H-1} w_{ha}^i)(g_a(f') + c_{Ha})] \times [f_a^i - f_a^{i\prime}]$$

$$- \sum_{i=1}^{k} \sum_{\omega \in \Omega} \lambda_\omega^i(d') \times (d_\omega^i - d_\omega^{i\prime}) \geq 0, \quad \forall (\tilde{f}, d) \in \mathcal{K}^1.$$

(7.31)

Similarly, since $(\tilde{f}'', d'')$ is also assumed to be a solution one must have that

$$\sum_{i=1}^{k}\sum_{a\in\mathcal{L}}\Big[w_{1a}^{i}(g_a(f'')+c_{1a})+w_{2a}^{i}(g_a(f'')+c_{2a})+\ldots$$

$$+(1-\sum_{h=1}^{H-1}w_{ha}^{i})(g_a(f'')+c_{Ha})\Big]\times[f_a^i-f_a^{i''}]$$

$$-\sum_{i=1}^{k}\sum_{\omega\in\Omega}\lambda_\omega^i(d'')\times(d_\omega^i-d_\omega^{i''})\ge 0,\quad\forall(\tilde{f},d)\in\mathcal{K}^1.\qquad(7.32)$$

Let $(\tilde{f}, d) = (\tilde{f}'', d'')$ and substitute into (7.31). Similarly, let $(\tilde{f}, d) = (\tilde{f}', d')$ and substitute into (7.32). Adding the two resulting inequalities, after algebraic simplifications, yields

$$\sum_{a\in\mathcal{L}}(g_a(f')-g_a(f''))\times(f_a'-f_a'')-\sum_{i=1}^{k}\sum_{\omega\in\Omega}(\lambda_\omega^i(d')-\lambda_\omega^i(d''))\times(d_\omega^{i'}-d_\omega^{i''})\le 0,$$

$$(7.33)$$

which is in contradiction to the assumption that g is strictly monotone increasing and that λ is strictly monotone decreasing. Thus, we must have that $(f', d') = (f'', d'')$. $\square$

Note that, given the proof of Theorem 7.5, one can immediately obtain the analogous uniqueness result for the fixed demand model governed by variational inequality (7.16a). Indeed, we now state the following corollary.

Corollary 7.1: Uniqueness of the Equilibrium Total Link Flow Pattern for the Fixed Demand Model in a Special Case
The total link flow pattern f^* induced by a solution $\tilde{f}^*$ to variational inequality (7.23a) in the case of generalized link cost functions C of the form (7.27) and (7.28) is guaranteed to be unique if g satisfies condition (7.29).

In addition, now the monotonicity property, as well as Lipschitz continuity, are derived. These properties will be used in establishing convergence of the algorithm in Section 7.4.

Theorem 7.6: Monotonicity for the Elastic Demand Model in the Special Case
Assume that the generalized cost functions C are as in (7.27) with the criteria functions differing on a given link only by the fixed cost terms as in (7.28). Assume that g is monotone increasing in f and that the inverse demand function is monotone decreasing, that is, that

$$-\langle\lambda(d^1)-\lambda(d^2), d^1-d^2\rangle\ge 0,\quad\forall d^1, d^2\in\mathcal{K}^1.$$

Then the function that enters the variational inequality problem (7.16b) governing the multiclass, multicriteria network equilibrium model with inverse demand functions is monotone.

Proof: One needs to establish that

$$\langle F(X^1) - F(X^2), X^1 - X^2 \rangle \geq 0, \quad \forall X^1, X^2 \in \mathcal{K}, \qquad (7.34)$$

where F, X, and $\mathcal{K}$ are as defined following (7.16b) and with C given by (7.27) and (7.28).

We have that

$$\langle F(X^1) - F(X^2), X^1 - X^2 \rangle$$

$$= \sum_{i=1}^{k} \sum_{a \in \mathcal{L}} \left[\left[w_{1a}^i (g_a(f^1) + c_{1a}) + w_{2a}^i (g_a(f^1) + c_{2a}) + \cdots \right.\right.$$

$$+ (1 - \sum_{h=1}^{H-1} w_{ha}^i)(g_a(f^1) + c_{Ha}) \Big]$$

$$- \left[w_{1a}^i (g_a(f^2) + c_{1a}) + w_{2a}^i (g_a(f^2) + c_{2a}) + \cdots \right.$$

$$\left.\left. + (1 - \sum_{h=1}^{H-1} w_{ha}^i)(g_a(f^2) + c_{Ha}) \right] \right] \times [f_a^{i1} - f_a^{i2}]$$

$$- \sum_{i=1}^{k} \sum_{w \in \Omega} (\lambda_w^i(d^1) - \lambda_w^i(d^2)) \times (d_w^{i1} - d_w^{i2}). \qquad (7.35)$$

But (7.35) is greater than or equal to zero, under the assumptions above (see also proof of Theorem 7.5), and, therefore, $F(X)$ is monotone. □

One may obtained the analogous result for the fixed demand model, using the same arguments as in the preceding proof but excluding the inverse demand function arguments. Indeed, we have:

Corollary 7.2: Monotonicity for the Fixed Demand Model in the Special Case
Assume that the generalized cost functions C are as in (7.27) with the criteria functions differing on a given link only by the fixed cost terms as in (7.28). Assume that g is monotone increasing in f. Then the function that enters the variational inequality problem (7.23b) governing the multiclass, multicriteria network equilibrium model with fixed demands is monotone.

The Lipschitz continuity result for the elastic demand model is now established.

Theorem 7.7: Lipschitz Continuity of F for the Elastic Demand Model
If the generalized link cost functions C and the inverse demand functions λ have bounded first-order derivatives, then the function $F(X)$ that enters the variational inequality (7.16b) is Lipschitz continuous, that is, there exists a positive constant L, such that

$$\|F(X^1) - F(X^2)\| \leq L\|X^1 - X^2\|, \quad \forall X^1, X^2 \in \mathcal{K}, \qquad (7.36)$$

where $\mathcal{K} = \mathcal{K}^1$.

Proof: Denote $F(X) = (F_1(X), \cdots, F_{kn+kJ}(X))^T$. Since $F_l(X) : R^{kn+kJ} \mapsto R^1$ is a smooth function, from the Taylor Theorem, one has that, for any $X^1, X^2 \in \mathcal{K}$, there exist $\xi_l \in R^{kn+kJ}$; $l = 1, \cdots, kn + kJ$, such that

$$F_l(X^1) - F_l(X^2) = \nabla F_l(\xi_l)(X^1 - X^2), \qquad l = 1, \cdots, kn + kJ. \qquad (7.37)$$

Let

$$\nabla F \equiv \begin{pmatrix} \nabla F_1(\xi_1) & & & & \\ & \ddots & & & \\ & & \nabla F_l(\xi_l) & & \\ & & & \ddots & \\ & & & & \nabla F_{kn+kJ}(\xi_{kn+kJ}) \end{pmatrix} \qquad (7.38)$$

Since the generalized link cost functions and the inverse demand functions have bounded first-order derivatives, there exists an $L \geq 0$, such that

$$\|\nabla F\| \leq L. \qquad (7.39)$$

Therefore, using (7.38) and the basic properties of the linear norm operator, one has the following:

$$\|F(X^1) - F(X^2)\| = \left\| \begin{pmatrix} \nabla F_1(\xi_1)(X^1 - X^2) \\ \nabla F_2(\xi_2)(X^1 - X^2) \\ \vdots \\ \nabla F_l(\xi_l)(X^1 - X^2) \\ \vdots \\ \nabla F_{kn+kJ}(\xi_{kn+kJ})(X^1 - X^2) \end{pmatrix} \right\|$$

$$= \|\nabla F(X^1 - X^2)\| \leq \|\nabla F\| \times \|X^1 - X^2\|. \qquad (7.40)$$

In view of (7.39), one can conclude that

$$\|F(X^1) - F(X^2)\| \leq L\|X^1 - X^2\|, \qquad \forall X^1, X^2 \in \mathcal{K}^1. \qquad (7.41)$$

$\square$

Using similar arguments as in the proof of Theorem 7.7 one can establish Lipschitz continuity of the function F governing the fixed demand model governed by variational inequality (7.23b).

Corollary 7.3: Lipschitz Continuity of F for the Fixed Demand Model

If the generalized link cost functions C have bounded first-order derivatives, then the function, $F(X)$, that enters the variational inequality (7.23b) is Lipschitz continuous, that is, there exists a positive constant L, such that

$$\|F(X^1) - F(X^2)\| \leq L\|X^1 - X^2\|, \quad \forall X^1, X^2 \in \mathcal{K}, \qquad (7.42)$$

where $\mathcal{K} = \mathcal{K}^2$.

7.3   Applications

In this section, two applications of the multiclass, multicriteria network equilibrium framework are presented. In Section 7.3.1, the fixed demand multicriteria network equilibrium model is applied to telecommuting versus commuting, whereas in Section 7.3.2, the elastic demand model is applied to teleshopping versus shopping.

7.3.1   Modeling Telecommuting versus Commuting Decision-Making

In this subsection, the fixed demand model is applied to telecommuting versus commuting decision-making. According to Hu and Young (1996), person-trips and person-miles of commuting increased between 1990 and 1995, both in absolute terms and as a share of all personal travel. Constituting 18 percent of all person-trips and 22 percent of all person-miles in 1995, commuting is the single most common trip purpose. Furthermore, as argued by Mokhtarian (1998) (see also Mokhtarian (1991)), it is very likely that a greater proportion of commute trips rather than other types of trips will be amenable to substitution through telecommunications. Consequently, telecommuting most likely has the highest potential for travel reduction of any of the telecommunication applications. Therefore, the study of telecommuting and its impacts is a subject worthy of continued interest and research. Furthermore, recent legislation that allows federal employees to select telecommuting as an option (see United States (2000)), underscores the practical importance of this topic.

The decision-makers in the context of this application are travelers, who seek to determine their *optimal* routes of travel from their origins, which are residences, to their destinations, which are their places of work.

Note that, in the supernetwork framework, a link may correspond to an actual physical link of transportation or an abstract or virtual link corresponding to a telecommuting link. Furthermore, the supernetwork representing the problem under study can be as general as necessary and a path may also consist of a set of links corresponding to physical and virtual transportation choices such as would occur if a worker were to commute to a work

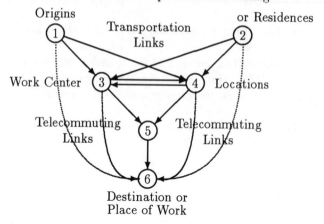

Fig. 7.1. A Conceptualization of Commuting versus Telecommuting

center from which she could then telecommute. In Figure 7.1, a conceptualization of this idea is provided.

Observe that, in Figure 7.1, nodes 1 and 2 represent locations of residences, whereas node 6 denotes the place of work. Work centers from which workers can telecommute are located at nodes 3 and 4 which also serve as intermediate nodes for transportation routes to work. The links: $(1,6)$, $(3,6)$, $(4,6)$, and $(2,6)$ are telecommunication links depicting virtual transportation to work via telecommuting, whereas all other links are physical links associated with commuting. Hence, the paths $(1,6)$ and $(2,6)$ consisting, respectively, of the individual single links represent "going to work" virtually whereas the paths consisting of the links $(1,3)$, $(3,6)$ and $(2,4)$, $(4,6)$ represent first commuting to the work centers located at nodes 3 and 4, from which the workers then telecommute. Finally, the remaining paths represent the commuting options for the residents at nodes 1 and 2. The conventional travel paths from node 1 to node 6 are as follows: $(1,3)$, $(3,5)$, $(5,6)$; $(1,3)$, $(3,4)$, $(4,5)$, $(5,6)$; $(1,4)$, $(4,5)$, $(5,6)$, and $(1,4)$, $(4,3)$, $(3,5)$, $(5,6)$. Note that there may be as many classes of users of this network as there are groups who perceive the trade-offs among the criteria in a similar fashion.

Of course, the network depicted in Figure 7.1 is illustrative, and the actual network can be much more complex with numerous paths depicting the physical transportation choices from one's residence to one's work location. Similarly, one can further complexify the telecommunication link/path options. Also, we emphasize, that a *path* within this framework is sufficiently general to also capture a choice of mode, which, in the case of transportation, could correspond to buses, trains, or subways (that is, public transit) and, of course, to the use of cars (i.e., private vehicles) (see also Chapter 3). Similarly, the concept of path can be used to represent a distinct telecommunications option.

In the model, since the decision-makers are travelers, the path flows and link flows by class would correspond, respectively, to the number of travelers of the class selecting a particular path and link. Hence, the conservation of flow equations (7.1) and (7.2) would apply and since we have assumed a fixed demand model (of course, one could also consider an elastic demand version, which would have location choice implications), the expression (7.3) must also be satisfied, with the travel demand d_ω^i associated with class i traveling between origin/destination pair ω assumed known and given.

The Criteria

We now turn to a discussion of the criteria, which one can expect to be reasonable in the context of decision-making in this particular application. Recall that the first multicriteria traffic network models, due to Schneider (1968) and Quandt (1967), considered two criteria and these were travel time and travel cost. Of course, telecommuting was not truly an option in those days. Dafermos (1981), Leurent (1993a, b), Marcotte (1998), as well as Nagurney (2000d) also considered those two criteria. Nagurney, Dong, and Mokhtarian (2000), in turn, focused on the development of an integrated multicriteria network equilibrium model, which was the first to consider telecommuting versus commuting trade-offs. They considered three criteria: travel time, travel cost, and an opportunity cost to trade-off the opportunity cost associated with not being physically able to interact with colleagues. Here, a fourth criterion is proposed, that of safety. Note, however, that the network equilibrium model with fixed demands in Section 7.1 can actually handle any number of criteria, provided that the number is finite.

Hence, consider the four criteria, given by (7.5) through (7.8), and representing, respectively, travel time, travel cost, the opportunity cost, and safety cost. Consider a generalized link cost for each class given by (7.9). Thus, the generalized cost on a path as perceived by a class of traveler is given by (7.12).

The behavioral assumption is that travelers of a particular class are assumed to choose the paths associated with their origin/destination pair so that the generalized cost on that path is minimal. An equilibrium is assumed to be reached when the multicriteria network equilibrium conditions (7.15) are satisfied. Hence, only those paths connecting an O/D pair are utilized such that the generalized costs on the paths, as perceived by a class, are equal and minimal. The governing variational inequality for this problem is given by (7.23a); equivalently, by (7.23b), and with the existence result following from Theorem 7.2 and the uniqueness result from Corollary 7.1.

7.3.2   Modeling Teleshopping versus Shopping Decision-Making

In this subsection, a multicriteria network equilibrium model for teleshopping versus shopping is proposed. The model generalizes the model proposed in

Nagurney, Dong, and Mokhtarian (2001a) to the case of elastic demands. Furthermore, destinations, which will now correspond to locations where the product is received, need not necessarily correspond to the same origin at which the shopping experience was initiated. Moreover, the number of origins to be distinct from the number of destinations.

Although there is now a growing body of transportation literature on telecommuting (cf. Mokhtarian (1998)), the topic of teleshopping, which is a newer concept, has received less attention to date. In particular, shopping refers to a set of activities in which consumers seek and obtain information about products and/or services, conduct a transaction transferring ownership or right to use, and spatially relocate the product or service to the new owner (Mokhtarian and Salomon (2002)). Teleshopping, in turn, refers to a case in which one or more of those activities is conducted through the use of telecommunication technologies. Today, much attention is focused on the Internet as the technology of interest, and Internet-based shopping is, indeed, increasing. In this setting, teleshopping represents the consumer's role in B2C electronic commerce. Although the model is in the context of Internet-based shopping, the model can apply more broadly.

Note that outside the work of Nagurney, Dong, and Mokhtarian (2001a), there has been essentially no study of the transportation impacts of teleshopping beyond speculation (e.g., Gould (1998), Mokhtarian and Salomon (2002)).

Assume that consumers are engaged in the purchase of a product which they do so in a repetitive fashion, say, on a weekly basis. The product may consist of a single good, such as a book, or a bundle of goods, such as food. Assume also that there are locations, both virtual and physical, where the consumers can obtain information about the product. The virtual locations are accessed through telecommunications via the Internet whereas the physical locations represent more classical shopping venues such as stores and require physical travel to reach.

The consumers may order/purchase the product, once they have selected the appropriate location, be it virtual or physical, with the former requiring shipment to the consumers' locations and the latter requiring, after the physical purchase, transportation of the consumer with the product to its final destination (which we expect, typically, to be his residence or, perhaps, place of work).

Refer to the network conceptualization of the problem given in Figure 7.2. We now identify the above concepts with the corresponding network component. The idea of such a shopping network was proposed in Nagurney, Dong, and Mokhtarian (2001a). Here, several generalizations are given.

Observe that the network depicted in Figure 7.2 consists of four levels of nodes with the first (top) level and the last (bottom) level corresponding to the locations (destinations) of the consumers involved in the purchase of the product. There are a total of $m + 2N + M$ nodes in the network with the number of consumer locations (origins) given by m and the number of

Locations of Consumers/Shoppers Before Shopping Experience

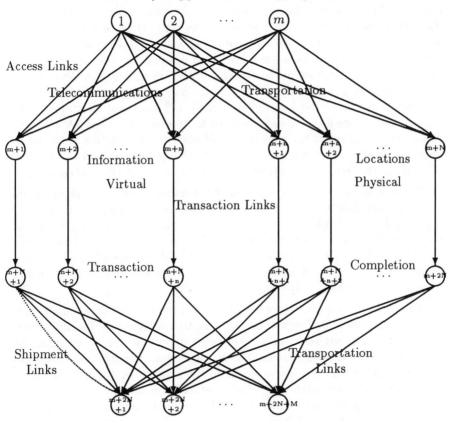

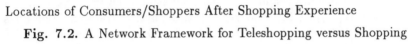

Locations of Consumers/Shoppers After Shopping Experience

Fig. 7.2. A Network Framework for Teleshopping versus Shopping

information locations given by N where N also corresponds to the number of shopping sites. The number of consumer locations associated with the destinations is given by M. Denote the consumer location nodes (before the shopping experience) at the top level of nodes by: $1, \ldots, m$, with a typical such node denoted by j. We emphasize that each location may have many consumers. The second level of nodes, in turn, corresponds to the information locations (and where the transactions also take place), with nodes $m + 1, \ldots, m + n$ representing the virtual or Internet-based locations; and nodes $m + n + 1, \ldots, m + N$ denoting the physical locations of information corresponding to stores, for example. Such a typical node is denoted by κ. The third level of nodes corresponds to the completion of the transaction with nodes $m + N + 1, \ldots, m + N + n$ corresponding to Internet sites where the product could have been purchased (and where it has been assumed that information has also been made available in the previous level of nodes); and nodes $m + N + n + 1, \ldots, m + 2N$ corresponding to the completion of the transaction at the physical stores. A typical such node is denoted by l. The bottom level of the nodes are enumerated as $m + 2N + 1, \ldots m + 2N + M$ and denote the locations of the consumers following the completion of the shopping experience. Note that we have, for flexibility purposes, let the number of nodes in the top level be distinct from the number at the bottom level.

We now discuss the links connecting the nodes in the network in Figure 7.2. There are four sets of links in the network. A typical link (j, κ) connecting a top level node (consumers' location) j to an information node κ at the second level corresponds to an *access* link for information. The links terminating in nodes $m + 1, \ldots, m + n$ of the second level correspond to telecommunication access links; and the links terminating in nodes $m + n + 1, \ldots, m + N$ correspond to (aggregated) transportation links.

As can be seen from Figure 7.2, from each second tier node κ there emanates a link to a node l, which corresponds to a completion of a transaction node. The first mn such links correspond to virtual orders, whereas the subsequent links denote physical orders/purchases. Finally, there are links emanating from the transaction nodes to the consumers' (final) destination nodes, with the links emanating from transaction nodes $m + N + 1, \ldots, m + N + n$ denoting shipment links (since the product, once ordered, must be shipped to the consumer); and the links emanating from transaction nodes $m + N + n + 1, \ldots, m + 2N + M$ representing physical transportation links to the consumers' destinations. Note that, in the case of the latter links, the consumers (after purchasing the product) transport it with themselves, whereas in the former case, the product is shipped to the consumers. Observe that in the supernetwork framework, we explicitly allow for alternative modes of shipping the product which is represented by an additional link (or links) connecting a virtual transaction node with the consumers' location.

The above network construction captures the *electronic dissemination* of goods (such as books or music, for example) in that an alternative shipment link in the bottom tier of links may correspond to the virtual or electronic shipment of the product.

Having fixed the above ideas we are now ready to present the notation which will allow us to clarify the costs, demands, and flows on the network. In addition, the behavior of the shoppers, who are assumed to be multicriteria decision-makers, is described. Recall that, as mentioned earlier, the shoppers can now shop from work and have their purchase delivered either to their work or to their home location.

An origin/destination pair in this network corresponds to a pair of nodes from the top tier in Figure 7.2 to the bottom tier. In the shopping network framework, a path consists of a sequence of choices made by a consumer. For example, the path consisting of the links $(1, m+1), (m+1, m+N+1), (m+N+1, m+2N+1)$ would correspond to consumers at location 1 accessing virtual location $m + 1$ through telecommunications, placing an order at the site for the product, and having it shipped to them. The path consisting of the links $(m, m + N)$, $(m + N, m + 2N)$, and $(m + 2N, m + 2N + M)$, on the other hand, could reflect that consumers at location m (which could be a work location or home) drove to the store at location $m + N$, obtained the information there concerning the product, completed the transaction, and then drove to node M. Note that a path represents a sequence of possible options for the consumers. The flows, in turn, reflect *how many* consumers of a particular class actually select the particular paths and links, with a zero flow on a path corresponding to the situation that no consumer elects to choose that particular sequence of links.

The conservation of flow equations associated with the different classes of shoppers are given by (7.1), (7.2), and (7.3).

The Criteria

The criteria that, it is reasonable to assume, are relevant to decision-making in this application are: time, cost, opportunity cost, and safety or security risk, that is, (7.5) through (7.8), where, in contrast to the telecommuting application time need not be restricted simply to *travel* time and, depending on the associated link, may include transaction time. In addition, the cost is not exclusively a travel cost but depends on the associated link and can include the transaction cost as well as the product price, or shipment cost. Moreover, the opportunity cost now arises when shoppers on the Internet cannot have the physical experience of trying the good or the actual sociableness of the shopping experience itself. Finally, the safety or security risk cost now can reflect not only the danger of certain physical transportation links but also the potential of credit card fraud, etc.

For example, an article in *The Economist* (2000b), on page 11, notes that "websites are not much good for replicating the social functions of shopping" and that "consumers are often advised against giving their credit-card numbers freely over the Internet, and this remains one of the most-cited reasons for not buying things online."

Assuming weights for each class, link, and criterion, a generalized link cost for each class and link is given by (7.9). The generalized path cost for a class of consumer is given by (7.12).

Also, assume, as given, the inverse demand functions which reflect the "price" that the consumers of each class and O/D pair are willing to pay for the shopping experience as functions of demand. Hence, assume inverse demand functions of the form (7.13).

The behavioral assumption is that consumers of a particular class are assumed to choose the paths associated with an O/D pair so that their generalized path costs are minimal. An equilibrium, hence, in the elastic demand model must satisfy conditions (7.14), which also require that if there is positive demand for a class and O/D pair, then the minimum generalized path cost is equal to the inverse demand for that class and O/D pair. The governing variational inequality is given by (7.16a); equivalently, (7.16b). The existence result appears in Theorem 7.4, and the uniqueness result in Theorem 7.5.

Before we present the algorithm it is worthwhile to note what kinds of products (and services) "sell well" electronically. In Chapter 6, we already mentioned that financial brokerages in 1999 were forecast to have online transactions values at just under $6 billion in the United States. According to the Boston Consulting Group, as cited in *The Economist* (2000b), computer hardware/software represents the largest segment with approximately $7.5 billion in transactions forecast in 1999 in the US; travel represents the second largest segment with only a slightly lower value in transactions; collectibles the fourth largest segment with approximately $5.5 billion; music/video the fifth largest segment, with approximately $1.75 billion, with books at about $1.5 billion. As noted therein, several of these "products" can be delivered over the Internet, notably, computer software, and, increasingly, airline tickets, and, as already mentioned, stockbroking services, as well as banking and insurance. Of course, books and newspapers are also being delivered in digitized form, when desired by the consumers.

7.4   The Algorithm

In this section, we show the realization of the modified projection method of Korpelevich (1977) for the solution of variational inequality problem (7.16a) and (7.23a). The modified projection method was also used in the computation of the supply chain network problems in Chapter 4, where, of course, the induced subproblems were different than those that occur below for multicriteria network equilibrium problems. Convergence results are also provided.

Modified Projection Method for the Solution of Variational Inequality (7.16a)

Step 0: Initialization

Set $(\tilde{f}^0, d^0) \in \mathcal{K}^1$. Let $\mathcal{T} = 1$, where $\mathcal{T}$ denotes an iteration and set α such that $0 < \alpha \le \frac{1}{L}$, where L is the Lipschitz constant for the problem (see (7.36)).

Step 1: Computation

Compute $(\bar{\tilde{f}}^{\mathcal{T}}, \bar{d}^{\mathcal{T}}) \in \mathcal{K}^1$ by solving the variational inequality subproblem:

$$\sum_{i=1}^{k} \sum_{a \in \mathcal{L}} (\bar{f}_a^{i\,\mathcal{T}} + \alpha C_a^i(\tilde{f}^{\mathcal{T}-1}) - f_a^{i\,\mathcal{T}-1}) \times (f_a^i - \bar{f}_a^{i\,\mathcal{T}})$$

$$+ \sum_{i=1}^{k} \sum_{\omega \in \Omega} (\bar{d}_\omega^{i\,\mathcal{T}} - \alpha \lambda_\omega^i(d^{\mathcal{T}-1}) - d_\omega^{i\,\mathcal{T}-1}) \times (d_\omega^i - \bar{d}_\omega^{i\,\mathcal{T}}) \ge 0, \quad \forall (\tilde{f}, d) \in \mathcal{K}^1.$$

$$(7.43)$$

Step 2: Adaptation

Compute $(\tilde{f}^{\mathcal{T}}, d^{\mathcal{T}}) \in \mathcal{K}^1$ by solving the variational inequality subproblem:

$$\sum_{i=1}^{k} \sum_{a \in \mathcal{L}} (f_a^{i\,\mathcal{T}} + \alpha C_a^i(\bar{\tilde{f}}^{\mathcal{T}}) - f_a^{i\,\mathcal{T}-1}) \times (f_a^i - f_a^{i\,\mathcal{T}})$$

$$+ \sum_{i=1}^{k} \sum_{\omega \in \Omega} (d_\omega^{i\,\mathcal{T}} - \alpha \lambda_\omega^i(\bar{d}^{\mathcal{T}}) - d_\omega^{i\,\mathcal{T}-1}) \times (d_\omega^i - d_\omega^{i\,\mathcal{T}}) \ge 0, \quad \forall (\tilde{f}, d) \in \mathcal{K}^1. \quad (7.44)$$

Step 3: Convergence Verification

If $|f_a^{i\,\mathcal{T}} - f_a^{i\,\mathcal{T}-1}| \le \epsilon$, $|d_\omega^{i\,\mathcal{T}} - d_\omega^{i\,\mathcal{T}-1}| \le \epsilon$, for all $i = 1, \cdots, k$; $\omega \in \Omega$, and all $a \in \mathcal{L}$, with $\epsilon > 0$, a pre-specified tolerance, then stop; otherwise, set $\mathcal{T} := \mathcal{T} + 1$, and go to Step 1.

The convergence result for the modified projection method for this model is now stated. Note that the algorithm may converge even for functions of more general form. Indeed, in Section 7.5.2 we apply this algorithm to a teleshopping versus shopping decision-making numerical example in which the functions are more general than those considered in Theorem 7.8. Nevertheless, Theorem 7.8 identifies specific functions for which convergence can be readily established.

Theorem 7.8: Convergence of the Modified Projection Method for the Elastic Demand Model

Assume that C takes the form of (7.27) and (7.28) and that the function g is monotone increasing. Assume that the inverse demand function λ is monotone decreasing. Also assume that C and λ have bounded first-order derivatives. Then the modified projection method described above converges to the solution of the variational inequality (7.16a) (and (7.16b)).

Proof: According to Korpelevich (1977), the modified projection method converges to the solution of the variational inequality problem, provided that the function that enters the variational inequality, F, is monotone and Lipschitz continuous and that a solution exists. Existence of a solution follows from Theorem 7.4. Lipschitz continuity, in turn, follows from Theorem 7.7 under the assumption that the generalized cost functions have bounded first-order derivatives, whereas monotonicity follows from Theorem 7.6. The conclusion follows. □

The realization of the modified projection method for the solution of variational inequality (7.23a) is also provided below, for completeness.

Modified Projection Method for the Solution of Variational Inequality (7.23a)

Step 0: Initialization

Set $\tilde{f}^0 \in \mathcal{K}^2$. Let $\mathcal{T} = 1$ and set α such that $0 < \alpha \leq \frac{1}{L}$, where L is the Lipschitz constant for the problem.

Step 1: Computation

Compute $\bar{\tilde{f}}^{\mathcal{T}} \in \mathcal{K}^2$ by solving the variational inequality subproblem:

$$\sum_{i=1}^{k} \sum_{a \in \mathcal{L}} (\bar{f}_a^{i\,\mathcal{T}} + \alpha C_a^i(\tilde{f}^{\mathcal{T}-1}) - f_a^{i\,\mathcal{T}-1}) \times (f_a^i - \bar{f}_a^{i\,\mathcal{T}}) \geq 0, \quad \forall \tilde{f} \in \mathcal{K}^2. \quad (7.45)$$

Step 2: Adaptation

Compute $\tilde{f}^{\mathcal{T}} \in \mathcal{K}^2$ by solving the variational inequality subproblem:

$$\sum_{i=1}^{k} \sum_{a \in \mathcal{L}} (f_a^{i\,\mathcal{T}} + \alpha C_a^i(\bar{\tilde{f}}^{\mathcal{T}}) - f_a^{i\,\mathcal{T}-1}) \times (f_a^i - f_a^{i\,\mathcal{T}}) \geq 0, \quad \forall \tilde{f} \in \mathcal{K}^2. \quad (7.46)$$

Step 3: Convergence Verification

If $|f_a^{i\,\mathcal{T}} - f_a^{i\,\mathcal{T}-1}| \leq \epsilon$, for all $i = 1, \cdots, k$, and all $a \in \mathcal{L}$, with $\epsilon > 0$, a pre-specified tolerance, then stop; otherwise, set $\mathcal{T} := \mathcal{T} + 1$, and go to Step 1.

Theorem 7.9: Convergence of the Modified Projection Method for the Fixed Demand Model

Assume that C takes the form of (7.27) and (7.28) and is monotone increasing. Also assume that C has bounded first-order derivatives. Then the modified projection method described above converges to the solution of the variational inequality (7.17a) (and (7.17b)).

Proof: Follows from Theorem 7.3 and Corollaries 7.2 and 7.3. □

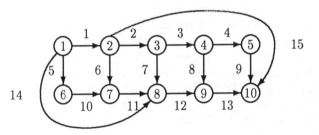

Fig. 7.3. Network Topology for Telecommuting versus Commuting Example

Note that the feasible sets underlying subproblems (7.43), (7.44), and (7.45), (7.46) are networks, of general form, in contrast to the networks of very special and simple structure underlying subproblems (4.45) and (4.46) induced by the modified projection method when applied to the static supply chain network model in Chapter 4. Nevertheless, each of these subproblems is actually a quadratic optimization problem with network structure and, hence, can be solved efficiently using algorithms that exploit this structure. We discuss this further when these algorithms are applied to specific numerical examples in the next section.

7.5 Numerical Examples

In this section, two numerical examples are presented, which illustrate, respectively, the telecommuting versus commuting model with fixed travel demands developed in Section 7.3.1 and the teleshopping versus shopping model with elastic demands described in Section 7.3.2. The numerical example for the former is given in Section 7.5.1, and for the latter, in Section 7.5.2.

Both numerical examples consist of two classes of decision-makers, each of which is faced with four criteria as outlined in the particular subsection. The modified projection method (both for the solution of (7.16a) and (7.23a)) was coded in FORTRAN and implemented on the DEC Alpha system at the University of Massachusetts at Amherst.

7.5.1 A Telecommuting versus Commuting Example

The first numerical example corresponds to the fixed demand model developed in Section 7.3.1, which is governed by variational inequality (7.23a); equivalently, (7.23b). Hence, to compute the equilibrium flow pattern for the problem, the modifed projection method for the solution of variational inequality (7.23a) was applied.

The first numerical example had the topology depicted in Figure 7.3. Links 1 through 13 are transportation links whereas links 14 and 15 are telecommunication links. The network consisted of ten nodes, fifteen links, and two O/D pairs where $\omega_1 = (1,8)$ and $\omega_2 = (2,10)$ with travel demands by class given by: $d^1_{\omega_1} = 10$, $d^1_{\omega_2} = 20$, $d^2_{\omega_1} = 10$, and $d^2_{\omega_2} = 30$. The paths connecting the O/D pairs were: for O/D pair ω_1: $p_1 = (1,2,7)$, $p_2 = (1,6,11)$, $p_3 = (5,10,11)$, $p_4 = (14)$, and for O/D pair ω_2: $p_5 = (2,3,4,9)$, $p_6 = (2,3,8,13)$, $p_7 = (2,7,12,13)$, $p_8 = (6,11,12,13)$, and $p_9 = (15)$. The weights were constructed as follows: For class 1, the weights were: $w^1_{1,1} = .25$, $w^1_{2,1} = .25$, $w^1_{3,1} = 1.$, $w^1_{1,2} = .25$, $w_{2,2} = .25$, $w^1_{3,2} = 1.$, $w^1_{1,3} = .4$, $w^1_{2,3} = .4$, $w^1_{3,3} = 1.$, $w^1_{1,4} = .5$, $w^1_{2,4} = .5$, $w^1_{3,4} = 2.$, $w^1_{1,5} = .4$, $w^1_{2,5} = .5$, $w^1_{3,5} = 1.$, $w^1_{1,6} = .5$, $w^1_{2,6} = .3$, $w^1_{3,6} = 2.$, $w^1_{1,7} = .2$, $w^1_{2,7} = .4$, $w^1_{3,7} = 1.$, $w^1_{1,8} = .3$, $w^1_{2,8} = .5$, $w^1_{3,8} = 1.$, $w^1_{1,9} = .6$, $w^1_{2,9} = .2$, $w^1_{3,9} = 2.$, $w^1_{1,10} = .3$, $w^1_{2,10} = .4$, $w^1_{3,10} = 1.$, $w^1_{1,11} = .2$, $w^1_{2,11} = .7$, $w^1_{3,11} = 1.$, $w^1_{1,12} = .3$, $w^1_{2,12} = .4$, $w^1_{3,12} = 1.$, $w^1_{1,13} = .2$, $w^1_{2,13} = .3$, $w^1_{3,13} = 2.$, $w^1_{1,14} = .5$, $w^1_{2,14} = .2$, $w^1_{3,14} = .1$, $w^1_{1,15} = .5$, $w^1_{2,15} = .3$, $w^1_{3,15} = .1$. All the weights $w^1_{4,a} = .2$ for all links a.

For class 2, the weights were: $w^2_{1,1} = .5$, $w^2_{2,1} = .5$, $w^2_{3,1} = .5$, $w^2_{1,2} = .5$, $w^2_{2,2} = .4$, $w^2_{3,2} = .4$, $w^2_{1,3} = .4$, $w^2_{2,3} = .3$, $w^2_{3,3} = .7$, $w^2_{1,4} = .3$, $w^2_{2,4} = .2$, $w^2_{3,4} = .6$, $w^2_{1,5} = .5$, $w^2_{2,5} = .4$, $w^2_{3,5} = .5$, $w^2_{1,6} = .7$, $w^2_{2,6} = .6$, $w^2_{3,6} = .7$, $w^2_{1,7} = .4$, $w^2_{2,7} = .3$, $w^2_{3,7} = .8$, $w^2_{1,8} = .3$, $w^2_{2,8} = .2$, $w^2_{3,8} = .6$, $w^2_{1,9} = .2$, $w^2_{2,9} = .3$, $w^2_{3,9} = .9$, $w^2_{1,10} = .1$, $w^2_{2,10} = .4$, $w^2_{3,10} = .8$, $w^2_{1,11} = .4$, $w^2_{2,11} = .5$, $w^2_{3,11} = .9$, $w^2_{1,12} = .5$, $w^2_{2,12} = .5$, $w^2_{3,12} = .7$, $w^2_{1,13} = .4$, $w^2_{2,13} = .6$, $w^2_{3,13} = .9$, $w^2_{1,14} = .3$, $w^2_{2,14} = .4$, $w^2_{3,14} = 1.$, $w^2_{1,15} = .2$, $w^2_{2,15} = .3$, $w^2_{3,15} = .2$. All the weights $w^2_{4,a} = .1$ for all links a.

The travel time functions and the travel cost functions for this example are reported in Table 7.2. The opportunity cost functions and the safety cost functions for the links for this example are reported in Table 7.3. The generalized link cost functions were constructed according to (7.9) using the weights given above.

Note that the opportunity costs associated with links 14 and 15 were high since these are telecommunication links and users by choosing these links forego the opportunities associated with working and associating with colleagues from a face to face perspective. Observe, however, that the weights for class 1 associated with the opportunity costs on the telecommunication links are low (relative to those of class 2). This has the interpretation that class 1 does not weight such opportunity costs highly and may, for example, prefer to be working from the home for a variety of reasons, including familial. Also, note that class 1 weights the travel time on the telecommunication links more highly than class 2 does. Furthermore, observe that class 1 weights the safety or security cost higher than class 2.

The convergence criterion was that the maximum of the absolute value of the path flows at two successive iterations was .0001. The modified projection method was initialized by equally distributing the demand for each class and

Table 7.2. The Travel Time and Travel Cost Functions for the Links for the Telecommuting Example

Link a	$t_a(f)$	$c_a(f)$
1	$.00005f_1^4 + 4f_1 + 2f_3 + 2$	$.00005f_1^4 + 5f_1 + 1$
2	$.00003f_2^4 + 2f_2 + f_5 + 1$	$.00003f_2^4 + 4f_2 + 2f_3 + 2$
3	$.00005f_3^4 + f_3 + .5f_2 + 3$	$.00005f_3^4 + 3f_3 + f_1 + 1$
4	$.00003f_4^4 + 7f_4 + 3f_1 + 1$	$.00003f_4^4 + 6f_4 + 2f_6 + 4$
5	$5f_5 + 2$	$4f_5 + 8$
6	$.00007f_6^4 + 3f_6 + f_9 + 4$	$.00007f_6^4 + 7f_6 + 2f_2 + 6$
7	$4f_7 + 6$	$8f_7 + 7$
8	$.00001f_8^4 + 4f_8 + 2f_{10} + 1$	$.00001f_8^4 + 7f_8 + 3f_5 + 6$
9	$2f_9 + 8$	$8f_9 + 5$
10	$.00003f_{10}^4 + 4f_{10} + f_{12} + 7$	$.00003f_{10}^4 + 6f_{10} + 2f_8 + 3$
11	$.00004f_{11}^4 + 6f_{11} + 2f_{13} + 2$	$.00004f_{11}^4 + 4f_{11} + 3f_{10} + 4$
12	$.00002f_{12}^4 + 4f_{12} + 2f_5 + 1$	$.00002f_{12}^4 + 6f_{12} + 2f_9 + 5$
13	$.00003f_{13}^4 + 7f_{13} + 4f_{10} + 8$	$.00003f_{13}^4 + 9f_{13} + 3f_8 + 3$
14	$f_{14} + 2$	$.1f_{14} + 1$
15	$f_{15} + 1$	$.2f_{15} + 1$

Table 7.3. The Opportunity Cost and Safety Cost Functions for the Links for the Telecommuting Example

Link a	$o_a(f)$	$s_a(f)$
1	$2f_1 + 4$	$f_1 + 1$
2	$3f_2 + 2$	$f_2 + 2$
3	$f_3 + 4$	$f_3 + 1$
4	$f_4 + 2$	$f_4 + 2$
5	$2f_5 + 1$	$2f_5 + 2$
6	$f_6 + 2$	$f_6 + 1$
7	$f_7 + 3$	$f_7 + 1$
8	$2f_8 + 1$	$2f_8 + 2$
9	$3f_9 + 2$	$3f_9 + 3$
10	$f_{10} + 1$	$f_{10} + 2$
11	$4f_{11} + 3$	$2f_{11} + 3$
12	$3f_{12} + 2$	$3f_{12} + 3$
13	$f_{13} + 1$	$f_{13} + 2$
14	$6f_{14} + 1$	$.5f_{14} + .1$
15	$7f_{15} + 4$	$.4f_{15} + .1$

Table 7.4. The Equilibrium Link Flows for the Telecommuting Example

Link a	Class 1 - f_a^{1*}	Class 2 - f_a^{2*}	Total flow - f_a^*
1	0.000	0.0000	0.0000
2	0.0000	24.0109	24.0109
3	0.0000	22.7600	22.7600
4	0.0000	17.3356	17.3356
5	0.0000	4.6901	4.6901
6	0.0000	5.9891	5.9891
7	0.0000	1.2509	1.2509
8	0.0000	5.4244	5.4244
9	0.0000	17.3556	17.3556
10	0.0000	4.6901	4.6901
11	0.0000	10.6792	10.6792
12	0.0000	7.2400	7.2400
13	0.0000	12.6644	12.6644
14	10.0000	5.3090	15.3099
15	20.0000	0.0000	20.0000

each O/D pair among the paths for that O/D pair. The parameter α in the modified projection method was set to .001 for this example. The modified projection metod was embedded with the equilibration algorithm of Dafermos and Sparrow (1969) (cf. Appendix C) for the solution of subproblems (7.45) and (7.46), which are equivalent to quadratic programming problems over a feasible set with network structure.

The modified projection method required 12 iterations for convergence. It yielded the equilibrium multiclass link flow and total link flow patterns reported in Table 7.4, which were induced by the equilibrium multiclass path flow pattern given in Table 7.5.

The generalized path costs were: for class 1, O/D pair ω_1:

$$C_{p_1}^1 = 13478.4365, \ C_{p_2}^1 = 11001.0342, \ C_{p_3}^1 = 8354.5420, \ C_{p_4}^1 = 1025.4167,$$

for class 1, O/D pair ω_2:

$$C_{p_5}^1 = 45099.8047, \ C_{p_6}^1 = 27941.5918, \ C_{p_7}^1 = 25109.3223, \ C_{p_8}^1 = 22631.9199,$$

$$C_{p_9}^1 = 2314.7222;$$

for class 2, O/D pair ω_1:

$$C_{p_1}^2 = 15427.5996, \ C_{p_2}^2 = 15427.2021, \ C_{p_3}^2 = 8721.8945, \ C_{p_4}^2 = 8721.3721,$$

and for class 2, O/D pair ω_2:

$$C_{p_5}^2 = 34924.6602, \ C_{p_6}^2 = 34924.6094, \ C_{p_7}^2 = 34925.3789, \ C_{p_8}^2 = 34924.9805,$$

Table 7.5. The Equilibrium Path Flows for the Telecommuting Example

Path p	Class 1 - x_p^{1*}	Class 2 - x_p^{2*}
p_1	0.0000	0.0000
p_2	0.0000	0.0000
p_3	0.0000	4.6901
p_4	10.0000	5.3099
p_5	0.0000	17.3357
p_6	0.0000	5.4244
p_7	0.0000	1.2509
p_8	0.0000	5.9892
p_9	20.0000	0.0000

$$C_{p_9}^2 = 41574.2617.$$

The combination of the modified projection method embedded with the equilibration algorithm for the solution of (7.45) and (7.46) yielded accurate solutions in a timely manner. Indeed, the equilibrium conditions were satisfied with good accuracy.

It is interesting to see the separation by classes in the equilibrium solution. Note that all members of class 1, whether residing at node 1 or node 2, were telecommuters, whereas all members of class 2 chose to commute to work. This outcome is realistic, given the weight assignments of the two classes on the opportunity costs associated with the links (as well as the weight assignments associated with the travel times). Of course, different criteria functions, as well as their numerical forms and associated weights, will lead to different equilibrium patterns.

This example demonstrates the flexibility of the modeling approach. Moreover, it allows one to conduct a variety of "what if" simulations in that one can modify the functions and the associated weights to reflect the particular telecommuting versus commuting scenario. For example, during a downturn in the economy, the opportunity costs associated with the telecommuting links may be high, and, also, different classes may weight this criteria on such links higher, resulting in a new solution. On the other hand, highly skilled employees who are in demand may have lower weights associated with such links in regard to the opportunity costs. This framework is, hence, sufficiently general to capture a variety of realistic situations while, at the same time, allowing decision-makers to identify their specific values and preferences.

7.5.2   A Teleshopping versus Shopping Example

In this subsection, a numerical teleshopping versus shopping example based on the model of Section 7.3.2 is presented, for which the equilibrium flow pattern is computed using the modified projection method described in the preceding section. Specifically, consider a situation in which there are consumers at two locations with the possibility of shopping virtually through telecommunications at two sites and physically at two other sites. Assume that there are two classes of shoppers. The shopping network for the problem is given in Figure 7.4. The network consists of two origin nodes at the top; two destination nodes at the bottom, with two O/D pairs given by: $\omega_1 = (1, 11)$ and $\omega_2 = (2, 12)$.

There is a total of twenty links in the network, where eight links (in the first set) are access links, four links (in the second set) are transaction links, and eight links (in the final set of links) are shipment/transportation links. In the first set of links, four links represent access links to the virtual sites through telecommunications and the remaining four links correspond to access links to the physical sites through transportation. The links have been enumerated in Figure 7.4 for data presentation purposes.

The modified projection method for the solution of variational inequality (7.16a) was implemented in FORTRAN and the Euler method (cf. Nagurney and Zhang (1996) and Appendix C) was embedded for the solution of variational inequality subproblems (7.43) and (7.44).

The convergence criterion was that the absolute value of the path flows at two successive iterations was less than or equal to ϵ with ϵ set to .0001. The α parameter in the modified projection method was set to .001. The demand for the product for each class of consumer was initialized to zero.

Denoting the O/D pairs by $\omega_1 = (1, 11)$ and $\omega_2 = (2, 12)$, the inverse demand functions of the two classes were $\lambda^1_{\omega_1}(d) = -.5d^1_{\omega_1} + 956$, $\lambda^1_{\omega_2}(d) = -.1d^1_{\omega_2} + 920$, and $\lambda^2_{\omega_1}(d) = -.2d^2_{\omega_1} + 580$, $\lambda^2_{\omega_2}(d) = -.1d^2_{\omega_2} + 1050$.

There were four paths connecting each O/D pair. The paths connecting O/D pair ω_1 were $p_1 = (1, 9, 13)$, $p_2 = (2, 10, 15)$, $p_3 = (3, 11, 17)$, and $p_4 = (4, 12, 19)$; whereas the paths connecting O/D pair ω_2 were $p_5 = (5, 9, 14)$, $p_6 = (6, 10, 16)$, $p_7 = (7, 11, 18)$, and $p_8 = (8, 12, 20)$. It was assumed that there were four criteria associated with each link and consisting, respectively, of time (criterion 1), monetary cost (criterion 2), an *opportunity* cost (criterion 3), and a safety or security cost (criterion 4).

The generalized link cost functions were constructed according to (7.9) using the weights given below, the time functions and the cost functions are reported in Table 7.6, and the opportunity and safety cost functions are reported in Table 7.7.

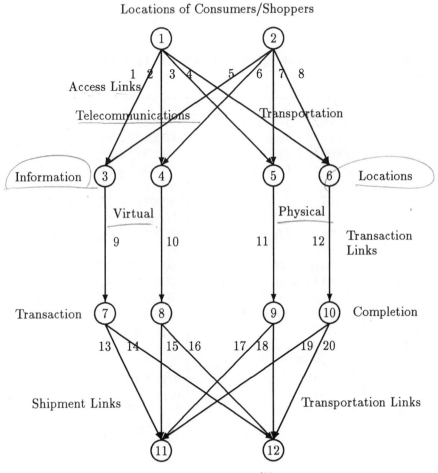

Fig. 7.4. The Network for the Teleshopping versus Shopping Example

Table 7.6. The Time and Cost Functions for the Links for the Teleshopping Example

Link a	$t_a(f)$	$c_a(f)$
1	$.00005f_1^4 + f_1 + f_2 + 5$	$.00005f_1^4 + 2f_1 + f_2 + 1$
2	$.00003f_2^4 + f_2 + .5f_5 + 1$	$.00003f_2^4 + 2f_2 + f_1 + 1$
3	$.00005f_3^4 + 4f_3 + f_4 + 1$	$.00005f_3^4 + 3f_3 + .5f_4 + 3$
4	$.00003f_4^4 + 6f_4 + 2f_5 + 4$	$.00003f_4^4 + 7f_4 + 3f_3 + 1$
5	$f_5 + 1$	$f_5 + 2$
6	$.00007f_6^4 + f_6 + .5f_2 + 1$	$.00007f_6^4 + 2f_6 + f_5 + 1$
7	$8f_7 + 7$	$4f_7 + 6$
8	$.00001f_8^4 + 7f_8 + 3f_5 + 6$	$.00001f_8^4 + 4f_8 + 2f_7 + 1$
9	$2f_9 + 1$	$2f_9 + 1$
10	$.00003f_{10}^4 + 2f_{10} + f_9 + 1$	$.00003f_{10}^4 + 2f_{10} + f_9 + 1$
11	$.00004f_{11}^4 + 2f_{11} + f_{10} + 4$	$.00004f_{11}^4 + 4f_{11} + 2f_{12} + 2$
12	$.00002f_{12}f^4 + 2f_{12} + f_{11} + 2$	$.00002f_{12}^4 + 4f_{12} + 2f_{11} + 1$
13	$.00003f_{13}^4 + 9f_{13} + 3f_{14} + 3$	$.00003f_{13}^4 + 3f_{13} + f_{14} + 2$
14	$5f_{14} + 3$	$4f_{14} + 2$
15	$6f_{15} + 4$	$4f_{15} + 1$
16	$10f_{16} + 10$	$2f_{16} + 10$
17	$5f_{17} + 10$	$5f_{17} + 10$
18	$f_{18} + 20$	$6f_{18} + 20$
19	$6f_{19} + 20$	$5f_{19} + 10$
20	$10f_{20} + 15$	$4f_{20} + 10$

Table 7.7. The Opportunity Cost and Safety Cost Functions for the Links for the Teleshopping Example

Link a	$o_a(f)$	$s_a(f)$
1	$2f_1 + 4$	$f_1 + 1$
2	$3f_2 + 2$	$f_2 + 2$
3	$f_3 + 1$	$f_3 + 1$
4	$f_4 + 1$	$f_4 + 1$
5	$2f_+5$	$f_5 + 1$
6	$3f_6 + 6$	$2f_6 + 1$
7	$f_7 + 1$	$f_7 + 1$
8	$f_8 + 1$	$f_8 + 1$
9	$5f_9 + 12$	$f_9 + 1$
10	$11f_{10} + 11$	$f_{10} + 11$
11	$f_{11} + 1$	$f_{11} + 1$
12	$f_{12} + 1$	$f_{12} + 1$
13	$f_{13} + 11$	$f_{13} + .5$
14	$6f_{14} + 21$	$2f_{14} + 1$
15	$7f_{15} + 14$	$f_{15} + .5$
16	$5f_{16} + 10$	$f_{16} + 1$
17	$f_{17} + 2$	$f_{17} + 1$
18	$2f_{18} + 1$	$f_{18} + 1$
19	$f_{19} + 1$	$f_{19} + 1$
20	$f_{20} + 1$	$f_{20} + 1$

The weights were constructed as follows. For class 1, the weights were:
$w_{1,1}^1 = .25$, $w_{2,1}^1 = .25$, $w_{3,1}^1 = 1.$, $w_{4,1}^1 = .2$ $w_{1,2}^1 = .25$, $w_{2,2}^1 = .25$, $w_{3,2}^1 = 1.$,
$w_{4,2}^1 = .2$, $w_{1,3}^1 = .4$, $w_{2,3}^1 = .4$, $w_{3,3}^1 = 1.$, $w_{4,3}^1 = .1$, $w_{1,4}^1 = .5$, $w_{2,4}^1 = .5$,
$w_{3,4}^1 = 2.$, $w_{4,4}^1 = .1$, $w_{1,5}^1 = .4$, $w_{2,5}^1 = .5$, $w_{3,5}^1 = 1.$, $w_{4,5}^1 = .1$, $w_{1,6}^1 = .5$,
$w_{2,6}^1 = .3$, $w_{3,6}^1 = 2.$, $w_{4,6}^1 = .1$, $w_{1,7}^1 = .2$, $w_{2,7}^1 = .4$, $w_{3,7}^1 = 1.$, $w_{4,7}^1 = .1$,
$w_{1,8}^1 = .3$, $w_{2,8}^1 = .5$, $w_{3,8}^1 = 1.$, $w_{4,8}^1 = .2$, $w_{1,9}^1 = .6$, $w_{2,9}^1 = .2$, $w_{3,9}^1 = 2.$,
$w_{4,9}^1 = .2$, $w_{1,10}^1 = .3$, $w_{2,10}^1 = .4$, $w_{3,10}^1 = 1.$, $w_{4,10}^1 = .3$, $w_{1,11}^1 = .2$, $w_{2,11}^1 = .7$,
$w_{3,11}^1 = 1.$, $w_{4,11}^1 = .3$, $w_{1,12}^1 = .3$, $w_{2,12}^1 = .4$, $w_{3,12}^1 = 1.$, $w_{4,12}^1 = .1$,
$w_{1,13}^1 = .2$, $w_{2,13}^1 = .3$, $w_{3,13}^1 = 2.$, $w_{4,13}^1 = .1$, $w_{1,14}^1 = .5$, $w_{2,14}^1 = .2$,
$w_{3,14}^1 = .1$, $w_{4,14}^1 = .1$, $w_{1,15}^1 = .5$, $w_{2,15}^1 = .3$, $w_{3,15}^1 = .1$, $w_{4,15}^1 = .1$,
$w_{1,16}^1 = 1.$, $w_{2,16}^1 = 1.$, $w_{3,16}^1 = 1.$, $w_{4,16}^1 = .2$, $w_{1,17}^1 = 1.$, $w_{2,17}^1 = 1.$,
$w_{3,17}^1 = 1.$, $w_{4,17}^1 = .2$, $w_{1,18}^1 = 1.$, $w_{2,18}^1 = 1.$, $w_{3,18}^1 = 1.$, $w_{4,18}^1 = .2$,
$w_{1,19}^1 = 1.$, $w_{2,19}^1 = 1.$, $w_{3,19}^1 = 1.$, $w_{4,19}^1 = .3$, $w_{1,20}^1 = 1.$, $w_{2,20}^1 = 1.$,
$w_{3,20}^1 = 1.$, $w_{4,20}^1 = .2$,

For class 2, the weights were: $w_{1,1}^2 = .5$, $w_{2,1}^2 = .5$, $w_{3,1}^2 = .5$, $w_{4,1}^2 = .1$,
$w_{1,2}^2 = .5$, $w_{2,2}^2 = .4$, $w_{3,2}^2 = .4$, $w_{4,2}^2 = .1$, $w_{1,3}^2 = .4$, $w_{2,3}^2 = .3$, $w_{3,3}^2 = .7$,
$w_{4,3}^2 = .1$, $w_{1,4}^2 = .3$, $w_{2,4}^2 = .2$, $w_{3,4}^2 = .6$, $w_{4,4}^2 = .1$, $w_{1,5}^2 = .5$, $w_{2,5}^2 = .4$,
$w_{3,5}^2 = .5$, $w_{4,5}^2 = .2$, $w_{1,6}^2 = .7$, $w_{2,6}^2 = .6$, $w_{3,6}^2 = .7$, $w_{4,6}^2 = .2$, $w_{1,7}^2 = .4$,
$w_{2,7}^2 = .3$, $w_{3,7}^2 = .8$, $w_{4,7}^2 = .1$, $w_{1,8}^2 = .3$, $w_{2,8}^2 = .2$, $w_{3,8}^2 = .6$, $w_{4,8}^2 = .1$,
$w_{1,9}^2 = .2$, $w_{2,9}^2 = .3$, $w_{3,9}^2 = .9$, $w_{4,9}^2 = .4$, $w_{1,10}^2 = .1$, $w_{2,10}^2 = .4$, $w_{3,10}^2 = .8$,
$w_{4,10}^2 = .4$, $w_{1,11}^2 = .4$, $w_{2,11}^2 = .5$, $w_{3,11}^2 = .9$, $w_{4,11}^2 = .3$, $w_{1,12}^2 = .5$,
$w_{2,12}^2 = .5$, $w_{3,12}^2 = .7$, $w_{4,12}^2 = .3$, $w_{1,13}^2 = .4$, $w_{2,13}^2 = .6$, $w_{3,13}^2 = .9$,
$w_{4,13}^2 = .1$, $w_{1,14}^2 = .3$, $w_{2,14}^2 = .4$, $w_{3,14}^2 = 1.$, $w_{4,14}^2 = .1$, $w_{1,15}^2 = .2$,
$w_{2,15}^2 = .3$, $w_{3,15}^2 = .2$, $w_{4,15}^2 = .2$, $w_{1,16}^2 = 1.$, $w_{2,16}^2 = 1.$, $w_{3,16}^2 = 1.$,
$w_{4,16}^2 = .2$, $w_{1,17}^2 = 1.$, $w_{2,17}^2 = 1.$, $w_{3,17}^2 = 1.$, $w_{4,17}^2 = .1$, $w_{1,18}^2 = 1.$,
$w_{2,18}^2 = 1.$, $w_{3,18}^2 = 1.$, $w_{4,18}^2 = .1$, $w_{1,19}^2 = 1.$, $w_{2,19}^2 = 1.$, $w_{3,19}^2 = 1.$,
$w_{4,19}^2 = .1$, $w_{1,20}^2 = 1.$, $w_{2,20}^2 = 1.$, $w_{3,20}^2 = 1.$, $w_{4,20}^2 = .1$.

The modified projection method converged in 93 iterations. It yielded the multiclass link flow and total flow pattern reported in Table 7.8. The equilibrium path flows, in turn, were as reported in Table 7.9.

The incurred generalized path costs were:
for class 1, O/D pair ω_1:

$$C_{p_1}^1 = 1099.8754, \quad C_{p_2}^1 = 950.3034, \quad C_{p_3}^1 = 963.5551, \quad C_{p_4}^1 = 975.1231,$$

for class 1, O/D pair ω_2:

$$C_{p_5}^1 = 920.8164, \quad C_{p_6}^1 = 1216.0173, \quad C_{p_7}^1 = 1047.4919, \quad C_{p_8}^1 = 1114.4659,$$

for class 2, O/D pair ω_1:

$$C_{p_1}^2 = 579.2358, \quad C_{p_2}^2 = 1795.4930, \quad C_{p_3}^2 = 970.5146, \quad C_{p_4}^2 = 947.5757,$$

and for class 2, O/D pair ω_2:

$$C_{p_5}^2 = 1144.5128, \quad C_{p_6}^2 = 1043.4633, \quad C_{p_7}^2 = 1067.9226, \quad C_{p_8}^2 = 1063.9229.$$

Table 7.8. The Equilibrium Link Flows for the Teleshopping Example

Link a	Class 1 - f_a^{1*}	Class 2 - f_a^{2*}	Total flow - f_a^*
1	0.000	0.4662	0.4662
2	1.2921	0.0000	1.2921
3	1.8871	0.0000	1.8871
4	0.6965	0.0000	0.6965
5	1.0004	0.0000	1.0004
6	0.0000	0.1612	0.1612
7	0.0000	0.1573	0.1573
8	0.0000	1.0884	1.0884
9	1.0040	0.4462	1.4666
10	1.2921	0.1612	1.4533
11	1.8871	0.1573	2.0444
12	0.6965	1.0884	1.7848
13	0.0000	0.4662	0.4662
14	1.0004	0.0000	1.0004
15	1.2921	0.0000	1.2921
16	0.0000	0.1612	.01612
17	1.8871	0.0000	1.8871
18	0.0000	0.1573	0.1573
19	0.6965	0.0000	0.6965
20	0.0000	1.0884	1.0884

The incurred inverse demands were:

$$\lambda_{\omega_1}^1 = 954.0622, \quad \lambda_{\omega_2}^1 = 919.9000, \quad \lambda_{\omega_1}^2 = 579.9067, \quad \lambda_{\omega_2}^2 = 1049.8593.$$

Here, note the separation of classes of consumers. Observe that, in the case of the first O/D pair, consumers of class 1 only utilized paths 2, 3, and 4, whereas consumers of class 2 only utilized path 1. Hence, for this O/D pair, consumers of class 2 all shopped on the Internet, whereas only some of the consumers of class 1 did, with others electing to select and purchase the product at physical locations. However, in the case of the second O/D pair, class 1 consumers only utilized path 5, whereas consumers of class 2 utilized paths 6, 7, and 8, only. Hence, in regard to the second O/D pair, consumers of class 1 now all elected to shop virtually. Thus, for the second O/D pair, consumers of class 2 now shopped both virtually and physically for the product.

This example is another illustration of the generality and the flexibility of the multicriteria network equilibrium framework for studying decision-making problems in the Information Age.

Of course, numerous and, in fact, an infinite, number of examples can be constructed to evaluate distinct teleshopping versus shopping scenarios.

Table 7.9. The Equilibrium Path Flows for the Teleshopping Example

Path p	Class 1 - x_p^{1*}	Class 2 - x_p^{2*}
p_1	0.0000	0.4663
p_2	1.2921	0.0000
p_3	1.8871	0.0000
p_4	0.6964	0.0000
p_5	1.0003	0.0000
p_6	0.0000	0.1613
p_7	0.0000	0.1573
p_8	0.0000	1.0883

What the multicriteria supernetwork approach allows one to do is to address the particular scenario under consideration. Also, we emphasize that the applications in Sections 7.3.1 and 7.3.2 are only two and a myriad of others can also be captured beneath such a supernetwork umbrella. Indeed, we expect that distance learning, for example, would be another relevant application. Furthermore, one can also extend the teleshopping versus shopping example in Section 7.3.2, with the appropriate addition of links, to allow for decision-makers to obtain information on the Internet, but to then purchase the product at a physical retail outlet, as has been occurring in the case, for example, of automobile purchases (see *The Economist* (2001a)). Indeed, Robert Wagoner, the CEO of General Motors, quoted on page 9 of that same source, states that "'almost all' prospective car buyers now look on the Internet first, and so turn up at the dealer's showroom knowing as much as he does about discounts and availability."

7.6   Sources and Notes

This chapter contains an extensive list of references to the literature as appropriate to the subject and material in the chapter and the book, at large. Here we have focused on fixed weights associated with the classes, links, and criteria. Recently, Nagurney, Dong, and Mokhtarian (2001b) proposed variable weights for multicriteria network equilibrium problems. Figures 7.1 and 7.2 appear in that paper, as well as some of the motivation for the applications, but the theoretical developments therein are for the variable weight models. This chapter, in contrast, synthesizes a variety of results in papers written by the authors with collaborators, provides proofs of the theoretical results, for completeness, and also includes new numerical examples. Table 7.1 is extracted from Nagurney and Dong (2000).

8 A Space-Time Network for Telecommuting versus Commuting

In this chapter, a supernetwork framework is presented for the study of telecommuting versus commuting decision-making over a fixed, multiperiod, time horizon, such as a work week. Hence, the model extends the telecommuting model of Section 7.3.1 to enable the prediction of not only the number of decision-makers of each class who will telecommute versus commute, but also the number of time periods, that is, days, they will do so. Having such information is not only important from a managerial perspective, but from an environmental one as well (cf. Nagurney (2000c) and Nagurney and Dong (2001)).

Clearly, both congestion and environmental issues associated with vehicle use are problems of major concern for our societies today. In recent years, there has been a growing interest in the development of rigorous tools for both congestion and emission control management (see, e.g., Nagurney (2000c) and the references therein). The development has been driven, in part, by legislation. For example, in the United States, the 1990 Clean Air Act Amendments (cf. U. S. DOT (1992a)) and the 1991 Intermodal Surface Transportation Efficiency Act (U. S. DOT (1992b)), in particular, have stimulated a growing interest in transportation management policies, which can affect the total vehicle exhaust emissions, and, consequently, the levels of air pollution.

However, for any policy to have an appropriate effect, it is imperative that the behavior of the individuals affected by the policy be taken into consideration. Moreover, in addressing telecommuting versus commuting issues and the impact on, for example, the environment, one must be cognizant also of the underlying network structure of the problems since certain paradoxical phenomena (see Chapter 12) may occur as regards transportation versus telecommunication trade-offs.

The topic of transportation and its relationships to telecommunications has been a subject of research interest for close to forty years (cf. Memmott (1963), Jones (1973), Khan (1976), Nilles, et al. (1976), Albertson (1977), and Harkness (1977)). Commuting, in particular, as one of the most common uses of transportation, and, telecommuting, made possible by the advent of technologies, have garnered special attention. Indeed, telecommuting has been explored in many studies in terms of its potential impact on reducing the negative effects of transportation such as congestion and environmental degradation due to pollution. For conceptual studies on this topic, see Salomon (1986), and Mokhtarian (1990); for empirical studies, see Nilles (1988), Mokhtarian (1991), and Mokhtarian, Handy, and Salomon (1995).

In Chapter 7, it was demonstrated that, through the use of appropriate criteria, the extension of the concept of a network to a supernetwork to include not only links associated with physical transportation but also links associated with telecommunications and, hence, virtual transportation, enabled one to predict the number of decision-makers of each class that would telecommute versus commute. Importantly, the model in Section 7.3.1 allowed each class of decision-maker to weight the criteria of travel time, travel cost, opportunity and safety costs in an individual fashion.

In this chapter, the more general question as to how many days (given, say, a weekly horizon) one can expect classes of individuals to telecommute or to commute is addressed. In the preceding chapter, in contrast, the focus was essentially on one time period (sufficiently long enough for the equilibrium to be achieved) with no allowance made for explicit decision-making over time. That approach, nevertheless, was an equilibrium one, as is the one described in this chapter. However, here the focus is not only on the question of whether or not to telecommute (versus commute) but how frequently this choice is made.

The crucial concept that is utilized in this chapter is that of a *space-time network* in order to abstract the decision-making not only over space, but also over time. The functions representing the criteria on the links of the network capture the dependence of the criteria on the flows over both space and over time. For example, there may be individuals of a class who select to telecommute five days of the work week, whereas others may choose to telecommute only one or two days.

The use of space-time networks was also made by Nagurney and Aronson (1989) and by Nagurney and Kim (1991) in order to formulate and study multiperiod spatial price equilibrium problems originated by Takayama and Judge (1971). A variety of other types of dynamic network models can be found in Powell, Odoni, and Jaillet (1995).

Given recent legislation that permits federal employees to select the telecommuting option, as well as a resurgence of interest on this topic (see Hafner (2000)), a theoretical framework that can model telecommuting versus commuting behavior over a time horizon is clearly also of practical relevance. The number of telecommuters in the USA (see Glater (2001)) has risen in the past decade from 4 million to 23.6 million. However, how often individuals choose to telecommute versus commute (and, typically, on what days) is still an open question both theoretically and empirically. Some recent summary survey results concerning telecommuting intensity can be found in International Telework Association & Council (2000). See also Shore (2000) for an overview of teleworking, which highlights that different workers may choose to telecommute a different number of days.

This chapter is organized as follows. In Section 8.1, the multiclass, multicriteria network equilibrium model and the space-time network which allows the conceptualization of the problem are presented. On such a supernetwork, a path corresponds to decision-making over different time periods. Here, for definiteness, the focus is on a time period being a day. However, the framework is more general and one need not limit oneself thus. Indeed, a period could correspond to a week with the overall time horizon under study then corresponding, say, to a month. Moreover, the concepts set forth here are relevant to other application domains outside of telecommuting versus commuting decision-making. What is necessary is that the decisions be of a repetitive nature. The governing equilibrium conditions are derived and two equivalent variational inequalities in path flows and in link loads, respectively, presented. We then describe experiences with telecommuting, sometimes also referred to as "teleworking," at AT&T and in Europe, in general, and in Scandinavia, in particular.

In Section 8.2, the connection between the model and the multicriteria network equilibrium model of Section 7.1 is made and some qualitative properties are presented. In Section 8.3, several numerical examples are presented for illustrative purposes.

8.1   The Model

In this section, the multiperiod, multiclass, multicriteria network equilibrium model for telecommuting versus commuting is developed. The notation is similar to that used in Chapter 7, but is recalled here for easy reference and for definiteness. Let T denote the finite-time horizon with, typically, T being set equal to 5 working days of the week, and use, without any loss in generality, the index $t = 1, 2, \ldots, T$, to denote the time period or day.

The Space-Time Network

Assume that there are n locations with a subset of the locations corresponding to residential locations, employment locations, teleworking centers, as well as intermediate locations for transportation (or telecommunications) purposes, respectively. The space-time network will consist of T subnetworks with each subnetwork t corresponding to the choices available within time period t. Index the locations for a subnetwork t of the space-time network corresponding

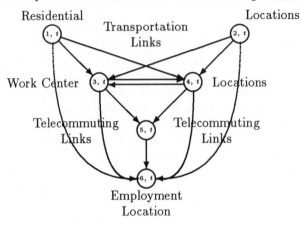

Fig. 8.1. A Subnetwork for the Conceptualization of Commuting versus Telecommuting within Time Period t

to time period t as follows: $(1,t), \ldots, (n,t)$; with t ranging from 1 through T. Assume that the number of locations within each subnetwork is fixed at n, which is also the number of nodes in each subnetwork. Hence, the total number of nodes in the space-time network will be equal to Tn.

We now discuss the links on the space-time network. The links will be links on each subnetwork plus connecting links which join two successive subnetworks. A link in the supernetwork framework can represent either a physical link corresponding to a classical transportation link or a *virtual* link corresponding to a telecommunication link which decision-makers can select as a telecommuting option. For example, in Figure 8.1, a conceptualization for period t of a telecommuting versus a commuting problem is depicted, which corresponds to subnetwork t. In Figure 8.1, nodes $(1,t)$ and $(2,t)$ depict the residential locations in time period (day) t; node $(6,t)$ denotes the employment location, and nodes $(3,t)$ and $(4,t)$ denote work center locations from which the decision-makers can telecommute. Hence, links $((1,t),(6,t))$, $((2,t),(6,t))$, $((3,t),(6,t))$, and $((4,t),(6,t))$ represent telecommuting links with all other links in Figure 8.1 being transportation links.

A sequence of links from a residential location to an employment location within a time period is termed a "route" and is denoted by r. Note that, as discussed in Chapter 3, a route can represent a mode of transportation in this context (for example, public or private). Furthermore, in our framework, since a mode of transportation includes telecommunications, a route can also represent a mode of telecommuting. Figure 8.1, hence, depicts the possible decisions, abstracted in Figure 7.1, but for a fixed time period t.

A space-time supernetwork for a time horizon T, thus, consists of T copies of a subnetwork t with t ranging from 1 through T to denote the subnetworks plus additional links to connect the subnetwork within a time period with the subsequent subnetwork. Consequently, from each employment location node in time period t, one needs to construct a link joining the appropriate residential location node in time period $t + 1$, where the residential and employment nodes have been identified as the locations where individuals live and work, respectively. We refer the reader to Figure 8.2 for the space-time supernetwork representation of the example given in Figure 8.1.

A path in the space-time supernetwork is now defined. A *path* is used to represent decisions over space and time and consists of a sequence of links (assumed acyclic) from a residential location node in period 1 to an employment location node in time period T. A residential location node in time period 1 is termed, henceforth, an *origin node* and the employment location node in time period T is a *destination node* with such a pair of nodes referred to as an *origin/destination* (O/D) pair. A path, thus, consists of a sequence of routes, which a decision-maker selects joined by the "connecting" links between the successive subnetworks. For example, cf. Figure 8.2, a decision-maker who selects the path consisting of the links: $(((1,1),(6,1));((6,1),(1,2));((1,2),(6,2));\ldots,((6,4),(1,5));((1,5),(6,5)))$ will telecommute each of the five days; other sequences of links represent other possible options.

Note that a path corresponding to a particular O/D pair must be constructed so that the appropriate residential location/employment location pair of nodes is included for each subnetwork. Otherwise, it would mean that one might switch within the time horizon either one's residential location, or one's employment location, or both. To fix this idea, a very simple example is presented in Figure 8.3 in which there are 3 residential locations and only a single employment location. Consider now the origin/destination pair of nodes $((1,1),(4,5))$ and note that there is only one path that connects this O/D pair and that satisfies the above restriction. It is drawn in bold-face in Figure 8.3.

The space-time supernetwork, hence, is a general network $G = [\mathcal{N}, \mathcal{L}]$, (but of special, multiperiod structure), where $\mathcal{N}$ denotes the set of nodes in the network and $\mathcal{L}$ the set of directed links. Now let a denote a link of the network connecting a pair of nodes and let p denote a path, consisting of a sequence of links connecting an origin/destination (O/D) pair of nodes. There are N links in the space-time network and N_P paths.

Let Ω denote the set of J O/D pairs. The set of paths connecting the O/D pair ω is denoted by P_ω and the entire set of paths in the network by P. For example, if there are N_r routes connecting a residential/employment location pair of nodes, then there will be N_r^T paths for the corresponding O/D pair, which, recall, consists of the residential location node in time period 1 and the employment location node in time period T.

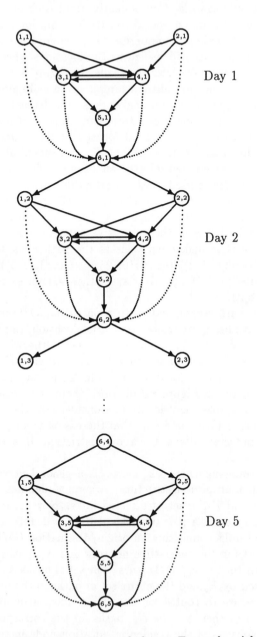

Fig. 8.2. A Space-Time Supernetwork for an Example with a 5 Day Time Horizon

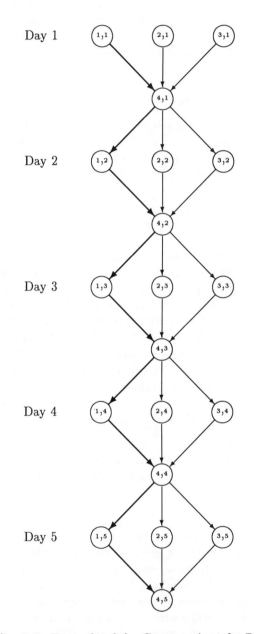

Fig. 8.3. Example of the Construction of a Path

The Conservation of Flow Equations

Assume that there are k classes of decision-makers in the supernetwork with a typical class denoted by i. Let f_a^i denote the flow of class i on link a and let x_p^i denote the nonnegative flow of class i on path p. The relationship between the link flows by class and the path flows is:

$$f_a^i = \sum_{p \in P} x_p^i \delta_{ap}, \quad \forall i, \quad \forall a \in \mathcal{L}, \tag{8.1}$$

where $\delta_{ap} = 1$, if link a is contained in path p, and 0, otherwise. Hence, the flow of a class of decision-maker on a link is equal to the sum of the flows of the class on the paths that contain that link.

In addition, let f_a denote the total flow on link a, where

$$f_a = \sum_{i=1}^{k} f_a^i, \quad \forall a \in \mathcal{L}. \tag{8.2}$$

Therefore, the total flow on a link is equal to the sum of the flows of all classes on that link. Group the class link flows into the kN-dimensional column vector $\tilde{f}$ with components $\{f_1^1, \ldots, f_N^1, \ldots, f_1^k, \ldots, f_N^k\}$ and the total link flows $\{f_1, \ldots, f_N\}$ into the N-dimensional column vector f. Also, group the class path flows into the kN_P-dimensional column vector $\tilde{x}$ with components $\{x_{p_1}^1, \ldots, x_{p_{N_P}}^k\}$. The travel demand associated with origin/destination (O/D) pair ω and class i will be denoted by d_ω^i. We group the travel demands into a column vector $d \in R^{kJ}$. Clearly, the travel demands must satisfy the following conservation of flow equations:

$$d_\omega^i = \sum_{p \in P_\omega} x_p^i, \quad \forall i, \forall \omega. \tag{8.3}$$

Hence, the demand is assumed to be fixed and known. Note that conservation of flow equations correspond, precisely, to equations (7.1) through (7.3), respectively.

Remark

In the model, it has been assumed that the choices available to the decision-makers in each time period are identical and, hence, the subnetworks comprising the supernetwork are as well. This is reasonable in regard to the application under consideration here, that is, telecommuting versus commuting decision-making. However, in the case of other applications, in which the space-time network can still abstract decision-making, the choices available in the time periods may be different and, therefore, the component subnetworks may have a distinct structure.

The Generalized Cost Structure

There are as many classes of decision-makers on this supernetwork as there are groups who perceive the trade-offs among travel cost, travel time, opportunity, and safety costs in a similar fashion.

We are now ready to describe the functions associated with the links. We emphasize that because of the structure of the space-time network the functions on the links are allowed to depend, in general, upon the flow on any link in the space-time network and, consequently, one can capture dependence over time since flows on distinct subnetworks correspond to flows in distinct time periods.

Assume, as given, a travel time function t_a associated with each link a in the network, where

$$t_a = t_a(f), \quad \forall a \in \mathcal{L}, \tag{8.4}$$

where (8.4) represents the time that it takes to traverse link a, and a travel cost function c_a associated with each link a, that is,

$$c_a = c_a(f), \quad \forall a \in \mathcal{L}, \tag{8.5}$$

with both these functions assumed to be continuous. Note that here, as was done in Chapter 7, we allow for the general situation in which both the travel time and the travel cost can depend on the entire link flow pattern. Note that similar functions were considered in Chapter 7, but now with the space-time network, such general functions can also be related to distinct time periods, since now a link corresponds to a decision not only in "space" but, also, in time.

In addition, in order to capture the opportunity costs associated with commuting versus telecommuting trade-offs, an opportunity cost o_a is associated with each link in the network, where

$$o_a = o_a(f), \quad \forall a \in \mathcal{L}, \tag{8.6}$$

as was also done in the telecommuting versus commuting model in Chapter 7.

Moreover, as was done in Section 7.3.1, let s_a denote the safety cost associated with link a, where

$$s_a = s_a(f), \quad \forall a \in \mathcal{L}. \tag{8.7}$$

Note that, in general, one need not associate the above functions with the connecting links. However, such a possibility is not excluded in order to enhance modeling flexibility.

Assume, as was the case in Chapter 7, that each class of decision-maker i has his own perception of the trade-offs among travel time, travel cost, opportunity cost, and safety cost associated with each link a, which are represented, respectively, by the nonnegative weights w_{1a}^i, w_{2a}^i, w_{3a}^i, and w_{4a}^i.

Here w^i_{1a} denotes the weight associated with class i's travel time on link a, w^i_{2a} denotes the weight associated with class i's travel cost on link a, w^i_{3a} denotes the weight associated with class i's opportunity cost on link a, and w^i_{4a} denotes the weight associated with its safety cost on link a.

Note that in order to model telecommuting versus commuting some links may only have opportunity costs associated with them whereas others may not even include opportunity costs (or have zero associated weights). Moreover, due to the structure of the space-time network one may have an opportunity cost in a specific time period depend on the flows of telecommuters in preceding and subsequent time periods. Thus, one can incorporate the costs associated with telecommuting in several time periods.

The generalized cost function of class i associated with link a, denoted by C^i_a, is defined as:

$$C^i_a = w^i_{1a} t_a + w^i_{2a} c_a + w^i_{3a} o_a + w^i_{4a} s_a, \quad \forall i, \quad \forall a \in \mathcal{L}. \tag{8.8}$$

In other words, as discussed in Chapter 7, the generalized cost on a link as experienced by a class of decision-maker is a weighting of the travel cost, travel time, opportunity cost, and safety cost on that link, which represent the criteria used in decision-making.

In view of (8.2)–(8.8), we may write

$$C^i_a = C^i_a(\tilde{f}), \quad \forall i, \quad \forall a \in \mathcal{L}, \tag{8.9}$$

and group the generalized link costs into the kN-dimensional row vector C with components $\{C^1_1, \ldots, C^1_N, \ldots, C^k_1, \ldots, C^k_N\}$.

Let V^i_p denote the generalized cost of class i associated with traversing path p, where

$$V^i_p = \sum_{a \in \mathcal{L}} C^i_a(\tilde{f}) \delta_{ap}, \quad \forall i, \forall p. \tag{8.10}$$

In this chapter, the notation V^i_p is utilized to denote a generalized cost on a path as perceived by a class of decision-maker, in contrast to the notation used in Chapter 7, which was C^i_p. This is done in order to emphasize that the generalized cost on a path can be over several time periods.

Hence, the generalized cost, as perceived by a class, associated with traversing a path is its weighting of the travel times, the travel costs, the opportunity costs, and the safety costs, on links which comprise the path, where the links in each subnetwork represent the possible choices available to the decision-maker within that time period. Group the generalized path costs into the column vector $V \in R^{kN_P}$.

The Behavioral Assumption

The behavioral assumption that is utilized here is precisely the one used in Section 7.1 for multicriteria network equilibrium problems in the case of fixed demands (cf. (7.15)) in that we assume that each class of decision-maker in the space-time network selects (subject to constraints) his "travel" path so as to minimize the generalized cost on the path, given that all other decision-makers have made their choices. As emphasized previously, paths in the space-time framework correspond to decisions not only over space but also over time. Hence, the use of this behavioral assumption is reasonable and classical, in a sense, but, at the same time, novel.

In particular, with the above notation, we have the following network equilibrium conditions for the problem outlined above:

Network Equilibrium Conditions

For each class i, for all O/D pairs $\omega \in \Omega$, and for all paths $p \in P_\omega$, the flow $\tilde{x}^*$ is said to be in equilibrium if the following condition holds:

$$V_p^i(\tilde{x}^*) \begin{cases} = \lambda_\omega^i, & \text{if} \quad x_p^{i*} > 0 \\ \geq \lambda_\omega^i, & \text{if} \quad x_p^{i*} = 0. \end{cases} \tag{8.11}$$

In other words, all utilized paths by a class connecting an origin/destination pair have equal and minimal generalized costs and these costs are equal to the disutility λ_ω^i associated with the class and O/D pair.

We now provide two alternative, but, equivalent, variational inequality formulations of the equilibrium conditions (8.11) in path flows and in link flows, respectively. From the path flow formulation one can construct a dynamic tatonnement process akin to dynamic traffic network models described in Nagurney and Zhang (1996) using the methodology of projected dynamical systems, which was also used in Chapters 5 and 6 to develop, respectively, dynamic supply chain and financial network models. The link flow formulation, on the other hand, will be utilized in Section 8.2 to obtain qualitative properties.

Specifically, in light of Theorem 7.2 (see also the proof of Theorem 7.1), one can write down immediately the variational inequality formulations below.

Theorem 8.1: Variational Inequality Formulations

A multicriteria, multiclass path flow pattern $\tilde{x}^* \in \mathcal{K}^1$ is a network equilibrium, that is, satisfies equilibrium conditions (8.11), if and only if it satisfies the variational inequality problem:

Path Flow Formulation

$$\sum_{i=1}^k \sum_{\omega \in \Omega} \sum_{p \in P_\omega} V_p^i(\tilde{x}^*) \times (x_p^i - x_p^{i*}) \geq 0, \quad \tilde{x} \in \mathcal{K}^1, \tag{8.12a}$$

where $\mathcal{K}^1 \equiv \{\tilde{x}|\tilde{x} \geq 0, \text{ and satisfies}(8.3)\}$, or, in standard variational inequality form:

$$\langle F(X^*), X - X^* \rangle \geq 0, \quad \forall X \in \mathcal{K}, \tag{8.12b}$$

where $F \equiv V$, $X \equiv \tilde{x}$, and $\mathcal{K} \equiv \mathcal{K}^1$, and $\langle \cdot, \cdot \rangle$ denotes the inner product in kN_P-dimensional space, or, equivalently, $\tilde{f}^* \in \mathcal{K}^2$ is an equilibrium link flow pattern if and only if it satisfies the variational inequality problem:

Link Flow Formulation

$$\sum_{i=1}^{k} \sum_{a \in \mathcal{L}} C_a^i(\tilde{f}^*) \times (f_a^i - f_a^{i*}) \geq 0, \quad \forall \tilde{f} \in \mathcal{K}^2, \tag{8.13a}$$

where $\mathcal{K}^2 \equiv \{\tilde{f} | \exists \tilde{x} \geq 0, \text{ and satisfies } (8.1), (8.2), (8.3)\}$, or, in standard variational inequality form:

$$\langle F(X^*), X - X^* \rangle \geq 0, \quad \forall X \in \mathcal{K}, \tag{8.13b}$$

where $F \equiv C$, $X \equiv \tilde{f}$, $\mathcal{K} \equiv \mathcal{K}^2$, and $\langle \cdot, \cdot \rangle$ denotes the inner product in kN-dimensional Euclidean space.

If there is only a single time period, then the model collapses to the telecommuting versus commuting model of Section 7.3.1.

In the next subsections, we describe experiences with telecommuting or teleworking in a US company, AT&T, and in Europe, at large, with a specific focus on the Scandinavian countries.

8.1.1 The Teleworking Experience at AT&T

According to an AT&T website (cf. AT&T (2001a)), telework participation at AT&T, based on a program established in 1992, reached an all time high in 2000, with 110 million miles of commuting avoided, and with a savings of approximately 50,000 tons of carbon dioxide, 5.1 million gallons of gasoline, 220,000 tons of hydrocarbons, 1.7 million tons of carbon monoxide, and 110,000 tons of nitrous oxide. The 2000 AT&T employee telework survey (see AT&T (2001b)) revealed that the number of AT&T employees who telework at least one day per month has increased to 56 percent, a 7 percent increase over the 49 percent reported in 1999. According to the same source, the number of frequent teleworkers, that is, those who work from home once a week or more also increased to 27 percent in 2000 from 24 percent in 1999. Those who telecommuted expressed such benefits as increased job satisfaction, work and family balance, productivity, as well as being able to attract and to keep good employees. According to this website "Like the Internet that enables it, telework is an excellent illustration of network economics."

8.1.2 The European Experience

The website (cf. AT&T (2001c)) states that, presently, 10 million Europeans telework. This number, nevertheless, represents only about 6 percent of the active workforce and, according to the European Union, is too small a participation to sustain a competitive economy. At a meeting in March, 2001, the heads of the European states gathered to discuss employment issues in the Information Society and, according to the same source, "pledged to give the majority of Europeans the option of teleworking by the end of this year." Indeed, as noted therein, in Europe, work practices, through the enablement of telecommunications, have taken a primary position in discussions at the European policy levels with four major reasons being: "the need to improve business efficiency, increase workforce mobility, include more working-age people in the workforce, and encourage sustainable development." According to Peter Johnston, head of the New Work Methods unit of the Information Society Directorate at the European Commission, quoted therein, "This new way of organizing work that we call telework gives such dramatic improvement in innovation and productivity that it is now essential to moving companies of all sizes to world levels" of competition.

In terms of the Scandinavian experience, in particular, presently 15 percent of the Swedish and the Finnish workforces has a telework arrangement, whereas the Danish government has reached an agreement with both employers and unions in terms of the delineation of responsibilities regarding telework arrangements.

Sirkka Heinonen, a senior research scientist at VTT Communites, the largest technological research center of the government in Finland, with a goal of building the Information Society, is quoted by AT&T (2001c) as saying "The greatest obstacles to telework in the future will be psychological, social and cultural," and not technical or economic. Indeed, in our model above, we explicitly allow distinct criteria in decision-making and different classes of decision-makers, which in this context are telecommuters or teleworkers, who can weight the criteria in an individual fashion. Hence, specifically, opportunity cost can include psychological and social factors. In addition, Heinonen recognized that for the employee, the greatest benefits are time, money and stress avoided by commuting less, coupled with more flexibility in balancing work and family issues. Above we have explicitly noted time and money (or cost) as criteria as regards telecommuting versus commuting decision-making. Nevertheless, she recognizes one of the major obstacles to telecommuting, that is, the workers' isolation and managers' fear of losing control of such workers. According to her, cited in that same source, as regards what can be done to relieve workers' isolation, "in Finland and most of Europe it can be overcome if we choose a telework model for just part of the time. The risk of isolation is highest if the employee teleworks all the time. But there is virtually no risk if it's just two days a week." Indeed, her studies have shown that in the context of telecommuting, one, two, or three days a week results in the greatest benefits for employees and employers alike.

The model above enables one to predict the number of individuals who will telecommute and the number of days that they will do so. In Section 8.3, we illustrate this through several numerical examples.

8.2   Qualitative Properties

Qualitative properties of the solution to variational inequality (8.13a) (equivalently, (8.13b)) follow directly from the results in Section 7.2 for the variational inequality (7.23a) (equivalently, (7.23b)). This is so since variational inequality (8.13a) coincides with variational inequality (7.23a).

Indeed, the following results are immediate.

Corollary 8.1: Existence
Let t, c, o, and s be given continuous functions. Then both variational inequality (8.12a) and variational inequality (8.13a) have at least one solution.

Proof: Follows from Theorem 7.3. □

We now turn to examining uniqueness. In particular, we consider a special case of the above model in which the uniqueness not of the vector of class link flows $\tilde{f}^*$ but of the total link flows f^* follows immediately from Corollary 7.1

Specifically, consider a generalized cost function of the form:

$$C_a^i = \psi_a^i t_a + \xi_a^i c_a + \delta_a^i o_a + (1 - \psi_a^i - \xi_a^i - \delta_a^i)s_a, \quad \forall a, i, \tag{8.14}$$

where

$$t_a = g_a(f) + \alpha_a, \, c_a = g_a(f) + \beta_a, \, o_a = g_a(f) + \gamma_a, s_a = g_a(f) + \theta_a, \quad \forall a \in \mathcal{L}. \tag{8.15}$$

Hence, the generalized cost function C_a^i for each class and link is a weighted average of the travel time, the travel cost, the opportunity cost, and the safety cost on a link. Moreover, the variable term is identical for the travel time, the travel cost, and the opportunity and safety cost on a given link. Here ψ_a^i, ξ_a^i, and δ_a^i are the link-dependent weights for class i decision-makers. Observe that the criteria functions are precisely of the form (7.27) and (7.28), where here the number of criteria H is equal to four. Assume now that t, c, o, and s are each strictly monotone in f, that is,

$$\langle t(f^1) - t(f^2), f^1 - f^2 \rangle > 0, \quad \forall f^1, f^2 \in \mathcal{K}^2, \quad f^1 \neq f^2, \tag{8.16}$$

$$\langle c(f^1) - c(f^2), f^1 - f^2 \rangle > 0, \quad \forall f^1, f^2 \in \mathcal{K}^2, \quad f^1 \neq f^2, \tag{8.17}$$

$$\langle o(f^1) - o(f^2), f^1 - f^2 \rangle > 0, \quad \forall f^1, f^2 \in \mathcal{K}^2, \quad f^1 \neq f^2, \tag{8.18}$$

and

$$\langle s(f^1) - s(f^2)), f^1 - f^2 \rangle > 0, \quad \forall f^2, f^2 \in \mathcal{K}^2, \quad f^1 \neq f^2. \tag{8.19}$$

Then we have the following.

Corollary 8.2: Uniqueness of the Total Link Flow Pattern in a Special Case
The total link flow pattern f^* induced by a solution $\tilde{f}^*$ to variational inequality (8.13a) in the case of generalized cost functions C of the form (8.14)

and (8.15), is guaranteed to be unique if the travel time, the travel cost, the opportunity cost, and the safety cost functions are each strictly monotone increasing in f as in (8.16)–(8.19), respectively.

Proof: Follows directly from Corollary 7.1. □

In addition, the monotonicity property as well as Lipschitz continuity are now presented. These conditions guarantee convergence of the modified projection method, which is applied in Section 8.3 to compute the solutions to several numerical examples.

Corollary 8.3: Monotonicity in a Special Case
Assume that the generalized cost functions C are as in (8.14) with the travel time, the travel cost, the opportunity cost functions, and the safety cost functions differing on a given link only by the fixed cost terms as in (8.15). Assume also that these functions are monotone increasing in f. Then the function that enters the variational inequality problem (8.13b) governing the multiperiod, multiclass, multicriteria traffic network equilibrium model is monotone.

Proof: The result is direct from Corollary 7.2. □

In addition, we have the following result which follows from Corollary 7.3:

Corollary 8.4: Lipschitz Continuity
If the generalized cost functions C have bounded first-order derivatives, then the function, $F(X)$, that enters the variational inequality (8.13b) is Lipschitz continuous.

8.3 Numerical Examples

In view of the results in Sections 8.1 and 8.2, one can apply the modified projection method as given in Section 7.4 to solve variational inequality (8.13a). Recall that this algorithm consists of the Initialization Step, the Computation Step (7.45), and the Adaptation Step (7.46).

In this section, hence, six numerical examples are presented for illustrative purposes. In particular, the examples are solved using the modified projection method as described in Section 7.4. For the solution of the variational inequality subproblems (7.45) and (7.46) (as was done for the single period telecommuting versus commuting numerical example in Section 7.5.1), we utilized the equilibration algorithm of Dafermos and Sparrow (1969) (see Appendix C), which was also used for the solution of the numerical example in Section 7.5.1. Note that the induced variational inequality subproblems are actually separable quadratic programming problems over a feasible set which is a network. The α parameter in the modified projection method was now set to .01, except where noted. The convergence criterion was that the absolute value of the flow for each class of decision-maker at two successive iterations was less than or equal to ϵ, with $\epsilon = .0001$. The space-time network for the numerical examples is given in Figure 8.4. In all the numerical examples, we assumed that the weights for all classes and links associated with the safety cost criterion (cf. (8.7) and (8.8)) were equal to zero. Hence, there is no need to consider the safety cost functions.

Example 8.1

The first numerical example is simple but serves to illustrate interesting features. It consists of a single class of decision-maker with a single residential location and a single employment location. The time horizon $T = 5$. Also, it is assumed that the choices available to the members of the class of decision-maker are expressed simply as whether to telecommute or to commute. The space-time network is given in Figure 8.4. It consists of ten nodes (since there are two nodes within each of the 5 time periods or days) with the top node in each subnetwork denoting the residential location and the bottom node in each subnetwork the employment location. There are 14 links in the supernetwork since there are two links for each of the five time periods and 4 connecting links. There are a total of 2^5 or 32 paths connecting the O/D pair $\omega = ((1,1),(2,5))$. The paths are enumerated and their link compositions given in Table 8.1.

The criteria were as described in Section 8.1 (and above) with the generalized link cost functions constructed according to (8.8) with the weights given by: For class 1, the weights were: $w_{1,1}^1 = .25$, $w_{2,1}^1 = .25$, $w_{3,1}^1 = 1.$, $w_{1,2}^1 = .25$, $w_{2,2} = .25$, $w_{3,2}^1 = 1.$, $w_{1,3}^1 = .4$, $w_{2,3}^1 = .4$, $w_{3,3}^1 = 1.$, $w_{1,4}^1 = .5$, $w_{2,4}^1 = .5$, $w_{3,4}^1 = 2.$, $w_{1,5}^1 = .4$, $w_{2,5}^1 = .5$, $w_{3,5}^1 = 1.$, $w_{1,6}^1 = .5$, $w_{2,6}^1 = .3$, $w_{3,6}^1 = 2.$, $w_{1,7}^1 = .2$, $w_{2,7}^1 = .4$, $w_{3,7}^1 = 1.$, $w_{1,8}^1 = .3$, $w_{2,8}^1 = .5$, $w_{3,8}^1 = 1.$, $w_{1,9}^1 = .6$, $w_{2,9}^1 = .2$, $w_{3,9}^1 = 2.$, $w_{1,10}^1 = .3$, $w_{2,10}^1 = .4$, $w_{3,10}^1 = 1.$, $w_{1,11}^1 = .2$, $w_{2,11}^1 = .7$, $w_{3,11}^1 = 1.$, $w_{1,12}^1 = .3$, $w_{2,12}^1 = .4$, $w_{3,12}^1 = 1.$, $w_{1,13}^1 = .2$, $w_{2,13}^1 = .3$, $w_{3,13}^1 = 2.$, $w_{1,14}^1 = .5$, $w_{2,14}^1 = .2$, $w_{3,14}^1 = .1$.

The travel time and travel cost functions on the links were as reported in Table 8.2 whereas the opportunity cost functions on the links were as reported in Table 8.3. The demand $d_\omega^1 = 100$.

The modified projection method converged in 28 iterations. It yielded the following equilibrium single class link flow (and total, since there is only one class) pattern:

$$f_1^* = 53.1127, \quad f_2^* = 46.8873, \quad f_3^* = 100.0000, \quad f_4^* = 53.7822,$$

$$f_5^* = 46.2178, \quad f_6^* = 100.0000, \quad f_7^* = 59.2427, \quad f_8^* = 40.7573,$$

$$f_9^* = 100.0000, \quad f_{10}^* = 57.6488, \quad f_{11}^* = 42.3512, \quad f_{12}^* = 100.0000,$$

$$f_{13}^* = 54.4498, \quad f_{14}^* = 45.5502,$$

which was induced by the equilibrium single-class path flow pattern:

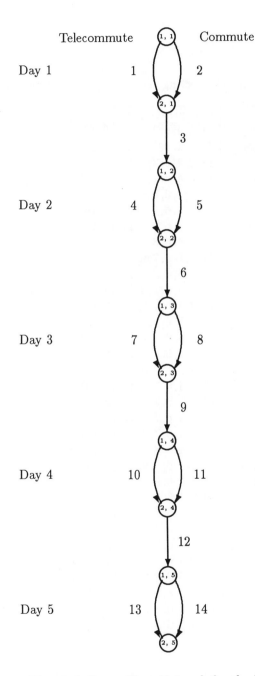

Fig. 8.4. Space-Time Network for the Examples

Table 8.1. Paths Connecting the Origin/Destination Pair

Path	Comprising Links
p_1	$(1, 3, 4, 6, 7, 9, 10, 12, 13)$
p_2	$(1, 3, 4, 6, 7, 9, 10, 12, 14)$
p_3	$(1, 3, 4, 6, 7, 9, 11, 12, 13)$
p_4	$(1, 3, 4, 6, 7, 9, 11, 12, 14)$
p_5	$(1, 3, 4, 6, 8, 9, 10, 12, 13)$
p_6	$(1, 3, 4, 6, 8, 9, 10, 12, 14)$
p_7	$(1, 3, 4, 6, 8, 9, 11, 12, 13)$
p_8	$(1, 3, 4, 6, 8, 9, 11, 12, 14)$
p_9	$(1, 3, 5, 6, 7, 9, 10, 12, 13)$
p_{10}	$(1, 3, 5, 6, 7, 9, 10, 12, 14)$
p_{11}	$(1, 3, 5, 6, 7, 9, 11, 12, 13)$
p_{12}	$(1, 3, 5, 6, 7, 9, 11, 12, 14)$
p_{13}	$(1, 3, 5, 6, 8, 9, 10, 12, 13)$
p_{14}	$(1, 3, 5, 6, 8, 9, 10, 12, 14)$
p_{15}	$(1, 3, 5, 6, 8, 9, 11, 12, 13)$
p_{16}	$(1, 3, 5, 6, 8, 9, 11, 12, 14)$
p_{17}	$(2, 3, 4, 6, 7, 9, 10, 12, 13)$
p_{18}	$(2, 3, 4, 6, 7, 9, 10, 12, 14)$
p_{19}	$(2, 3, 4, 6, 7, 9, 11, 12, 13)$
p_{20}	$(2, 3, 4, 6, 7, 9, 11, 12, 14)$
p_{21}	$(2, 3, 4, 6, 8, 9, 10, 12, 13)$
p_{22}	$(2, 3, 4, 6, 8, 9, 10, 12, 13)$
p_{23}	$(2, 3, 4, 6, 8, 9, 11, 12, 13)$
p_{24}	$(2, 3, 4, 6, 8, 9, 11, 12, 14)$
p_{25}	$(2, 3, 5, 6, 7, 9, 10, 12, 13)$
p_{26}	$(2, 3, 5, 6, 7, 9, 10, 12, 14)$
p_{27}	$(2, 3, 5, 6, 7, 9, 11, 12, 13)$
p_{28}	$(2, 3, 5, 6, 7, 9, 11, 12, 14)$
p_{29}	$(2, 3, 5, 6, 8, 9, 10, 12, 13)$
p_{30}	$(2, 3, 5, 6, 8, 9, 10, 12, 14)$
p_{31}	$(2, 3, 5, 6, 8, 9, 11, 12, 13)$
p_{32}	$(2, 3, 5, 6, 8, 9, 11, 12, 14)$

Table 8.2. The Travel Time and Travel Cost Functions for the Links

Link a	$t_a(f)$	$c_a(f)$
1	$.00005f_1^4 + .5f_1 + .1f_2 + .2$	$.00005f_1^4 + f_1 + .5f_2 + 1$
2	$.00005f_2^4 + 2f_2 + f_1 + 1$	$.00005f_2^4 + 5f_2 + 2f_1 + 2$
3	0.0000	0.0000
4	$.00005f_4^4 + .5f_4 + .1f_5 + .2$	$.00005f_4^4 + f_4 + .5f_5 + 1$
5	$.00005f_5^4 + 2f_5 + f_4 + 1$	$.00005f_5^4 + 2f_4 + 5f_5 + 2$
6	0.0000	0.0000
7	$.00005f_7^4 + .5f_7 + .1f_8 + .2$	$.00005f_7^4 + f_7 + + .5f_8 + 1$
8	$.00005f_8^4 + 2f_8 + f_7 + 1$	$.00005f_8^4 + 5f_8 + 2f_7 + 2$
9	0.0000	0.0000
10	$.00005f_{10}^4 + .5f_{10} + .1f_{11} + .2$	$.00005f_{10}^4 + f_{10} + .5f_{11} + 1$
11	$.00005f_{11}^4 + 2f_{11} + f_{10} + 1$	$.00005f_{11}^4 + 5f_{11} + 2f_{10} + 2$
12	0.0000	0.0000
13	$.00005f_{13}^4 + .5f_{13} + .1f_{14} + .2$	$.00005f_{13}^4 + f_{13} + .5f_{14} + 1$
14	$.00005f_{14}^4 + 2f_{14} + f_{13} + 1$	$.00005f_{14}^4 + 5f_{14} + 2f_{13} + 2$

$$x_{p_1}^{1*} = 8.8423, \quad x_{p_2}^{1*} = 3.1286, \quad x_{p_3}^{1*} = 3.2258, \quad x_{p_4}^{1*} = 3.1458,$$

$$x_{p_5}^{1*} = 3.1435, \quad x_{p_6}^{1*} = 3.0630, \quad x_{p_7}^{1*} = 1.9958, \quad x_{p_8}^{1*} = 3.1984,$$

$$x_{p_9}^{1*} = 3.1874, \quad x_{p_{10}}^{1*} = 3.6961, \quad x_{p_{11}}^{1*} = 3.2472, \quad x_{p_{12}}^{1*} = 3.1638,$$

$$x_{p_{13}}^{1*} = 2.8312, \quad x_{p_{14}}^{1*} = 2.9486, \quad x_{p_{15}}^{1*} = 2.7673, \quad x_{p_{16}}^{1*} = 1.580,$$

$$x_{p_{17}}^{1*} = 3.8039, \quad x_{p_{18}}^{1*} = 3.4827, \quad x_{p_{19}}^{1*} = 3.3014, \quad x_{p_{20}}^{1*} = 3.4188,$$

$$x_{p_{21}}^{1*} = 3.0862, \quad x_{p_{22}}^{1*} = 3.0025, \quad x_{p_{23}}^{1*} = 2.5539, \quad x_{p_{24}}^{1*} = 1.3897,$$

$$x_{p_{25}}^{1*} = 3.0516, \quad x_{p_{26}}^{1*} = 4.2542, \quad x_{p_{27}}^{1*} = 3.1870, \quad x_{p_{28}}^{1*} = 3.1062,$$

$$x_{p_{29}}^{1*} = 3.1035, \quad x_{p_{30}}^{1*} = 3.0237, \quad x_{p_{31}}^{1*} = 3.1221, \quad x_{p_{32}}^{1*} = 0.0000.$$

All the path generalized costs on used paths, that is, those with positive flow, were equal to 1999.4 (approximately to 4 decimal places).

We now discuss the results. Note that only one path, and that is path p_{32}, which represents commuting all 5 days of the week was not used. This means that *none* of the decision-makers in this example opt to commute five days of the week. Path p_1, on the other hand, represents the option of telecommuting 5 days of the week and only 8.8423 (see $x_{p_1}^{1*}$) elect this option. This is, nevertheless, under the demand $d_w^1 = 100$, the most popular choice since the largest number of decision-makers make this choice over the 5 day horizon. The next least popular choice (outside of path p_{32} which is not used)

Table 8.3. The Opportunity Cost Functions for the Links

Link a	$o_a(f)$
1	$.4f_1 + .2f_4 + .2$
2	$.2f_2 + .1f_5 + 1$
3	0.0000
4	$.3f_4 + .2f_1 + 1$
5	$f_5 + f_2 + 1$
6	0.0000
7	$.5f_7 + .1f_4 + .2$
8	$2f_8 + f_5 + 1$
9	0.0000
10	$.5f_{10} + .1f_7 + .2$
11	$f_{11} + .4f_8 + 1$
12	0.0000
13	$.4f_{13} + .1f_{10} + .2$
14	$.2f_{14} + .1f_{11} + 1$

is represented by path p_{16} which has the flow $x_{p_{16}}^{1*} = 1.580$. This represents the following decision: to telecommute on the first day of the week, and to commute on the remaining four days. This may have the interpretation that this class of decision-maker likes to work at home at the beginning of the week (following the weekend, say).

Example 8.2

The following change was then made to the data in Example 8.1. We increased the demand d_ω^1 from 100 to 300. The modified projection method converged in 5 iterations and yielded the following equilibrium path flow pattern: only path p_{24} was used and it, hence, had all the demand assigned to it, that is, $x_{p_{24}}^{1*} = 300$, with all other path flows being, thus, equal to zero. Path p_{24} represents the following decision(s): to commute on days 1, 3, 4, and 5, and to telecommute on day 2. Path p_{24} had a generalized path cost of 1915.2499, and all other paths (which were unused) had (substantially) higher generalized path costs.

Example 8.3

In the third numerical example, another class of decision-maker was added and denoted by class 2, whose weights were as follows: $w_{1,1}^2 = .5$, $w_{2,1}^2 = .3$, $w_{3,1}^2 = .1$, $w_{1,2}^2 = 1.$, $w_{2,2}^2 = 1.$, $w_{3,2}^2 = 1.$, $w_{1,3}^2 = 1.$, $w_{2,3}^2 = 1.$, $w_{3,3}^2 = 1.$, $w_{1,4}^2 = 1.$, $w_{2,4}^2 = 1.$, $w_{3,4}^2 = 1.$, $w_{1,5}^2 = 1.$, $w_{2,5}^2 = 1.$, $w_{3,5}^2 = 1.$, $w_{1,6}^2 = .5$, $w_{2,6}^2 = .5$, $w_{3,6}^2 = .5$, $w_{1,7}^2 = .5$, $w_{2,7}^2 = .4$, $w_{3,7}^2 = .4$, $w_{1,8}^2 = .4$, $w_{2,8}^2 = .3$, $w_{3,8}^2 = .2$, $w_{1,9}^2 = .3$, $w_{2,9}^2 = .2$, $w_{3,9}^2 = .6$, $w_{1,10}^2 = .5$, $w_{2,10}^2 = .4$, $w_{3,10}^2 = .5$, $w_{1,11}^2 = .7$, $w_{2,11}^2 = .6$, $w_{3,11}^2 = .7$, $w_{1,12}^2 = .4$, $w_{2,12}^2 = .3$, $w_{3,12}^2 = .8$,

$w_{1,13}^2 = .3$, $w_{2,13}^2 = .2$, $w_{3,13}^2 = .6$, $w_{1,14}^2 = .2$, $w_{2,14}^2 = .3$, $w_{3,14}^2 = .9$.

The remainder of the data was as in Example 8.1. The demand for class 2 was $d_\omega^2 = 100$.

We now present and discuss the results obtained by an application of the modified projection method which converged in 7 iterations. Recall that in Example 8.1, when there was only a single class of decision-maker, then path p_{32} was the only path that was not used by class 1. Now, however, with the introduction of a new class of decision-maker, the following equilibrium pattern was obtained: for class 1, *only* path p_{32} was used and, hence, $x_{p_{32}}^{1*} = 100$, with an associated generalized path cost given by $V_{p_{32}}^1 = 1200.0499$; all other generalized path costs were higher for this class since those paths were not used. Class 2 also only utilized path p_{32} and, hence, the flow for class 2 on that path was $x_{p_{32}}^{2*} = 100$. Its generalized cost was $V_{p_{32}}^2 = 1953.9998$, with the other unused paths having higher generalized costs for this class. Interestingly, with the addition of a new class of decision-maker the equilibrium pattern for class 1 changed entirely. Also, interestingly, despite different weights associated with the criteria both decision-makers of class 1 and of class 2 chose to commute 5 days a week!

Example 8.4

The following perturbation to the data was then made. We increased the demand for class 1 to 300, that is, $d_\omega^1 = 300$, but kept the demand for class 2 as in Example 8.3, that is, $d_\omega^2 = 100$. The new equilibrium pattern was computed by the modified projection method in 2 iterations. Now both class 1 and class 2 used solely path p_{24}, where, recall, that this path corresponds to telecommuting on the second day of the week and commuting on the remaining 4 days. Interestingly, both classes of decision-makers selected the same option, again.

Example 8.5

We then proceeded to increase the demand for class 2 to 300, that is, $d_\omega^2 = 300$, with the other data as in the example immediately preceding. The modified projection method converged in 4 iterations and the solution stayed the same as in the preceding example.

Example 8.6

The demands for both classes were then decreased, so that $d_\omega^1 = 30$ and $d_\omega^2 = 30$, with all other data remaining as in Example 8.3. Interestingly, except for one path, which was used by both classes, the other paths used were distinct for each class. The modified projection method converged in 243 iterations and yielded the following path flow pattern.

For class 1:

$$x_{p_1}^{1*} = .3359, \quad x_{p_2}^{1*} = 1.9953, \quad x_{p_9}^{1*} = 1.4688, \quad x_{p_{10}}^{1*} = 2.7508,$$

$$x_{p_{17}}^{1*} = 1.8524, \quad x_{p_{18}}^{1*} = 4.1009, \quad x_{p_{25}}^{1*} = 2.4664, \quad x_{p_{26}}^{1*} = 15.0296,$$

with all other path flows for this class being equal to zero. The generalized path costs on the used paths was approximately 644.95 for all such paths.

For class 2:

$$x_{p_1}^{2*} = 4.3939, \quad x_{p_3}^{2*} = 4.3290, \quad x_{p_5}^{2*} = 7.740, \quad x_{p_7}^{2*} = 13.5531,$$

with all other path flows for this class being equal to zero. The generalized path costs on the used paths was 809.95, approximately.

Note that both classes used path 1, that is, there were members of each class who sought to telecommute all five days. However, all other paths used by class 2 were distinct from those chosen by class 1.

For completeness, we also report the computed equilibrium multiclass link flow pattern and the total link flow pattern.

Link flows for class 1:

$$f_1^{1*} = 6.5508, \quad f_2^{1*} = 23.4492, \quad f_3^{1*} = 30.0000, \quad f_4^{1*} = 8.2845,$$

$$f_5^{1*} = 21.7155, \quad f_6^{1*} = 30.0000, \quad f_7^{1*} = 30.0000, \quad f_8^{1*} = 0.0000,$$

$$f_9^{1*} = 30.0000, \quad f_{10}^{1*} = 30.0000, \quad f_{11}^{1*} = 0.0000, \quad f_{12}^{1*} = 30.0000,$$

$$f_{13}^{1*} = 6.1235, \quad f_{14}^{1*} = 23.8765.$$

Link flows for class 2:

$$f_1^{2*} = 30.0000, \quad f_2^{2*} = 0.0000, \quad f_3^{2*} = 30.0000, \quad f_4^{2*} = 30.0000,$$

$$f_5^{2*} = 0.0000, \quad f_6^{2*} = 30.0000, \quad f_7^{2*} = 8.7229, \quad f_8^{2*} = 21.2771,$$

$$f_9^{2*} = 30.0000, \quad f_{10}^{2*} = 12.1179, \quad f_{11}^{2*} = 17.8821, \quad f_{12}^{2*} = 30.0000,$$

$$f_{13}^{2*} = 30.0000, \quad f_{14}^{2*} = 0.0000,$$

and the total link flows:

$$f_1^* = 36.5508, \quad f_2^* = 23.4492, \quad f_3^* = 60.0000, \quad f_4^* = 38.2845,$$

$$f_5^* = 21.7155, \quad f_6^* = 60.0000, \quad f_7^* = 38.7229, \quad f_8^* = 21.2771,$$

$$f_9^* = 60.0000, \quad f_{10}^* = 42.1179, \quad f_{11}^* = 17.8821, \quad f_{12}^* = 60.0000,$$

$$f_{13}^* = 36.1235, \quad f_{14}^* = 23.8765.$$

As can be seen from the total link flows, over two-thirds of the decision-makers chose to telecommute on the fourth day, with telecommuting being selected by more than half of the decision-makers on any given day. Hence, the number of commuters is lowest on day four and highest on day five.

8.4   Sources and Notes

The concept of a space-time network for modeling decision-making as regards telecommuting versus commuting in a multicriteria network equilibrium framework is due to Nagurney, Dong, and Mokhtarian (2001c) from which the numerical example in Section 8.3 is also taken. In this chapter, however, we include the safety cost criterion and relate the model to the framework described in Chapter 7. In addition, we now interpret the space-time network as a supernetwork.

9 Urban Location and Transportation in the Information Age

This chapter describes, through rigorous modeling and analysis, how transportation and location decisions, relevant to the Information Age, can be made endogenously in a supernetwork framework. Specifically, the multicriteria network equilibrium framework of Chapter 7 is retained, telecommuting is still an option with the advent of telecommunication networks, but now the supernetwork concept is used to capture location decisions as well.

The study of urban transportation and associated locational decisions has a long history, beginning with the contributions of Beckmann, McGuire, and Winsten (1956), who provided the basic framework for the formulation and analysis of transportation flows between origins and destination pairs over realistic networks. Further contributions to residential location and transportation research in the network equilibrium vein were made by Florian, Nguyen, and Ferland (1975), Dafermos (1976), Evans (1976), Boyce and Southworth (1979), Los (1979), Boyce (1980), and Boyce, et al. (1983), Lundqvist and Mattsson (1983), Lundqvist, Mattsson, and Kim (1998).

As noted by Kim (1983), efforts to combine transportation and land use problems, in general, and transportation and residential location problems, in particular, have had a long tradition, wherein residential location is viewed as consisting of trade-offs between the cost of the journey to work and residential benefits. More recent research has focused on the development of even more general models to handle a variety of cost and demand structures (cf. Safwat and Magnanti (1988), Kim (1989), Boyce and Mattsson (1999)) as well as to expand the scale of tractable problems (see Wegener (1986), Anderstig and Mattsson (1998), Yang and Meng (1998), Eliasson and Mattsson (2000)) and to include environmental and sustainability issues (see Johansson and Mattsson (1995), Lundqvist (1996, 1998, 1999), and the references therein).

The supernetwork model described in this chapter has the following features:

a. It allows each class of decision-maker to have his own set of criteria associated with the transportation *and* the location decisions and the number of criteria need only be finite. Possible criteria associated with route choice may include travel time, travel cost, environmental cost (associated with emissions), opportunity cost associated with telecommuting, etc. Relevant criteria associated with location choice, on the other hand, as regards residential location, may include land use cost, attractiveness of the surrounding area, safety, proximity to like-minded individuals, etc. Appropriate criteria associated with employment location may include attractiveness of the work environment, opportunities for advancement, salary scale, etc.

b. It allows for the selection of residential locations, or employment destinations, or both, in addition to the optimal routes of travel within the same framework, through the use of appropriate generalized cost functions which are distinct for each class of decision-maker, and through the application of a supernetwork formalism which interprets a *path* in a general fashion, and

c. It combines the option of telecommuting in the Information Age into the location/transportation network equilibrium framework.

The chapter is organized as follows. In Section 9.1, the multiclass, multicriteria network equilibrium models of location/transportation are developed, and the equilibrium conditions derived for three distinct scenarios. The variational inequality formulations of the governing equilibrium conditions are also provided. We then describe some experiences of both employees and employers in terms of location and transportation issues in the Silicon Valley and in Kista Science City outside Stockholm, Sweden.

In Section 9.2, some qualitative properties are given. In Section 9.3, an algorithm is proposed for the computation of the equilibrium patterns and then applied, in Section 9.4, to numerical examples for illustration purposes.

9.1 The Multicriteria Network Models of Location and Transportation

In this section, the multiclass, multicriteria network equilibrium models of location and transportation are constructed. As mentioned earlier, the focus is on three distinct scenarios, which are:

Scenario 1: Employment Location and Route Selection Decision-makers have predetermined origins (residential locations) and are free to select their destinations (employment locations) as well as their travel routes,

Scenario 2: Residential Location and Route Selection Decision-makers have predetermined destinations (employment locations) and are free to choose their origins (residential locations) as well as their travel routes.

Scenario 3: Residential Location, Employment Location, and Route Selection Decision-makers are free to select their origins (residential locations) and their destinations (employment locations), in addition to their travel routes.

Next, the notation is presented which is then utilized to formalize the model constructions for the problems underlying the above three scenarios. Moreover, we show how the problems can be visualized and studied on appropriately constructed supernetworks with the proper identification of the paths.

The models will allow each class of decision-maker to make the locational and transportation decisions based on his own set of criteria, which will permit the preception of, for example, travel cost and travel time, as well as other costs, such as opportunity cost, on a link in an individual manner.

The Notation

We now introduce the notation and then provide the specific problems that correspond to the above three scenarios. The notation is similar to that in Chapter 7, but with the additions and modifications necessary to this new application setting.

Consider a general network $G = [\mathcal{N}, \mathcal{L}]$, where $\mathcal{N}$ denotes the set of nodes in the network and $\mathcal{L}$ the set of directed links. Let a denote a link of the network connecting a pair of nodes and let p denote a path, assumed to be acyclic, consisting of a sequence of links connecting an origin/destination (O/D) pair of nodes. There are n links in the network and n_P paths. The set of paths in the network is denoted by P. Let Y denote the set of origin nodes and Z the set of destination nodes. Let P_y denote the set of paths originating in node y and let P_z denote the set of paths terminating in node z.

The Supernetwork Transformations

We now describe the supernetwork transformations for the three scenarios above which will allow one to associate criteria for the distinct classes not only with their transportation decisions but also with their locational decisions.

Note that a path consists of a sequence of links from an origin to a destination. In this framework, as has been emphasized throughout this book, a link may correspond to an actual physical link of transportation or an abstract or virtual link corresponding to a telecommunications link. Moreover, in order to be able to incorporate explicit criteria associated with location decisions (which we expect to be a function of the flows), we associate (and construct) with each employment location node z' (in the case of Scenario 1) a new link (z', z), which abstracts the employment location decision associated with location z'. The nodes z are, hence, termed destination nodes. Similarly, in the case of Scenario 2, construct, for each residential node y', a new link (y, y'), which allows one to abstract the residential location decision associated with location y'. The nodes y are, henceforth, referred to

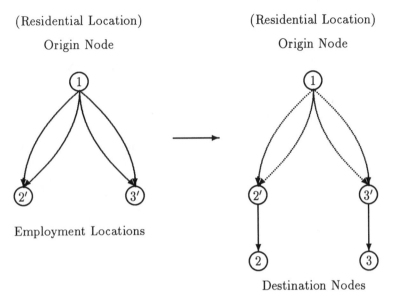

Fig. 9.1. Supernetwork Transformation for an Example of Scenario 1

as origins. Finally, in the case of Scenario 3, in which both residential and employment location decisions are to be made, we construct from each employment location node z' a new link (z', z) and to each residential location node a new link (y, y'). The nodes y are then referred to as origin nodes and the nodes z as destination nodes. A path, hence, will include not only links corresponding to *transportation* links but also to *location* links. Note that in this supernetwork framework transportation is viewed broadly in that it subsumes telecommunications as a mode. Also, as discussed in Chapters 7 and 8, multiclass, multicriteria network equilibrium models, as is our framework here, subsume multiple forms of transportation (such as private and public) in that a "path" in this context may correspond to a mode of transportation. In addition, since the emphasis here is on transportation and location decisions in the Information Age, the concept of path may also be applied to an alternative mode of telecommuting through telecommunications.

Illustrations of the appropriate constructions for the three distinct scenarios are given in Figures 9.1 through 9.3 for specific network examples.

For example, in Figure 9.1, the scenario is represented in which there is a single residential location, which corresponds to the origin node 1, and two possible employment locations denoted by nodes $2'$ and $3'$. In order to be able to model the employment locational choices, construct, as depicted in the second network in Figure 9.1, which is a supernetwork, two destination

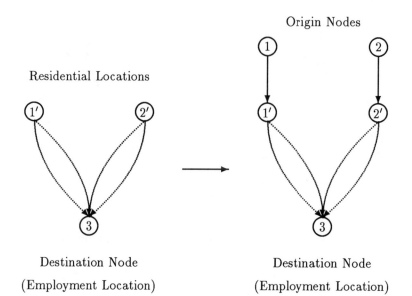

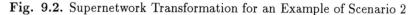

Fig. 9.2. Supernetwork Transformation for an Example of Scenario 2

nodes 2 and 3 and links joining, respectively, node 2′ with node 2 and node 3′ with node 3. As will be shown later, we will associate with the links (2′, 2) and (3′, 3) appropriate criteria which correspond to criteria associated with the classes' employment locational decisions. The links connecting node 1 with nodes 2′ and 3′ denote transportation/telecommmunication links. A path in this network is, hence, a sequence of links from the origin node to a destination node and consists of both transportation and employment location links.

The first network depicted in Figure 9.2, represents an example of Scenario 2, in which there is a single employment location corresponding to destination node 3 and two residential locations corresponding, respectively, to nodes 1′ and 2′. The links joining nodes 1′ and 2′ with node 3 represent transportation/telecommunication options. The second network depicted in Figure 9.2 shows the supernetwork transformation, through the addition of nodes 1 and 2 with links joining these nodes to nodes 1′ and 2′, respectively, which will allow us to associate explicit criteria associated with residential locational choices for the different classes. Note that now nodes 1 and 2 are termed origin nodes. A path (cf. the second network in Figure 9.2) joining an origin node to the destination node consists of a residential locational link plus a transportation/telecommunication link.

The first network in Figure 9.3 depicts an example illustrating Scenario

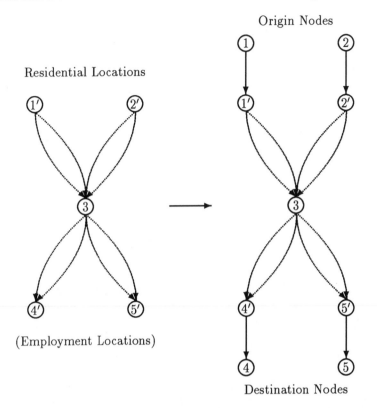

Fig. 9.3. Supernetwork Transformation for an Example of Scenario 3

3, in which both residential and employment locations are to be determined in addition to the routes of travel. In this example, there are two residential locations and two employment locations with the links joining nodes $1'$ and $2'$ to node 3 and node 3 to nodes $4'$ and $5'$ representing transportation/telecommunication options. The second network in Figure 9.3, in turn, represents the supernetwork transformation through the addition of origin nodes 1 and 2 and destination nodes 4 and 5. A path in such a network consists, hence, of links corresponding to a residential location option, the transportation/telecommunication option sequence, as well as the employment location option.

We next describe the flows on the network which correspond to the number of decision-makers selecting particular options and making specific locational and transportation decisions. We also discuss criteria that such decision-makers may utilize in making their decisions.

The Conservation of Flow Equations

Assume, as has been done throughout this part of the book, that there are k classes of decision-makers in the network with a typical class denoted by i.

Let f_a^i denote the flow of class i on link a and let x_p^i denote the nonnegative flow of class i on path p. The relationship between the link flows by class and the path flows is:

$$f_a^i = \sum_{p \in P} x_p^i \delta_{ap}, \quad \forall i, \quad \forall a \in \mathcal{L}, \tag{9.1}$$

where $\delta_{ap} = 1$, if link a is contained in path p, and 0, otherwise. Hence, as discussed both in Chapters 7 and 8, the flow of a class of decision-maker on a link is equal to the sum of the flows of the class on the paths that contain that link.

In addition, let f_a denote the total flow on link a, where

$$f_a = \sum_{i=1}^{k} f_a^i, \quad \forall a \in \mathcal{L}. \tag{9.2}$$

Thus, the total flow on a link is equal to the sum of the flows of all classes on that link. Group the class link flows into the kn-dimensional column vector $\tilde{f}$ with components $\{f_1^1, \ldots, f_n^1, \ldots, f_1^k, \ldots, f_n^k\}$ and the total link flows $\{f_1, \ldots, f_n\}$ into the n-dimensional column vector f. Also, group the class path flows into the kn_P-dimensional column vector $\tilde{x}$ with components $\{x_{p_1}^1, \ldots, x_{p_{n_P}}^k\}$.

The total number of decision-makers of class i associated with origin node y will be denoted by O_y^i. Note that the value of O_y^i will correspond to the number of individuals of class i at residential location y' who seek to make both an employment location decision as well as a transportation route decision. The total number of decision-makers of class i associated with destination node z will be denoted by D_z^i. Note that the value of D_z^i corresponds to the number of individuals of class i at employment location z' who seek to make both a residential location decision and a transportation route decision. Group the trip productions into a column vector $O \in R_+^{kJ}$, and the trip attractions into the column vector $D \in R_+^{kJ}$ and assume that these values are given and fixed.

Clearly, the following conservation of flow equations must be satisfied:

$$O_y^i = \sum_{p \in P_y} x_p^i, \quad \forall i, \forall y, \tag{9.3}$$

$$D_z^i = \sum_{p \in P_z} x_p^i, \quad \forall i, \forall z. \tag{9.4}$$

Moreover, if T^i denotes the total number of decision-makers of class i in the network, that is, the total number of individuals of a class who must make a residential location decision, an employment location decision, as well as a transportation route decision connecting their residential location to their employment location, one must also have that:

$$T^i = \sum_{y \in Y} O^i_y = \sum_{z \in Z} D^i_z = \sum_{p \in P} x^i_p, \quad \forall i. \tag{9.5}$$

Clearly, conservation of flow equations (9.3) correspond to Scenario 1, conservation of flow equations (9.4) to Scenario 2, and conservation of flow equations to Scenario 3.

The Criteria

We are now ready to describe the functions associated with the links, which consist, through the appropriate supernetwork transformation, of either transportation or locational links. In particular, assume (as was also done in Chapters 7 and 8) that there are H criteria, with H being a finite number, which the decision-makers may utilize in their locational/transportation decision-making with a typical criterion denoted by h. As before, let C_{ha} denote criterion h associated with link a, where:

$$C_{ha} = C_{ha}(f), \quad \forall a \in \mathcal{L}, \tag{9.6}$$

where C_{ha} is assumed to be a continuous function.

For example, as discussed in Chapters 7 and 8, criterion 1 may be time, in which case, one would have:

$$C_{1a} = C_{1a}(f) = t_a(f), \quad \forall a \in \mathcal{L}, \tag{9.7}$$

where $t_a(f)$ denotes the time associated with traversing link a. As argued in the two preceding chapters, in the case of a link corresponding to physical transportation, such as commuting, such a function may be higher than in the case of a link corresponding to telecommuting.

Another relevant criterion for such decision-making would be cost, that is, one may have:

$$C_{2a} = C_{2a}(f) = c_a(f), \quad \forall a \in \mathcal{L}, \tag{9.8}$$

which would reflect (depending on the link a) a transportation cost, or access cost in the case of a telecommunications link, or land-use price in the case of a residential location link. In addition, another relevant criterion in evaluating telecommuting versus commuting options is opportunity cost since one may expect that this cost would be high in the case of telecommuting (since one cannot benefit from the collegiality of the work environment) and lower in the case of commuting. Hence, the third criterion may be opportunity cost where:

$$C_{3a} = C_{3a}(f) = o_a(f), \quad \forall a \in \mathcal{L}, \tag{9.9}$$

with $o_a(f)$ denoting the opportunity cost associated with link a.

Finally, a decision-maker may wish to associate a safety cost with locations and with transportation in which case the fourth criterion may be:

$$C_{4a} = C_{4a}(f) = s_a(f), \quad \forall a \in \mathcal{L}, \tag{9.10}$$

where $s_a(f)$ denotes a safety cost measure associated with link a.

Note that the criteria associated with locational decisions need not be the same as those associated with transportation decisions.

Assume that each class of decision-maker has a potentially different perception of the trade-offs among the criteria, which are represented by the nonnegative weights $w_{1a}^i, \ldots, w_{Ha}^i$. Hence, w_{1a}^i denotes the weight on link a associated with criterion 1 for class i, w_{2a}^i denotes the weight associated with criterion 2 for class i, and so on. As described also in Chapters 7 and 8, observe that the weights are link-dependent and can, hence, incorporate specific link-dependent factors which could include for a particular class factors such as safety, convenience, and sociability.

Similar to the manner in Chapters 7 and 8, construct then the *generalized* cost of class i associated with link a and denoted by C_a^i as:

$$C_a^i = \sum_{h=1}^{H} w_{ha}^i C_{ha}, \quad \forall i, \quad \forall a \in \mathcal{L}. \tag{9.11}$$

In lieu of (9.2), one may write

$$C_a^i = C_a^i(\tilde{f}), \quad \forall i, \quad \forall a \in \mathcal{L}, \tag{9.12}$$

and group the generalized link costs into the kn-dimensional column vector C with components $\{C_1^1, \ldots, C_n^1, \ldots, C_1^k, \ldots, C_n^k\}$.

Let now V_p^i denote the generalized cost of class i associated with path p in the supernetwork where:

$$V_p^i = \sum_{a \in \mathcal{L}} C_a^i(\tilde{f}) \delta_{ap}, \quad \forall i, \quad \forall p. \tag{9.13}$$

Therefore, the generalized cost associated with a class and a path is that class's weighted combination of the various criteria on the links that comprise the path. Here the notation V_p^i is used in a location/transportation path context (see also (8.10)), in contrast to its context in Chapter 8.

Note, from the structure of the criteria on the links as expressed by (9.6) and the generalized cost structure assumed for the different classes on the links according to (9.11) and (9.13), that, as in Chapters 7 and 8, it is explicitly being assumed that the relevant criteria are functions of the flows on the links where, recall, that the flows correspond to the number of decision-makers of a particular class that select a particular link.

In terms of the above terminology and notation, the three scenarios lead to the following location/transportation problems:

Problem 1: Given the vector O, determine the vector of path flows $\tilde{x}$.

Problem 2: Given the vector D, determine the vector of path flows $\tilde{x}$.

Problem 3: Given the vector T, determine the vector of path flows $\tilde{x}$.

We now discuss the behavioral assumption underlying the above three problems and state the governing equilibrium conditions.

The Behavioral Assumption

The behavioral assumption which is applied here has also been used by Dafermos (1976) (see also Chapter 3) in the context of single-criteria, fixed demand integrated traffic network equilibrium models. Note that those models, however, preceded the application of variational inequality theory (cf. Dafermos (1980, 1982)) which is the methodology that is adopted in the subsequent section in order to formulate the governing equilibrium conditions. Analogous behavioral assumptions have been applied in a variety of network equilibrium contexts in the preceding chapters in this part of the book.

Specifically, the behavioral assumption utilized is similar to that underlying traffic assignment models (see also, Beckmann, McGuire, and Winsten (1956)) in that it is assumed that each class of user in the network selects (subject to constraints) his origin (in the case of Scenario 2), or his destination (in the case of Scenario 1), or both (in the case of Scenario 3), and his travel route so as to minimize the generalized cost on the path, given that all other users have made their choices. Moreover, each path consists of one (as in Problems 1 and 2) or two (as in Problem 3) locational decisions.

In particular, the following are the multiclass, multicriteria network equilibrium conditions for the three problems outlined above.

Multiclass, Multicriteria Network Equilibrium Conditions

Problem 1: For each class i, for all origins $y \in Y$, and for all paths $p \in P_y$, the flow pattern $\tilde{x}^*$ is said to be in equilibrium if the following conditions hold:

$$V_p^i(\tilde{f}^*) \begin{cases} = \lambda_y^i, & \text{if} \quad x_p^{i*} > 0 \\ \geq \lambda_y^i, & \text{if} \quad x_p^{i*} = 0. \end{cases} \tag{9.14}$$

In this scenario, the equilibrium is characterized by all utilized paths for a given class emanating from a given origin node having equal and minimal generalized costs.

Problem 2: For each class i, for all destinations $z \in Z$, and for all paths $p \in P_z$, the flow pattern $\tilde{x}^*$ is said to be in equilibrium if the following conditions hold:

$$V_p^i(\tilde{f}^*) \begin{cases} = \lambda_z^i, & \text{if} \quad x_p^{i*} > 0 \\ \geq \lambda_z^i, & \text{if} \quad x_p^{i*} = 0. \end{cases} \tag{9.15}$$

Hence, in this case, all the generalized costs on paths for each class terminating in each destination node are equal and minimal.

Problem 3: For each class i, the flow pattern $\tilde{x}^*$ is said to be in equilibrium if the following conditions hold:

$$V_p^i(\tilde{f}^*) \begin{cases} = \lambda^i, & \text{if } x_p^{i*} > 0 \\ \geq \lambda^i, & \text{if } x_p^{i*} = 0. \end{cases} \tag{9.16}$$

Equilibrium conditions (9.16) state that for each class, the generalized path costs are equal and minimal.

We now define the feasible sets $\mathcal{K}^i$; $i = 1, 2, 3$, underlying the respective problems as $\mathcal{K}^1 \equiv \{\tilde{f} | \tilde{x} \geq 0$, and $(9.1), (9.2), (9.3)$, hold$\}$, $\mathcal{K}^2$ is defined similarly except that, rather than (9.3) holding, (9.4) must now hold, whereas $\mathcal{K}^3$ requires that (9.5) be satisfied instead.

We present the variational inequality formulations of the equilibrium conditions governing Problems 1 through 3 below. Specifically, in light of Theorem 7.2, one can write down immediately the variational inequality formulations for the above three problems.

Theorem 9.1: Variational Inequality Formulations

The variational inequality formulations of the multiclass multicriteria network equilibrium model(s) with location/transportation satisfying equilibrium conditions (9.14), or (9.15), or (9.16), respectively, for Problems i; $i = 1, 2, 3$: are given by: determine $\tilde{f} \in \mathcal{K}^i$, satisfying

$$\sum_{i=1}^{k} \sum_{a \in \mathcal{L}} C_a^i(\tilde{f}^*) \times (f_a^i - f_a^{i*}) \geq 0, \qquad \forall \tilde{f} \in \mathcal{K}^i; \tag{9.17a}$$

equivalently, in standard variational inequality form:

$$\langle F(X^*), X - X^* \rangle \geq 0, \quad \forall X \in \mathcal{K}, \tag{9.17b}$$

where $F \equiv C$, $X \equiv \tilde{f}$, and $\mathcal{K} \equiv \mathcal{K}^i; i = 1, 2, 3$.

Note that although the structure of the function F that enters each of the variational inequalities corresponding to the three distinct problems is identical, the feasible sets $\mathcal{K}^1$, $\mathcal{K}^2$, and $\mathcal{K}^3$, are distinct.

Remark

Observe that, in the case of the construction of the supernetworks underlying Problems 1, 2, and 3, we could have simply constructed, respectively, for Problem 1: a single super destination node, with links from the employment location nodes to the super destination node; for Problem 2: a single super source node, with links joining the super source node to each residential location node; and, finally, for Problem 3: a super source and a super destination node with links joining the former with the residential locations and with links from the employment locations to the latter. Then, we could have defined origin/destination pairs accordingly with there being only one destination, in effect, on such a supernetwork for Problem 1; only 1 origin node for the supernetwork for Problem 2; and only 1 origin node and 1 destination node for the supernetwork for Problem 3. An analogous construction was done by Dafermos (1976) (see also Chapter 3). However, she assumed that there were no criteria associated with such "added" abstract links and, consequently, no expressions to allow for explicit location criteria. The above supernetwork constructions are done so for conceptualization and notational simplicity, although they do result in more nodes than are truly necessary.

For example, in the case of the second network in Figure 9.1, the links emanating from nodes $2'$ and $3'$ could terminate, instead, in a single super (destination) node, whereas the links terminating in nodes $1'$ and $2'$ in the second network in Figure 9.2, could have originated in a single super (origin) node. In the case of the second network in Figure 9.3, on the other hand, one could have constructed a single super source node (rather than nodes 1 and 2) and had links then emanating from it to nodes $1'$ and $2'$. Also, one could have constructed a single super destination node (rather than nodes 4 and 5) with links from nodes $4'$ and $5'$ to it.

One could then define the origin/destination pairs accordingly, and the models would collapse to the multicriteria network equilibrium model with origin/destination pairs and fixed demands outlined in Section 7.1.

9.1.1   Some Practical Experiences from Employees and Employers

As noted in the AT&T (2001c) website, "the fundamental economic driver of employment...has traditionally been intertwined with location. People move to cities or suburbs in search of employment, while people move from urban areas to suburbs in search of a higher quality of life – but there must be work within driving distance. Businesses may even take advantage of this talent pool." Sprint PCS is a US company which has opened nine major US customer service centers in three years. According to Lyne (2000), Sprint notes that "getting the right labor and the right facility, make up about 90% of a call center's major considerations." One criteria that the company considers is easy accessibility and an area with a short distance for transportation. The company contends that call center employees, typically not college graduates, will not commute more than 25 or 30 minute due to a saturated market of call centers, where they can always find another one in another part of the city. (This nicely illustrates, for example, Scenario 2, in which the employees have their residences but need to determine the employment locations and their optimal routes of travel between.) Hence, Sprint, which does not operate on regular business hours, typically locates its call centers not in the Central Business District. In addition, it shows that firms in making their location decisions must also consider transportation time and costs not only as regards their product deliveries, say, but also of their employees.

9.1.1.1 Silicon Valley and Congestion

A report recently released by the Joint Venture: Silicon Valley Network, a regional organization and the A. T. Kearney consulting firm, as quoted in the Modesto Bee Online (2001), states that Silicon Valley "could lose its place as the world's premier high-tech zone because of the high costs of living and doing business here, a shortage of qualified workers and worsening traffic." The median home price in Santa Clara County, in which San Jose, the largest city in northern California is located passed $500,000 in 2001. Moreover, it is not uncommon for workers to commute two hours from less expensive areas such as Modesto. That study, based on interviews with executives of more than 100 companies, recognizes that companies want more collaboration with goverments to assist in the timely building of affordable housing and to reduce traffic congestion.

According to the Silicon Valley/San Jose Business Journal (2001), congestion in the San Francisco-Oakland Bay area costs an estimated $3 billion annually in wasted fuel and lost time. In San Jose, the figure is $1.25 billion. The traffic congestion in the Bay, as measured in the Texas Transportation Institute's annual Mobility Study and also reported in the article, is now the second worst in the nation, after Los Angeles. According to Tapan Munroe, the chief economist with Pacific Gas & Electric Co. quoted in the Los Altos Town Crier (1998), "The challenges are traffic, shortages in skilled workforce, affordable housing and air quality." He sees telecommuting as one solution to the Silicon Valley traffic congestion but also recognizes that there are barriers to its use.

Interestingly, and, not unexpectedly, the recent downturn in the economy as reported on SiliconValley.com (2001), may be having an effect on travel times with the layoffs in the dot.com companies. Anecdotal evidence and interviews with commuters suggest that the flow of traffic there has improved. Others, however, dispute this conclusion. Nevertheless, the importance of location decisions coupled with transportation decisions are clearly revealed in the realities of Silicon Valley and its economy.

9.1.1.2 Kista Science City

Kista Science City, located outside Stockholm, in Sweden, is considered to be the fifth largest information technology cluster in the world. Stockholm is noted as a world leader in information technology and Kista acts as the headquarters for its information technology (IT) activity. As discussed by the Stockholm's City Planning Administration (2001), there are several reasons why this particular area has become an IT cluster and these include: a high degree of both national and international attraction; unique resources of human capital; it is easily accessible by public transport, by car, or by air, with Arlanda Airport located nearby; and it is characterized by a high degree of competence within the telecommunications sector with business, and universities and research institutions in proximity.

Its development has been considered a success, with a greater number of businesses locating in the area, with more youths studying past high school, and a renewal in residential areas and enhanced shopping districts. Nevertheless, despite the positives from such expansion due to IT, Stockholm is now beginning to face some of the same problems as Silicon Valley, although nowhere to the same degree. There has been an increase in traffic congestion and high housing prices, and workers have started shifting their residential locations. For additional background on transportation and location decision-making in the Information Age, see Ramjerdi (1999).

9.1.2 Location and Internet Congestion

Throughout this book, we have been emphasizing supernetworks for decision-making and the similarities as well as differences between transportation networks and telecommunication networks. We now provide some illustrative examples which demonstrate that, even in terms of travel time on the Internet (see the cost criterion (9.7)), location does matter.

According to the AT&T (2001d) website "Even on the Net, life is a highway. You may not have a windshield or a rearview mirror in your face, but the Traffic's real. And so is the wait." The article proceeds to say that teleworkers/telecommuters, by definition, are not faced with a daily commute but they still may "find themselves in virtual traffic much of the time." For example, just as vehicular traffic has peaks and valleys throughout the day, and decision-makers may determine their times of departure (and arrivals) accordingly, so the Internet, as well is subject to traffic peaks and valleys and this aspect can affect one's productivity. For example, the article advises that, depending upon where you live, that is, your residential location, you may be able to find some "shortcuts" through the Internet traffic jams. Indeed, individuals connected online in the US Eastern time zone typically find the Internet fastest early in the morning whereas Pacific time zone workers find the web slowest in the morning, but somewhat faster later in the workday when the "Eastern zone is off-hours, Europe's asleep, and Asia's just awakening."

Hence, according to the article the old saying "'Think globally, act locally' has new meaning in Internet time. You may find that by planning your Net time around your geographic locale and network traffic peaks, you can get more done in less time..."

9.2 Qualitative Properties

In this section, some qualitative properties of the solutions to the variational inequality problems (9.17) are presented.

In particular, by referring to Theorem 7.3, one can immediately present the following result since the feasible set underlying each of the three variational inequality problems is compact, that is, closed and bounded, and the generalized cost functions are assumed to be continuous.

Theorem 9.2: Existence
The solutions to each of the three variational inequalities given in (9.17a) are guaranteed to exist.

We now (as was done in Chapters 7 and 8) consider a generalized class cost function on a link a for class i of the *special* form:

$$C_a^i = w_{1a}^i C_{1a} + w_{2a}^i C_{2a} + \ldots + w_{(H-1)a}^i C_{(H-1)a} + (1 - \sum_{h=1}^{H-1} w_{ha}^i) C_{Ha}, \quad \forall i, \forall a \in \mathcal{L},$$

(9.18)

where

$$C_{ha} = g_a(f) + g_{ha}, \quad \forall a \in \mathcal{L}, \forall h,$$ (9.19)

that is, each criterion differs from any other on a link solely by the fixed cost term g_{ha}. Each of the weights preceding the respective criterion is assumed to be nonnegative. Note that these are precisely of the form (7.27) and (7.28).

Uniqueness of the total link load pattern then is immediate from Corollary 7.1, under the assumption that the function g is strictly monotone and the functions are as given in (9.18) and (9.19); equivalently, as given by (7.27) and (7.28). Monotonicity of the function F, in turn, in the case of such special functions follows from Corollary 7.2, provided that g is monotone increasing and, again, of the special form above. Lipschitz continuity of F then follows from Corollary 7.3, provided that the generalized link cost functions have bounded first-order derivatives. In this case, the generalized link cost functions need only be as given by (9.11).

9.3   The Algorithm

An explicit statement of the modified projection method for the solution of variational inequality problems (9.17a) for the multicriteria network equilibrium models of location and transportation is now given. In view of the results in Section 9.3, and those in Section 7.4 (cf. (7.45) and (7.46)), the statement of the algorithm is as follows, with convergence results as in Theorem 7.9, but over the appropriate feasible set.

Modified Projection Method for the Solution of Variational Inequalities (9.17a)

Step 0: Initialization
Set $\tilde{f}^0 \in \mathcal{K}^i; i = 1, 2, 3$. Let $\mathcal{T} = 1$, where $\mathcal{T}$ is the iteration counter and set α such that $0 < \alpha \leq \frac{1}{L}$, where L is the Lipschitz constant for the problem.

Step 1: Computation

Compute $\bar{f}^T \in \mathcal{K}^i; i = 1, 2, 3$, by solving the variational inequality subproblem:

$$\sum_{i=1}^{k} \sum_{a \in \mathcal{L}} (\bar{f_a^i}^T + \alpha(C_a^i(\bar{f}^{T-1})) - f_a^{iT-1}) \times (f_a^i - \bar{f_a^i}^T) \geq 0, \quad \forall \tilde{f} \in \mathcal{K}^i; i = 1, 2, 3.$$

(9.20)

Step 2: Adaptation

Compute $\tilde{f}^T \in \mathcal{K}^i; i = 1, 2, 3$, by solving the variational inequality subproblem:

$$\sum_{i=1}^{k} \sum_{a \in \mathcal{L}} (f_a^{iT} + \alpha(C_a^i(\bar{\tilde{f}}^T)) - f_a^{iT-1}) \times (f_a^i - f_a^{iT}) \geq 0, \quad \forall \tilde{f} \in \mathcal{K}^i; i = 1, 2, 3.$$

(9.21)

Step 3: Convergence Verification

If $|f_a^{iT} - f_a^{iT-1}| \leq \epsilon$, for all $i = 1, \cdots, k$, and all $a \in \mathcal{L}$, with $\epsilon > 0$, a pre-specified tolerance, then stop; otherwise, set $T := T + 1$, and go to Step 1.

9.4 Numerical Examples

In this section, three numerical examples, which illustrate Scenario 3 are presented. They consist of two classes of decision-makers. Hence, in these examples we seek to determine the equilibrium residential locations, employment locations, as well as the routes utilized in between by each class. The examples are stylized, but reinforce the concepts introduced earlier. Of course, a change in the input data will result in a distinct equilibrium solution as we show by perturbing the data and computing the solutions to two variants of the first example.

Specifically, the modified projection method was applied to solve variational inequality (9.17a) discussed in the preceding section in order to compute the multiclass, multicriteria network equilibrium pattern where the feasible set $\mathcal{K} = \mathcal{K}^3$. The convergence criterion was that the absolute value of the path flows of each class at two successive iterations was less than or equal to ϵ with ϵ set to 10^{-4}. The α parameter used in the modified projection method was set to .01. The demand was equally distributed among all the paths to construct the initial path flow pattern. For the solution of the variational inequality subproblems (9.20) and (9.21), which are equivalent to quadratic programming problems, we utilized the equilibration method of Dafermos and Sparrow (1969) (see Appendix C) as was also done for the telecommuting examples in Chapters 7 and 8.

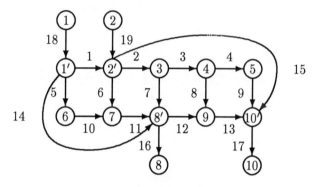

Fig. 9.4. Supernetwork for the Numerical Examples

The modified projection method, embedded with the equilibration algorithm, was coded in FORTRAN and the system utilized was a DEC Alpha Series 2000 at the University of Massachusetts at Amherst.

The examples had the supernetwork topology depicted in Figure 9.4. It corresponds to Scenario/Problem 3 in which the total number of decision-makers of each class is known. Nodes 1' and 2' represent the two residential locations, and the origin nodes are, hence, nodes 1 and 2. Nodes 8' and 10' are the employment locations with abstract nodes 8 and 10 being then the corresponding destination nodes. Links 1 through 13 are transportation links whereas links 14 and 15 are telecommunication links to depict telecommuting options. Links 16 and 17, in turn, represent the employment location links whereas links 18 and 19 denote the residential location links.

Example 9.1

In the first example, the total numbers of decision-makers in the two classes were $T^1 = 1200$ and $T^2 = 600$. In the subsequent two examples, these numbers were varied. In Table 9.1, the eighteen paths connecting the origin nodes 1 and 2 with the destination nodes 8 and 10, along with the links comprising the paths, are given. The paths were enumerated using a path-generation routine in the code.

The criteria were as follows. For links 1 through 15, with links 1 through 13 denoting transportation links and links 14 and 15 denoting telecommunication links to represent a telecommuting option, we considered three criteria: transportation time, transportation cost, and an opportunity cost. In the case of links 14 and 15 the transportation time would correspond to

Table 9.1. Paths in the Supernetwork

Path	Comprising Links
p_1	$(18, 1, 2, 3, 4, 9, 17)$
p_2	$(18, 1, 2, 3, 8, 13, 17)$
p_3	$(18, 1, 2, 7, 12, 13, 17)$
p_4	$(18, 1, 2, 7, 16)$
p_5	$(18, 1, 6, 11, 12, 13, 17)$
p_6	$(18, 1, 6, 11, 16)$
p_7	$(18, 1, 15, 17)$
p_8	$(18, 5, 10, 11, 12, 13, 17)$
p_9	$(18, 5, 10, 11, 16)$
p_{10}	$(18, 14, 12, 13, 17)$
p_{11}	$(18, 14, 16)$
p_{12}	$(19, 2, 3, 4, 9, 17)$
p_{13}	$(19, 2, 3, 8, 13, 17)$
p_{14}	$(19, 2, 7, 12, 13, 17)$
p_{15}	$(19, 2, 7, 16)$
p_{16}	$(19, 6, 11, 12, 13, 17)$
p_{17}	$(19, 6, 11, 16)$
p_{18}	$(19, 15, 17)$

Table 9.2. The Generalized User Link Cost Functions for the Two Classes

Link a	Class 1 - C_a^1	Class 2 - C_a^2
1	$.25t_1(f) + .25c_1(f) + o_1(f)$	$.5t_1(f) + .5c_1(f) + .5o_1(f)$
2	$.25t_2(f) + .25c_2(f) + o_2(f)$	$.5t_2(f) + .4c_2(f) + .4o_2(f)$
3	$.4t_3(f) + .4c_3(f) + o_3(f)$	$.4t_3(f) + .3c_3(f) + .7o_3(f)$
4	$.5t_4(f) + .5c_4(f) + 2o_4(f)$	$.3t_4(f) + .2c_4(f) + .6o_4(f)$
5	$.4t_5(f) + .5c_5(f) + o_5(f)$	$.5t_5(f) + .4c_5(f) + .5o_5(f)$
6	$.5t_6(f) + .3c_6(f) + 2o_6(f)$	$.7t_6(f) + .6c_6(f) + .7o_6(f)$
7	$.2t_7(f) + .4c_7(f) + o_7(f)$	$.4t_7(f) + .3c_7(f) + .8o_7(f)$
8	$.3t_8(f) + .5c_8(f) + o_8(f)$	$.3t_8(f) + .2c_8(f) + .6o_8(f)$
9	$.6t_9(f) + .2c_9(f) + 2o_9(f)$	$.2t_9(f) + .3c_9(f) + .9o_9(f)$
10	$.3t_{10}(f) + .4c_{10}(f) + o_{10}(f)$	$.1t_{10}(f) + .4c_{10}(f) + .8o_{10}(f)$
11	$.2t_{11}(f) + .7c_{11}(f) + o_{11}(f)$	$.4t_{11}(f) + .5c_{11}(f) + .9o_{11}(f)$
12	$.3t_{12}(f) + .4c_{12}(f) + o_{12}(f)$	$.5t_{12}(f) + .5c_{12}(f) + .7o_{12}(f)$
13	$.2t_{13}(f) + .3c_{13}(f) + 2o_{13}(f)$	$.4t_{13}(f) + 6c_{13}(f) + .9o_{13}(f)$
14	$.5t_{14}(f) + .2c_{14}(f) + .1o_{14}(f)$	$.3t_{14}(f) + .4c_{14}(f) + o_{14}(f)$
15	$.5t_{15}(f) + .3c_{15}(f) + .1o_{15}(f)$	$.2t_{15}(f) + .3c_{15}(f) + 2o_{15}(f)$
16	$h_{16}(f) + ca_{16}(f) + oc_{16}(f)$	$h_{16}(f) + ca_{16}(f) + oc_{16}(f)$
17	$h_{17} + ca_{17}(f) + oc_{17}(f)$	$h_{17}(f) + ca_{17}(f) + oc_{17}(f)$
18	$tc_{18}(f) + .5cl_{18}(f) + ca_{18}(f)$	$tc_{18}(f) + cl_{18}(f) + ca_{18}(f)$
19	$tc_{19}(f) + .5cl_{19}(f) + ca_{19}(f)$	$tc_{19}(f) + cl_{19}(f) + ca_{19}(f)$

the access time, whereas the transportation cost would correspond to the telecommunication cost. The opportunity costs, in turn, enable one to better model commuting versus telecommuting trade-offs. For example, one can expect the opportunity cost associated with a telecommunications link to be higher than that of a transportation link since telecommuters do not have the opportunity of meeting in person with colleagues.

In Table 9.2, we give the structure (cf. (9.11)) of the generalized user link class cost functions for the two classes of decision-makers in the example and its variants. For links 1 through 15 the criteria for a link a were: transportation time, denoted by t_a, transportation cost, denoted by $c_a(f)$, and opportunity cost, denoted by $o_a(f)$. For links 16 and 17 the criteria were for a typical link a: health cost, denoted by $h_a(f)$, cost of amenities, denoted by $ca_a(f)$, and opportunity cost, denoted by $oc_a(f)$. For links 18 and 19 the criteria for a link a were: telecommunications access cost, denoted by $tc_a(f)$, cost of living, denoted by $cl_a(f)$, and cost of amenities $ca_a(f)$. The numbers preceding the particular criterion are the weight of the criterion for that particular class and link.

The specific criterion functions used in the example and its variants are given in Tables 9.3 through 9.5.

Table 9.3. The Criterion Functions for the Transportation/Telecommuting Links

Link a	$t_a(f)$	$c_a(f)$	$o_a(f)$
1	$.00005f_1^4 + 4f_1 + 2f_3 + 2$	$.00005f_1^4 + 5f_1 + 1$	$2f_1 + 4$
2	$.00003f_2 + 2f_2 + f_5 + 1$	$.00003f_2^4 + 4f_2 + 2f_3 + 2$	$3f_2 + 2$
3	$.00005f_3^4 + f_3 + .5f_2 + 3$	$.00005f_3^4 + 3f_3 + f_1 + 1$	$f_3 + 4$
4	$.00003f_4^4 + 7f_4 + 3f_1 + 1$	$.00003f_4^4 + 6f_4 + 2f_6 + 4$	$f_4 + 2$
5	$5f_5 + 2$	$4f_5 + 8$	$2f_5 + 1$
6	$.00007f_6^4 + 3f_6 + f_9 + 4$	$.00007f_6^4 + 7f_6 + 2f_2 + 6$	$f_6 + 2$
7	$4f_7 + 6$	$8f_7 + 7$	$f_7 + 3$
8	$.00001f_8^4 + 4f_8 + 2f_{10} + 1$	$.00001f_8^4 + 7f_8 + 3f_5 + 6$	$2f_8 + 1$
9	$2f_9 + 8$	$8f_9 + 5$	$3f_9 + 2$
10	$.00003f_{10}^4 + 4f_{10} + f_{12} + 7$	$.00003f_{10}^4 + 6f_{10} + 2f_8 + 3$	$f_{10} + 1$
11	$.00004f_{11}^4 + 6f_{11} + 2f_{13} + 2$	$.00004f_{11} + 4f_{11} + 3f_{10} + 4$	$4f_{11} + 3$
12	$.00002f_{12}f^4 + 4f_{12} + 2f_5 + 1$	$.00002f_{12} + 6f_{12} + 2f_9 + 5$	$3f_{12} + 2$
13	$.00003f_{13}^4 + 7f_{13} + 4f_{10} + 8$	$.00003f_{13}^4 + 9f_{13} + 3f_8 + 3$	$f_{13} + 1$
14	$f_{14} + 2$	$.1f_{14} + 1$	$6f_{14} + 1$
15	$f_{15} + 1$	$.2f_{15} + 1$	$7f_{15} + 4$

Table 9.4. The Criterion Functions for the Employment Locational Links

Link a	$h_a(f)$	$ca_a(f)$	$oc_a(f)$
16	$3f_{16} + 10$	$f_{16} + 1$	$f_{16} + 1$
17	$2f_{17} + 4$	$f_{17} + 1$	$2f_{17} + 2$

Table 9.5. The Criterion Functions for the Residential Locational Links

Link a	$tc_a(f)$	$cl_a(f)$	$ca_a(f)$
18	$5f_{18} + 10$	$10f_{18} + 1$	$f_{18} + 1$
19	$f_{19} + 1$	$f_{19} + 1$	$5f_{19} + 10$

Note that the opportunity costs associated with links 14 and 15 were high since these are telecommunication links and users by choosing these links forego the opportunities associated with working and associating with colleagues from a face to face perspective. Observe, however, that the weights for class 1 associated with the opportunity costs on the telecommunication links are low (relative to those of class 2). This has the interpretation that class 1 does not weight such opportunity costs highly and may, for example, prefer to be working from the home for a variety of reasons, including family. Also, note that class 1 weights the transportation time on the telecommunication links more highly than class 2 does and, thus, cares about congestion more on such a link.

In terms of the criteria associated with the employment location links 16 and 17, each class of decision-maker weighted each of the three criteria equally and identically. On the other hand, in terms of the residential location links 18 and 19, although members of class 2 weighted each of the associated criteria identically, the members of class 1 weighted the cost of living lower.

The modified projection method required 211 iterations for convergence. It yielded the equilibrium multiclass link flow and total flow pattern reported in Table 9.6. The equilibrium path flow pattern induced by the equilibrium multiclass link flow pattern is reported in Table 9.7.

The generalized path costs were: for class 1: $V_{p_{11}}^1 = 12563.9092$, $V_{p_{18}}^1 = 12563.8154$, with all generalized costs on other paths exceeding the above values (since class 1 only utilized paths p_{11} and p_{18}), and for class 2: $V_{p_9}^2 = 19403.773$, $V_{p_{11}}^2 = 19403.2637$, $V_{p_{12}}^2 = 19403.3535$, $V_{p_{13}}^2 = 19403.3535$, $V_{p_{15}}^2 = 19403.2520$, $V_{p_{17}}^2 = 19403.3379$, with generalized costs on other paths exceeding the above since the other paths were not utilized by class 2.

The combination of the modified projection method embedded with the equilibration method yielded accurate solutions.

Note that location link 16 had approximately the same number of decision-makers selecting it (i.e., employment location 8'), as were attracted to employment location link 17 (that is, employment location 10'). However, the number of decision-makers selecting residential location link 18 corresponding to residential location 1' was substantially lower than the number selecting locational link 19 corresponding to residential location 2'. Also, interestingly, according to the total flow on link 14, there were about 660 telecommuters out of a population of 678 from residential location 1'. In terms of residential location 2', 914 decision-makers out of about 1121 (see the total flows on links 15 and 19) chose to telecommute to work.

In regards to the employment locational decisions, only approximately 18 out of 600 members of class 2 selected employment location link 17, that is, employment location 10', with approximately 582 selecting employment location link 16, that is, employment location 8'. On the other hand, about 914 out of 1200 decision-makers of class 1 selected employment location link 17, that is, employment location 10'. Furthermore, essentially all decision-

Table 9.6. The Equilibrium Link Flows for Example 9.1

Link a	Class 1 - f_a^{1*}	Class 2 - f_a^{2*}	Total flow - f_a^*
1	0.0000	0.0000	0.0000
2	0.0000	128.9642	128.0642
3	0.0000	17.7903	17.7903
4	0.0000	11.6516	11.6516
5	0.0000	17.9881	17.9881
6	0.0000	79.1368	79.1368
7	0.0000	110.2739	110.2739
8	0.0000	6.1387	6.1387
9	0.0000	11.6516	11.6516
10	0.0000	17.9881	17.9881
11	0.0000	97.1250	97.1250
12	0.0000	0.0000	0.0000
13	0.0000	6.1387	6.1387
14	285.4840	374.8107	660.2947
15	914.5154	0.0000	914.5154
16	285.4840	582.2097	867.6937
17	914.5154	17.7903	932.3057
18	285.4840	392.7989	678.2829
19	914.5154	207.2010	1121.7163

Table 9.7. The Equilibrium Path Flows for Example 9.1

Path p	Class 1 - x_p^{1*}	Class 2 - x_p^{2*}
p_1	0.0000	0.0000
p_2	0.0000	0.0000
p_3	0.0000	0.0000
p_4	0.0000	0.0000
p_5	0.0000	0.0000
p_6	0.0000	0.0000
p_7	0.0000	0.0000
p_8	0.0000	0.0000
p_9	0.0000	17.9881
p_{10}	0.0000	0.0000
p_{11}	286.4840	374.8107
p_{12}	0.0000	11.6516
p_{13}	0.0000	6.1387
p_{14}	0.0000	0.0000
p_{15}	0.0000	110.2739
p_{16}	0.0000	0.0000
p_{17}	0.0000	79.1368
p_{18}	914.5154	0.0000

Table 9.8. The Equilibrium Link Flows for Example 9.2

Link a	Class 1 - f_a^{1*}	Class 2 - f_a^{2*}	Total flow - f_a^*
1	0.0000	0.0000	0.0000
2	0.0000	204.1477	204.1477
3	0.0000	0.0000	0.0000
4	0.0000	0.0000	0.0000
5	0.0000	27.2801	27.2801
6	0.0000	128.6633	128.6633
7	0.0000	204.1477	204.1477
8	0.0000	0.0000	0.0000
9	0.0000	0.0000	0.0000
10	0.0000	27.2801	27.2801
11	0.0000	155.9434	155.9434
12	0.0000	0.0000	0.0000
13	0.0000	0.0000	0.0000
14	961.7896	2639.8948	3601.6843
15	5038.199	0.0000	5038.1992
16	961.7896	2999.9858	3961.7754
17	5038.1992	0.0000	5038.199
18	961.7896	2667.1748	3628.9644
19	5038.199	332.8109	5371.0103

makers of class 1 chose to telecommute, whereas only about two-thirds of class 2 elected this option.

We then proceeded to construct two variants of the preceding example by varying the demands associated with the two classes.

Example 9.2

In the second example, the data were kept as in the preceding example, but now we increased the total numbers of the two classes five-fold, yielding $T^1 = 6000$ and $T^2 = 3000$. An application of the modified projection method with the α parameter now set to .001 converged in 1384 iterations and yielded the new equilibrium link flow and path flow patterns reported in Tables 9.8 and 9.9, respectively.

The generalized path costs were: for class 1: $V_{p_{11}}^1 = 63786.1719$, $V_{p_{18}}^1 = 63784.8867$, with all generalized costs on other paths exceeding the above values (since class 1 only utilized paths p_{11} and p_{18}), and for class 2: $V_{p_9}^2 = 100733.0391$, $V_{p_{11}}^2 = 100732.9844$, $V_{p_{15}}^2 = 100733.8438$, $V_{p_{17}}^2 = 100733.9375$, with generalized costs on other paths exceeding the above since the other paths were not utilized by class 2. As expected, with the greater number of decision-makers, the generalized path costs increased, due to the criterion functions being increasing functions of the flows.

Table 9.9. The Equilibrium Path Flows for Example 9.2

Path p	Class 1 - x_p^{1*}	Class 2 - x_p^{2*}
p_1	0.0000	0.0000
p_2	0.0000	0.0000
p_3	0.0000	0.0000
p_4	0.0000	0.0000
p_5	0.0000	0.0000
p_6	0.0000	0.0000
p_7	0.0000	0.0000
p_8	0.0000	0.0000
p_9	0.0000	27.2801
p_{10}	0.0000	0.0000
p_{11}	961.7896	2639.8948
p_{12}	0.0000	0.0000
p_{13}	0.0000	0.0000
p_{14}	0.0000	0.0000
p_{15}	0.0000	204.1477
p_{16}	0.0000	0.0000
p_{17}	0.0000	128.6633
p_{18}	5038.1992	0.0000

Note that, with the increased number of totals of decision-makers in both classes, employment location $10'$ was now relatively more attractive than location $8'$ (and more attractive than it had been in the preceding example with lower total numbers of decision-makers). This is due to the fact that as the employment locations became more congested the costs associated with location $10'$ were lower (see the corresponding criterion functions for links 16 and 17). On the other hand, residential location $2'$ now became relatively more attractive than residential location $1'$ (cf. the total flows on links 19 and 18, respectively). Again, this can be explained by the form of the criterion functions associated with the residential locational links. As in the preceding example, essentially all the decision-makers of class 1 chose to telecommute. A higher proportion of the decision-makers of class 2 now also chose to telecommute and this is most likely due to increasing congestion. Interestingly, class 2 chose to telecommute exclusively using telecommunications link 14, whereas the majority of class 1 telecommuted using telecommunications link 15.

Example 9.3

We then constructed another variant of the first example by considering Example 9.2 but now interchanging the total numbers in each class. Thus, we decreased T^1 to 3000 but increased T^2 to 6000. The decision-makers of class 2 now outnumber the decision-makers of class 1. An application of the modified projection method to this new problem with $\alpha = .001$ resulted in convergence in 1033 iterations and yielded the new equilibrium link load and path flow patterns reported in Tables 9.10 and 9.11, respectively.

Note that now all members of class 1 chose to telecommute using telecommunications link 15, whereas members of class 2 telecommuted using both link 14 and link 15. Employment locations $10'$ and $8'$ were now almost equally attractive and had a similar number of employees. Members of class 1 now all located at residential location $2'$, members of class 2 now preferred residential location $1'$ and whereas in Variant 1 they had preferred residential location $2'$.

The generalized path costs were now: for class 1: $V_{p_{18}}^1 = 57247.3125$, with all generalized costs on other paths exceeding the above values (since class 1 only utilized path p_{18}), and for class 2: $V_{p_9}^2 = 115393.0313$, $V_{p_{11}}^2 = 115393.0313$, $V_{p_{12}}^2 = 115394.0000$, $V_{p_{13}}^2 = 115393.5391$, $V_{p_{15}}^2 = 115393.0859$, $V_{p_{17}}^2 = 115393.2422$, $V_{p_{18}}^2 = 115393.8672$, with generalized costs on other paths exceeding the above since the other paths were not utilized by class 2.

Again, the modified projection method yielded accurate solutions. Note that although the monotonicity condition was not verified a priori and, in fact, the criterion functions were much more general than those for which monotonicity was established, the algorithm, nevertheless, converged. Hence, one can expect it to be applicable to a greater range of problems than those for which theoretical results have been established. This holds also in the case of the numerical examples in Chapters 7 and 8.

Table 9.10. The Equilibrium Link Flows for Example 9.3

Link a	Class 1 - f_a^{1*}	Class 2 - f_a^{2*}	Total flow - f_a^*
1	0.0000	0.0000	0.0000
2	0.0000	219.1261	219.1261
3	0.0000	46.7751	46.7751
4	0.0000	28.3570	28.3570
5	0.0000	20.3091	20.3091
6	0.0000	141.6093	141.6093
7	0.0000	172.3510	172.3510
8	0.0000	18.4181	18.4181
9	0.0000	28.3570	28.3570
10	0.0000	20.3091	20.3091
11	0.0000	161.9184	161.9184
12	0.0000	0.0000	0.0000
13	0.0000	18.4181	18.4181
14	0.0000	4146.6807	4146.6807
15	30000.00	1472.080	4472.2119
16	0.0000	4480.9502	4480.9502
17	30000.00	1518.9832	4518.9873
18	0.0000	4166.9897	4166.9897
19	30000.00	1832.9434	4832.9473

Table 9.11. The Equilibrium Path Flows for Example 9.3

Path p	Class 1 - x_p^{1*}	Class 2 - x_p^{2*}
p_1	0.0000	0.0000
p_2	0.0000	0.0000
p_3	0.0000	0.0000
p_4	0.0000	0.0000
p_5	0.0000	0.0000
p_6	0.0000	0.0000
p_7	0.0000	0.0000
p_8	0.0000	0.0000
p_9	0.0000	0.3091
p_{10}	0.0000	0.0000
p_{11}	0.0000	4146.6807
p_{12}	0.0000	28.3570
p_{13}	0.0000	18.4181
p_{14}	0.0000	0.0000
p_{15}	0.0000	172.3510
p_{16}	0.0000	0.0000
p_{17}	0.0000	141.6093
p_{18}	3000.00	1472.2080

9.5   Sources and Notes

The models described in this chapter are due to Nagurney and Dong (2002). The presentation of them here is novel and is done in a supernetwork framework. Moreover, additional figures are presented for exposition purposes as well as examples from practice. The numerical examples in this chapter are taken from the above source.

Note that in this chapter the fixed demand case has been considered. One could also construct elastic analogues of the models considered here and apply the theoretical results for the elastic demand multicriteria network equilibrium model obtained in Chapter 7. Indeed, such an approach was used by Nagurney, Dong, and Mokhtarian (2000) to construct integrated network equilibrium models but within the application setting of telecommuting versus commuting decision-making.

Part IV New Directions

10 Supernetworks of Producers and Consumers

With this chapter, we begin the fourth, and, final, part of this book. Specifically, the chapters in this part focus on new directions in that they provide syntheses or extensions of ideas found in Parts II and III or new application areas. This chapter formulates a multitiered supernetwork in which the decision-makers on each of the two tiers of the network are multicriteria ones. Chapter 11 returns to the topic of financial decision-making, but now introduces variable weights associated with the criteria. Chapter 12, on the other hand, illustrates, through the application area of the environment, how careful one needs to be in addressing decision-making in the Information Age. It presents paradoxes that can occur in networks, in particular, in supernetworks, which combine aspects of transportation and telecommunication networks. Chapter 12 then shows how policies can be used to circumvent such paradoxes and demonstrates that behavior modification in the form of the inclusion of environmental criteria in decision-making can have the same effect.

This chapter describes a supernetwork framework for the formulation, analysis, and computation of solutions to problems in which the firms and the consumers are multicriteria decision-makers. The problems are multitiered but consist of two tiers of decision-makers, in particular, the firms and the consumers, in contrast to the multitiered supernetworks studied in supply chains in Chapters 4 and 5, which consisted of three or more tiers. Moreover, in this chapter, the decision-makers are multicriteria ones.

In particular, the firms, which are spatially separated, and the consumers, located at the demand markets, each face multiple criteria in making their production/consumption decisions. It is assumed that each firm seeks to maximize his profit, where profit is the difference between the revenue and costs, which include not only production cost but also the total processing costs associated with selecting different shipment options to each demand market. The shipment alternatives to each demand market are represented by links characterized by specific transportation cost and transportation time functions. Hence, a specific shipment option or link may have a low associated transportation time but a high transportation cost whereas another may have a high associated transportation time and a low cost. Each firm also seeks to maximize its output (and, in effect, its market share). An individual firm assigns its own weights to the two criteria of profit maximization and output maximization.

The consumers, in turn, correspond to different classes and weight the transportation time and transportation cost associated with obtaining the product from each firm in an individual manner. Thus, one class of consumer may be more time-sensitive in obtaining the product, whereas another may be more cost-sensitive. The consumers of each class, therefore, base their consumption decisions not only on the price set by the producers but also on the *generalized* cost, which includes the transportation time and cost associated with obtaining the product at a particular demand market from a specific firm.

This chapter brings together multicriteria decision-makers on the production side and on the consumption side in a network economic framework. Chapters 7 through 9, on the other hand, focused on the consumption side, whether the topic was telecommuting, teleshopping, or location and transportation decisions. Other applications of multicriteria decision-making in a spatial context can be found in the edited volume of Stewart and van den Honert (1998) and the references therein.

The chapter is organized as follow. In Section 10.1, the multicriteria spatial network model with firms and consumers is presented. The supernetwork is a bipartite one with multiple links connecting the top-tier nodes corresponding to the firms and the bottom-tier nodes denoting the demand markets with the links representing different shipment alternatives. The variational inequality formulation of the governing equilibrium conditions is then derived, which yields both the product shipment (and production) pattern as well as the demand price pattern. We then discuss some of the realities of shipping goods in the Information Age with examples from railroading and trucking.

In Section 10.2, the focus is on the "statics," whereas in Section 10.3, a tatonnement process in commodity shipment and price variables is proposed and its projected dynamical system formulation given. Dynamic models were also developed in Chapters 5 and 6 using this methodology for supply chain networks with electronic commerce and for financial networks with intermediation, respectively.

In Section 10.5, the Euler method is proposed for the time-discretization of the dynamic adjustment process. We also provide conditions for convergence and then apply the method in Section 10.5 to several numerical examples, in which the weights associated with the different criteria are allowed to vary.

10.1   The Model with Multicriteria Producers and Consumers

In this section, the supernetwork model with multicriteria producers and multicriteria consumers is developed. The production side is first addressed and then the consumption side. Subsequently, the integrated supernetwork model is constructed and the variational inequality formulation of the governing equilibrium conditions derived.

The Production Side

Assume that a certain homogeneous product is produced by m firms and is consumed by consumers located at n demand markets. We denote a typical firm by i and a typical demand market by j. Let q_i denote the nonnegative production output of firm i. Group the production outputs of all firms into the column vector $q \in R_+^m$. Assume that each firm i is faced with a production cost function f_i, which we assume can depend, in general, on the entire vector of production outputs, that is,

$$f_i = f_i(q), \quad \forall i. \tag{10.1}$$

Each firm can ship the product to each demand market using one (or more) of o possible shipment alternatives, which can represent mode/route alternatives. Denote a typical shipment alternative by l. Associated with firm i selecting shipment alternative l to demand market j is the total shipment processing cost, denoted by tc_{ijl}, and given by:

$$tc_{ijl} = \hat{c}_{ijl}(q_{ijl})q_{ijl}, \tag{10.2}$$

where $\hat{c}_{ijl}$ denotes the unit cost of processing the shipment of the product from firm i to demand market j using alternative l and q_{ijl} denotes the quantity of the product produced by firm i and shipped to demand market j using alternative l.

To help fix ideas and to aid in the construction of the supernetwork, the shipment alternatives associated with firm i and demand market j are depicted as links in Figure 10.1 and, henceforth, the shipment alternatives are alternatively referred to as links.

The quantity produced by firm i must satisfy the following conservation of flow equation:

$$q_i = \sum_{j=1}^{n} \sum_{l=1}^{o} q_{ijl}, \tag{10.3}$$

which states that the quantity produced by firm i is equal to the sum of the quantities shipped from the firm to all demand markets via all the shipment alternatives.

The total costs incurred by a firm i, thus, are equal to the sum of the firm's production cost plus the total cost of processing the shipments of the

Firm i

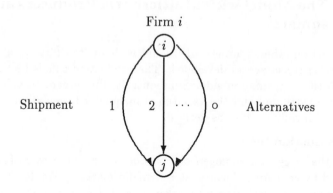

Demand Market j

Fig. 10.1. Network Structure of Shipment Alternatives for Firm i to Demand Market j

product along all shipment links to all demand markets. The firm's revenue, in turn, is equal to the price charged for the product times the total quantity consumed of the product from the firm at all the demand markets. Let ρ^*_{ijl} denote the price charged for the product by the producer i for shipment to demand market j via alternative l (i.e., the supply price). Then the criterion of profit maximization for firm i can be expressed as:

$$\text{Maximize} \quad \sum_{j=1}^{n}\sum_{l=1}^{o} \rho^*_{ijl} q_{ijl} - f_i(q) - \sum_{j=1}^{n}\sum_{l=1}^{o} \hat{c}_{ijl}(q_{ijl})q_{ijl}, \qquad (10.4)$$

subject to $q_{ijl} \geq 0$, for all j, l, and satisfying constraint (10.3). We discuss how the supply price ρ^*_{ijl} is determined later in this section when the supernetwork model is described. Hence, the prices (see also Stevens (1961)) are allowed to explicitly vary by location of the producer/demand market/shipment alternatives. This kind of flexibility/generality was also permitted in the supply chain models in Chapters 4 and 5.

In addition, since *multicriteria* decision-making on the production side is being considered, assume that each firm seeks to maximize its production output, that is, firm i seeks to also:

$$\text{Maximize} \quad \sum_{j=1}^{n}\sum_{l=1}^{o} q_{ijl}, \qquad (10.5)$$

subject to $q_{ijl} \geq 0$ for all j, l.

Of course, a firm may have a different criterion than that of output maximization, as well as other criteria overall. However, here, for definiteness, and for purposes of model development and analysis, we consider the above two specific criteria.

We now describe how to construct a value function associated with the two criteria facing each firm, that is, profit maximization, and output maximization. Each firm i associates a nonnegative weight w_i with the output maximization criterion, with the weight associated with the profit maximization criterion serving as the numeraire and being set equal to 1. Then, we construct a value function for each firm (cf. Fishburn (1970), Chankong and Haimes (1983), Yu (1985), Keeney and Raiffa (1993)) using a constant additive weight value function. Consequently, the multicriteria decision-making problem for firm i is transformed into:

$$\text{Maximize} \quad \sum_{j=1}^{n}\sum_{l=1}^{o} \rho_{ijl}^* q_{ijl} - f_i(q) - \sum_{j=1}^{n}\sum_{l=1}^{o} \hat{c}_{ijl}(q_{ijl})q_{ijl} + w_i \sum_{j=1}^{n}\sum_{l=1}^{o} q_{ijl},$$

$$(10.6)$$

subject to $q_{ijl} \geq 0, \forall j, l$, and satisfying (10.3).

According to (10.6), each firm has its own production cost function, its own total shipment processing cost function, as well as its weight associated with the second criterion.

The firms are assumed to behave in a noncooperative manner in the sense of Cournot (1838) and Nash (1950, 1951), seeking to determine their own optimal production and shipment quantities. If the production cost function for each firm is continuously differentiable and convex, as is the total shipment processing cost function, the optimality conditions (see Dafermos and Nagurney (1987), Nagurney (1999), Gabay and Moulin (1980), and Appendix B) take the form of a variational inequality problem given by: determine $(q^*, Q^*) \in K$, such that

$$\sum_{i=1}^{m} \left[\frac{\partial f_i(q^*)}{\partial q_i} - w_i \right] \times [q_i - q_i^*] + \sum_{i=1}^{m}\sum_{j=1}^{n}\sum_{l=1}^{o} \left[\frac{\partial \hat{c}_{ijl}(q_{ijl}^*)}{\partial q_{ijl}} q_{ijl}^* + \hat{c}_{ijl}(q_{ijl}^*) - \rho_{ijl}^* \right]$$

$$\times [q_{ijl} - q_{ijl}^*] \geq 0, \qquad\qquad \forall (q, Q) \in K, \qquad (10.7)$$

where Q denotes the mno-dimensional column vector of product shipments, and $K \equiv \{(q, Q) | Q \geq 0, \text{ and satisfies } (10.3)\}$.

The Consumption Side

We now describe the consumers located at the demand markets. Assume that there are k classes of consumers, with a typical class denoted by r, at each of the n demand markets. Each class of consumer takes into account in making consumption decisions not only the prices charged for the product by the firms but also the transportation time and transportation cost to obtain the product. Hence, they, as are the firms, are multicriteria decision-makers. Let c_{ijl} denote the transportation cost associated with shipping the product from firm i to demand market j along link l. Assume that the transportation cost is continuous and of the form:

$$c_{ijl} = c_{ijl}(q_{ijl}), \quad \forall i, j, l. \tag{10.8}$$

In addition, let t_{ijl} denote the transportation time associated with shipping the product from firm i to j via l, where the function is continuous and of the form:

$$t_{ijl} = t_{ijl}(q_{ijl}), \quad \forall i, j, l. \tag{10.9}$$

Let q_{ijlr} denote the quantity of the product shipped from i to j via l and going to class r, where:

$$q_{ijl} = \sum_{r=1}^{k} q_{ijlr}, \quad \forall i, j, l, \tag{10.10}$$

that is, the total amount of the product shipped between a firm and a demand market along a link is equal to the sum of all the class product shipments shipped on that link.

Assume now that members of a class of consumer at each demand market perceive the transportation cost and the transportation time associated with obtaining the product in an individual manner and weight these two criteria, which they wish to minimize, accordingly. In particular, let w_{jr}^1 denote the nonnegative weight associated with the transportation cost as perceived by class r at demand market j and let w_{jr}^2 denote the nonnegative weight associated with the transportation time as perceived by class r at demand market j. Thus, the *generalized* cost as perceived by class r at demand market j of obtaining the product from firm i via shipment alternative l is given by the expression:

$$w_{jr}^1 c_{ijl}(q_{ijl}) + w_{jr}^2 t_{ijl}(q_{ijl}).$$

Let now λ_{jr} denote the *generalized* demand price of the product as perceived by class r at demand market j and group the generalized demand prices into the column vector $\lambda \in R_+^{nk}$. Further, denote the demand of class r at demand market j by d_{jr} and assume, as given, the continuous demand functions:

$$d_{jr} = d_{jr}(\lambda), \quad \forall j, r. \tag{10.11}$$

The classes of consumers located at the demand markets take the price charged by the producers for the product (with shipment along l), which, recall was denoted by ρ_{ijl}^*, plus the generalized cost as perceived by the class associated with shipping the product to the demand market, in making their consumption decisions. In equilibrium, we know that this sum must be equal to the demand price that the consumers of that class are willing to pay to obtain the product. Hence, the equilibrium condition takes the form: For all i, j, l, r:

$$\rho_{ijl}^* + w_{jr}^1 c_{ijl}(q_{ijl}^*) + w_{jr}^2 t_{ijl}(q_{ijl}^*) \begin{cases} = \lambda_{jr}^*, & \text{if} \quad q_{ijlr}^* > 0 \\ \geq \lambda_{jr}^*, & \text{if} \quad q_{ijlr}^* = 0, \end{cases} \tag{10.12}$$

and

$$
d_{jr}(\lambda^*) \begin{cases} = \displaystyle\sum_{i=1}^{m}\sum_{l=1}^{o} q_{ijlr}^*, & \text{if} \quad \lambda_{jr}^* > 0 \\[2ex] \leq \displaystyle\sum_{i=1}^{m}\sum_{l=1}^{o} q_{ijlr}^*, & \text{if} \quad \lambda_{jr}^* = 0. \end{cases} \tag{10.13}
$$

Conditions (10.13) state that if the demand price for the product of a class at a demand market is positive, then the sum of the product shipments for that class from the firms along all shipment alternatives is precisely equal to the demand for that class and demand market at the equilibrium demand price vector. If the equilibrium demand price for that class and demand market is zero, then there may be an excess of product shipments over the demand for that class and demand market.

Using similar arguments as in the proofs of variational inequality formulations for the supply chain model with electronic commerce (see also Samuelson (1952), Takayama and Judge (1971), Nagurney, Dong, and Zhang (2000), Nagurney and Dong (2000)), one can conclude that the vector $(\hat{Q}^*, \lambda^*)$, where $\hat{Q}$ is the $mnok$-dimensional vector of class product shipments with component $ijlr$ given by q_{ijlr}, satisfies conditions (10.12) and (10.13) if and only if it satisfies the variational inequality problem:

$$
\sum_{i=1}^{m}\sum_{j=1}^{n}\sum_{l=1}^{o}\sum_{r=1}^{k} \left[\rho_{ijl}^* + w_{jr}^1 c_{ijl}(q_{ijl}^*) + w_{jr}^2 t_{ijl}(q_{ijl}^*) - \lambda_{jr}^* \right] \times \left[q_{ijlr} - q_{ijlr}^* \right]
$$

$$
- \sum_{j=1}^{n}\sum_{r=1}^{k} \left[d_{jr}(\lambda^*) - \sum_{i=1}^{m}\sum_{l=1}^{o} q_{ijlr}^* \right] \times \left[\lambda_{jr} - \lambda_{jr}^* \right] \geq 0, \quad \forall(\hat{Q}, \lambda) \in \mathcal{K}, \tag{10.14}
$$

where $\mathcal{K} \equiv \{(\hat{Q}, \lambda) | (\hat{Q}, \lambda) \in R_+^{mnok+nk}\}$.

The Supernetwork Model

We now present the supernetwork model which synthesizes the optimality conditions of the multicriteria firms and the equilibrium conditions of the multiclass, multicriteria consumers on the bipartite supernetwork. Hence, to obtain an equilibrium of the spatial network system, one must have that the sum of the optimality conditions of the firms as given by (10.7) and the equilibrium conditions of the consumers as in (10.14) is satisfied.

In Figure 10.2, we depict the structure of the supernetwork system, consisting of all the firms, all the demand markets and classes of consumers, and all the shipment alternatives. Note that the network is bipartite, akin to the classical spatial price equilibrium network given in Samuelson (1952) except that there are multiple links connecting each top-tier node with each bottom-tier node to represent shipment alternatives. We emphasize here that the links are used to represent transportation/shipment choices, which are aggregated, the number of which can be as numerous as needed in order to capture the variety of alternatives.

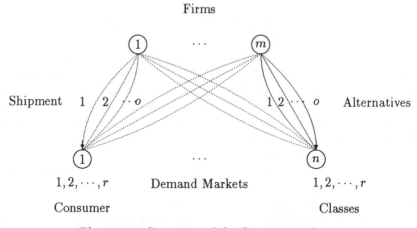

Fig. 10.2. Structure of the Supernetwork

Remark

Each shipment link can be disaggregated to represent in greater detail the transportation/shipment choices, as was depicted graphically in the case of the physical links for the supply chains in Figure 5.8. The literature, beginning with the work of Florian and Los (1982) (see also Dafermos and Nagurney (1984a) and Nagurney (1999), and the references therein) includes a variety of spatial network models in which the firms, often referred to as "producers," are connected to the demand markets via explicit transportation networks. In the case of freight networks, in particular, one may also introduce explicit carriers and shippers (see Friesz, Gottfried, and Morlok (1986)). Such agents may also be multicriteria decision-makers. We discuss two freight carriers later in this section.

First, however, we have to handle a minor technicality. In order to be able to construct a single variational inequality problem governing both the production and the consumption sides and to put it into standard form with a reduced number of variables, note that both the firm production output quantities and their product shipments to the demand markets are related to the class product shipments by (10.3) and (10.10), respectively. Hence, let

$$\frac{\partial \hat{f}_i(\hat{Q})}{\partial q_{ijlr}} \equiv \frac{\partial f_i(q)}{\partial q_i}, \quad \forall i, j, l, r, \tag{10.15}$$

and

$$mtc_{ijlr}(\hat{Q}) \equiv \frac{\partial \hat{c}_{ijl}(q_{ijl})}{\partial q_{ijl}} \times q_{ijl} + \hat{c}_{ijl}(q_{ijl}), \quad \forall i, j, l, r. \tag{10.16}$$

The term mtc_{ijlr} denotes the marginal cost of processing the shipment of the product from i to j via l for class r. In addition, define the generalized cost gc_{ijlr} for obtaining the product by class r at demand market j from firm i using shipment alternative or link l as:

$$gc_{ijlr}(\hat{Q}) \equiv w_{jr}^1 c_{ijl}(q_{ijl}) + w_{jr}^2 t_{ijl}(q_{ijl}), \quad \forall i, j, l, r. \tag{10.17}$$

Definition 10.1: The Equilibrium

An equilibrium of the spatial economy consisting of multicriteria producers and consumers is attained when the sum of the optimality conditions for all firms, as denoted by inequality (10.7), and the spatial equilibrium conditions, as represented by inequality (10.14), are satisfied by the class product shipment variables and the demand price variables.

We now combine the optimality conditions for the firms, as represented by the solution of variational inequality (10.7), with the equilibrium conditions of the consumers, as expressed by the variational inequality (10.14), and use the identities (10.15), (10.16), and (10.17), to yield a single inequality in class product shipment variables and class demand price variables:

$$\sum_{i=1}^{m}\sum_{j=1}^{n}\sum_{l=1}^{o}\sum_{r=1}^{k} \left[\frac{\partial \hat{f}_i(\hat{Q}^*)}{\partial q_{ijlr}} + mtc_{ijlr}(\hat{Q}^*) - w_i - \rho_{ijl}^* \right] \times \left[q_{ijlr} - q_{ijlr}^* \right]$$

$$+ \sum_{i=1}^{m}\sum_{j=1}^{n}\sum_{l=1}^{o}\sum_{r=1}^{k} \left[\rho_{ijl}^* + gc_{ijlr}(\hat{Q}^*) - \lambda_{jr}^* \right] \times \left[q_{ijlr} - q_{ijlr}^* \right]$$

$$- \sum_{j=1}^{n}\sum_{r=1}^{k} \left[d_{jr}(\lambda^*) - \sum_{i=1}^{m}\sum_{l=1}^{o} q_{ijlr}^* \right] \times \left[\lambda_{jr} - \lambda_{jr}^* \right] \geq 0, \quad \forall (\hat{Q}, \lambda) \in \mathcal{K}. \tag{10.18}$$

Before inequality (10.18) is further simplified in order to obtain the governing variational inequality of the entire supernetwork system, we analyze inequality (10.18) from an economic perspective. From the first term in (10.18) (which is equivalent to the left-hand side of (10.7)) one can infer that the price ρ_{ijl}^* charged by a firm i for the product to consumers at demand market j using shipment along l must be precisely equal to the firm's marginal cost of production plus the marginal of the total cost of shipment processing via l minus the weight associated with the output maximization criterion (if the product shipment is positive between the firm/demand market pair along the link and for that class). If the weight is precisely zero, then one simply recovers the well-known economic result that the price that the producers charge for the product is equal to their marginal costs, if there is a positive output of the quantity, which here means that there is a positive amount of the product shipped via a particular link to a class at a demand market. Otherwise, if the marginal costs associated with that combination of product/shipment alternative/class/demand market exceed the supply price that the consumers are willing to pay for the product, then there will be zero of that product shipped on that link from that firm to the class at that demand market.

Hence, in equilibrium, according to (10.18), if q^*_{ijlr} is positive then $\rho^*_{ijl} = \frac{\partial \hat{f}_i(\hat{Q}^*)}{\partial q_{ijlr}} + mtc_{ijlr}(\hat{Q}^*) - w_i$. Also, from the second term in (10.18) (which is equivalent to the first term in (10.14)), one can infer that, $\rho^*_{ijl} = \lambda^*_{jr} - gc_{ijlr}(\hat{Q}^*)$, in this case, as well. Thus, one can easily recover the supply prices ρ^*_{ijl} for all i, j, l, once we have obtained the solution. Simplifying now (10.18) further, yields the following variational inequality formulation.

Theorem 10.1: Variational Inequality Formulation
A multiclass product shipment and demand price pattern $(\hat{Q}^*, \lambda^*) \in \mathcal{K}$ is an equilibrium according to Definition 10.1 if and only if it satisfies the variational inequality problem:

$$\sum_{i=1}^{m} \sum_{j=1}^{n} \sum_{l=1}^{o} \sum_{r=1}^{k} \left[\frac{\partial \hat{f}_i(\hat{Q}^*)}{\partial q_{ijlr}} + mtc_{ijlr}(\hat{Q}^*) - w_i + gc_{ijlr}(\hat{Q}^*) - \lambda^*_{jr} \right]$$

$$\times \left[q_{ijlr} - q^*_{ijlr} \right]$$

$$- \sum_{j=1}^{n} \sum_{r=1}^{k} \left[d_{jr}(\lambda^*) - \sum_{i=1}^{m} \sum_{l=1}^{o} q^*_{ijlr} \right] \times \left[\lambda_{jr} - \lambda^*_{jr} \right] \geq 0, \quad \forall (\hat{Q}, \lambda) \in \mathcal{K}, \quad (10.19)$$

or, equivalently, in standard form:

$$\langle F(X^*), X - X^* \rangle \geq 0, \quad \forall X \in \mathcal{K}, \tag{10.20}$$

where $\mathcal{K}$ is the $mnok+nk$-dimensional column vector consisting of the vectors $(\hat{Q}, \lambda)$ and $F(X)$ is the $mnok + nk$-dimensional column vector such that $F \equiv (F^1, F^2)$ where F^1 is the $mnok$-dimensional vector with $ijlr$-th component given by:

$$\frac{\partial \hat{f}_i(\hat{Q})}{\partial q_{ijlr}} + mtc_{ijlr}(\hat{Q}) - w_i + gc_{ijlr}(\hat{Q}) - \lambda_{jr}$$

and F^2 is the nk-dimensional vector with component jr given by: $-d_{jr}(\lambda) + \sum_{i=1}^{m} \sum_{l=1}^{o} q_{ijlr}$. Recall that $\langle \cdot, \cdot \rangle$ here denotes the inner product in $(mnok + nk)$-dimensional Euclidean space.

Proof: The result follows, after algebraic simplification, from (10.18). □

10.1.1   Some Experiences from Freight Carriers

We now describe some experiences regarding the shipment of freight using two alternatives: trains and trucks. Although trains are considered to be cheaper as movers of freight and also more energy efficient, trucks are considered to be faster and can pick up and deliver from door to door. Trucks appear to have an advantage in today's market, given the importance of speed in supply chain management, according to Robert Blanchard, principal of the railroad consulting firm, The Blanchard Co., cited in Bryce (2001). He estimates that in the US, "The intercity freight market is worth \$500 billion per year...Railroads have 7% of that." He notes that the challenge is for the railroads to acquire a greater share.

10.1.1.1   Railroads as Freight Movers in the Information Age

The railroad industry in the United States is highly centralized, as compared to the trucking industry, with only seven major railroads that haul freight with, notable among them, The Burlington Northern and Santa Fe Railway, Norfolk Southern Railway, and the Union Pacific Railroad, among them. The trucking industry, on the other hand, is characterized by hundreds of smaller, independent haulers, and dozens of large and medium-sized long-haul and local trucking companies. Interestingly, although many websites now are devoted to servicing the trucking industry, it is just fairly recently that the railroads have taken advantage of the web. Indeed, for instance, although Covisint (see Section 5.1.1.1), formed by the big automakers, made its debut in February 2000, the comparable website for the railroad industry, named, Rail Marketplace.com, only made its debut in April, 2001. As noted by John Lanigan, CEO of Logistics.com, in Bryce (2001), "Web markets go after industries where there are lots of buyers," and, hence, developers of software for web products have focused on the trucking sector rather than on the railroads.

Nevertheless, things are changing. Not only are the big railroads beginning to follow their own Internet strategies, but according to the article by Bryce (2001), they are also cooperating on a site to make it simpler for shippers to use rail service. This is especially important since in North America, nearly half of all the freight moved by rail is handled by more than one railroad. The website, Steelroads, is supported by the seven major railroads, made its debut in February 2000 and provides pricing, tracking and service data from more than 300 major freight rail carriers in the US, Canada, and Mexico.

10.1.1.2   Trucking and Congestion

The interstate, known as I-95, slices through the commercial corridor between Maine and Virginia, which, according to Kennedy (2000), contains almost a quarter of the US population. Kennedy (2000) states that I-95 is the major highway connecting 13 major airports, 11 major seaports, and more than 24 railroad stations. In addition, 30,000 miles of other roads tend to, in one way or another, "flow" into I-95. Traffic experts consider this highway, the busiest and most overburdened one in the nation. It is the only major highway linking the states of the Eastern Seaboard of the United States.

This route is becoming so congested that it is having adverse effects on the flow of freight. For example, near Greenwich, Connecticut, in 1985, only 80,000 vehicles traveled on I-95, whereas today the number is closer to 130,000 vehicles, and, according to the same article, the estimate is for 172,000 vehicles by the year 2020, which is three times the number of residents in that town. On the other hand, south of Washington, where I-95 intersects with the Capital Beltway, there are as many as 400,000 vehicles daily, at what is considered to be the largest highway interchange in the world. Not too far from this point, this interstate goes over the Potomac River via the Woodrow Wilson Bridge, which was designed to carry 75,000 vehicles per day and now handles 190,000 a day,

Mr. Dick Chartier, a United Parcel Service (UPS) truck driver, who drives a UPS truck from Providence, Rhode Island to Secaucus, New Jersey, is quoted in Kennedy (2000) as saying that his truck is his "living room for 10 hours every day. Or 11. Or 12. Or longer, if there is rain or snow or road work or, God forbid, even a minor accident ahead of him." In snow, the round-trip drive from Warwick, Rhode Island to Secaucus, New Jersey, has taken 17 hours and he has had to sleep in his truck. Indeed, safety is also a big issue, with 3,000 people having died on this highway in the past decade. Nevertheless, this interstate is considered less congested than the San Diego Freeway in Los Angeles, California or the Southwest Freeway in Houston, Texas.

10.2   Qualitative Properties

In this section, some qualitative properties of the solution to variational inequality (10.19) are provided, in particular, existence and uniqueness results. In addition, some properties of the function F (cf. (10.20)) that enters the variational inequality of interest here are also obtained.

Since the feasible set $\mathcal{K}$ is not compact we cannot derive existence simply from the assumption of continuity of the functions. Nevertheless, one can impose a rather weak condition to guarantee existence of a solution pattern (as has also been done in a variety of "elastic demand" models in preceding chapters).

Let

$$\sigma_b = \{(\hat{Q}, \lambda)|0 \leq Q \leq b_1; \ 0 \leq \lambda \leq b_2\}, \tag{10.21}$$

where b is a positive scalar and $\hat{Q} \leq b_1, \lambda \leq b_2$ means that $q_{ijlr} \leq b_1$ and $\lambda_{jr} \leq b_2$ for all i, j, l, r. Then $\mathcal{K}_b = \mathcal{K} \cup \sigma_b$ is a bounded closed convex subset of $R^{mnok+nk}$. Thus, the following variational inequality

$$\langle F(X^b), X - X^b \rangle \geq 0, \quad \forall X^b \in \mathcal{K}_b, \tag{10.22}$$

admits at least one solution $X^b \in \mathcal{K}_b$, from the standard theory of variational inequalities, since $\mathcal{K}_b$ is compact and F is continuous. Following Kinderlehrer and Stampacchia (1980) (see also Theorems 4.2 and 4.3), one then has:

Theorem 10.2

Variational inequality (10.19) admits a solution if and only if there exists a $b > 0$, such that variational inequality (10.22) admits a solution in K_b with

$$\hat{Q}^b < b_1, \quad \lambda^b < b_2. \tag{10.23}$$

Theorem 10.3: Existence

Suppose that there exist positive constants M, N, R with $R > 0$, such that:

$$\frac{\partial \hat{f}_i(\hat{Q})}{\partial q_{ijlr}} + mtc_{ijlr}(\hat{Q}) + gc_{ijlr}(\hat{Q}) - w_i > R, \quad \forall \hat{Q} \text{ with } q_{ijlr} \geq N, \quad \forall i, j, l, r,$$

$$\tag{10.24}$$

$$d_{jr}(\lambda) \leq N, \quad \forall \lambda \text{ with } \lambda_{jr} > M, \quad \forall j, r. \tag{10.25}$$

Then variational inequality (10.19) admits at least one solution.

Proof: Under conditions (10.24) and (10.25) one can construct a $b > 0$ so that (10.23) holds and existence then follows from Theorem 10.2. See also existence proof of Theorem 4.3. □

Assumptions (10.24) and (10.25) are reasonable from an economics perspective, since when the product shipment between a pair of markets is large, one can expect the corresponding supply price or the generalized cost to be bounded from below by a positive value. Moreover, in the case where the demand price of the product as perceived by a class at a demand market is high, one can expect that the demand for the product by that class will be low at that market.

We now recall a definition which was also used for the analysis of the supply chain network models in Chapter 4.

Definition 10.2 (see also Definition 4.2): Additive Production Cost

Suppose that for each firm i, the production cost f_i is additive, that is

$$f_i(q) = f_i^1(q_i) + f_i^2(\bar{q}_i), \tag{10.26}$$

where $f_i^1(q_i)$ is the internal production cost that depends solely on its own output level q_i, which may include the production operation and the facility maintenance, etc., and $f_i^2(\bar{q}_i)$ is the interdependent part of the production cost that is a function of all the other firms' output levels $\bar{q}_i = (q_1, \cdots, q_{i-1}, q_{i+1}, \cdots, q_m)$ and reflects the impact of the other firms production pattern on firm i's cost. This interdependent part of the production cost may describe the competition for the resources, consumption of the homogeneous raw materials, etc.

Theorem 10.4: Monotonicity

Suppose that the production cost functions $f_i; i = 1, ..., m$, are additive, as defined in Definition 10.2, and $f_i^1; i = 1, ..., m$, are convex functions. Suppose, also, that, for all i, j and l, the transportation cost c_{ijl} and the transportation time t_{ijl} have the same congestion function b_{ijl}, that is,

$$c_{ijl}(q_{ijl}) = b_{ijl}(q_{ijl}) + c_{ijl}^0, \tag{10.27}$$

$$t_{ijl}(q_{ijl}) = b_{ijl}(q_{ijl}) + t_{ijl}^0. \tag{10.28}$$

In addition, assume that

(i) the congestion functions $b_{ijl}(q_{ijl})$ form a monotone increasing function of shipments $q_{ijl}, \forall i, j, l$;

(ii) the total shipment processing cost tc_{ijl} is convex for all i, j, l;
(iii) the class demand functions (10.11) are monotone decreasing with respect to the class demand price vector λ.

Finally, assume that the weights associated with the transportation costs and transportation times as perceived by the classes of consumers at the demand markets are as follows: $w_{jr}^1 = (1 - w_{jr})$ and $w_{jr}^2 = w_{jr}$ for all j, r.

Then, the vector function F that enters the variational inequality (10.20) is monotone, that is,

$$\langle F(X^1) - F(X^2), X^1 - X^2 \rangle \geq 0, \quad \forall X^1, X^2 \in \mathcal{K}.$$

Proof: We have, for any $X^1, X^2 \in \mathcal{K}$,

$$\langle F(X^1) - F(X^2), X^1 - X^2 \rangle$$

$$= \sum_{i=1}^{m} \sum_{j=1}^{n} \sum_{l=1}^{o} \sum_{r=1}^{k} \left[\frac{\partial \hat{f}_i(\hat{Q}^1)}{\partial q_{ijlr}} - \frac{\partial \hat{f}_i(\hat{Q}^2)}{\partial q_{ijlr}} \right] \times [q_{ijlr}^1 - q_{ijlr}^2]$$

$$+ \sum_{i=1}^{m} \sum_{j=1}^{n} \sum_{l=1}^{o} \sum_{r=1}^{k} \left[mtc_{ijlr}(\hat{Q}^1) - mtc_{ijlr}(\hat{Q}^2) \right] \times [q_{ijlr}^1 - q_{ijlr}^2]$$

$$+ \sum_{i=1}^{m} \sum_{j=1}^{n} \sum_{l=1}^{o} \sum_{r=1}^{k} \left[gc_{ijlr}(\hat{Q}^1) - gc_{ijlr}(\hat{Q}^2) \right] \times [q_{ijlr}^1 - q_{ijlr}^2]$$

$$- \sum_{j=1}^{n} \sum_{r=1}^{k} [d_{jr}(\lambda^1) - d_{jr}(\lambda^2)] \times [\lambda_{jr}^1 - \lambda_{jr}^2]$$

$$= (I) + (II) + (III) - (IV). \tag{10.29}$$

First, it follows from the additive production cost assumption and equations (10.3) and (10.10), that

$$\frac{\partial \hat{f}_i(\hat{Q})}{\partial q_{ijlr}} = \frac{\partial \hat{f}_i^1(\hat{Q})}{\partial q_{ijlr}} = f_i^{1'}(q_i), \quad \forall i, j, l, r. \tag{10.30}$$

Therefore, the first item on the right-hand side of (10.29) can be simplified to

$$(I) = \sum_{i=1}^{m} [f_i^{1'}(q_i^1) - f_i^{1'}(q_i^2)] \times [q_i^1 - q_i^2], \tag{10.31}$$

which is nonnegative if f_i^1 is convex for each i.

Secondly, as defined by (10.16), mtc_{ijlr} is the derivative of tc_{ijl}, which is convex under the condition of the theorem. Therefore, it follows from classic convex analysis (cf. Bazaraa, Sherali, and Shetty (1993) and Appendix A) that

$$(II) = \left[mtc_{ijlr}(\hat{Q}^1) - mtc_{ijlr}(\hat{Q}^2) \right] \times [q_{ijlr}^1 - q_{ijlr}^2]$$

$$= \left[tc_{ijl}'(q_{ijl}^1 - q_{ijl}^2) \right] \times [q_{ijl}^1 - q_{ijl}^2] \geq 0. \tag{10.32}$$

Thirdly, noting the same monotone congestion factors for transportation costs and transportation times for all shipments q_{ijl} from firm i to market j via link l, one has

$$(III) = \sum_{i=1}^{m} \sum_{j=1}^{n} \sum_{l=1}^{o} \sum_{r=1}^{k} [gc_{ijl}(q_{ijl}^1) - gc_{ijl}(q_{ijl}^2)] \times [q_{ijlr}^1 - q_{ijlr}^2]$$

$$= \sum_{i=1}^{m} \sum_{j=1}^{n} \sum_{l=1}^{o} [c_{ijl}(q_{ijl}^1) - c_{ijl}(q_{ijl}^2)] \times [\sum_{r=1}^{k} (1 - w_{jr})(q_{ijlr}^1 - q_{ijlr}^2)]$$

$$+ \sum_{i=1}^{m} \sum_{j=1}^{n} \sum_{l=1}^{o} [t_{ijl}(q_{ijl}^1) - t_{ijl}(q_{ijl}^2)] \times [\sum_{r=1}^{k} w_{jr}(q_{ijlr}^1 - q_{ijlr}^2)]$$

$$= \sum_{i=1}^{m} \sum_{j=1}^{n} \sum_{l=1}^{o} [b_{ijl}(q_{ijl}^1) - b_{ijl}(q_{ijl}^2)] \times [q_{ijl}^1 - q_{ijl}^2] \geq 0.$$

Finally, (IV) is negative because the demand functions are assumed to be monotone decreasing with respect to the generalized prices.

In conclusion, the right-hand side of (10.29) is nonnegative; namely, F is monotone. $\square$

Under stronger assumptions, one has the following result:

Theorem 10.5: Strict Monotonicity
Suppose that the production cost functions $f_i; i = 1, ..., m$, are additive, as defined in Definition 10.2, and $f_i^1; i = 1, ..., m$, are convex functions. Suppose,

also, that, for all i, j and l, the transportation cost c_{ijl} and the transportation time t_{ijl} have the same congestion functions b_{ijl}, that is,

$$c_{ijl}(q_{ijl}) = b_{ijl}(q_{ijl}) + c_{ijl}^0,$$

$$t_{ijl}(q_{ijl}) = b_{ijl}(q_{ijl}) + t_{ijl}^0.$$

In addition, assume

(i) the congestion functions $b_{ijl}(q_{ijl})$ form a monotone increasing function of shipments $q_{ijl}, \forall i, j, l$;

(ii) the total shipment processing cost tc_{ijl} is convex for all i, j, l, and at least one of (i) or (ii) is a strict condition;

(iii) the class market demand functions (10.11) are strictly monotone decreasing with respect to the class demand price vector λ.

Further, assume that the transportation cost and time weights are as in Theorem 10.4.

Then, the vector function F that enters the variational inequality (10.20) is strictly monotone with respect to (Q, λ).

Proof: It is clear that, under the conditions of Theorem 10.5, for any two distinct (Q^1, λ^1), (Q^2, λ^2), either (IV) will be negative, or one of (II) and (III) will be positive, whichever corresponds to the strict condition, as in the proof of Theorem 10.4. Therefore, the right-hand side of (10.29) must be positive. Hence, by definition, F is strictly monotone. □

Theorem 10.5 is used in establishing convergence of the algorithmic scheme in Section 10.4.

Theorem 10.6: Uniqueness

Under the same conditions as imposed in Theorem 10.5, the solutions to the variational inequality (10.20) are unique in all the shipments from every firm to every demand market via every link, and are unique in prices at every demand market for every class.

Proof: The theorem follows as a corollary of the previous theorem, since strict monotonicity of the governing function implies uniqueness of the corresponding variational inequality. □

10.3   The Dynamics

In this section, a dynamic counterpart of the model developed in Section 10.1 is presented. First, the dynamics underlying the multiclass product shipments are described and then the dynamics underlying the multiclass demand market prices. The dynamics are, subsequently, unified by presenting the projected dynamical systems model whose set of stationary points coincides with the set of solutions to variational inequality (10.19).

The Dynamics of the Multiclass Product Shipments

The dynamic model presented here assumes that the multiclass product shipments adjust according to the difference between the generalized demand price for each class and demand market plus the weight for each firm associated with the output maximization criterion and the sum of the marginal costs of the firm in question (which, recall, is equal to the supply price) and the generalized cost associated with the market pair, class, and shipment alternative combination. Mathematically, we have that: For each (i, j, l, r):

$$\dot{q}_{ijlr}(t) = \begin{cases} \lambda_{jr}(t) + w_i - \frac{\partial \hat{f}_i(\hat{Q}(t))}{\partial q_{ijlr}} - mtc_{ijlr}(\hat{Q}(t)) - gc_{ijlr}(\hat{Q}(t)), \\ \quad \text{if } q_{ijlr}(t) > 0, \\ \max\{0, \lambda_{jr}(t) + w_i - \frac{\partial \hat{f}_i(\hat{Q}(t))}{\partial q_{ijlr}} - mtc_{ijlr}(\hat{Q}(t)) - gc_{ijlr}(\hat{Q}(t))\}, \\ \quad \text{if } q_{ijlr}(t) = 0. \end{cases}$$

$$(10.33)$$

According to (10.33) the product shipment for a class between a pair of firm and demand markets using shipment alternative l will increase if the demand price of the class at the demand market exceeds the supply price plus the generalized cost associated with shipping the product from the supply market. On the other hand, the product shipment for that class will decrease if the supply price plus the generalized cost exceeds the demand price that the consumers of that class are paying at the demand market. Note also that (10.33) guarantees that the product shipments can never be negative, which would violate feasibility.

The Demand Price Dynamics

The demand market prices for a class, in turn, evolve as follows:

$$\dot{\lambda}_{jr}(t) \begin{cases} = d_{jr}(\lambda(t)) - \sum_{i=1}^{m} \sum_{l=1}^{o} q_{ijlr}(t), & \text{if } \lambda_{jr}(t) > 0, \\ = \max\{0, d_{jr}(\lambda(t)) - \sum_{i=1}^{m} \sum_{l=1}^{o} q_{ijlr}(t)\}, & \text{if } \lambda_{jr}(t) = 0. \end{cases}$$

$$(10.34)$$

According to (10.34), the demand price of the product for a class at a demand market will increase if the demand exceeds the supply of the product for that class at the demand market; it will decrease if the supply exceeds the demand. Moreover, (10.34) guarantees that the demand price at the demand market for each class will not be negative.

Hence, this adjustment process is in concert with those proposed by Nagurney, Takayama, and Zhang (1995a, b) for (single-criteria) spatial price equilibrium problems as well as for spatial oligopolies by Nagurney, Dupuis, and Zhang (1994) (see also Chapter 5 for the dynamic supply chain model).

The Projected Dynamical System

The dynamic model described by (10.33) and (10.34) can now be rewritten as a projected dynamical system defined by the following initial value problem:

$$\dot{X} = \Pi_{\mathcal{K}}(X, -F(X)), \quad X(0) = X_0, \tag{10.35}$$

where $\Pi_{\mathcal{K}}$ is the projection operator of $-F(X)$ onto $\mathcal{K}$ at X and $X_0 = (Q_0, \lambda_0)$ is the initial point corresponding to the initial multiclass product shipment and demand price pattern. The trajectory of (10.35) describes the dynamic evolution of and the dynamic interactions between the product shipment and the price patterns. Recall that a projected dynamical system differs from a classical dynamical system in that the right-hand side in (10.35) is discontinuous due to the explicit incorporation of the constraint set, where here the constraint set through the reformulated variational inequality (10.19) is the nonnegative orthant.

Theorem 10.7
The set of stationary points of the projected dynamical system (10.35) coincides with the set of solutions of the variational inequality (10.19).

Proof: According to the fundamental theorem of projected dynamical systems (see Appendix B), X^* is a stationary point of the projected dynamical system (10.35) if and only if it is a solution to the variational inequality (10.19). $\square$

10.4   The Discrete-Time Algorithm

In this section, the Euler method is proposed for the computation of the equilibrium pattern. The algorithm provides a discretization of the continuous time adjustment process given in Section 10.3. The algorithm computes a solution to variational inequality (10.19) and, in addition, provides a discrete-time approximation to the projected dynamical system (10.35), the stationary points of which (cf. Theorem 10.7) coincide with the solutions of variational inequality (10.19).

Its statement in the general form for the solution of variational inequality (10.20) and for the time discretization of the corresponding projected dynamical system (see also Appendix C) is given by:

$$X^{\tau+1} = P_{\mathcal{K}}(X^\tau - \alpha_\tau F(X^\tau)), \tag{10.36}$$

where τ denotes an iteration (or time period) and $\{a_\tau\}$ is a sequence of positive scalars to be discussed later. This algorithm (in different realizations) has also been used to compute solutions to dynamic supply chain network problems in Chapter 5 and to dynamic financial network problems with intermediation in Chapter 6.

In particular, in the context of the supernetwork problem with multicriteria producers and consumers, formulated as (10.19), with F above taking the form as defined following (10.20), the projection operation takes on a very simple form for computational purposes, and, hence, the multiclass product shipments as well as the demand market prices can be computed at an iteration in closed form as follows.

Computation of Multiclass Product Shipments

For all i, j, l, r, compute:

$$q_{ijlr}^{\tau+1} = \max\{0, \alpha_\tau(\lambda_{jr}^\tau + w_i - \frac{\partial \hat{f}_i(\hat{Q}^\tau)}{\partial q_{ijlr}} - mtc_{ijlr}(\hat{Q}^\tau) - gc_{ijlr}(\hat{Q}^\tau)) + q_{ijlr}^\tau\},$$

(10.37)

Computation of Demand Market Prices

For all j, r, compute:

$$\lambda_{jr}^{\tau+1} = \max\{0, \alpha_\tau(d_{jr}(\lambda^\tau) - \sum_{i=1}^m \sum_{l=1}^o q_{ijlr}^\tau) + \lambda_{jr}^\tau\}.$$

(10.38)

Hence, although the proof of convergence of the algorithm, as will be shown below, is rather technical, the actual realization of the algorithm is remarkably simple (as was also the case for the realization of the Euler method in the context of the dynamic supply chain model in Chapter 5).

Of course, steps (10.37) and (10.38) can also be interpreted as a discrete-time adjustment process. Indeed, according to (10.37), the multiclass product shipments at a given iteration (or time period) are updated according to the difference between the price at the demand market plus the weight and the various marginal costs (taking into consideration also the commodity shipment from the previous period). The demand market prices for a class, in turn, according to (10.38) are updated according to the difference between the demand and the amount consumed by that class at the demand market at the preceding time period (with the price at the preceding time period also being enterred in).

In what follows, the convergence of the Euler method given by (10.37) (10.38) will be established, for the sake of rigor. See also Sections 5.3 and 6.3. It is rather technical and can be omitted by those not interested.

Theorem 10.8: Convergence
Assume that all the conditions of Theorem 10.5 hold true. In addition, assume that

(1) for every i, j, l

$$\frac{\partial \hat{f}_i(\hat{Q})}{\partial q_{ijlr}} + mtc_{ijlr}(\hat{Q}) + gc_{ijlr}(\hat{Q})$$

(10.39)

uniformly approaches infinity as q_{ijl} tends to infinity;

(2) for every j, r, $d_{jr}(\lambda)$ uniformly approaches zero as λ_{jr} approaches infinity; and

(3) the stepsizes $\{\alpha_\tau\}$ for the Euler method satisfy

$$\lim_{\tau \to \infty} \alpha_\tau = 0$$

(10.40)

$$\sum_{\tau=1}^{\infty} \alpha_\tau = \infty. \tag{10.41}$$

Then, the Euler method given by iteration (10.37) and (10.38) converges to a solution of the variational inequality (10.20).

Proof: According to Theorem C.1 in Appendix C, the convergence of the Euler method can be ensured if Assumption C.1 of the same Appendix holds true, where Assumption C.1 is comprised of five parts. Part 1, which deals with the choice of stepsizes is exactly (10.40) and (10.41), conditions which have already been imposed here. Part 2 is satisfied automatically for the Euler method.

In what follows, we will prove that Part 3, Part 4 and Part 5 of Assumption C.1 hold true under the condition of the present theorem.

Recall Part 3 of Assumption C.1 in that the ω-limit set of the constraint $\mathcal{K}$ is contained in the set of stationary points of the projected dynamical system (10.35). Let $X(t) = (\hat{Q}(t), \lambda(t))_{t \geq 0}$ denote the solution trajectory of (10.35). It uniquely determines the trajectory $(Q(t), \lambda(t))_{t \geq 0}$, where $Q(t) = \{q_{ijl}(t); i = 1, ..., m; j = 1, ..., n; l = 1, ..., o\}$ is induced by (10.10). Let $X^* = (\hat{Q}^*, \lambda^*)$ be a solution to variational inequality problem (10.20) and let Q^* be induced by (10.10). In light of Theorem 10.5, F is strictly monotone with respect to (Q, λ). This implies (cf. Theorem B.9) that (Q^*, λ^*) is a global monotone attractor, namely,

$$Q(t) \longrightarrow Q^*, \quad \lambda(t) \longrightarrow \lambda^*, \quad \text{as} \quad t \longrightarrow \infty. \tag{10.42}$$

In addition, Theorem 10.6 ensures the uniqueness of (Q^*, λ^*) for all solutions to variational inequality problem (10.20). Now let $(\bar{Q}, \bar{\lambda})$ be an ω-limit point of $\mathcal{K}$. Then, by (10.42) one has

$$\bar{q}_{ijl} = q_{ijl}^*, \forall i, \forall j, \forall l, \tag{10.43}$$

$$\bar{\lambda}_{jr} = \lambda_{jr}^*, \forall j, \forall r. \tag{10.44}$$

In the sequel, we show that let $(\bar{Q}, \bar{\lambda})$ solves variational inequality problem (10.20), or, equivalently, it satisfies the following equilibrium conditions:

$$\frac{\partial \hat{f}_i(\hat{Q})}{\partial q_{ijlr}} + mtc_{ijlr}(\hat{Q}) - w_i + gc_{ijlr}(\hat{Q}) \begin{cases} = \lambda_{jr}, & \text{if} \quad q_{ijlr} > 0 \\ \geq \lambda_{jr}, & \text{if} \quad q_{ijlr} = 0, \end{cases} \tag{10.45}$$

and

$$d_{jr}(\lambda) \begin{cases} = \sum_{i=1}^{m} \sum_{l=1}^{o} q_{ijlr}, & \text{if} \quad \lambda_{jr} > 0 \\ \leq \sum_{i=1}^{m} \sum_{l=1}^{o} q_{ijlr}, & \text{if} \quad \lambda_{jr} = 0. \end{cases} \tag{10.46}$$

Note that the left-hand side of (10.45) is, indeed, a function of Q, which can be denoted by $H_{ijlr}(Q)$ for simplicity. Therefore, it follows from (10.43) and (10.44) that both the left-hand side and the right-hand side of (10.45) should assume the same value when evaluated at $(\bar{Q}, \bar{\lambda})$ and at (Q^*, λ^*). However, as a solution to variational inequality problem (10.20), (Q^*, λ^*) satisfies (10.45). Hence, the only possibility that $(\bar{Q}, \bar{\lambda})$ violates the equilibrium condition (10.45) occurs when the following is true:

$$H_{ijlr}(\bar{Q}) - \bar{\lambda}_{jr} = H_{ijlr}(Q^*) - \lambda_{jr}^* > 0, \quad \text{and} \quad \bar{q}_{ijlr} > 0. \tag{10.47}$$

Expression (10.47) would imply, by the definition of ω-limit point, the existence of an unbounded time sequence $\{t_v\}_{v \geq 0}$ such that

$$q_{ijlr}(t_v) \longrightarrow \bar{q}_{ijlr} \quad \text{as} \quad v \longrightarrow \infty. \tag{10.48}$$

Consequently, for all large enough v, one would have

$$q_{ijlr}(t_v) \geq \frac{1}{2} \bar{q}_{ijlr} > 0. \tag{10.49}$$

On the other hand, however, (10.42) and (10.47) suggest that there exist $T_0 > 0$ and $\epsilon > 0$ such that

$$\lambda_{jr}(t) - H_{ijlr}(t) \leq -\epsilon, \quad \forall t \geq T_0. \tag{10.50}$$

In view of (10.33), (10.50) implies

$$q_{ijlr}(t) \longrightarrow 0, \quad \text{as} \quad t \longrightarrow \infty, \tag{10.51}$$

which contradicts (10.49). Therefore, (10.47) cannot be true. Namely, $(\bar{Q}, \bar{\lambda})$ satisfies equilibrium condition (10.45).

In a similar way, one can show that $(\bar{Q}, \bar{\lambda})$ also satisfies equilibrium condition (10.46). Hence, it has been proved that every ω-limit point of the constraint set solves variational inequality (10.20), or, equivalently, it belongs to the set of stationary points of the projected dynamical system (10.35). Thus, it has been shown that Part 3 of Assumption C.1 holds.

Next, it will be proved that Part 4 of Assumption C.1 holds true. First, it will be shown that $\{\lambda^T\}$ is bounded. Under the conditions of the theorem, it is clear that the demand function $d(\lambda)$ is bounded from above. Denote its upper bound by D_1, that is,

$$d_{jr}(\lambda) \leq D_1, \quad \forall j, r, \quad \forall \lambda. \tag{10.52}$$

In light of (10.40), there exists a large enough N_1 such that

$$\alpha_\tau \leq \frac{1}{2D_1}, \quad \forall \tau \geq N_1. \tag{10.53}$$

Assume that the λ components in the first N_1 iterations of the Euler method are bounded by M_1; that is,

$$\lambda_{jr}^\tau \le M_1, \quad \forall j, r, \quad \forall \tau \le N_1. \tag{10.54}$$

Under the condition of the theorem that d is strictly monotone decreasing and uniformly goes to zero when λ_{jr} approaches infinity, one should have a sufficiently large number M_2 so that $M_2 \ge M_1$ and

$$d_{jr}(\lambda) \le \sum_{i=1}^m \sum_{l=1}^o q_{ijlr} \tag{10.55}$$

holds for all λ with $\lambda_{jr} \ge M_2$.

It is now claimed that all λ_{jr}^τ generated by the Euler method are bounded by $2M_2$; that is,

$$\lambda_{jr}^\tau \le 2M_2, \quad \forall j, r, \quad \forall \tau. \tag{10.56}$$

In view of (10.54), (10.56) holds true for all $\tau \le N_1$. So, we only need to show (10.56) for $T = N_1 + k$; $k = 1, 2, \dots$ This can be done inductively. Suppose that (10.56) holds for all $\tau \le N_1 + k$. For any given pair of (j, r), we distinguish between two cases.

Case (i) If $M_2 \le \lambda_{jr}^{\tau+k} \le 2M_2$, then, in light of (10.55), the Euler iteration (10.38) gives

$$\lambda_{jr}^{\tau+k+1} = \lambda_{jr}^{\tau+k} + \alpha_{\tau+k}(d_{jr}(\lambda^{\tau+k}) - \sum_{i=1}^m \sum_{l=1}^o q_{ijlr}^{\tau+k}) < \lambda_{jr}^{\tau+k} \le 2M_2. \tag{10.57}$$

Case (ii) If $\lambda_{jr}^{\tau+k} < M_2$, then, one has the following estimate for the Euler iteration (10.38), in light of (10.52), (10.53), and (10.54):

$$\lambda_{jr}^{\tau+k+1} \le \lambda_{jr}^{\tau+k} + \alpha_\tau d_{jr}(\lambda^{\tau+k})$$

$$\le \lambda_{jr}^{\tau+k} + \frac{1}{2D_1} d_{jr}(\lambda^{\tau+k}) \le \lambda_{jr}^{\tau+k} + \frac{1}{2} \le 2M_2. \tag{10.58}$$

Concluding (10.57) and (10.58) by induction, (10.56) has been proved.

We now turn to proving that the q_{ijlr} components of the Euler sequence are also bounded.

In light of (10.40), there exists a large enough N_2 such that

$$\alpha_\tau \le \frac{1}{2(b + 2M_2)}, \quad \forall \tau \ge N_2, \tag{10.59}$$

where M_2 denotes the upper bound as in (10.46) for all the λ components of the Euler sequence and $b = \max_i\{w_i\}$. Assume that the q components in the first N_2 iterations of the Euler method are bounded by M_3; that is,

$$q_{ijlr}^\tau \le M_3, \quad \forall i, j, l, r, \quad \forall \tau \le N_2. \tag{10.60}$$

Under the condition of the theorem that

$$\frac{\partial \hat{f}_i(\hat{Q})}{\partial q_{ijlr}} + mtc_{ijlr}(\hat{Q}) + gc_{ijlr}(\hat{Q})$$

uniformly approaches infinity as q_{ijl} tends to infinity, one should have a sufficiently large number M_4 so that $M_4 \geq M_3$ and that

$$\lambda_{jr} + w_i - \frac{\partial \hat{f}_i(\hat{Q})}{\partial q_{ijlr}} - mtc_{ijlr}(\hat{Q}) - gc_{ijlr}(\hat{Q}) \leq 0 \qquad (10.61)$$

holds for all $\hat{Q}$ with $q_{ijlr} \geq M_4$. It is now claimed that all q_{ijlr}^τ generated by the Euler method are bounded by $2M_4$. In other words,

$$q_{ijlr}^\tau \leq 2M_4, \quad \forall i,j,l,r, \quad \forall \tau. \qquad (10.62)$$

According to (10.60), (10.62) is valid for all $\tau \leq N_2$. So, one only needs to show (10.62) for $\tau = N_2 + k; \ k = 1, 2, \dots$. This can be done inductively. Suppose that (10.62) holds for all $\tau \leq N_1 + k$. For any given (i,j,l,r), one can distinguish between two cases.

Case (i) If $M_4 \leq q_{ijlr}^{\tau+k} \leq 2M_4$, then it follows from (10.51) that the Euler iteration (10.37) gives

$$q_{ijlr}^{\tau+k+1} \leq q_{ijlr}^{\tau+k} + \alpha_{\tau+k}(\lambda_{jr}^{\tau+k} + w_i - \frac{\partial \hat{f}_i(\hat{Q}^{\tau+k})}{\partial q_{ijlr}} - mtc_{ijlr}(\hat{Q}^{\tau+k}) - gc_{ijlr}(\hat{Q}^{\tau+k}))$$

$$\leq q_{ijlr}^{\tau+k} \leq 2M_4. \qquad (10.63)$$

Case (ii) If $q_{ijlr}^{\tau+k} \leq M_4$, then one has the following estimate for the Euler iteration (10.37), in light of (10.59) and (10.60),

$$q_{ijlr}^{\tau+k+1} \leq q_{ijlr}^{\tau+k} + \alpha_{\tau+k}(\lambda_{jr}^{\tau+k} + w_i) \leq q_{ijlr}^{\tau+k} + \alpha_{\tau+k}(2M_2 + b) \leq M_4 + \frac{1}{2} \leq 2M_4.$$
$$(10.64)$$

Concluding (10.63) and (10.64) by induction, it has been shown that (10.62) is valid for all τ. that is, Part 4 of Assumption C.1 holds true.

Finally, Part 5 of Assumption C.1 holds when F is monotone (Nagurney and Zhang (1996), Proposition 4.2). Hence, according to Theorem 10.4, this part is valid under the condition of the present theorem.

The proof is complete. $\square$

10.5 Numerical Examples

In this section, several numerical examples are presented. In particular, supernetwork problems consisting of two firms, two demand markets, and with

Firms

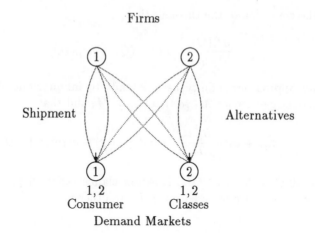

Shipment   Alternatives

1,2   1,2
Consumer   Classes
Demand Markets

Fig. 10.3. Supernetwork for the Examples

two available shipping alternatives from each firm to each demand market were considered. Hence, the supernetwork structure of the problem was as depicted in Figure 10.3. There were two classes of consumers.

The Euler method was implemented in FORTRAN and the computer system used was a DEC Alpha located at the University of Massachusetts at Amherst. The convergence criterion was that $|q_{ijlr}^\tau - q_{ijlr}^{\tau-1}| \le \epsilon$, for all i, j, l, r, and $|\lambda_{jr}^\tau - \lambda_{jr}^{\tau-1}| \le \epsilon$ for all j, r, with $\epsilon = .0001$. The Euler method was initialized as follows: all initial product shipments and class demand market generalized prices were set equal to zero. The sequence $\{\alpha_\tau\} = .1 \times \{1, \frac{1}{2}, \frac{1}{2}, \frac{1}{3}, \frac{1}{3}, \frac{1}{3}, \dots\}$.

Example 10.1

The first example served as a baseline, from which several additional examples were constructed by varying specific parameters. The production cost functions of the two firms were given by:

$$f_1(q) = 2.5q_1^2 + q_1q_2 + 2q_1, \quad f_2(q) = 2.5q_2^2 + q_1q_2 + 2q_2.$$

The unit shipment processing cost functions and the transportation cost and time functions were as given in Table 10.1.

The class demand functions were:

$$d_{11}(\lambda) = -2\lambda_{11} - 1.5\lambda_{21} + 1000, \quad d_{21}(\lambda) = -2\lambda_{21} - 1.5\lambda_{11} + 1000,$$

$$d_{12}(\lambda) = -2\lambda_{12} - 1.5\lambda_{22} + 1000, \quad d_{22}(\lambda) = -2\lambda_{22} - 1.5\lambda_{12} + 1000.$$

The weights were all equal to 1, that is: $w_1 = w_2 = 1$, and $w_{11}^1 = w_{12}^1 = w_{21}^1 = w_{22}^1 = w_{11}^2 = w_{12}^2 = w_{21}^2 = w_{22}^2 = 1$.

Table 10.1. The Unit Shipment Processing Cost, Transportation Cost, and Transportation Time Functions

i,j,l	$\hat{c}_{ijl}$	c_{ijl}	t_{ijl}
$1,1,1$	$q_{111}+1$	$q_{111}+5$	$2q_{111}+10$
$1,1,2$	$.5q_{12}+.5$	$3q_{112}+15$	$q_{112}+3.5$
$1,2,1$	$q_{121}+1$	$q_{121}+5$	$2q_{121}+10$
$1,2,2$	$.5q_{122}+.5$	$3q_{122}+15$	$q_{122}+3.5$
$2,1,1$	$q_{211}+1$	$q_{211}+5$	$2q_{211}+10$
$2,1,2$	$.5q_{212}+5$	$3q_{212}+15$	$q_{212}+3.5$
$2,2,1$	$q_{221}+1$	$q_{221}+5$	$2q_{221}+10$
$2,2,2$	$.5q_{222}+.5$	$3q_{222}+15$	$q_{222}+3.5$

Table 10.2. The Equilibrium Multiclass Product Shipment Pattern for Example 10.1

Shipment	Class $r=1$	Class $r=2$
q^*_{111r}	4.668	4.668
q^*_{112r}	4.368	4.368
q^*_{112r}	4.668	4.668
q^*_{122r}	4.368	4.368
q^*_{211r}	4.668	4.668
q^*_{212r}	4.368	4.368
q^*_{221r}	4.668	4.668
q^*_{222r}	4.368	4.368

In this baseline numerical example, one can see that shipment alternative 2, although faster than shipment alternative 1 (since its transportation time was lower) had a higher transportation cost. This is reasonable, since one can expect that in order to obtain the good more quickly, one may have to pay a higher cost.

The Euler method converged in 273 iterations and yielded the multiclass product shipment pattern reported in Table 10.2.

The equilibrium (total) product shipment pattern (cf. (10.10)) was given by:

$$q^*_{111} = 9.336, \quad q^*_{112} = 8.736, \quad q^*_{121} = 9.336, \quad q^*_{122} = 8.736,$$

$$q^*_{211} = 9.336, \quad q^*_{212} = 8.736, \quad q^*_{221} = 9.336, \quad q^*_{222} = 8.736.$$

The computed equilibrium class demand prices at the two demand markets were:

$$\lambda^*_{11} = 280.542, \quad \lambda^*_{12} = 280.542, \quad \lambda^*_{21} = 280.542, \quad \lambda^*_{22} = 280.542.$$

Table 10.3. The Equilibrium Multiclass Product Shipment Pattern for Example 10.2

Shipment	Class $r = 1$	Class $r = 2$
q^*_{111r}	9.301	0.000
q^*_{112r}	0.942	7.784
q^*_{112r}	9.30	0.000
q^*_{122r}	0.942	7.784
q^*_{211r}	9.301	0.000
q^*_{212r}	0.942	7.784
q^*_{221r}	9.301	0.000
q^*_{222r}	0.942	7.784

The computed equilibrium production outputs of the firms were, hence:

$$q^*_1 = q^*_2 = 36.144.$$

We also, for completeness, provide the firms' prices associated with the demand markets and the two shipment alternatives, that is, the ρ^*_{ij1} and the ρ^*_{ij2}, for $i = 1, 2$ and $j = 1, 2$. Specifically, $\rho^*_{ij1} = 237.534$ and $\rho^*_{ij2} = 227.099$, for $i = 1, 2$ and $j = 1, 2$, which represent the price that the firm i charges to the consumers at demand market j for the product, if delivered using shipment alternative 1 or 2, respectively. Of course, the consumers also have to pay the incurred cost of transportation. Note that, for exposition purposes, the firms' production cost functions are identical as are their shipment processing cost functions to a given demand market via a shipment alternative, and the demand functions are identical for each class and demand market. However the transportation time and cost functions differ for each of the two shipment alternatives and, hence, the prices that the firms charge differ solely (in this stylized example) by shipment alternative.

The above results are reasonable given the proposed underlying functions for this numerical example.

Example 10.2

In the second example, the following sensitivity analysis was conducted. All the data were as in Example 10.1, except that now it was assumed that members of class 2 are more time-sensitive to the delivery of the product than they were in Example 10.1. Hence, we altered the appropriate weights and now had $w^2_{12} = 1.1$ and $w^2_{22} = 1.1$.

The Euler method converged in 7028 iterations and yielded the equilibrium multiclass product shipment pattern reported in Table 10.3.

The equilibrium (total) product shipment pattern induced by the above multiclass pattern was:

$$q^*_{111} = 9.300, \quad q^*_{112} = 8.726, \quad q^*_{121} = 9.300, \quad q^*_{122} = 8.726,$$

Table 10.4. The Equilibrium Multiclass Product Shipment Pattern for Example 10.3

Shipment	Class $r = 1$	Class $r = 2$
q_{111r}^*	4.851	4.851
q_{112r}^*	4.551	4.551
q_{112r}^*	4.851	4.851
q_{122r}^*	4.551	4.551
q_{211r}^*	4.637	4.637
q_{212r}^*	4.337	4.337
q_{221r}^*	4.637	4.637
q_{222r}^*	4.337	4.337

$$q_{211}^* = 9.300, \quad q_{212}^* = 8.726, \quad q_{221}^* = 9.300, \quad q_{222}^* = 8.726.$$

The computed equilibrium class demand prices at the two demand markets were:

$$\lambda_{11}^* = 279.837, \quad \lambda_{12}^* = 281.291, \quad \lambda_{21}^* = 279.837, \quad \lambda_{22}^* = 281.291.$$

The computed equilibrium production outputs of the firms were, hence:

$$q_1^* = q_2^* = 36.054.$$

The equilibrium supply prices were:

$$\rho_{ij1}^* = 236.93 \text{ and } \rho_{ij2}^* = 226.55 \text{ for } i = 1, 2; j = 1, 2.$$

Note that (cf. Table 10.3) now all members of class 2 shifted their orders for the commodity so that at each demand market only the lower transportation time links were used for the deliveries to this class of consumer.

Example 10.3

In the third example, we did the following sensitivity analysis. We kept all the data as in Example 10.1, except that now we assumed that firm 1 has altered its market share weight from 1 to 10, that is, now $w_1 = 10$.

The Euler method converged in 416 iterations and yielded the equilibrium multiclass product shipment pattern given in Table 10.4.

The above multiclass product shipment pattern corresponds to the following total product shipment pattern (cf. (10.10)):

$$q_{111}^* = 9.702, \quad q_{112}^* = 9.102, \quad q_{121}^* = 9.702, \quad q_{122}^* = 9.102,$$

$$q_{211}^* = 9.274, \quad q_{212}^* = 8.674, \quad q_{221}^* = 9.274, \quad q_{222}^* = 8.674.$$

The computed equilibrium class demand prices at the two demand markets were:

$$\lambda_{11}^* = 280.455, \quad \lambda_{12}^* = 280.455, \quad \lambda_{21}^* = 280.455, \quad \lambda_{22}^* = 280.455.$$

The computed equilibrium production outputs of the firms were, hence:

$$q_1^* = 37.609, \quad q_2^* = 35.895.$$

The equilibrium firm supply prices were:
for firm 1:

$$\rho_{111}^* = \rho_{121}^* = 236.347 \text{ and } \rho_{112}^* = \rho_{122}^* = 225.54;$$

for firm 2:

$$\rho_{211}^* = \rho_{221}^* = 237.633 \text{ and } \rho_{212}^* = \rho_{222}^* = 227.260.$$

Hence, each firm now charged a different price according to the shipment alternative to a given demand market.

Observe that the total output of firm 1 now increased in comparison to its output in Example 10.1, whereas that of firm 2 decreased. The change in the class demand prices, in turn, was negligible.

10.6   Sources and Notes

This chapter is based on the paper of Nagurney, Zhang, and Dong (2002). Here the results are framed as a supernetwork. We emphasize that time and cost associated with product deliveries are of particular importance in the Information Age in regard to decision-making not only on the consumption side but also on the production side. Hence, we have included such criteria explicitly in our model.

11 Multicriteria Decision-Making in Financial Networks

In this chapter, we return to the subject of finance, which was the topic of Chapter 6. However, in this chapter, the focus is on multicriteria decision-making in a financial context, rather than decision-making on multitiered financial networks. In addition, in contrast to the models developed in Chapters 7 through 10 in this book, now the weights associated with the criteria are no longer assumed to be fixed, but, rather, are allowed to be variable.

Since the pioneering work of Markowitz (1952) that unveiled modern portfolio theory, there have been many extensions made to the original model in order, for example, to explain the individual's asset-holding behavior and to develop normative rules for asset selection. Markowitz's model was based on mean-variance portfolio selection, where the average and the variability of portfolio returns were determined in terms of the mean and the variance of the corresponding investments.

In particular, two criteria or objectives have played major roles in portfolio model building and these are: the maximization of the returns as reflected in the mean and the minimization of the risk as measured by the variance of the return. However, most of the model extensions in the literature have assumed a fixed trade-off between these two criteria, that is, constant weights, and, in most cases, *equal* weights (see, e.g., Sharpe (1964), Lintner (1965), Pogue (1970), Francis and Archer (1979), among others). Nevertheless, the importance of the mean and the variance as perceived by an investor or sector in practice may vary according to the values that they assume. For example, one would expect that more emphasis will be given to reducing the risk when it is high than when it is low, and more attention will be paid to the return when it is low. This kind of rationality argues for a *state-dependent* trade-off between the mean and the variance, or, in other words, variable weights for the two criteria in the value function. Indeed, the optimal solution derived in a bicriteria financial model with a fixed trade-off can, very possibly, be unacceptable in practice.

Hence, in this framework, it is a bi-objective decision problem that each sector faces in maximizing its return and, simultaneously, in minimizing its risk. Consequently, each financial sector manages its portfolio investment towards these two objectives, subject to the prices of the instruments, which follow the laws of supply and demand, and which, we expect, eventually, to yield a financial equilibrium.

To date, there has been minimal research conducted on the modeling and analysis of financial equilibrium insofar as the modeling of the financial sectors' multicriteria decision-making or the incorporation of a multicriteria perspective into the sectors' value functions is concerned. For a rigorous treatment of multicriteria decision making and computational procedures, along with applications to finance, in which fixed weights are assumed, we refer the reader to the book by Rustem (1998) and the references therein. Additional references to multicriteria decision-making and finance, but in the context of a single decision-maker, include the work of Muhleman, Locketta, and Gear (1978), Lee and Chesser (1980), Spronk (1981), Colson and De Bruyn (1983), Rios-Garcia and Rio Insura (1983), Martel, Khoury, and Bergeron (1988), Cosset, Siskos, and Zopounidis (1992), and Zopounidis (2001), among others.

This chapter is motivated by the need to fill this void by presenting a financial equilibrium model with a class of value functions with state-dependent weights that addresses the perspective of the individual sectors' bicriteria decision-making, and by providing the qualitative analysis. Specifically, the modeling approach in this chapter seeks to advance the work of Nagurney, Dong, and Hughes (1992) in general financial equilibrium modeling by introducing a class of value functions with state-dependent weights for bicriteria decision-making of each financial sector.

Recall that Nagurney, Dong, and Hughes (1992) presented a financial equilibrium model in an economy with multiple financial sectors and multiple instruments, which largely extended the work of the Capital Asset Pricing Model (CAPM) (cf. Sharpe (1964), Lintner (1965), and Mossin (1966)) by relaxing several key assumptions including homogeneous expectations and the existence of a risk-free asset. However, in that model, the decision of each sector's portfolio selection was based on the standard Markowitz mean-variance model with weights equal to one assigned to the two criteria.

This chapter is organized as follows. In Section 11.1, a bicriteria decision model of an individual financial sector is presented, in which the sector seeks an optimal portfolio composition in terms of assets and liabilities. We recall the basic concepts of a value function and its variable weights from the multicriteria decision-making literature (see also, e.g., Keeney and Raiffa (1993)). We then give an example to show why constant weight value functions may not reveal a financial sector's preference in regards to the return and the risk, and, therefore, it is appropriate to introduce state-dependent weights for the value functions in financial decision-making. A class of value functions with state-dependent weights is then proposed for the modeling of the individual sector's decision-making problem in selecting its optimal portfolio. The portfolio optimization problem for each sector is then constructed using the derived value function and a qualitative property established. This portfolio optimization model for a sector is utilized in the subsequent financial equilibrium derivation and analysis in Section 11.2.

In Section 11.2, the optimality conditions for each sector are derived and the economic system conditions governing the prices presented. The financial equilibrium is defined from the perspective of the individual sectors' decision-making. A variational inequality formulation of the governing equilibrium conditions is given in Section 11.3. We also obtain some qualitative properties of the financial equilibrium pattern, in particular, existence and uniqueness results. Section 11.4 considers some practical aspects regarding the measurement of risk in the twenty-first century and an application to Asian economies. Section 11.5 presents some concluding comments.

11.1　The Bicriteria Portfolio Selection Model

We first construct, in Subsection 11.1.1, the basic problem facing a sector in an economy in regards to the optimal portfolio composition determination by identifying two objectives and the constraints faced by a typical sector. We then turn, in Section 11.1.2, to the derivation of an appropriate value function, which is both price-dependent and risk-penalizing. Subsequently, in Section 11.2, we present the portfolio selection model in which we replace the two criteria with the value function for each sector to be optimized. We also establish that the value function is strictly concave for each sector with respect to asset and liability holdings. Finally, we present the necessary and sufficient conditions for an optimal portfolio for each sector.

11.1.1　The Portfolio Selection Model with Two Objectives

In this subsection, the basic notation which will be utilized to construct the complete financial equilibrium model in Section 11.2 is presented. We then focus on the portfolio selection problem facing a typical sector.

Consider an economy consisting of m sectors, with a typical sector denoted by i, and n financial instruments, with a typical instrument denoted by j. In this economy each sector can hold some combination of the n instruments as both assets and liabilities. Let x_{ij} denote the volume of instrument j held in sector i's portfolio as an asset, and let y_{ij} denote the volume of instrument j held in sector i's portfolio as a liability. Group the assets in sector i's portfolio into a column vector $x_i \in R^n$ and the liabilities into the column vector $y_i \in R^n$. Furthermore, group the sector asset vectors into a column vector $x \in R^{mn}$, and the sector liability vectors into the vector $y \in R^{mn}$

Each financial sector decides its portfolio composition. The performance of a future portfolio may be evaluated under two criteria: the mean and the uncertainty surrounding the mean. Each sector's uncertainty, or risk, with respect to the future value of the portfolio is assessed by a variance-covariance matrix. Let Q^i denote the $2n \times 2n$ variance-covariance matrix with regard to sector i's assets and liabilities.

In this model, it is assumed that the total volume of each balance sheet side is exogenous and fixed. Moreover, under the assumption of perfect competition, each sector will behave as if it has no influence on instrument prices or on the behavior of the other sectors. Let r_j denote the price of instrument j, and group the instrument prices into the vector $r \in R^n$.

A given financial sector i strives to increase its return and to decrease its risk. Therefore, an individual sector faces a bi-objective decision-making problem, with the first objective $z_1^i = \begin{pmatrix} x_i \\ y_i \end{pmatrix}^T Q^i \begin{pmatrix} x_i \\ y_i \end{pmatrix}$ denoting the risk to be minimized, and the second objective $z_2^i = \sum_{j=1}^{n} r_j(x_{ij} - y_{ij})$ denoting the return to be maximized. Inevitably, there is a trade-off between the two objectives in that high return usually involves high risk.

The bi-objective portfolio problem for sector i is, thus, given by:

$$\text{Minimize} \quad z_1^i = \begin{pmatrix} x_i \\ y_i \end{pmatrix}^T Q^i \begin{pmatrix} x_i \\ y_i \end{pmatrix}$$

$$\text{Maximize} \quad z_2^i = \sum_{j=1}^{n} r_j(x_{ij} - y_{ij})$$

subject to:

$$\sum_{j=1}^{n} x_{ij} = S^i \qquad (11.1)$$

$$\sum_{j=1}^{n} y_{ij} = S^i$$

$$x_{ij} \geq 0, \quad y_{ij} \geq 0; \quad j = 1, \ldots, n. \qquad (11.2)$$

Constraints (11.1) are the accounting identity reflecting that the accounts for sector i must balance, where S^i is the total financial volume held by sector i. Constraints (11.2) are the nonnegativity assumption. Let K_i denote the closed convex set of (x_i, y_i) satisfying the constraints (11.1) and (11.2). Since Q^i is a variance-covariance matrix one can assume that it is positive-definite.

In the next subsection, we construct price-dependent and risk-penalizing value functions for each sector, which allow for greater flexibility and realism in modeling than the constant or equal weight terms associated with the above two objectives.

11.1.2 Value Functions with Variable Weights

In this subsection, appropriate value functions for the sectors in the economy are constructed. We begin with some fundamentals of value functions.

Value functions have been studied extensively and used for decision problems with multiple criteria (cf. Fishburn (1970), Chankong and Haimes (1983), Yu (1985), Keeney and Raiffa (1993)). In particular, assume that there are q criteria to be maximized, that more is better for each, and v is called a value function for the q criteria if it is a real-valued function defined on the set of all the possible outcomes such that $v(z_1^1, \cdots, z_q^1) > v(z_1^2, \cdots, z_q^2)$ if and only if $(z_1^1, \cdots, z_q^1)$ is preferred to $(z_1^2, \cdots, z_q^2)$. Nevertheless, theoretically, strong assumptions are, typically, required to ensure the existence of a value function in order to represent the preference structure (cf. Zeleny (1982), Yu (1985)).

A constant additive weight value function is given by:

$$v(z_1, \cdots, z_q) = w_1 z_1 + \cdots + w_q z_q \qquad (11.3)$$

where the weights w_i's are independent of the z_i's. A special example of a constant weight value function is the one with equal weights. Value functions with equal weights have been employed in financial applications by, among others, Sharpe (1964), Lintner (1965), Pogue (1970), Francis and Archer (1979), and Rustem (1998).

A deficiency of a constant weight value function in the modeling of portfolio evaluation can be seen in the following example. The example is for illustrative purposes and shows that at times the constant weight value function cannot reveal an investor's preference. In practice, there are many approaches that can be used in assessing a value function (cf. Yu and Zhang (1992)).

An Example

Suppose that a sector is choosing between two investment plans, Plan A and Plan B, and assesses that Plan A has a risk $z_1^A = 15$, and a return $z_2^A = 100$, and Plan B has a risk $z_1^B = 0$ (no risk), and a return $z_2^B = 80$.

We first note that risk is minimized (rather than maximized) and, hence, in constructing a value function with constant weights we must multiply the risk by a minus one. Using then the constant weights as in (11.3), one would have concluded that

$$v(z_1^A, z_2^A) = -z_1^A + z_2^A = -15 + 100 = 85$$

is better than

$$v(z_1^B, z_2^B) = -z_1^B + z_2^B = -0 + 80 = 80.$$

Obviously, this is in contradiction to a common perception in the evaluation of these two plans. A proper value function should, in this case, impose a higher weight for z_1^A than that for z_1^B, as a penalty for higher risk.

It is clear that, in practice, more attention will generally be given to reduce the risk when the risk is high. This kind of decision rationality argues that the value function should penalize the states with high risk by imposing a greater weight to z_1 of high risks than to those z_1 with low risks. We now introduce a class of state-dependent weight value functions which may better describe the sector's behavior than the constant weight value functions.

Definition 11.1: Risk-Penalizing Weight
$w_1^i = w_1^i(z_1^i)$ is called a *risk-penalizing weight* for sector i, if w_1^i is a strictly increasing, convex, and smooth function, and $w_1^i \geq 0$, where z_1^i is the expected risk of the portfolio selection $(x_i, y_i) \in K_i, \forall i$.

Definition 11.2: Price-Dependent Weight
$w_2^i = w_2^i(r)$ is called a *price-dependent weight* for sector i, if it is smooth, where $w_2^i \geq 0, r \in R_+^n$.

Definition 11.3: Price-Dependent and Risk-Penalizing Value Function
A value function v^i for sector i is called *price-dependent and risk-penalizing* if

$$v^i = -w_1^i(z_1^i)z_1^i + w_2^i(r)z_2^i, \qquad (11.4)$$

where w_1^i, w_2^i are defined as above.

In such a state-dependent value function, w_1^i represents the importance of the risk perceived by sector i, that is, the marginal value for each unit decrement of z_1^i at the state (z_1^i, z_2^i). Analogously, w_2^i represents the importance of the return perceived by investor i at the current state (z_1^i, z_2^i), that is, the marginal value for each unit increment of z_2^i at (z_1^i, z_2^i).

The risk-penalizing value function is naturally named to reflect the risk-averse attitude of a financial sector which would devalue any alternative of high risk by imposing an increasing marginal penalty to it. The price dependency, in turn, stems from the consideration that the perceived marginal value of the expected return should be evaluated according to the financial sector's knowledge of the prices of the various financial instruments in the market. Such knowledge may be established over the history of the performance of these financial instruments and efforts are needed to prevent an overemphasis of the marginal value of the return due to a suspiciously high price. In the context of perfect competition and complete markets, every financial sector has the same access to the information. Therefore, $w_2^i(r)$ should be the same for every sector i. Let's denote it, thus, as $w_2(r)$.

An Example of Linear Function Weights

A simple example of weight function w_1^i defined in Definition 11.1 could be $w_1^i(z_1^i) = c^i z_1^i$, where c^i is a constant and $c^i \geq 0$. An example of w_2^i defined in Definition 11.2 could be $w_2^i(r) = c$, where c is constant and $c \geq 0$, $\forall i$.

Then the value function for sector i could be written as:

$$v^i = -w_1^i(z_1^i)z_1^i + w_2^i(r)z_2^i$$

$$= -c^i z_1^i \times z_1^i + c z_2^i$$

$$= -c^i {z_1^i}^2 + c z_2^i$$

$$= -c^i \left(\begin{pmatrix} x_i \\ y_i \end{pmatrix}^T Q^i \begin{pmatrix} x_i \\ y_i \end{pmatrix} \right)^2 + c \sum_{j=1}^n r_j(x_{ij} - y_{ij}).$$

We now use the above weight functions to revise the previous example.

The Example Revisited

Suppose that, in the previous example, a sector imposes a risk-penalizing weight in his value function, and let $w_1(z_1) = z_1$ (which is convex and strictly increasing). Suppose also that the prices are the same for the two portfolios in the example and the price-dependent weight at that price is 1. Then, the value function for that institution is

$$v(z_1, z_2) = -z_1 \times z_1 + z_2.$$

Therefore, the value of (z_1^A, z_2^A) perceived by this institution would now be

$$v(z_1^A, z_2^A) = -15 \times 15 + 100 = -125$$

and the value of (z_1^B, z_2^B) becomes

$$v(z_1^B, z_2^B) = -0 \times 0 + 80 = 80.$$

One sees that with a proper penalty for risk incorporated into the value function plan B would be preferred to plan A, which is in agreement with common sense.

Note, further, that a constant weight value function oversimplifies a price-dependent and risk-penalizing value function, where $w_1^i(z_1^i) = w_1^i$, $w_2^i(r) = w_2^i$, and

$$v^i = -z_1^i + z_2^i$$

$$= -\begin{pmatrix} x_i \\ y_i \end{pmatrix}^T Q^i \begin{pmatrix} x_i \\ y_i \end{pmatrix} + \sum_{j=1}^n r_j(x_{ij} - y_{ij})$$

is a $(1,1)$ constant weight value function for each sector i (see, e.g., Nagurney, Dong, and Hughes (1992)).

11.1.3   The Portfolio Selection Model with Value Functions

We are now ready to present a modification of the bi-objective portfolio optimization problem presented in Section 11.1.1, which includes the above-derived value function for a sector. Such a model will be used in our subsequent financial equilibrium analysis in Section 11.2.

The bi-objective decision-making problem for sector i can be converted to a single objective decision-making problem in the above defined price-dependent and risk-penalizing value function as follows:

$$\text{Maximize } v^i \quad = \quad -w_1^i(z_1^i)z_1^i + w_2(r)z_2^i \tag{11.5}$$

subject to:

$$\sum_{j=1}^{n} x_{ij} = S^i$$

$$\sum_{j=1}^{n} y_{ij} = S^i$$

$$x_{ij} \geq 0, \quad y_{ij} \geq 0; \quad j = 1, \ldots, n.$$

We now state and prove a basic result, which will be utilized to derive the optimality conditions for each sector, and, ultimately, in Section 11.2, the variational inequality formulation of the governing equilibrium conditions.

Theorem 11.1
The value function $v^i(x_i, y_i, r)$ defined in (11.4) is strictly concave with respect to $(x_i, y_i) \in K_i, \forall i$.

Proof: Let $g^i(z_1^i) = w_1^i(z_1^i)z_1^i$. Since $w_1^i(z_1^i)$ is strictly increasing and non-negative, and $z_1^i > 0$, one has that

$$\frac{dg^i(z_1^i)}{dz_1^i} = \left(\frac{dw_1^i(z_1^i)}{dz_1^i}z_1^i + w_1^i(z_1^i) \right) > 0. \tag{11.6}$$

$$\frac{d^2g^i(z_1^i)}{dz_1^{i\,2}} = \left(\frac{d^2w_1^i(z_1^i)}{dz_1^{i\,2}}z_1^i + 2\frac{dw_1^i(z_1^i)}{dz_1^i} \right) > 0, \tag{11.7}$$

because $w_1^i(z_1^i)$ is convex and strictly increasing.

Combining (11.6) and (11.7), one knows that $g^i : R \mapsto R$ is nondecreasing and strictly convex, whereas $z_1^i : K_i \mapsto R$ is convex with respect to $(x_i, y_i) \in K_i$ because the variance-covariance matrix is positive-definite.

Hence, the composition of $h^i(x_i, y_i) \equiv -g^i \circ z_1^i$ is strictly concave with respect to $(x_i, y_i) \in K_i$. Since $w_2(r)z_2^i$ is linear with respect to (x_i, y_i), the theorem is proved. $\square$

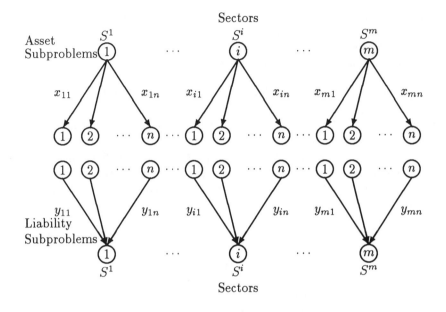

Fig. 11.1. Network Structure of the Sectors' Optimization Problems

In Figure 11.1, the network structure of the sectors' portfolio optimization problems is presented. Indeed, the budget constraints as given in problem (11.5) have the interpretation of conservation of flow constraints in that the amount of financial funds held by a sector must be equal to the amount allocated in the different financial instruments held as assets and as liabilities.

Hence, Figure 11.1 represents the structure of the financial economy out of equilibrium. A variety of financial network models (without, however, the multicriteria perspective taken here) can be found in Nagurney and Siokos (1997) and the references therein. Indeed, Nagurney, Dong, and Hughes (1992) identified and exploited the network structure of general financial equilibrium problems in the case of multiple sectors and multiple instruments.

11.2   Variational Inequality Formulation

In this section, the optimality conditions for each sector are presented as well as the economic system conditions governing the prices of the financial instruments. The financial equilibrium is then defined. We derive the variational inequality formulation of the equilibrium conditions and, subsequently, utilize this formulation to obtain qualitative properties of the equilibrium pattern, including existence and uniqueness results.

Optimality Conditions for Each Sector

Since, as established in Theorem 11.1, $v^i(x, y, r)$ is strictly concave with respect to $(x_i, y_i) \in K_i$, the necessary and sufficient conditions (cf. Appendix A) for $(x_i^*, y_i^*) \in K_i$ to be an optimal portfolio for sector i in problem (11.5) are that the following inequality is satisfied:

$$-\nabla_{x_i} v^i(x_i^*, y_i^*, r^*) \cdot (x_i - x_i^*) - \nabla_{y_i} v^i(x_i^*, y_i^*, r^*) \cdot (y_i - y_i^*) \geq 0, \quad \forall (x_i, y_i) \in K_i,$$
(11.8)

where $\nabla_X f(X)$ denotes the gradient of the vector f with respect to the components of the vector X.

In view of the composition $h^i(x_i, y_i) \equiv -g^i \circ z_1^i$ defined in the proof of Theorem 11.1, the value function in (11.5), and the two criteria z_1^i and z_2^i given prior to (11.1), one has that (11.8) is equivalent to the following inequality:

$$-[\nabla_{x_i} h^i(x_i^*, y_i^*) + w_2(r^*)r^*] \cdot (x_i - x_i^*) - [\nabla_{y_i} h^i(x_i^*, y_i^*) - w_2(r^*)r^*] \cdot (y_i - y_i^*) \geq 0,$$

$$\forall (x_i, y_i) \in K_i.$$
(11.9)

Economic System Conditions

We now turn to the determination of the inequalities governing the instrument prices in the economy. These prices provide feedback from the economic system to the sectors in regard to the equilibration of the total assets and total liabilities of each instrument. Here it is assumed that there is free disposal and that, therefore, the prices will be nonnegative. The economic system conditions insuring market clearance then take on the following form.

For each instrument j; $j = 1, \ldots, n$:

$$\sum_{i=1}^{m} x_{ij}^* - \sum_{i=1}^{m} y_{ij}^* \begin{cases} = 0, & \text{if } r_j^* > 0 \\ \geq 0, & \text{if } r_j^* = 0. \end{cases}$$
(11.10)

In other words, if the market clears for a given instrument, then its price must be positive; on the other hand, if there is excess supply of that instrument in the economy, then its price must be zero. Combining the above derived inequalities, we have the following.

Definition 11.4: Financial Equilibrium

A vector $(x^*, \ y^*, \ r^*) \in K \equiv \prod_{i=1}^{m} K_i \times R_+^n$ is an equilibrium of the above financial model if and only if it satisfies inequalities (11.8) and (11.10) for all sectors $i; i = 1, \ldots, m$, and all instruments $j; j = 1, \cdots, n$, simultaneously.

We are now ready to establish the variational inequality governing the equilibrium conditions of the financial model.

Theorem 11.2: Variational Inequality Formulation
A vector of sector assets and liabilities, and instrument prices $(x^*, y^*, r^*) \in \mathcal{K}$ is a financial equilibrium if and only if it satisfies the variational inequality problem: determine $(x_i^*, y_i^*, r^*) \in \mathcal{K}$, such that

$$-\sum_{i=1}^{m}[\nabla_{x_i} v^i(x_i^*, y_i^*, r^*)] \cdot [x_i - x_i^*] - \sum_{i=1}^{m}[\nabla_{y_i} v^i(x_i^*, y_i^*, r^*)] \cdot [y_i - y_i^*]$$

$$+\sum_{j=1}^{n}[\sum_{i=1}^{m}(x_{ij}^* - y_{ij}^*)] \times [r_j - r_j^*] \geq 0, \quad \forall(x, y, r) \in \mathcal{K}. \tag{11.11}$$

Proof: Assume that $(x^*, y^*, r^*) \in \mathcal{K}$ is an equilibrium. Then inequalities (11.8) and (11.10) hold for all sectors i and all instruments j. Hence, from (11.8), after summing over all sectors, we obtain:

$$-\sum_{i=1}^{m}[\nabla_{x_i} v^i(x_i^*, y_i^*, r^*)] \cdot [x_i - x_i^*] - \sum_{i=1}^{m}[\nabla_{y_i} v^i(x_i^*, y_i^*, r^*)] \cdot [y_i - y_i^*] \geq 0,$$

$$\forall(x, y) \in \prod_{i=1}^{m} K_i. \tag{11.12}$$

Also, from inequality (11.10) one can conclude that

$$\sum_{i=1}^{m}(x_{ij}^* - y_{ij}^*) \times (r_j - r_j^*) \geq 0, \quad \forall r_j \geq 0,$$

and, therefore,

$$\sum_{j=1}^{n}\sum_{i=1}^{m}(x_{ij}^* - y_{ij}^*) \times (r_j - r_j^*) \geq 0, \quad \forall r \in R_+^n. \tag{11.13}$$

Summing now inequalities (11.12) and (11.13), one obtains the variational inequality (11.11).

We now establish that a solution to (11.11) will also satisfy equilibrium conditions (11.8) (or (11.9)), and (11.10).

If $(x^*, y^*, r^*) \in \mathcal{K}$ is a solution of (11.11), if we let $x_i = x_i^*$, $y_i = y_i^*$, for all i, and substitute the resultants in (11.11), yields:

$$\sum_{j=1}^{n}\sum_{i=1}^{m}(x_{ij}^* - y_{ij}^*) \times (r_j - r_j^*) \geq 0, \quad \forall r \in R_+^n, \tag{11.14}$$

which implies conditions (11.10).

Similarly, if we let $r_j = r_j^*$, for all j, in which case substitution into (11.11) yields:

$$-\sum_{i=1}^{m}[\nabla_{x_i}v^i(x_i^*, y_i^*, r^*)] \cdot [x_i - x_i^*] - \sum_{i=1}^{m}[\nabla_{y_i}v^i(x_i^*, y_i^*, r^*)] \cdot [y_i - y_i^*] \geq 0,$$

$$\forall(x, y) \in \prod_{i=1}^{m} K_i, \tag{11.15}$$

which implies that (11.8) must hold. □

Variational Inequality Formulation of Financial Equilibrium with a Class of Linear Function Weights

We now consider a value function described in Section 11.1.2 and give the explicit form of the variational inequality formulation of the equilibrium conditions in this case. In particular, assume that $w_1^i(z_1^i) = c^i z_1^i$, and $w_2(z_2^i) = c$, $c^i \geq 0$, and $c \geq 0$. Then the variational inequality (11.11) takes the explicit form:

$$\sum_{i=1}^{m}\sum_{j=1}^{n}\left\{4c^i \begin{pmatrix} x_i^* \\ y_i^* \end{pmatrix}^T Q^i \begin{pmatrix} x_i^* \\ y_i^* \end{pmatrix} \left[Q_{(11)_j}^i{}^T \cdot x_i^* + Q_{(21)_j}^i{}^T \cdot y_i^*\right] - cr_j^*\right\}$$

$$\times [x_{ij} - x_{ij}^*]$$

$$+\sum_{i=1}^{m}\sum_{j=1}^{n}\left\{4c^i \begin{pmatrix} x_i^* \\ y_i^* \end{pmatrix}^T Q^i \begin{pmatrix} x_i^* \\ y_i^* \end{pmatrix} \left[Q_{(22)_j}^i{}^T \cdot x_i^* + Q_{(12)_j}^i{}^T \cdot y_i^*\right] + cr_j^*\right\}$$

$$\times [y_{ij} - y_{ij}^*]$$

$$+\sum_{j=1}^{n}\sum_{i=1}^{m}(x_{ij}^* - y_{ij}^*) \times (r_j - r_j^*) \geq 0, \quad \forall(x, y, r) \in \mathcal{K},$$

where Q^i has been partitioned as $Q^i = \begin{pmatrix} Q_{11}^i & Q_{12}^i \\ Q_{21}^i & Q_{22}^i \end{pmatrix}$, and $Q_{\alpha\beta_j}^i$ denotes the jth column of $Q_{\alpha\beta}^i$, with $\alpha, \beta = 1, 2$.

Now the qualitative properties of the equilibrium pattern are addressed through the study of variational inequality (11.11). We first establish that the variational inequality (11.11) can be reformulated as a variational inequality problem over a compact (and convex) set. This then allows us, subsequently, to establish the existence of an equilibrium pattern through the application of a classical existence result from the theory of variational inequalities.

Theorem 11.3

If $(x^*, y^*, r^*) \in \mathcal{K}$ is an equilibrium, that is, satisfies variational inequality (11.11), then the equilibrium asset and liability pattern (x^*, y^*) is a solution to the variational inequality problem: determine $(x^*, y^*) \in \hat{S}$, satisfying:

$$-\sum_{i=1}^{m} \nabla_{x_i} h^i(x_i^*, y_i^*) \cdot (x_i - x_i^*) - \sum_{i=1}^{m} \nabla_{y_i} h^i(x_i^*, y_i^*) \cdot (y_i - y_i^*) \geq 0, \quad \forall(x,y) \in \hat{S},$$

$$(11.16)$$

where $\hat{S} \equiv \{(x,y) | (x,y) \in \prod_{i=1}^{m} K_i; \sum_{i=1}^{m} x_{ij} - \sum_{i=1}^{m} y_{ij} \geq 0; \ j = 1, \ldots, n\}$, and is non-empty.

Conversely, if (x^*, y^*) is a solution of (11.16), there exists an $r^* \in R_+^n$, such that (x^*, y^*, r^*) is a solution of (11.11) and, thus, an equilibrium.

Proof: The proof of this theorem is analogous to that of Theorem 6.3 in Nagurney and Siokos (1997). $\square$

Variational inequality (11.11) is now put into standard form. First, define the m-dimensional column vector

$$v \equiv (v^1(x_1, y_1, r), \ldots, v^m(x_m, y_m, r))^T.$$

Then, define the vector $X \equiv (x, y, r)$ and the column vector $F(X)$ where

$$F(X) \equiv \begin{bmatrix} -\nabla_X v(x, y, r) \\ -\nabla_Y v(x, y, r) \\ \sum_{i=1}^{m}(x_{i1} - y_{i1}) \\ \vdots \\ \sum_{i=1}^{m}(x_{in} - y_{in}) \end{bmatrix}_{2mn+n}$$

$$(11.17)$$

Consequently, (11.11) can be written as:
Determine $X^* \in \mathcal{K}$ satisfying:

$$\langle F(X^*), X - X^* \rangle \geq 0, \quad \forall X \in \mathcal{K}.$$

$$(11.18)$$

Henceforth, we refer to variational inequality (11.18) as VI$(F, \mathcal{K})$.

Now two standard theorems in variational inequality theory are presented (see also Appendix B).

Theorem 11.4: Existence

If $\mathcal{K}$ is a compact convex set and $F(X)$ is continuous on $\mathcal{K}$, then the variational inequality problem VI$(F, \mathcal{K})$ admits at least one solution X^*.

Theorem 11.5: Uniqueness

Suppose that $F(X)$ is strictly monotone on $\mathcal{K}$. Then the solution to the VI$(F, \mathcal{K})$ problem is unique, if one exists.

According to Theorem 11.1, $-h^i(x_i, y_i)$ is strictly convex on K_i for all i. Therefore, the function $F(X)$ that enters the variational inequality (11.18) is strictly monotone. Combining the above Theorems 11.3, 11.4, and 11.5, one can conclude the following theorem immediately.

Theorem 11.6: Existence and Uniqueness
The equilibrium asset, liability, and price pattern (x^*, y^*, r^*) exists and the equilibrium asset and liability pattern (x^*, y^*) is unique.

Before identifying the supernetwork structure of the financial economy in equilibrium, we establish the following result.

Theorem 11.7
In equilibrium, the market clears for each instrument, that is,

$$\sum_{i=1}^{m}(x_{ij}^* - y_{ij}^*) = 0, \quad j = 1, \ldots, n. \tag{11.19}$$

Proof: One can easily observe that from the constraints in problem (11.5) that the following expression must hold:

$$\sum_{i=i}^{m}\sum_{j=1}^{n}(x_{ij}^* - y_{ij}^*) = 0. \tag{11.20}$$

If we assume now that for some instrument k we have, that, in equilibrium,

$$\sum_{i=1}^{m}(x_{ik}^* - y_{ik}^*) > 0, \tag{11.21}$$

then, according to (11.20), this would imply that for some other instrument l, we would then have to have that:

$$\sum_{i=1}^{m}(x_{il}^* - y_{il}^*) < 0, \tag{11.22}$$

which is in contradiction to equilibrium condition (11.10) being satisfied for every instrument price. Hence, we must have that

$$\sum_{i=1}^{m}(x_{ij}^* - y_{ij}^*) = 0, \tag{11.23}$$

for every instrument j; $j = 1, \ldots, n$. □

Since, according to Theorem 11.8, the market clears for each financial instrument, this implies that the supply of each financial instrument (the assets) is equal to the demand for each financial instrument (the liabilities) and,

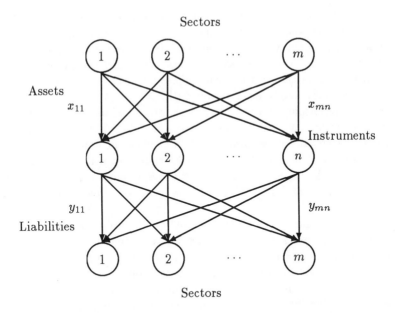

Fig. 11.2. The Supernetwork Structure of the Financial Economy at Equilibrium

hence, according to network theory the flows into the corresponding instrument node must be equal to the flows out. Therefore, as illustrated in Figure 11.2, the individual networks comprising the sectors' optimization problems in Figure 11.1, "merge" into the supernetwork depicted in Figure 11.2 at equilibrium. Hence, the subnetworks evolve over time into the supernetwork depicted in Figure 11.2.

Related network constructions for a variety of financial equilibrium problems with similar budgetary constraints can be found in Nagurney and Siokos (1997).

11.3   Measurement of Financial Risk in the Twenty-First Century

Alan Greenspan, the Chairman of the Federal Reserve Board in the United States, at a conference sponsored by the Office of the Controller of the Currency in Washington, DC, on October 14, 1999 (see Federal Reserve Board (1999)), offered his perspective on the fundamental sources of financial risk as well as the value added of banks and other financial intermediaries. In particular, as is well known, he reiterated that risk is inherent in all business and financial activity. Moreover, he noted that the evaluation of risk "is a key element in all estimates of wealth" due to such uncertainties as whether any specific nonfinancial asset will be productive, what kinds of flows of returns an asset may generate, and uncertainties relating to the economy at large and to asset values, in general. He utilized a metaphor derived from networks to describe the risk of an asset as being the potential for "actual results to deviate from the path" where an investor would seek to estimate the most likely long-term earnings path.

Mr. Greenspan, in the same speech, described one of the roles of financial intermediation, in turn, as being that of redistributing risk among people with different attitudes towards risk, a facet of our model. As stated by him, "Any means that shifts from those who choose to withdraw from those more willing to take it on permits increased investment without significantly raising the perceived degree of discomfort from risk that the population overall experiences."

Moreover, he explicitly emphasized the importance of information technology in financial decision-making today in that information is critical to the evaluation of risk and reduces the uncertainties and, hence, the variances, that are utilized in directing portfolio decisions.

Finally, he emphasized that during a financial crisis, as represented by several international ones in recent years, risk aversion increases dramatically, and this presents challenges from a risk management perspective. In our variable weight framework, increased risk is weighted more highly.

11.3.1 Experiences from Asian Economies

We now provide an illustration of some of the above concepts in which it is apparent that when the risk is perceived as being higher, individuals give more attention to the risk relative to the rate of return of their portfolios and, hence, variable weights, rather than fixed weights are used in the determination of the trade-off between return and risk, that is, the value functions.

Appel (2000) reported that, in November 2000, fund management companies such as HSBC Asset Management (Hong Long) Ltd., Investec Asset Management Asia, OCBC Asset Management Ltd., and UOB Asset Management Ltd. launched funds that guaranteed repayment to investors who would keep their funds invested for the two to three year life of the funds. The Development Bank of Singapore (DBS), in turn, went further in announcing the "first and only unit trust" to guarantee a yearly return of between 2.4 percent and 3.5 percent, depending on the length of time of the investment, and more if stocks should rally. According to Teng Ngiek Lian, the chief executive of Value Partners Singapore Ltd., as cited in the same article, fund managers apparently believe that the stomache-churning volatility in stock through that year is making investors receptive to products that offer fewer gains in return for assurances of less pain. According to Stuart Aldcroft, the managing director of Investec Asset Management in Hong Kong (see Appel (2000)) during volatile stock markets even the less-aggressive funds that investment houses historically offer can strike investors as being high-risk.

11.4   Concluding Comments

In this chapter, we presented a financial equilibrium model with multiple sectors and multiple financial instruments, in which each sector faces a bicriteria decision-making problem of portfolio selection in order to maximize returns and to minimize risk. Unlike the earlier literature (cf. Nagurney and Siokos (1997) and the references therein) we no longer assume equal and constant weights (typically set to one) associated with the objectives.

In particular, a class of value functions with variable weights was studied and employed for the model, which is more general than the value function with constant weights, which has been used in models in the existing literature. The class of price-dependent and risk-penalizing value functions proposed here reflects the common attitude in portfolio composition theory that would devalue a portfolio with particularly high risk. It also incorporates the fact that the perceived marginal value of the expected return is dependent on the financial sectors' knowledge of the various instruments' prices in the market. Therefore, the price-dependent, risk-penalizing value functions discussed in this paper are believed to better represent reality, as well as practice.

This chapter offers a methodology to study financial equilibrium problems in which bicriteria decision-making is the underlying structure. It would be interesting to further model and analyze financial equilibria in which sectors have more criteria than two in their portfolio selection decisions. For example, Chow (1995) extended Markowitz's standard model by including the so-called tracking error as another criteria in portfolio selection.

In addition, as discussed in Hallerbach and Spronk (2000), risk analysis within a multicriteria decision-making framework is also relevant to applications outside of finance, but with concepts from finance, nevertheless, serving as a pillar.

11.5   Sources and Notes

This chapter is based on the paper of Dong and Nagurney (2001). It focuses on the modeling and qualitative aspects of a multicriteria financial equilibrium model in which the weights are no longer fixed but are, rather, variable. Here, however, we explicitly identify the network structure of the problem both out of and in equilibrium and also discuss some illustrative examples from practice.

Nagurney, Dong, and Mokhtarian (2001b) recently introduced variable weights for the study of multiclass, multicriteria network equilibrium models, which are extensions of the fixed demand and elastic demand models in Chapter 7. They then applied such models to teleshopping versus shopping and telecommuting versus commuting decision-making.

In both the financial equilibrium model developed in this chapter and the one formulated and studied in Chapter 6, the importance of decentralized decision-making was recognized. Interestingly, although the model of this chapter does not consider intermediaries, the structure of the supernetwork as depicted in Figure 11.2 is similar to the logistics network (see Figure 6.1) underlying the dynamic financial network model with intermediation. In this chapter, however, we have focused on financial instruments as asset and as liability holdings whereas in Chapter 6 the emphasis was on the transformation of financial flows. Additional background on financial equilibrium modeling and computation, can be found in Nagurney (1994), Nagurney and Siokos (1997), and Nagurney (2001). For additional reading on decentralized decision-making in the context of finance, see Bernholz (1990). For further reading on how the information revolution has narrowed space and time and its effects on financial innovation and the future of money, see Dorn (1997).

12 Paradoxes and Policies

This chapter turns to another area of application of supernetworks – that of the environment. Specifically, we consider supernetworks in which certain links correspond to telecommunication links and are characterized by a zero emission factor, that is, irregardless of the flow on such links the total emissions generated by the use of such links is zero. We identify three distinct paradoxical phenomena that can occur in such networks, which demonstrate that so-called "improvements" to the network may result in increases in total emissions generated.

Congested urban transportation networks represent large-scale networks in which the behavior of the individual users or travelers has implications for the society as a whole. For example, the negative effects of vehicle use, notably in terms of congestion and pollution, are now well established. Indeed, congestion in the United States results in $100 billion in lost productivity annually with the figure being approximately $150 billion in Europe. Moreover, cars and other motor vehicles are responsible for at least 50 percent of the air pollution in urban areas (see *The Economist* (1996, 1997)). The World Health Organization (WHO) (cf. Nagurney (2000c)) has estimated that only about 20 percent of the world's town residents enjoy good enough air quality as measured by the levels of emissions. Specifically, motor vehicles generate about 15 percent of the world's emissions of carbon dioxide, the principal global warming gas, 50 percent of the nitrogen oxide emissions, which in combination with other pollutants form nitric acid, which then falls to earth as acid rain, and 90 percent of the carbon monoxide (cf. Button (1990)).

Clearly, both congestion and environmental issues associated with vehicle use are problems of major concern for our societies today. In recent years, there has been a growing interest in the development of rigorous tools for both congestion and emission control management (see, e.g., Nagurney (2000c) and the references therein). For any policy, however, to have an appropriate effect, it is imperative that the behavior of the individuals affected by the policy be taken into consideration. Moreover, in order to investigate telecommuting versus commuting and/or teleshopping versus shopping in the context of environmental impacts one must be able to capture the decision alternatives within the same framework, such as through the supernetwork framework promulgated in this book.

As noted in Chapter 3, the study of paradoxes in traffic networks dates to Braess (1968) who presented an example in which, assuming user-optimizing behavior (cf. Beckmann, McGuire, and Winsten (1956), Dafermos and Sparrow (1969), and Chapter 3) on the part of the travelers, the addition of a link results in all travelers being worse off from a cost perspective. That example has stimulated much research in sensitivity analysis and in the identification of analogous paradoxical phenomena not only in transportation networks (see Murchland (1970), Fisk (1979), Steinberg and Zangwill (1983), Dafermos and Nagurney (1984b,c), Frank (1992), Pas and Principio (1996), among others), but also in other network settings, including telecommunication networks (cf. Cohen and Kelly (1990), Korilis, Lazar, and Orda (1999)).

Recently, Nagurney (2000e) identified emission paradoxes which can arise in transportation networks in that so-called "improvements" to the transportation network, in the form of a road addition, or decrease in travel demand, for example, may result in an increase in the total emissions generated. In this chapter, we take up the question of whether networks with zero emission links (such as those corresponding to telecommunication links) and including a variety of supernetworks as discussed in Parts II and III of this book, may also result in counterintuitive phenomena as regards the emissions generated.

The chapter is organized as follows. In Section 12.1, we recall the basic network (single-class) equilibrium model with fixed demand, which was introduced in Chapter 3, to which we then add an environmental component. In Section 12.2, we identify three distinct paradoxical phenomena which can occur in supernetworks with zero emission links. We also revisit an example given by Nagurney (2000c) and show that, if a certain link's emission factor is reduced to zero, the total emissions will not increase. We then prove that, for a special network case, the addition of a zero emission link never results in an increase in total emissions.

Subsequently, we consider the paradoxes and establish, in Section 12.3, an emission pricing policy which guarantees that such paradoxes will not occur. Finally, in Section 12.4, it is demonstrated that the pricing policy is equivalent to a particular weight assignment associated with the emissions generated if the users of the supernetwork are now assumed to be multicriteria decision-makers who seek not only to minimize their costs but also not to exceed an imposed environmental emissions upper bound.

12.1   The Network Equilibrium Model with Emissions

Before presenting the paradoxes in the next section, we first describe the basic network equilibrium model with fixed demands and with emissions.

The model was also used as the basic framework for the identification of emission paradoxes in Nagurney (2000e). Here, however, we interpret a link in a more general fashion, in particular, in a supernetwork context, and let a link, as has been done in Chapters 4 through 9, correspond to a means of access between nodes which can reflect either physical transportation or virtual transportation as through telecommunications.

This model serves as the foundation for the identification of counterintuitive phenomena in Section 12.2. The notation is similar to that utilized in Chapter 3 and is as follows. Consider a network $\mathcal{G} = [\mathcal{N}, \mathcal{L}]$ consisting of the set of nodes $\mathcal{N}$ and a set of directed links $\mathcal{L}$. Let a, b, etc., denote the links and let p, q, etc., denote the paths, which are assumed to be acyclic. Note that, as mentioned above, a link may correspond to either a transportation link or to a telecommunication link. Assume that there are J origin/destination (O/D) pairs in the network, with a typical O/D pair denoted by ω, and the set of O/D pairs denoted by Ω. Let P_ω denote the set of paths connecting O/D pair ω and let P denote the set of paths in the network.

A path in this supernetwork model, hence, consists of a sequence of links to get from an origin to a destination where a link may be either a transportation or a telecommunication link. For example, in a telecommuting application (see Figure 7.1) a single link connecting an origin (place of residence) to a destination (work location) may correspond to a telecommunication link whereby decision-makers can telecommute, as opposed to physically commute. Similarly, in a teleshopping application (see Figure 7.2), such a link may correspond to placing a virtual order rather than driving to a store to shop. Recall that in the supernetwork depicted in Figure 7.1 the paths consisting of the links joining nodes 1 and 6 and nodes 2 and 6 correspond to telecommunication links which can represent telecommuting options for residents located, respectively at nodes 1 and 2. The other paths joining nodes 1 and 2 and consisting of links: $(1,3), (3,6); (1,3), (3,5), (5,6); (1,4),$ $(4,5), (5,6),$ and $(1,4), (4,6)$ would correspond to transportation routes for the commuters between nodes 1 and 2. Similarly, one can construct the paths connecting origin node 2 with destination node 6 and corresponding to exclusively transportation links.

The flow on a link a is denoted by f_a, and the user cost associated with traversing link a by c_a. Group the link flows into a column vector $f \in R^n$, and the link user costs into a column vector $c \in R^n$, where n is the number of links in the network. The user cost on a link will, in general, depend upon the entire link flow pattern, that is,

$$c = c(f), \tag{12.1}$$

where c is a known smooth function. A user traversing path p incurs a user cost C_p, where

$$C_p(f) = \sum_{a \in L} c_a(f) \delta_{ap}, \tag{12.2}$$

where $\delta_{ap} = 1$, if link a is contained in path p, and 0, otherwise.

Assume fixed demands for the origin/destination pairs, as was done also in the fixed demand, but multicriteria, network model described in Section 7.1, where the demand for O/D pair ω is denoted by d_ω. The nonnegative flow on path p is denoted by x_p, with the path flows grouped into a column vector $x \in R_+^{n_P}$, where n_P denotes the number of paths in the network. The following conservation of flow equations must be satisfied by the flows in the network:

$$d_\omega = \sum_{p \in P_\omega} x_p, \quad \forall \omega \in \Omega, \tag{12.3}$$

and

$$f_a = \sum_{p \in P} x_p \delta_{ap}, \quad \forall a \in \mathcal{L}. \tag{12.4}$$

As discussed in earlier chapters, the conservation of flow equation (12.3) states that the sum of the path flows on paths connecting an O/D pair must be equal to the demand for that O/D pair. Equation (12.4), in turn, says that the flow on a link equals the sum of the path flows on paths that use that link. Let $\mathcal{K}$ denote the feasible set where $\mathcal{K} \equiv \{f \mid$ there exists a vector $x \geq 0$, and satisfying (12.3) and (12.4)$\}$.

Recall now the well-known network equilibrium conditions (see also Chapter 3 and Chapter 7), which are equally applicable to more general supernetwork setting which includes not only transportation links but also telecommunication links:

Definition 12.1: Fixed Demand Network Equilibrium
For every O/D pair $\omega \in \Omega$ and each path $p \in P_\omega$:

$$C_p(f^*) \begin{cases} = \lambda_\omega, & \text{if } x_p^* > 0 \\ \geq \lambda_\omega, & \text{if } x_p^* = 0, \end{cases} \tag{12.5}$$

that is, only those paths that have minimal and equal user costs for each O/D pair are utilized.

As discussed in Chapter 3 (see also Appendix B), the network equilibrium conditions satisfying (12.5) were shown by Smith (1979) and Dafermos (1980) to satisfy the finite-dimensional *variational inequality problem*.

Theorem 12.1 Variational Inequality Formulation of Fixed Demand Network Equilibrium
A vector $f^* \in \mathcal{K}$ is a network equilibrium link flow pattern if and only if it satisfies the variational inequality problem:

$$\langle c(f^*), f - f^* \rangle \geq 0, \quad \forall f \in \mathcal{K}, \tag{12.6}$$

where $\langle \cdot, \cdot \rangle$ denotes the inner product in R^n.

Recall that, in the special and simplest case in which the user link cost functions (12.1) are separable and increasing functions of the link flows (see

Chapter 3), the network equilibrium coincides with the solution to the convex optimization problem:

$$\text{Minimize}_{f \in \mathcal{K}} \quad \sum_{a \in \mathcal{L}} \int_0^{f_a} c_a(y)dy. \tag{12.7}$$

We now discuss the emission factors. Let h_a denote the emission factor associated with link a with the total emissions generated on link a being given by $h_a f_a$. The total emissions generated by the flow on the network, denoted by E, are then given by $E = \sum_{a \in \mathcal{L}} h_a f_a$ (cf. Glover and Brzezinski (1989), DeCorla-Souza, et al. 1995, Anderson, et al. (1996) and Allen (1996)).

12.2 Paradoxes on Supernetworks with Zero Emission Links

Three distinct paradoxes in supernetworks in which there exists a zero emission link are now identified. Such a link, for example, could correspond to a telecommunication link in a supernetwork. We also revisit an example by Nagurney (2000c) which illustrated another paradox.

Paradox 1: The Addition of a Zero Emission Link Results in an Increase in Total Emissions with No Change in Demand

Consider the Braess (1968) network, which is illustrated in Figure 12.1 and represents the original network before the addition of link e and after such an addition.

Consider now the first network depicted in Figure 12.1 in which there are 4 links: a, b, c, d; 4 nodes: 1, 2, 3, 4, and a single O/D pair $\omega_1 = (1, 4)$. There are, thus, 2 paths available to users between this O/D pair: $p_1 = (a, c)$ and $p_2 = (b, d)$. The user link cost functions are $c_a(f_a) = 10f_a$, $c_b(f_b) = f_b + 50$, $c_c(f_c) = f_c + 50$, $c_d(f_d) = 10f_d$, and the fixed demand $d_{\omega_1} = 6$. Assume that the emission factors on the links are given by $h_a = .2$, $h_b = .1$, $h_c = .1$, and $h_d = .2$. Clearly, the user-optimized flow pattern, satisfying equilibrium conditions (12.5) is $x_{p_1}^* = 3$, $x_{p_2}^* = 3$, with equilibrium link flows $f_a^* = 3$, $f_b^* = 3$, $f_c^* = 3$, $f_d^* = 3$, and with associated equilibrium path costs $C_{p_1} = 83$ and $C_{p_2} = 83$. The total number of emissions generated by the equilibrium link flow pattern is $E = .2(3) + .1(3) + .1(3) + .2(3) = 1.8$.

Now, as illustrated in Figure 12.1, consider the addition of a new link "e", joining node 2 to node 3 to the original network. Assume that link e has an emission factor $h_e = 0$ and a user cost $c_e(f_e) = f_e + 10$. The addition of this link creates a new path $p_3 = (a, e, d)$ that is available to the users of the network. Assume also that the demand d_{ω_1} remains unchanged at 6 units of flow.

The equilibrium path flow pattern on the new network is $x_{p_1}^{**} = 2$, $x_{p_2}^{**} = 2$, $x_{p_3}^{**} = 2$, with equilibrium link flows $f_a^{**} = 4$, $f_b^{**} = 2$, $f_c^{**} = 2$, $f_e^{**} = 2$, $f_d^{**} = 4$, and with associated equilibrium path costs $C_{p_1} = C_{p_2} = C_{p_3} = 92$.

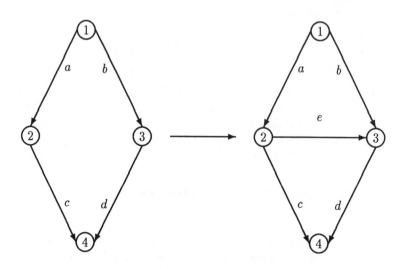

Fig. 12.1. Supernetwork Topology for Paradox 1

The total emissions generated in the new network are equal to 2, a value greater than the total generated in the original network. Hence, the addition of a new link with zero emissions makes not only everyone worse off in terms of cost but also in terms of the emissions generated.

Nagurney (2000e) considered the same network topologies and cost and demand structure in her first paradoxical example therein but assumed that the emission factor on link e was positive.

Paradox 2: A Decrease in Demand on a Supernetwork with a Zero Emission Link May Result in an Increase in Emissions

We now illustrate a second paradox regarding a supernetwork with a zero emission link in which a decrease in the demand for an origin/destination pair, joined by a single path consisting of a single link with a zero emission factor, results in an increase in total emissions.

Consider the supernetwork depicted in Figure 12.2. The user link cost functions are $c_a(f_a) = f_a + 1$, $c_b(f_b) = f_b + 4$, and $c_c(f_c) = f_c + 1$. There are two origin/destination pairs $\omega_1 = (1, 2)$ and $\omega_2 = (1, 3)$. The path connecting O/D pair ω_1, p_1, consists of the single link a. The paths connecting O/D pair ω_2 are $p_2 = (a, c)$ and $p_3 = b$. The demands in the original problem are $d_{\omega_1} = 1$ and $d_{\omega_2} = 2$. The emission factors on the links are $h_a = 0.$, $h_b = .01$, and $h_c = .5$. Hence, link a may correspond to a telecommunication link.

The network equilibrium path flow pattern is $x^*_{p_1} = 1$, $x^*_{p_2} = 1$, $x^*_{p_3} = 1$, with induced link flow pattern $f^*_a = 2$, $f^*_b = f^*_c = 1$. The path user costs are: for O/D pair ω_1: $C_{p_1} = 3$, and for O/D pair ω_2: $C_{p_2} = C_{p_3} = 5$. The total emissions generated: $E = .02 + .01 + .5 = .51$.

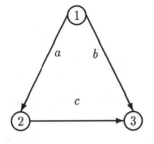

Fig. 12.2. Supernetwork Topology for Paradox 2

We now consider a decrease in demand associated with O/D pair ω_1 with the new demand $d_{\omega_1} = .5$ and all other data remain the same. The new network equilibrium path flow pattern is $x_{p_1}^{**} = .5$, $x_{p_2}^{**} = 1.1666...,,$ $x_{p_3}^{**} = .833...$, with induced equilibrium link flow pattern $f_a^{**} = 1.666...$, $f_b^{**} = .833...$, $f_c^{**} = 1.166...$ The new path user costs are: for O/D pair ω_1: $C_{p_1} = 2.666...$, and for O/D pair ω_2: $C_{p_2} = C_{p_3} = 4.833....$ The total emissions now generated: $E = 0.000... + .00833... + .5830 = .59133....$

Hence, the total emissions have increased from .51 to .59133... even though the demand has decreased. Moreover, the costs for paths between the two origin/destination pairs have decreased. Nagurney (2000e) considered the above network example except in the case where $h_a = .01$ and obtained a similar result. The above result is, hence, much stronger.

Paradox 3: Adding a New Path which Consists Solely of a Zero Emission Link and which Shares No Links with Any Other Path May Result in an Increase in Emissions

We now illustrate a third paradox regarding a supernetwork in which the addition of a new path consisting solely of a zero emission results in an increase in total emissions.

Consider the first network depicted in Figure 12.3. The user link cost functions are $c_a(f_a) = f_a + 10$, $c_b(f_b) = 3f_a + 3f_b$. There is a single origin/destination pair: $\omega_1 = (1, 2)$. The paths connecting the O/D pair are $p_1 = a$ and $p_2 = b$. The demand in this network $d_{\omega_1} = 5$. The emission factors on the links are $h_a = 0.1$, $h_b = .5$.

The network equilibrium path flow pattern is $x_{p_1}^* = 5$, $x_{p_2}^* = 0$, with induced link flow pattern $f_a^* = 5$, $f_b^* = 0$. The path user costs are $C_{p_1} = 15$, and $C_{p_2} = 15$. The total emissions generated: $E^* = .5 + 0 = .5$.

We now add a new link c, as depicted in the second network in Figure 12.3, which directly connects the O/D pair and which consists exclusively of a zero emission link, that is, $h_c = 0$. The user cost function on link c is

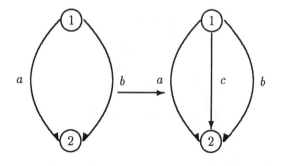

Fig. 12.3. Supernetwork Topology for Paradox 3

$c_c(f_c) = f_c + 11$. There are now three paths connecting the O/D pair, with $p_3 = c$.

The new network equilibrium link flow pattern is $f_a^{**} = 2$, $f_b^{**} = 2$, and $f_c^{**} = 1$. The path user travel costs are $C_{p_1} = C_{p_2} = C_{p_3} = 12$. The total emissions now generated: $E = 0.2 + 1.0 + 0.0 = 1.2$. Hence, the equilibrium path costs have decreased. However, the total emissions have increased from .5 to 1.2 even though a new disjoint path (that is, a path that has no links in common with any other path) with zero emissions was added.

A Paradox Revisited: A Reallocation of Users from an Origin/Destination Pair of Higher Total Emissions to One of Lower Total Emissions

We now revisit an example termed "Paradox 4" in Nagurney (2000c). Although therein it was presented as a multimodal example, given the proposed link cost structure, we can make copies of the multimodal network (cf. Chapter 3) as given in Figure 12.4 to obtain the supernetwork representation. There are, hence, two origin/destination pairs in the supernetwork with $\omega_1 = (1,2)$ and $\omega_2 = (3,4)$. The paths are $p_1 = a$, $p_2 = b$, $p_3 = c$, and $p_4 = d$. Assume that the demands are given by $d_{\omega_1} = 10$ and $d_{\omega_2} = 5$.

The user link cost functions are $c_a(f_a) = f_a + 5$, $c_b(f_b) = f_b + 5$, $c_c(f_c) = f_c + 10$, and $c_d(f_d) = f_d + 5$. The emission factors associated with the links are $h_a = 0.2$, $h_b = 0.2$, $h_c = .4$, and $h_d = .1$.

It is straightforward to verify that the network equilibrium pattern is given by $x_{p_1}^* = 5$, $x_{p_2}^* = 5$, $x_{p_3}^* = 0$, $x_{p_4}^* = 5$, with associated equilibrium link flow pattern $f_a^* = 5$, $f_b^* = 5$, $f_c^* = 0$, and $f_d^* = 5$, and user path costs $C_{p_1} = C_{p_2} = 10$, and $C_{p_3} = C_{p_4} = 10$.

The total emissions due to users between O/D ω_1 are $h_a f_a^* + h_b f_b^* = 1 + 1 = 2$, whereas the total emissions due to users between O/D pair ω_2 are

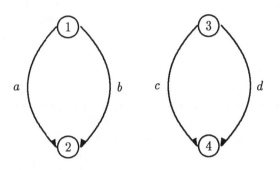

Fig. 12.4. Supernetwork Topology for a Revisited Paradox

$h_c f_c{}^* + h_d f_d{}^* = 0 + 0 = 0$, with the total emissions generated equal to 2.

Nagurney (2000c) considered a transfer of 2.5 units of demand from O/D pair ω_1 to O/D pair ω_2 so that the new demands were given by: $d_{\omega_1} = 7.5$ and $d_{\omega_2} = 7.5$. The new network equilibrium pattern is then $x_{p_1}^{**} = 3.75$, $x_{p_2}^{**} = 3.75$, $x_{p_3}^{**} = 1.25$, and $x_{p_4}{}^* = 6.25$, with associated link flow pattern $f_a^{**} = 3.75$, $f_b^{**} = 3.75$, $f_c^{**} = 1.25$, $f_d^{**} = 6.25$, and user path costs $C_{p_1} = C_{p_2} = 8.75$ and $C_{p_3} = C_{p_4} = 11.25$. The total emissions are now equal to 2.625, which exceed those prior to the demand transfer.

However, if we modify the emission factor on link 4 from $h_4 = .1$ to $h_4 = 0$, then the original total emissions generated (before the reallocation of the demand) would be 2 which would precisely the total emissions generated after the reallocation. Hence, the paradox would not apply in the case of such a zero emission link.

Conjecture

The results concerning the revisited example strongly suggest that if a link with zero emissions is added to a network so that it connects an origin/destination pair directly (and its user link cost function and that of the other links is separable), then the total emissions cannot increase with such a network design change. This conjecture is also motivated by the result of Dafermos and Nagurney (1984c) who established that the addition of a route connecting an origin/destination pair of nodes in a transportation network such that the new route has no links in common with the original network can never result in an increase in travel costs for the users of that O/D pair even though the user link cost functions are of the form given by (12.1). In that setting, the addition of a route could correspond to a highway, whereas in our setting the addition of such a link/route where we now include the emission factor equal to zero could correspond to a telecommunication link for telecommuting purposes. Interestingly, Korilis, Lazar, and Orda (1999) discuss a similar result in the context of telecommunication networks. Note that here we also have to have particular cost functions since Paradox 3 provides a counterexample to this result holding in the general case of nonseparable (and asymmetric) functions.

We now establish the following result.

Theorem 12.2: Special Supernetwork Topology and Cost Structure for the Reduction of Emissions with a New Zero Emission Link

If there are only disjoint paths connecting an O/D pair in a supernetwork and the cost function on each link is separable and an increasing function of the flow, then adding a new zero emission link which connects the O/D directly will not increase the total emissions, provided that the demand is fixed.

Proof: Let (f^*, λ^*) and (f^{**}, λ^{**}) denote, respectively, the equilibrium link flow pattern and equilibrium cost for the original network and the network with an additional zero emission link.

If a new link is added to the network which connects the O/D pair directly, the equilibrium cost will not increase (see Dafermos and Nagurney (1984c)), that is,

$$\lambda^* \leq \lambda^{**}.$$

Since all the paths are disjoint, then, for simplicity, we can assume that there is only one link in each path (possibly after some aggregation). Using (12.5), it is easy to obtain that if $f_a^* = 0$, then $f_a^{**} = 0$. Therefore,

$$c_a(f_a^*) \geq c_a(f_a^{**}), \qquad \text{for all} \quad a \in \mathcal{L}.$$

Since c_a is an increasing function of flow f_a, one can conclude that $f_a^* \leq f_a^{**}$ for all a. Hence, the total emissions E which are equal to $\sum_a h_a f_a$ will not increase with the additional zero emission link. $\square$

12.3   An Emission Pricing Policy to Circumvent Paradoxes

In this section, we show that an emission pricing policy originally proposed in Nagurney (2000c) can be used to circumvent paradoxes. In particular, it guarantees that a certain level of emissions is not exceeded. An application of the pricing policy can then be used to guarantee that the paradoxes described in Section 12.2 do not occur. Here we illustrate how this is accomplished.

Specifically, we first consider, for simplicity, problem (12.7), in which it is assumed that, for now, the user link cost functions are separable and given by:

$$c_a = c_a(f_a), \quad \forall a \in \mathcal{L}. \tag{12.8}$$

To problem (12.7), which is the optimization reformulation of the network equilibrium conditions (12.5) in the case of functions of the form (12.8), we then append an environmental constraint of the form:

$$\sum_{a \in \mathcal{L}} h_a f_a \leq \bar{Q}, \tag{12.9}$$

where $\bar{Q}$ denotes the desired upper bound on the emissions. Constraint (12.9) guarantees that the total emissions generated in the network do not exceed the desired upper bound.

After making the substitution for the link flows $f_a = \sum_{p \in P} x_p \delta_{ap}$, $\forall a \in \mathcal{L}$, in the objective function (12.7) and in constraint (12.9) (in order to simplify the derivation), one obtains, hence, the following problem:

$$\text{Minimize} \quad \sum_{a \in \mathcal{L}} \int_0^{\sum_{p \in P} x_p \delta_{ap}} c_a(y) dy \tag{12.10}$$

subject to:

$$\sum_{p \in P_\omega} x_p = d_\omega, \quad \forall \omega \in \Omega, \tag{12.11}$$

$$\sum_{a \in \mathcal{L}} h_a \sum_{p \in P} x_p \delta_{ap} \leq \bar{Q}, \tag{12.12}$$

$$x_p \geq 0, \quad \forall p \in P. \tag{12.13}$$

Since the user link cost functions are increasing functions of the flow, the objective function is convex and the constraints, which are linear, are also convex. Hence, the Kuhn-Tucker optimality conditions for this problem (see also Appendix A) take the form $x^* \in R_+^{n_P}$ is an optimal solution if it satisfies the demands and satisfies the following system of equalities and inequalities: for each O/D pair $\omega \in \Omega$ and each path $p \in P_\omega$:

$$\bar{C}_p(x^*, \tau^*) = C_p(x^*) + \tau^* \sum_{a \in \mathcal{L}} h_a \delta_{ap} \begin{cases} = \hat{\lambda}_\omega, & \text{if } x_p^* > 0 \\ \geq \hat{\lambda}_\omega, & \text{if } x_p^* = 0, \end{cases} \tag{12.14}$$

where τ^* is the Lagrange multiplier associated with the environmental constraint (12.12).

Condition (12.14) states that all used paths connecting an O/D pair have equal and minimal *generalized* costs on their paths where the generalized cost on a path p is denoted by $\bar{C}_p$. The generalized user cost on a path includes both the user cost on a path as in (12.2) plus the term $\tau^* \sum_{a \in \mathcal{L}} h_a \delta_{ap}$. If we interpret τ^* as the marginal cost of emission abatement, then the term $\tau^* \sum_{a \in \mathcal{L}} h_a \delta_{ap}$ corresponds to the true cost associated with emission generation by a user of path p.

In addition, for optimality to hold, one must also have that:

$$\bar{Q} - \sum_{a \in \mathcal{L}} h_a \sum_{p \in P} x_p^* \delta_{ap} \begin{cases} = 0, & \text{if } \tau^* > 0 \\ \geq 0, & \text{if } \tau^* = 0. \end{cases} \tag{12.15}$$

We now propose the following emission pricing policies, which are equivalent, but which are, respectively, path-based and link-based. Letting $h_p = \sum_{a \in \mathcal{L}} h_a \delta_{ap}$ denote the emissions generated on path p by a user, then setting a price of $\tau^* h_p$ for each user of a path p and on all paths $p \in P$, where τ^* satisfies (12.14) and (12.15) guarantees that the users of the network will select their paths according to (12.14) and (12.15) and will not exceed the emission bound $\bar{Q}$.

Similarly, since the cost on a path is equal to the sum of the costs on its links as in (12.2), a link emission pricing policy, satisfying (12.14) and (12.15) would charge $\tau^* h_a$ for each user of link a in the network and for all links $a \in \mathcal{L}$.

The imposition of either the above path or link emission pricing policy would guarantee that the desired emission bound would not be exceeded. The users of the network, assuming as we have throughout, would behave in a user-optimizing fashion and would then select their paths according to (12.14).

We refer, henceforth, to conditions (12.14) and (12.15) as the equilibrium conditions under the above emission pricing policy (either path- or link-based).

Observe that conditions (12.14) and (12.15), although derived from an optimization problem, may be interpreted as *equilibrium conditions* and are also applicable in the case of user link cost functions of the general form given by (12.1). We assume such functions from this point on.

Moreover, conditions (12.14) and (12.15) can also be formulated as a variational inequality problem. Indeed, we have the following:

Theorem 12.3: Variational Inequality Formulation of Network Equilibrium in the Presence of an Emission Pricing Policy
A path flow and price pattern $(x^*, \tau^*) \in \mathcal{K}^1$ is an equilibrium of the network equilibrium model with an emission pricing policy described above if and only if it is a solution to the variational inequality problem:

Path Flow Formulation

$$\sum_{\omega \in \Omega} \sum_{p \in P_\omega} \left[C_p(x^*) + \tau^* \sum_{a \in \mathcal{L}} h_a \delta_{ap} \right] \times \left[x_p - x_p^* \right]$$

$$+ \left[\bar{Q} - \sum_{a \in \mathcal{L}} h_a \sum_{p \in P} x_p^* \delta_{ap} \right] \times \left[\tau - \tau^* \right] \geq 0, \forall (x, \tau) \in \mathcal{K}^1, \qquad (12.16)$$

where $\mathcal{K}^1 \equiv \bar{K}^1 \times R_+^1$ and $\bar{K}^1 \equiv \{x | x \geq 0 \text{ and satisfies} (12.11)\}$, or, equivalently, $(f^*, \tau^*) \in \mathcal{K}^2$ is an equilibrium link flow and price pattern if and only if it satisfies the variational inequality problem:

Link Flow Formulation

$$\sum_{a \in \mathcal{L}} [c_a(f^*) + \tau^* h_a] \times [f_a - f_a^*] + \left[\bar{Q} - \sum_{a \in \mathcal{L}} h_a f_a^* \right] \times [\tau - \tau^*] \geq 0, \quad \forall (f, \tau) \in \mathcal{K}^2,$$
(12.17)

where $\mathcal{K}^2 \equiv \bar{K}^2 \times R_+^1$ and $\bar{K}^2 \equiv \{f | \exists \, an \, x \geq 0 \, satisfying \, (12.4), (12.11)\}$.

Proof: See proof of Theorem 5.1 in Nagurney (2000c).

Variational inequality (12.17) can be solved by the modified projection method of Korpelevich (1977), embedded with the equilibration algorithm of Dafermos and Sparrow (1969) (see Appendix C). We now apply this combination in order to compute the new equilibrium link flow pattern and price pattern for each of the three paradoxes discussed in Section 12.2.

Resolution of Paradox 1 through Pricing

Recall that, in Paradox 1, the addition of a new link with zero emissions results in an increase in total emissions from the original level of 1.8 to the new level of 2. In order to avoid the paradox we impose a $\bar{Q} = 1.8$ and solve variational inequality (12.17) in order to obtain the link-pricing policy.

An application of the modified projection method yielded the following solution: $x_{p_1}^* = x_{p_2}^* = 3.00$, and $x_{p_3}^* = 0.00$ and link flow pattern: $f_a^* = f_b^* = f_c^* = f_d^* = 3.00$ and $f_e^* = 0.00$. The computed $\tau^* = 130.035$. The generalized costs on the paths (cf. (12.14)), after the imposition of the pricing policy, were given by $\bar{C}_{p_1} = \bar{C}_{p_2} = 122.012$ and $\bar{C}_{p_3} = 122.019$. Hence, under the emission pricing policy the new link e was not used.

The total emissions generated were 1.8, which was precisely equal to the bound desired and the value before the addition of the new link.

Resolution of Paradox 2 through Pricing

We then applied the emission link-pricing policy described above to resolve Paradox 2, where a decrease in demand for an O/D pair with a zero emission link yielded an increase in total emissions. Here, we set $\bar{Q} = .51$ which was the value of total emissions generated before the demand decrease. We solved variational inequality (12.17) for this example with the remainder of the data as described in the Paradox 2 example after the demand decrease. The modified projection method yielded the following solution: $x_{p_1}^* = .50$, $x_{p_2}^* = x_{p_3}^* = 1.00$, and $f_a^* = 1.50$, $f_b^* = 1.00$, and $f_c^* = 1.00$. The computed $\tau^* = 1.0395$. The generalized costs on the paths were given by: $\bar{C}_{p_1} = 2.5$, $\bar{C}_{p_2} = \bar{C}_{p_3} = 5.01$. The total emissions generated under the pricing policy were equal to .51.

Resolution of Paradox 3 through Pricing

Recall that, in Paradox 3, the addition of a path consisting of a single link connecting an O/D pair and with a zero emission factor, such that the path had no links in common with any other path, results in an increase in total emissions. Solving now variational inequality (12.17) by the modified projection method for the data given in that example for the network after the addition of the path and with the original emission bound $\bar{Q} = .5$ yielded the following solution: $x_{p_1}^* = 2.2400$, $x_{p_2}^* = .5519$, and $x_{p_3}^* = 2.208$, with link loads: $f_a^* = 2.2408$, $f_b^* = .5519$, and $x_{p_3}^* = 2.208$. The computed $\tau^* = 9.6841$ yielding generalized path costs given by $\bar{C}_{p_1} = \bar{C}_{p_2} = \bar{C}_{p_3} = 13.21$. This pricing policy resulted in total emissions as in the original problem before the path addition and equal to .5.

12.4   Multicriteria Decision-Making and Emission Policies

In the network equilibrium model described in Section 12.1, it was assumed that the users of the network consider the cost on the path as in (12.2) as the criterion and, assuming user-optimizing behavior, seek to determine their cost-minimizing paths of travel according to network equilibrium conditions (12.5).

As discussed in Part III of this book, there has been renewed interest in modeling user-optimizing behavior under the assumption that, in the case of networks, users may take not only their cost into consideration but other criteria such as time as well as opportunity cost in the context of telecommuting versus commuting. In the context of environmental issues, a natural criterion, in addition to cost, would be to minimize the emissions generated. Interestingly, such a criterion was also proposed by Tzeng and Chen (1993) but in a system-optimizing setting (see Chapter 3) in which the users or travelers in the network could be directed to the paths so that the total system cost and emissions generated would be minimized.

Here we make the following connection: the emission pricing policy coinciding with the solution of equilibrium conditions (12.14) and (12.15) has the interpretation of the solution to a *multicriteria network equilibrium problem* (see also Chapter 7), whose solution coincides with variational inequality (12.16) or (12.17), provided that the weight, which is assumed to be the same for all users of the network, is equal to the value given by τ^*.

Hence, we propose the following multicriteria network equilibrium model. Assume that the notation is as in Sections 11.1 and 11.3 but now assume that users of the supernetwork (which, recall, can consist of both telecommunication and transportation links) seek not only to minimize the cost associated with the path from their origin to their destination, but are now also environmentally conscious and, hence, seek to choose a path so that the total emissions generated do not exceed a desired upper bound.

Assume also that each user of the network has a weight τ associated with the emissions that he generates on a path. Hence, his multicriteria disutility associated with a path p is given by:

$$C_p(x) + \tau h_p, \quad \forall p \in P, \tag{12.18}$$

where we have used, as previously, the relationship $h_p = \sum_{a \in \mathcal{L}} h_a \delta_{ap}$ to denote the emissions generated by an individual on path p. In this multicriteria decision-making setting, the network equilibrium conditions (12.5) will now take the form:

For each O/D pair $\omega \in \Omega$ and each path $p \in P_\omega$:

$$C_p(x^*) + \tau h_p \begin{cases} = & \bar{\lambda}_\omega, \quad \text{if } x_p^* > 0 \\ \geq & \bar{\lambda}_\omega, \quad \text{if } x_p^* = 0. \end{cases} \qquad (12.19)$$

Observe that in this multicriteria model there is a single-class of decision-maker, in contrast to the multicriteria network equilibrium models in Part II of this book.

Clearly, if the weight τ in (12.18) is set precisely to τ^*, where τ^* corresponds to the marginal cost of emission abatement as in (12.14) and (12.15), then the multicriteria network equilibrium pattern satisfying (12.19) will coincide with the network equilibrium pattern under the emission pricing policy satisfying (12.14) and (12.15).

Thus, if there is no emission pricing policy in place, but, rather, users of the network are now multicriteria decision-makers and explicitly take into consideration not only the cost on a path but also the emissions generated, the desired outcome, that is, not exceeding the emission bound $\bar{Q}$, can be attained as well. Note that it is imperative, however, that the weight τ that the users associate with their emission generation coincides with τ^*. Hence, this value gives us a measure of how environmentally conscious the users need to be in order to have the "standard" achieved independently by the users through their behavior and without any policy imposition.

12.5   Sources and Notes

The results in this paper are due to Nagurney and Dong (2001). We note that the book by Dhanda, Nagurney, and Ramanujam (1999) contains a variety of environmental network models, which are constructed on abstract networks. However, the focus there is not on transportation versus telecommunications issues. In this book we elevate decision-making in the Information Age to decision-making on supernetworks.

Appendix A Optimization Theory

In this appendix, we provide the fundamentals of optimization theory at a level utilized in Parts I – IV of this book. The goal of this appendix, along with Appendix B, is to provide the minimal mathematical background needed for an adequate understanding of the models in this book. Appendix C then provides some basics of algorithms, notably, of the type used for the solution of the models in this book. The reader may skip this appendix at first reading and may refer back to it as needed.

We now recall some basic definitions and results from convexity theory and mathematical optimization at a level that is relevant to the material presented in this book. The results are standard. For a more detailed presentation of the aforementioned areas, we refer the reader to the books by Bradley, Hax, and Magnanti (1977), Bazaraa, Jarvis, and Sherali (1990), and Bazaraa, Sherali, and Shetty (1993). We begin with some basic concepts from convexity theory and then proceed to optimization theory.

Convexity theory plays a fundamental role in optimization theory and we begin with basic definitions.

Definition A.1: A Convex Set
A set $K \subset R^n$ is called a convex set if, given any two vectors X_1 and X_2 in K, $\lambda X_1 + (1 - \lambda)X_2 \in K$, for every $\lambda \in [0,1]$.

In the special case of two dimensions, that is, when one is dealing with a set $K \in R^2$, simply stated, a set is convex if the line that connects any two points in that set also lies in the interior of that set.

Example A.1: A Convex Set

For example, consider the set K consisting of x_1, x_2, such that $x_1 \geq 0$ and $x_2 \geq 0$. Moreover, assume that x_1 and x_2 must also satisfy the constraint:

$$x_1 + x_2 \leq 5.$$

Clearly, the set K is convex.

Certain functions that arise often in the models developed in this book are now defined.

Definition A.2: A Continuous Function
A function $f : K \mapsto R$ is said to be continuous at $X \in K$, if for any given $\epsilon > 0$, there is a $\delta > 0$, such that $\psi \in K$ and $\|\psi - X\| < \delta$, imply that $|f(\psi) - f(X)| < \epsilon$.

Definition A.3: A Differentiable Function
Consider a nonempty set K such that $K \subset R^n$, a column vector X lying in the interior of K, and let f be a function such that $f : K \mapsto R$. Then f is said to be differentiable, if there exists a column vector $\nabla f(X) \in R^n$, called the gradient of f at X, and defined as:

$$\nabla f(X)^T = \left(\frac{\partial f(X)}{\partial X_1}, \frac{\partial f(X)}{\partial X_2}, \cdots, \frac{\partial f(X)}{\partial X_n} \right), \qquad (A.1)$$

and a function $\beta(X;y) \to 0$ as $y \to x$ such that

$$f(y) = f(X) + \langle \nabla f(X), (y - X) \rangle + \|y - X\|\beta(X;y), \quad \forall y \in K, \qquad (A.2)$$

where $\langle \cdot, \cdot \rangle$ denotes the inner product in the n-dimensional Euclidean space.

Definition A.4: A Twice Differentiable Function
The function f is said to be twice differentiable at X if, in addition to the gradient vector, there exists an $n \times n$ matrix $H(X)$, called the Hessian matrix of the function f at X, defined as:

$$H = \begin{pmatrix} \frac{\partial^2 f}{\partial X_1 \partial X_1} & \frac{\partial^2 f}{\partial X_1 \partial X_2} & \cdots & \frac{\partial^2 f}{\partial X_1 \partial X_n} \\ \frac{\partial^2 f}{\partial X_2 \partial X_1} & \frac{\partial^2 f}{\partial X_2 \partial X_2} & \cdots & \frac{\partial^2 f}{\partial X_2 \partial X_n} \\ \vdots & \ddots & \ddots & \vdots \\ \frac{\partial^2 f}{\partial X_n \partial X_1} & \cdots & \cdots & \frac{\partial^2 f}{\partial X_n \partial X_n} \end{pmatrix}, \qquad (A.3)$$

and a function $\beta(X;y) \to 0$ as $y \to X$ such that:

$$f(y) = f(X) + \langle \nabla f(X), (y - X) \rangle$$

$$+ \frac{1}{2} (y - X)^T H(X) (y - X) + \|y - X\|^2 \beta(X;y), \quad \forall y \in K. \qquad (A.4)$$

Example A.2
An example of a twice differentiable function in two dimensions is: $f(x) = 5x_1^2 + 8x_2^2$.

Definition A.5: Convex and Concave Functions

Let K be a nonempty convex set and consider a function $f : K \mapsto R$. Then the function $f(X)$ is said to be a convex function on K if for any two distinct points $X_1, X_2 \in K$, and for all $\lambda \in [0, 1]$, the following holds:

$$f\left[\lambda X_2 + (1 - \lambda) X_1\right] \leq \lambda f(X_2) + (1 - \lambda) f(X_1). \tag{A.5}$$

The function f is said to be strictly convex on K if the above inequality holds as a strict inequality. A function $f(X)$ is said to be concave (strictly concave) if $-f(X)$ is convex (strictly convex).

In other words, in two dimensions, a function $f(X)$ is convex (concave) if a line segment joining any two points $[X_1, f(X_1)]$, $[X_2, f(X_2)]$ on the surface of $f(X)$ lies on or above (below) that surface.

The previous definition can be used directly to establish whether a function is convex or not. For example, if one assumes that the function $f(X)$ is continuous and that it has second-order partial derivatives over K, then an alternative way to determine whether a function is convex or not is to evaluate whether the Hessian of the function is positive semidefinite or not. In particular, if the Hessian matrix H of second-order partial derivatives is positive semidefinite, then $f(X)$ is convex, and if H is negative semidefinite, then $f(x)$ is concave. Recall that a matrix is positive (negative) definite if all its eigenvalues are positive (negative) or, equivalently, if all of its principal determinants have positive (negative) value. A matrix is positive semidefinite if all its eigenvalues are nonnegative as are all of its principal determinants.

Example A.3: A Convex Function

Consider the function $f(x_1, x_2) = 3x_1^2 + 4x_2^2$, whose Hessian matrix is:

$$H = \begin{pmatrix} 6 & 0 \\ 0 & 8 \end{pmatrix}.$$

This Hessian matrix is a diagonal matrix with positive elements on the diagonal and, hence, positive definite, so f is clearly convex and, in fact, it is strictly convex.

Definition A.6: Quasiconvex and Quasiconcave Functions

Let K be a nonempty convex set and consider a function $f : K \mapsto R$. The function $f(X)$ is said to be a quasiconvex function on K, if for any two distinct points $X_1, X_2 \in K$, and $\forall \lambda \in [0, 1]$, we have:

$$f\left[\lambda X_2 + (1 - \lambda) X_1\right] \leq maximum\ (f(X_1), f(X_2)).$$

The function $f(X)$ is said to be quasiconcave on K if $-f(X)$ is quasiconvex.

Definition A.7: Pseudoconvex and Pseudoconcave Functions

Let K be a nonempty convex set and consider a function $f : K \mapsto R$, which is differentiable on K. Then the function $f(X)$ is said to be a pseudoconvex function on K, if for any two distinct points $X_1, X_2 \in K$, with $\langle \nabla f(X_1), X_2 - X_1 \rangle \geq 0$, we have $f(X_2) \geq f(X_1)$.

The function $f(X)$ is said to be pseudoconcave on K if $-f(X)$ is pseudoconvex.

One of the principal goals of economics and engineering, as well as operations research and management science, is the determination of an optimal solution for a series of different problems. We now present some of the fundamentals of optimization theory in addition to some of the concepts and ideas that are utilized throughout this book. We also present some examples for illustrative purposes.

An optimization problem in R^n is a problem in which one seeks to optimize a function f, which is said to be the *objective function*, subject to some constraints. For example, an objective function may represent profits to be maximized or costs or risk to be minimized. Constraints, in turn, can reflect budget or other resource constraints. A point $X^0 \in R^n$ is called a *feasible solution* to the optimization problem if it satisfies all the constraints of the problem. Moreover, a point $X^* \in R^n$ is called an *optimal solution* to the optimization problem if it is a feasible solution and it provides the best possible value for the objective function.

There are different classes of optimization problems, depending on the structure of the objective function and the constraints. For example, if the objective function is linear, as are the constraints, and the variables are continuous (rather than discrete), then the problem is a *linear* programming problem, whose principal method of solution is the simplex method (see Bazaraa, Jarvis, and Sherali (1990)). On the other hand, if either the objective function or the constraints are nonlinear expressions of the variables, then the problem is a *nonlinear* programming problem. For further details, see Bazaraa, Sherali, and Shetty (1993). Clearly, the classical system-optimization problems as well as the optimization reformulation of the symmetric user-optimization problem (see Chapter 3) are nonlinear programming problems.

A well-known case of a nonlinear programming problem occurs when the objective function is quadratic and the constraints are linear, in which case we have a quadratic programming problem. The classical traffic network equilibrium problems with linear and symmetric user link cost functions (for which an optimization reformulation exists (see Chapter 3)) as well as a variety of portfolio optimization problems (see Chapter 11) are examples of quadratic programming problems. In Appendix C, we provide equilibration algorithms which can be applied to solve quadratic programming problems with network structure, such as those encountered in problems in this text.

On the other hand, if one or more of the variables in a problem are constrained to be discrete, that is, to take on integer values, then one has an *integer* programming problem at hand. We do not consider such problems in this book.

A.1   Karush-Kuhn-Tucker Optimization Conditions

In this subsection, we discuss important conditions for optimality, but we first present some basic definitions.

Definition A.8: Global Maximum and Minimum
The function $f : K \mapsto R^n$ is said to take its global maximum at point X^* if

$$f(X) \leq f(X^*), \quad \forall X \in K. \tag{A.6}$$

Similarly, the function $f : K \mapsto R^n$ is said to take its global minimum at point ψ^* if:

$$f(\psi) \geq f(\psi^*), \quad \forall \psi \in K. \tag{A.7}$$

Definition A.9: Local Maximum and Minimum
The function $f : K \mapsto R^n$ is said to take its local maximum at point X^* if there exists a $\delta > 0$ such that for every $X \neq X^*$ that belongs to K and is in a δ-neighborhood of X^*, the following holds:

$$f(X) \leq f(X^*), \quad \forall X \in (K \cap B(X^*, \delta)), \tag{A.8}$$

where $B(X^*, \delta)$ denotes the ball with center X^* and radius δ.
Similarly, the function $f : K \mapsto R^n$ is said to take its local minimum at point ψ^* if there exists a $\delta > 0$ such that for every $\psi \neq \psi^*$ that belongs to K and is in a δ-neighborhood of ψ^*, the following holds:

$$f(\psi) \geq f(\psi^*), \quad \forall \psi \in (K \cap B(\psi^*, \delta)). \tag{A.9}$$

Karush-Kuhn-Tucker (KKT) Conditions

Karush (1939) and Kuhn and Tucker (1951) independently proposed a set of necessary and sufficient conditions for an optimal solution of a general mathematical optimization problem. Their work provided the mathematical framework upon which the qualitative theory as well as the computational methods in optimization have been based. In this subsection, a compact presentation of these conditions is given for reference purposes.

Karush-Kuhn-Tucker Necessary Conditions

Let $\mathcal{K}$ be a nonempty open set such that $\mathcal{K} \subset R^n$, and let $\{f : R^n \mapsto R\}$, $\{g_i : R^n \mapsto R\}$ for $i = 1, 2, \ldots, m$, and $\{h_j : R^n \mapsto R\}$ for $j = 1, 2, \ldots, t$. Moreover, consider the general optimization problem of the following form:

$$\text{Minimize} \quad f(X)$$

subject to:

$$g_i(X) \leq 0, \quad \text{for} \quad i = 1, 2, \ldots, m,$$

$$h_j(X) = 0, \quad \text{for} \quad j = 1, 2, \ldots, t,$$

$$X \in \mathcal{K}.$$

Let X^* be a feasible solution and let $I = \{i : g_i(X^*) = 0\}$. Furthermore, assume that f and g_i are differentiable at X^* for $i \in I$, and that the g_i are continuous at X^* for $i \in I$. Finally, assume that the h_j are continuously differentiable at X^* for all $j = 1, 2, \ldots, t$. Further, suppose that $\nabla g_i(X^*)$ for $i \in I$ and $\nabla h_j(X^*)$ for $j = 1, 2, \ldots, t$, are linearly independent. If X^* locally solves the minimization problem then there exist unique scalars v_i^* for $i \in I$, and γ_j^* for $j = 1, 2, \ldots, t$, such that:

$$\nabla f(X^*) + \sum_{i=1}^{m} v_i^* \nabla g_i(X^*) + \sum_{j=1}^{t} \gamma_j^* \nabla h_j(X^*) = 0 \qquad (A.10)$$

$$v_i^* g_i(X^*) = 0, \text{ for } i = 1, 2, \ldots, m \qquad (A.11)$$

$$v_i^* \geq 0, \text{ for } i = 1, 2, \ldots, m. \qquad (A.12)$$

The scalars v_i^* and γ_j^* are called *Lagrange* multipliers. Note that there is one Lagrange multiplier associated with each constraint and that they represent the marginal rate of change in the objective function f with respect to each per unit change in the right-hand side of the corresponding constraint. Lagrange multipliers have important economic interpretations, as revealed in different models that are presented in the this book.

Any point that satisfies the KKT conditions is called a *KKT point*.

An optimization problem sometimes includes nonnegativity constraints for the variables involved, that is, $X \geq 0$. Such inequality constraints are especially relevant in supernetworks since we need to ensure, for example, that the flows on the network, which are physical entities, be they decision-makers, products, or prices, are nonnegative. Clearly, the KKT conditions that were just presented will still hold. Many times, however, for reasons of convenience and simplicity, the Lagrange multipliers associated with the nonnegativity constraints are eliminated, and the conditions are reduced to:

$$\nabla f(X^*) + \sum_{i=1}^{m} v_i^* \nabla g_i(X^*) + \sum_{j=1}^{t} \gamma_j^* \nabla h_j(X^*) \geq 0 \qquad (A.13)$$

$$\left[\nabla f(X^*) + \sum_{i=1}^{m} v_i^* \nabla g_i(X^*) + \sum_{j=1}^{t} \gamma_j^* \nabla h_j(X^*) \right]^T X^* = 0 \qquad (A.14)$$

$$v_i^* g_i(X^*) = 0, \text{ for } i = 1, \ldots, m \qquad (A.15)$$

$$v_i^* \geq 0, \text{ for } i = 1, \ldots, m. \qquad (A.16)$$

A geometric interpretation of the KKT conditions is that a vector X^* is a KKT point if and only if $-\nabla f(X^*)$ lies in the cone spanned by the gradients of the binding constraints, that is, those constraints that hold as equalities.

Karush-Kuhn-Tucker Sufficient Conditions

Let, again, $\mathcal{K}$ be a nonempty open set such that $\mathcal{K} \subset R^n$, and let $\{f : R^n \mapsto R\}$, $\{g_i : R^n \mapsto R\}$ for $i = 1, 2, \ldots, m$ and $\{h_j : R^n \mapsto R\}$ for $j = 1, 2, \ldots, t$. Moreover, consider, once again, the general optimization problem of the following form:

$$\text{Minimize} \quad f(X)$$

subject to:

$$g_i(X) \leq 0, \quad \text{for} \quad i = 1, 2, \ldots, m$$

$$h_j(X) = 0, \quad \text{for} \quad j = 1, 2, \ldots, t,$$

$$X \in \mathcal{K}.$$

Let X^* be a feasible solution, and let $I = \{i : g_i(X^*) = 0\}$. Assume that the KKT conditions hold at X^*. In other words, assume that there exist scalars $\overline{v}_i \geq 0$ with $i \in I$ and $\overline{\gamma}_j$ with $j = 1, 2, \ldots, t$, such that

$$\nabla f(X^*) + \sum_{i \in I} \overline{v}_i \nabla g_i(X^*) + \sum_{j=1}^{t} \overline{\gamma}_j \nabla h_j(X^*) = 0. \qquad (A.17)$$

Let $J = \{j : \overline{\gamma}_j > 0\}$ and $L = \{j : \overline{\gamma}_j < 0\}$. Further, suppose that f is pseudoconvex at X^*, the constraints g_i are quasiconvex at X^* for $i \in I$, h_j is quasiconvex for the $j \in J$ and quasiconcave for the $j \in L$. Then X^* is a global optimal solution to the general minimization problem.

For a maximization problem, the KKT conditions are similar, where now the function f has to be pseudoconcave.

Definition A.10: Lagrangian Function
Consider, once again, the general minimization problem described previously. Then the function such that:

$$\phi(X, v, \gamma) = f(X) + \sum_{i=1}^{m} v_i g_i(X) + \sum_{j=1}^{t} \gamma_j h_j(X) \qquad (A.18)$$

is said to be the Lagrangian function of the general optimization problem.

If we let X^* be a KKT point to the general optimization problem with v^*, γ^* being the Lagrange multipliers that correspond to the constraints of the problem, then the function:

$$L(X) \equiv \phi(X, v^*, \gamma^*) = f(X) + \sum_{i \in I} v_i^* g_i(X) + \sum_{j=1}^{t} \gamma_j^* h_j(X) \qquad (A.19)$$

is said to be the restricted Lagrangian function.

Let $\nabla^2 L$ denote the Hessian of (A.19). Then if $\nabla^2 L$ is:

- positive semidefinite for all X in the feasible set, X^* is a global minimum;

- positive semidefinite for all X in the feasible set and in a δ-neighborhood $B(X^*, \delta)$, for a $\delta > 0$, X^* is a local minimum;

- positive definite, X^* is a strict local minimum.

A.2   Optimization Examples

In this subsection, several examples are presented in order to illustrate some of the above concepts.

Example A.4: Profit Maximization

Consider a perfectly competitive firm that produces a single product, where q denotes the production output of the firm, and $f(q)$ denotes the production cost associated with producing q. Assume that the production cost function is convex in the production output. Let ρ^* denote the price of the product. Assume that the firm wishes to maximize profit, where profit is the difference between the revenue and the production cost. Then the optimization problem faced by the firm is:

$$\text{Maximize} \quad \rho^* q - f(q)$$

subject to:

$$q \geq 0.$$

Since the objective function that is being maximized is concave and the feasible set is convex, the Karush-Kuhn-Tucker optimality conditions here, which are both necessary and sufficient for an optimal q^*, take the form:

$$\left[\frac{\partial f(q^*)}{\partial q} - \rho^* \right] \geq 0,$$

$$\left[\frac{\partial f(q^*)}{\partial q} - \rho^* \right] q^* = 0,$$

$$q^* \geq 0.$$

Indeed, the conditions have the following interpretation: The firm will produce, that is, $q^* > 0$, if the marginal cost of production, given by $\frac{\partial f(q^*)}{\partial q}$, is precisely equal to the price of the good ρ^*; if the marginal cost of production exceeds the price that the consumers are willing to pay for the product, then the firm will not produce the product.

Example A.5: Total Cost Minimization

Consider a shipper overseeing a network consisting of two nodes, denoted by 1 and 2, and three links connecting the nodes, denoted by a, b, and c. The flows on the links are denoted, respectively, by f_a, f_b, and f_c. Let d denote the demand for the product, which is shipped from node 1 to node 2. This demand must be equal to the sum of the shipments. Let $\hat{c}_a$, $\hat{c}_b$, and $\hat{c}_c$ denote the total costs associated with shipping the flows over the links a, b, and c, respectively. Assume that the total cost functions, which are functions of the flow on each link, are convex and continuously differentiable.

Assume that the shipper wishes to deliver the product so that the total cost associated with shipping is minimized.

Then the shipper's optimization problem is to:

$$\text{Minimize} \quad \hat{c}_a(f_a) + \hat{c}_b(f_b) + \hat{c}_c(f_c)$$

subject to:

$$f_a + f_b + f_c = d,$$

$$f_a \geq 0, \quad f_b \geq 0, \quad f_c \geq 0.$$

Since the objective function that one wishes to minimize is convex and continuously differentiable and the feasible set is convex, the KKT optimality conditions are both necessary and sufficient and are given by:

$$\left[\frac{\partial \hat{c}_a(f_a^*)}{\partial f_a} + \gamma^* \right] \geq 0, \quad \left[\frac{\partial \hat{c}_a(f_a^*)}{\partial f_a} + \gamma^* \right] f_a^* = 0,$$

$$\left[\frac{\partial \hat{c}_b(f_b^*)}{\partial f_b} + \gamma^* \right] \geq 0, \quad \left[\frac{\partial \hat{c}_b(f_b^*)}{\partial f_b} + \gamma^* \right] f_b^* = 0,$$

$$\left[\frac{\partial \hat{c}_c(f_c^*)}{\partial f_c} + \gamma^* \right] \geq 0, \quad \left[\frac{\partial \hat{c}_c(f_c^*)}{\partial f_c} + \gamma^* \right] f_c^* = 0,$$

$$f_a^* + f_b^* + f_c^* = d,$$

$$f_a^* \geq 0, \quad f_b^* \geq 0, \quad f_c^* \geq 0,$$

where γ^* is the Lagrange multiplier associated with the demand constraint. The optimality conditions reveal that for all used links, that is, for all links with positive flow in the optimal solution, the marginals of the total costs on those links are equal and minimal.

Appendix B Variational Inequalities and Dynamical Systems

In this appendix, we provide a brief overview of finite-dimensional variational inequality theory and projected dynamical systems theory, with a focus on the qualitative aspects. In Appendix C, we then discuss computational procedures. For a more thorough treatment of the theory, algorithms, as well as additional applications, and proofs, see the books by Nagurney (1999) and by Nagurney and Zhang (1996). The book on sustainable transportation networks by Nagurney (2000c) discusses a variety of transportation/environmental applications formulated as such problems. For applications to environmental networks, see the book by Dhanda, Nagurney, and Ramanujam (1999). For applications to financial networks, see the book by Nagurney and Siokos (1997).

Section B.1 focuses on variational inequality problems while Section B.2 discusses projected dynamical systems and identifies their relationship to the former.

B.1 Variational Inequalities

Variational inequalities were introduced by Hartman and Stampacchia (1966), mainly for the study of problems arising in the field of mechanics. The research focused on infinite-dimensional variational inequalities, rather than on finite-dimensional variational inequalities, which are the kind utilized in this book. The book by Kinderlehrer and Stampacchia (1980) provides an introduction to infinite-dimensional variational inequality problems.

Smith (1979) presented a formulation of the equilibrium conditions of the traffic network equilibrium problem that were then identified as a finite-dimensional variational inequality by Dafermos (1980). From this connection, much research has been conducted on such variational inequality problems and many applications, ranging from oligopolistic market equilibrium problems to general economic and financial equilibrium problems, have been studied, both qualitatively and computationally, using this methodology.

Variational inequality theory is a powerful tool for the study of many equilibrium problems, since the variational inequality problem contains, as special cases, important problem classes which are widely utilized in economics and in engineering, such as systems of nonlinear equations, optimization problems, and complementarity problems. Moreover, the problem is related to fixed point problems. Indeed, it has been utilized to formulate equilibrium problems governed by entirely distinct equilibrium concepts, including: Wardrop (1952) equilibrium governing congested urban traffic networks (cf. Smith (1979) and Dafermos (1980)), spatial price equilibrium (cf. Samuelson (1952), Takayama and Judge (1971), Florian and Los (1982)), and oligopolistic market equilibrium (cf. Gabay and Moulin (1980)), governed by the Cournot (1838)–Nash (1950) equilibrium. In this book, we show how variational inequality theory can be utilized in the study of supernetworks, and, in particular, multitiered and multicriteria supernetworks.

We first present the formal definition of a variational inequality problem and then discuss the relationship between the variational inequality problem and optimization problems. The definition of a variational inequality problem can also be found in Chapter 3.

Definition B.1: The Variational Inequality Problem
The finite-dimensional variational inequality problem, VI($F, \mathcal{K}$), is to determine a vector $X^* \in \mathcal{K}$, such that:

$$\langle F(X^*), X - X^* \rangle \geq 0, \quad \forall X \in \mathcal{K}, \tag{B.1}$$

where F is a given continuous function from $\mathcal{K}$ to R^N, $\mathcal{K}$ is a given closed convex set, and $\langle \cdot, \cdot \rangle$ denotes the inner product in R^N.

The variational inequality problem has a geometric interpretation. In particular, it states that $F(X^*)$ is "orthogonal" to the feasible set $\mathcal{K}$ at the point X^*. In Figure B.1, the geometric interpretation is provided.

In order to emphasize the relationship between the variational inequality problem and optimization problems, we now present the following results. Proofs can be found in Kinderlehrer and Stampacchia (1980) and in Nagurney (1999).

Relationship between the Variational Inequality Problem and Optimization Problems

We now present the relationship between variational inequality problems and optimization problems. Specifically, note that a variational inequality problem contains an optimization problem as a special case.

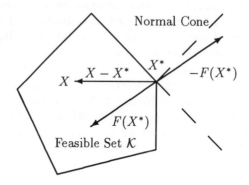

Fig. B.1. Geometric Interpretation of VI($F, \mathcal{K}$)

Proposition B.1

Let X^* be the solution to the following optimization problem:

$$\text{Minimize} \quad f(X) \tag{B.2}$$

subject to:

$$X \in \mathcal{K},$$

where f is a continuously differentiable function, and $\mathcal{K}$ is closed and convex. Then X^* is a solution of the variational inequality problem:

$$\langle \nabla f(X^*), X - X^* \rangle \geq 0, \quad \forall X \in \mathcal{K}, \tag{B.3}$$

where $\nabla f(X^*)$ denotes the gradient of f with respect to X with components:

$$\nabla f(X)^T = \left(\frac{\partial f(X^*)}{\partial X_1}, \frac{\partial f(X^*)}{\partial X_2}, \ldots, \frac{\partial f(X^*)}{\partial X_N} \right).$$

Proposition B.2

If $f(X)$ is a convex function and X^* is a solution to VI($\nabla f, \mathcal{K}$) given by (B.3), then X^* is a solution to the optimization problem (B.2).

In the special case, when $\mathcal{K} = R^N$, then the above optimization problem (B.2) is an *unconstrained* problem.

On the other hand, if a certain symmetry condition holds, the variational inequality problem can also be reformulated as an optimization problem.

Theorem B.1
Assume that $F(X)$ is continuously differentiable on $\mathcal{K}$ and that the Jacobian matrix:

$$\nabla F(X) = \left\{ \begin{array}{ccc} \frac{\partial F_1}{\partial X_1} & \cdots & \frac{\partial F_1}{\partial X_N} \\ \vdots & & \vdots \\ \frac{\partial F_N}{\partial X_1} & \cdots & \frac{\partial F_N}{\partial X_N} \end{array} \right\} \tag{B.4}$$

is symmetric and positive semidefinite, so that F is convex. Then there exists a real-valued function $f : \mathcal{K} \mapsto R$ satisfying

$$\nabla f(X) = F(X) \tag{B.5}$$

with X^* the solution of $\mathrm{VI}(F, \mathcal{K})$ also being the solution of the optimization problem (B.2).

Hence, one can see that the variational inequality problem encompasses the optimization problem and that the variational inequality problem can be reformulated as a convex optimization problem only when the symmetry and the positive semidefiniteness conditions hold.

Therefore, the variational inequality problem is a more general problem in that it can also handle a function $F(X)$ with an asymmetric Jacobian, that is, when (cf. (B.4)): $\frac{\partial F_i}{\partial X_j} \neq \frac{\partial F_j}{\partial X_i}$, for i, j. Historically, many equilibrium problems were reformulated as optimization problems under the symmetry and positive semidefiniteness condition, including the traffic network equilibrium problem (cf. Beckmann, McGuire, and Winsten (1956)). See Chapter 3 for further details and background. This assumption, however, is restrictive in many application settings, specifically, in the case of supernetworks since it cannot adequately handle asymmetric cost functions as well as multiple modes and multiple classes on the networks realistically. Hence, the appeal of the use of the variational inequality formulation and associated theory.

Variational Inequality Formulation of a Class of Constrained Optimization Problem

We now present a result (see Bertsekas and Tsitsiklis (1989)) that demonstrates how a class of constrained optimization problem over specific types of constraints can be formulated as a variational inequality problem.

Consider the convex constrained optimization problem:

$$\text{Minimize} \quad \sum_{i=1}^{m} f_i(X_i) \tag{B.6}$$

subject to:

$$a_j^T X \leq b_j, \quad j = 1, \ldots, r \tag{B.7}$$

$$X_i \in K_i, \quad i = 1, \ldots, m,$$

where $f_i : R^{n_i} \mapsto R$ is a convex differentiable function and a_j^T is a row vector of coefficients corresponding to the j-th constraint, and X is vector consisting of the vectors; $\{X_1, \ldots, X_m\}$. Then this problem is equivalent to the variational inequality problem of finding $X_i^* \in K_i$ and $u_j^* \geq 0$, such that

$$\sum_{i=1}^{m} \langle (\nabla f_i(X_i^*) + \sum_{j=1}^{r} u_j^* a_{ji})^T, (X_i - X_i^*) \rangle + \sum_{j=1}^{r} (b_j - a_j^T X^*) \times (u_j - u_j^*) \geq 0,$$

$$(B.8)$$

$$\forall X_i \in K_i, \quad u_j \geq 0, \quad \forall j.$$

Note that u_j^* is the Lagrange multiplier in the solution associated with inequality constraint j in the minimization problem. The coefficient a_{ji} corresponds to the ith component of the vector a_j. This problem can be solved using the modified projection method discussed in Appendix C.

B.1.1   Qualitative Properties

We now present some basic qualitative properties of variational inequality problems. Specifically, we discuss the issues of existence and uniqueness of a solution. Definitions which are referred to in discussions of the convergence of algorithms are also included. All the theoretical results presented in this subsection, along with all the corresponding proofs, can be found in Kinderlehrer and Stampacchia (1980) and Nagurney (1999).

The existence of a solution to a variational inequality problem follows from continuity of the function F entering the variational inequality, provided that the feasible set $\mathcal{K}$ is compact (that is, closed and bounded, in the case of R^N), as stated in the following theorem.

Theorem B.2: Existence under Compactness and Continuity

If $\mathcal{K}$ is a compact convex set and $F(X)$ is continuous on $\mathcal{K}$, then the variational inequality problem $\mathrm{VI}(F, \mathcal{K})$ admits at least one solution X^*.

Note that in the network equilibrium problem with fixed demands (see Chapters 3 and 7), the feasible set underlying the problem is compact and, hence, existence of a solution to the variational inequality formulation of the problem follows solely from the assumption that the user link cost functions are continuous functions of the flows.

If the feasible set $\mathcal{K}$ is unbounded, then we have:

Theorem B.3

$\mathrm{VI}(F, \mathcal{K})$ *admits a solution if and only if there exists an $R > 0$ and a solution X_R^* of $\mathrm{VI}(F, S)$, such that $\|X_R^*\| < R$, where $S = \{X : \|X\| \leq R\}$.*

Such a condition was utilized by Dafermos (1986) to establish the existence of a solution to the variational inequality governing the elastic demand network equilibrium problem in which the demands, rather than the disutilities are given (see also Nagurney (1999) and Chapters 4 and 7).

The existence, as well as the uniqueness, of a solution to a variational inequality problem is directly related to certain monotonicity conditions. Indeed, monotonicity plays a role in variational inequality theory that is similar to the role that convexity plays in optimization theory. Hence, this is a property that we establish in many of the models in this book, under reasonable assumptions.

We recall some basic definitions and will later discuss some qualitative results.

Definition B.2: Monotonicity
$F(X)$ *is said to be monotone on* $\mathcal{K}$ *if:*

$$\langle F(X^1) - F(X^2), X^1 - X^2 \rangle \geq 0, \quad \forall X^1, X^2 \in \mathcal{K}. \qquad (B.9)$$

Definition B.3: Strict Monotonicity
$F(X)$ *is strictly monotone on* $\mathcal{K}$ *if:*

$$\langle F(X^1) - F(X^2), X^1 - X^2 \rangle > 0, \quad \forall X^1, X^2 \in \mathcal{K}, \quad X^1 \neq X^2. \qquad (B.10)$$

Definition B.4: Strong Monotonicity
$F(X)$ *is strongly monotone on* $\mathcal{K}$*, if for some* $\alpha \geq 0$*:*

$$\langle F(X^1) - F(X^2), X^1 - X^2 \rangle \geq \alpha \|X^1 - X^2\|, \quad \forall X^1, X^2 \in \mathcal{K}. \qquad (B.11)$$

We now present the first uniqueness result in the following theorem.

Theorem B.4: Uniqueness under Strict Monotonicity
If $F(X)$ *is strictly monotone on the feasible set* $\mathcal{K}$*, then if a solution to* VI$(F, \mathcal{K})$ *exists, it is unique.*

For example, uniqueness of the equilibrium link flow pattern in a fixed demand network equilibrium problem (see Dafermos (1980), and Nagurney (1999) and Chapter 3) is guaranteed under the assumption of strict monotonicity of the user link travel cost functions.

Under the strong monotonicity assumption on the function $F(\cdot)$, one obtains both the existence and the uniqueness of a solution.

Theorem B.5: Existence and Uniqueness under Strong Monotonicity
If $F(X)$ *is strongly monotone on the feasible set* $\mathcal{K}$*, then there exists precisely one solution* X^* *to* VI$(F, \mathcal{K})$*.*

Strong monotonicity of the user link cost functions as well as minus the disutility functions guarantees, in the case of the elastic demand network equilibrium problem (see Dafermos (1982), Nagurney (1999), and Chapter 3), both the existence and the uniqueness of an equilibrium link flow and demand pattern. In the case of the elastic demand network equilibrium problem, the feasible set is no longer compact, as was the case in the fixed demand network equilibrium problem and, hence, a stronger condition (such as strong monotonicity) is needed to guarantee the existence of a solution. Moreover, strong monotonicity also guarantees uniqueness of the solution.

In many cases, computational algorithms and, in particular, the modified projection method used to solve many of the supernetwork models in this book, require, for convergence purposes, that the function F that enters the variational inequality problem is Lipschitz continuous, that is:

Definition B.5: Lipschitz Continuity
$F(X)$ is Lipschitz continuous on $\mathcal{K}$ if there exists a constant $L > 0$, such that:

$$\|F(X^1) - F(X^2)\| \leq L\|X^1 - X^2\|, \quad \forall X^1, X^2 \in \mathcal{K}, \qquad (B.12).$$

where L is referred to as the Lipschitz constant.

We also, for definiteness, recall the definition of a norm projection.

Definition B.6: Norm Projection
Let $\mathcal{K}$ be a closed convex set in R^N. Then for each $X \in R^N$, there is a unique point $y \in \mathcal{K}$, such that

$$\|X - y\| \leq \|X - z\|, \quad \forall z \in \mathcal{K}, \qquad (B.13)$$

and y is known as the orthogonal projection of X on the set $\mathcal{K}$ with respect to the Euclidean norm, that is,

$$y = P_{\mathcal{K}}X = \arg\min_{z \in \mathcal{K}}\|X - z\|. \qquad (B.14)$$

B.2 Projected Dynamical Systems

In this section, we review some results in the development of a tool for the study of equilibrium problems in a dynamic setting, known as *projected dynamical systems* theory (see Nagurney and Zhang (1996) and Dupuis and Nagurney (1993)). One of the notable features of this tool is its relationship to the variational inequality problem. Projected dynamical systems theory, however, extends the static study of equilibrium states by introducing an additional time dimension in order to allow for the analysis of disequilibrium behavior that precedes the equilibrium. Such a tool is used, for example, in this book in Chapter 5 to develop a dynamic supply chain network model with electronic commerce and in Chapter 6 to formulate a dynamic financial network model with intermediation. In addition, this methodology is utilized in Chapter 10 to formulate a dynamic supernetwork model with multicriteria producers and consumers.

Let $\mathcal{K} \subset R^N$ be closed and convex. Denote the boundary and the interior of $\mathcal{K}$, respectively, by $\partial \mathcal{K}$ and $\mathcal{K}^0$. Given $X \in \partial \mathcal{K}$, define the set of inward normals to $\mathcal{K}$ at X by

$$n(X) = \{\gamma : \|\gamma\| = 1, \text{ and } \langle \gamma, X - y \rangle \leq 0, \forall y \in \mathcal{K}\}.$$

For notational convenience, we define $n(X)$ to be $\{\gamma : \|\gamma\| = 1\}$ for X in the interior of $\mathcal{K}$.

When $\mathcal{K}$ is a convex polyhedron, $\mathcal{K}$ takes the form $\cap_{i=1}^{N} \mathcal{K}_i$, where each $\mathcal{K}_i$ is a closed half-space with inward normal n_i. Let P be the norm projection, defined in Definition B.6.

Note that if $y \in \mathcal{K}$, then $P(y) = y$, and if $y \notin \mathcal{K}$, then $P(y) \in \partial \mathcal{K}$, and $P(y) - y = \alpha \gamma$ for some $\alpha > 0$ and $\gamma \in n(P(y))$.

Given $X \in \mathcal{K}$ and $v \in R^N$, define the projection of the vector v at X (with respect to $\mathcal{K}$) by

$$\Pi_{\mathcal{K}}(X, v) = \lim_{\delta \to 0} \frac{(P_{\mathcal{K}}(X + \delta v) - X)}{\delta}. \tag{B.15}$$

The class of ordinary differential equations of interest here takes the form:

$$\dot{X} = \Pi_{\mathcal{K}}(X, -F(X)), \quad X(0) = X_0 \in \mathcal{K}, \tag{B.16}$$

where $\mathcal{K}$ is a closed convex set, corresponding to the constraint set in a particular application, and $F(X)$ is a vector field defined on $\mathcal{K}$. We refer to the ordinary differential equation in (B.16) as ODE$(F, \mathcal{K})$.

Observe that the right-hand side of the ordinary differential equation (B.16) is associated with a projection operator and is, hence, discontinuous on the boundary of $\mathcal{K}$. Therefore, one needs to explicitly state what one means by a solution to an ODE with a discontinuous right-hand side.

Definition B.7: A Projected Dynamical System
Define the projected dynamical system (PDS) $X_0(t) : \mathcal{K} \times R \mapsto \mathcal{K}$ *as the family of solutions to the Initial Value Problem* (IVP)*(B.16) for all* $X_0 \in \mathcal{K}$.

It is apparent from the definition that $X_0(0) = X_0$. For convenience, we sometimes write $X_0 \cdot t$ for $X_0(t)$ and say, interchangeably, that X^* is an equilibrium or stationary point of the PDS$(F, \mathcal{K})$.

The behavior of the dynamical system is now described. See Figure B.2 for a graphical depiction. If $X(t)$ lies in the interior of the feasible set $\mathcal{K}$, then the evolution of the solution is given by $F : \dot{X} = -F(X)$. However, if the vector field $-F$ drives X to the boundary of $\mathcal{K}$, that is, for some t one has

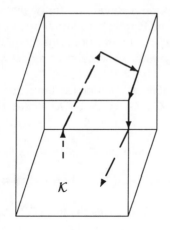

Fig. B.2. The Evolution of a Trajectory in $\mathcal{K}$

$X(t) \in \partial\mathcal{K}$ and $-F(X(t))$ points "out" of $\mathcal{K}$, the right-hand side of (B.16) becomes the projection of $-F$ onto $\partial\mathcal{K}$. In this case, the solution to (B.16) then evolves along a "section" of $\partial\mathcal{K}$, that is, $\partial\mathcal{K}_i$, for some i. Later, the solution may re-enter the interior of $\mathcal{K}$, or it may enter a lower dimensional part of the boundary of $\mathcal{K}$.

We now define a stationary or an equilibrium point.

Definition B.8: A Stationary Point or an Equilibrium Point
The vector $X^* \in \mathcal{K}$ is a stationary point or an equilibrium point of the projected dynamical system PDS$(F, \mathcal{K})$ *if*

$$0 = \Pi_{\mathcal{K}}(X^*, -F(X^*)).$$

Hence, we say that X^* is a stationary point or an equilibrium point if, once the projected dynamical system is at X^*, it will remain at X^* for all future times.

From Definition B.8 it is clear that X^* is an equilibrium point of the projected dynamical system PDS$(F, \mathcal{K})$ if the vector field F vanishes at X^*. The contrary, however, is only true when X^* is an interior point of the constraint set $\mathcal{K}$. Indeed, when X^* lies on the boundary of $\mathcal{K}$, we may have $F(X^*) \neq 0$.

It is worth emphasizing that for classical dynamical systems, the necessary and sufficient condition for an equilibrium point is that the vector field vanishes at that point, that is, that $0 = -F(X)$.

The relationship between the ODE$(F, \mathcal{K})$ and the VI$(F, \mathcal{K})$ is given in the following theorem.

Theorem B.6
Assume that $\mathcal{K}$ is a convex polyhedron. Then the stationary points of the ODE$(F, \mathcal{K})$ coincide with the solutions of VI$(F, \mathcal{K})$.

We emphasize here that the constraint set underlying supernetwork problems is precisely a convex polyhedron.

Before stating the fundamental theorem of projected dynamical systems, we introduce the following assumption needed for the theorem.

Assumption B.1: Linear Growth Condition
There exists a $B < \infty$ such that the vector field $-F : R^N \mapsto R^N$ satisfies the linear growth condition: $\|F(X)\| \leq B(1 + \|X\|)$ for $X \in \mathcal{K}$, and also

$$\langle -F(X) + F(y), X - y \rangle \leq B\|X - y\|^2, \quad \forall X, y \in \mathcal{K}. \tag{B.17}$$

Theorem B.7: Existence, Uniqueness, and Continuous Dependence
Assume Assumption B.1. Then
(i) For any $X_0 \in \mathcal{K}$, there exists a unique solution $X_0(t)$ to the initial value problem (B.16);
(ii) If $X_k \to X_0$ as $k \to \infty$, then $X_k(t)$ converges to $X_0(t)$ uniformly on every compact set of $[0, \infty)$.

The second statement of Theorem B.7 is sometimes called the continuous dependence of the solution path to ODE$(F, \mathcal{K})$ on the initial value. As a consequence of Theorem B.7, the PDS$(F, \mathcal{K})$ is well defined and inhabits $\mathcal{K}$ whenever Assumption B.1 holds.

Lipschitz continuity implies Assumption B.1 and is, therefore, a sufficient condition for the fundamental properties of projected dynamical systems stated in Theorem B.7.

B.2.1   Stability Results

In this section, for completeness, we recall some recently obtained stability results using monotonicity conditions. Stability analysis is crucial to the understanding of dynamic models. For example, one may wish to answer such questions as: if a supernetwork system starts near an equilibrium, will it stay at that point forever, and, given the current state of the system, will it asymptotically approach an equilibrium? Stability results are used in this book in Chapter 10 in the proof of convergence for a computational procedure.

Definition B.9
For any subset A of R^N, the ω-limit set of A is defined by

$$\omega(A) = \{y : \exists X_k \in A, t_k \to \infty, \text{ such that } X_k \cdot t_k \to y, \text{ as } k \to \infty\}.$$

We will use $B(X, r)$, hereafter, to denote the open ball with radius r and center X.

Definition B.10: Stable/Unstable Equilibrium Point
An equilibrium point X^* is stable if for any $\epsilon > 0$, there exists a $\delta > 0$ such that for all $X \in B(X^*, \delta)$ and $t \geq 0$

$$X \cdot t \in B(X^*, \epsilon).$$

The equilibrium point X^* is unstable if it is not stable.

Definition B.11: Asymptotically Stable Equilibrium Point
An equilibrium point X^* is asymptotically stable if it is stable and there exists a $\delta > 0$ such that for all $X \in B(X^*, \delta)$

$$\lim_{t \to \infty} X \cdot t \longrightarrow X^*.$$

Definition B.12: Monotone Attractor
An equilibrium point X^* is a monotone attractor if there exists a $\delta > 0$ such that for all $X \in B(X^*, \delta)$

$$d(X, t) = \|X \cdot t - X^*\| \tag{B.18}$$

is a nonincreasing function of t; X^* is a global monotone attractor if $d(X, t)$ is nonincreasing in t for all $X \in \mathcal{K}$.

Definition B.13: Strictly Monotone Attractor
An equilibrium point X^* is a strictly monotone attractor if there exists a $\delta > 0$ such that for all $X \in B(X^*, \delta)$, $d(X, t)$ is monotonically decreasing to zero in t; X^* is a strictly global monotone attractor if $d(X, t)$ is monotonically decreasing to zero in t for all $X \in \mathcal{K}$.

We now present local and global stability directly under various monotonicity conditions.

Theorem B.8
Suppose that X^* solves VI$(F, \mathcal{K})$. If $F(X)$ is locally monotone at X^*, then x^* is a monotone attractor for the PDS$(F, \mathcal{K})$; if $F(X)$ is monotone, then X^* is a global monotone attractor.

Theorem B.9
Suppose that X^* solves VI$(F, \mathcal{K})$. If $F(X)$ is locally strictly monotone at X^*, then X^* is a strictly monotone attractor; if $F(X)$ is strictly monotone at X^*, then X^* is a strictly global monotone attractor.

In Appendix C, we describe a variety of algorithms for the solution of variational inequality problems, projected dynamical systems, as well as optimization problems with network structure of the type encountered in this book.

Appendix C Algorithms

The results in the previous appendix are useful not only in the qualitative analysis of solutions to variational inequality problems and projected dynamical systems, but also in providing conditions for establishing the convergence of algorithms. In this appendix, we present some of the basic algorithmic schemes, with special emphasis on algorithms that are used to compute equilibrium patterns in models discussed in this book.

In Section C.1, we focus on algorithms for variational inequality problems. In Section C.2, we consider the approximation of projected dynamical systems through discrete-time algorithms, which also, ultimately, determine an equilibrium or stationary point and, hence, also determine the solution to the associated variational inequality problems.

C.1 Algorithms for Variational Inequalities

In this section, we focus on algorithms that are relevant for the solution of the models in this book. In particular, the algorithms resolve a variational inequality problem, typically, into a series of simpler variational inequality problems, which, in turn, can usually be reformulated as optimization problems. The conditions of convergence are also discussed. For a variety of different algorithms applied to a plethora of equilibrium problems, including traffic network equilibrium problems, spatial price equilibrium problems, as well as oligopolistic market equilibrium problems, see Nagurney (1999).

As already mentioned, variational inequality algorithms resolve the variational inequality subproblem into simpler variational inequality subproblems, which are, typically, optimization problems. Hence, the overall efficiency of a variational inequality algorithm will depend upon the optimization algorithm used at each iteration. The subproblems often have a special structure and special purpose algorithms that unveil the structure can be used to solve the embedded mathematical programming problems to achieve further efficiencies. In particular, in the supernetwork problems considered in this text, the underlying structure is that of a network and, for completeness, and easy reference, we also present some network-based optimization algorithms in Section C.3.

We now present two computational algorithms, the projection method and the modified projection method, along with their convergence conditions.

Projection methods resolve a variational inequality problem (B.1) into, typically, a series of quadratic programming problems. Projection methods have been successfully implemented for the computation of a variety of equilibrium problems, including traffic network equilibrium problems (cf. Dafermos (1980, 1982, 1983) Nagurney (1999), and the references therein).

We now present a typical iteration of the projection method.

The Projection Method

The typical iteration, $\mathcal{T}$, of a projection method, following the initialization step, can be stated as follows:

$$X^{\mathcal{T}} = P_{\mathcal{K}}(X^{\mathcal{T}-1} - \alpha G^{-1} F(X^{\mathcal{T}-1})), \qquad (C.1)$$

where G is a symmetric $N \times N$ positive definite matrix, $\alpha > 0$, and $P_{\mathcal{K}} X$ is the orthogonal projection of X on the set $\mathcal{K}$, where recall that (cf. Definition B.6):

$$y = P_{\mathcal{K}} X = \arg \min_{z \in \mathcal{K}} \|X - z\|.$$

The subproblem, at an iteration $\mathcal{T}$, induced by (C.1), consists of the solution of the following minimum norm problem:

$$\min_{X \in \mathcal{K}} \|X - (X^{\mathcal{T}-1} - \alpha G^{-1} F(X^{\mathcal{T}-1}))\|, \qquad (C.2)$$

or, equivalently, to the solution of the strictly convex quadratic programming problem:

$$\min_{X \in \mathcal{K}} \frac{1}{2} \langle X, X \rangle - \langle (X^{\mathcal{T}-1} - \alpha G^{-1} F(X^{\mathcal{T}-1})), X \rangle. \qquad (C.3)$$

In the special case, where $\mathcal{K}$ is the nonnegative orthant, that is, when $\mathcal{K} = R^N_+$, then the projection operation becomes particularly simple. In this case, an iteration of the projection method (C.1) takes on the following closed form expression:

$$(X^{\mathcal{T}})_i = \begin{cases} (X^{\mathcal{T}-1} - \alpha G^{-1} F(X^{\mathcal{T}-1}))_i, & \text{if } (X^{\mathcal{T}-1} - \alpha G^{-1} F(X^{\mathcal{T}-1}))_i \geq 0, \\ 0, & \text{otherwise,} \end{cases}$$

$$(C.4)$$

for $i = 1, \ldots, N$.

Hence, in the case that the feasible set $\mathcal{K}$ is the nonnegative orthant, a simple formula is required in order to compute the iterate $\{X^{\mathcal{T}}\}$. It should also be noted that the evaluation of each $(X^{\mathcal{T}})_i; i = 1, \ldots, N$, can be done both independently and simultaneously.

The convergence of the projection method is guaranteed (cf. Bertsekas and Tsitsiklis (1989)) provided that the function F is both strongly monotone (see Definition B.4) and Lipschitz continuous (see Definition B.5), for any $\alpha \in (0, \alpha^0]$, such that the mapping induced by the projection is a contraction mapping with respect to the norm $\| \cdot \|_G$. The sequence $\{X^T\}$ generated by the projection algorithm then converges to the solution of X^*.

On the other hand, if the function F is not strongly monotone, but, rather, is only monotone (see Definition B.2) and satisfies the Lipschitz continuity condition, then the modified method of Korpelevich (1977) guarantees convergence to a solution to the variational inequality problem, provided, of course, that a solution exists. However, if the function F is monotone, rather than strongly monotone, then a unique solution is no longer guaranteed.

The modified projection method is presented next since it is used frequently in this book.

The Modified Projection Method

The typical iteration of the modified projection method, following the initialization with a feasible solution, is as follows:

$$X^T = P_\mathcal{K}(X^{T-1} - \alpha F(\bar{X}^{T-1})), \qquad (C.5)$$

where $\bar{X}^{T-1}$ is given by:

$$\bar{X}^{T-1} = P_\mathcal{K}(X^{T-1} - \alpha F(X^{T-1})), \qquad (C.6)$$

and α is a positive scalar, such that $\alpha \in (0, \frac{1}{L}]$, where L is the Lipschitz constant in Definition B.5. Also, note that $G^{-1} = I$ (see (C.1) in the Projection Method).

Other variational inequality algorithms, such as the relaxation method, as well as a variety of decomposition methods, both serial and parallel, can be found in Nagurney (1999) and the references therein.

C.2   Algorithms for Projected Dynamical Systems

In this section, we recall a recently introduced general iterative scheme designed to estimate stationary points of the projected dynamical system (B.16); equivalently, to determine solutions to the variational inequality problem (B.1). The algorithms induced by what we term the PDS general iterative scheme can be interpreted as discrete time approximations to the continuous time model given by (B.16).

The PDS general iterative scheme for obtaining a solution to (B.1) takes the following form.

The PDS General Iterative Scheme

Step 0: Initialization

Start with an $X^0 \in \mathcal{K}$. Set $\tau := 0$.

Step 1: Computation

Compute $X^{\tau+1}$ by solving the variational inequality problem:

$$X^{\tau+1} = P_{\mathcal{K}}(X^\tau - \alpha_\tau F_\tau(X^\tau)), \qquad (C.7)$$

where $\{\alpha_\tau; \tau = 1, 2, \ldots\}$ is a sequence of positive scalars and the sequence of vector fields $\{F_\tau(\cdot); \tau = 1, 2, \ldots\}$ are "approximations" to $F(\cdot)$.

Step 2: Convergence Verification

If $|X^{\tau+1} - X^\tau| \leq \epsilon$, for some $\epsilon > 0$, a prespecified tolerance, then stop; otherwise, set $\tau := \tau + 1$, and go to Step 1.

We first give the precise conditions for the convergence theorem and a general discussion of the conditions. Subsequently, several examples of the functions $\{F_\tau(\cdot); \tau = 1, 2, \ldots\}$ are given.

The following notation is needed for the statement of Assumption C.1.

For each $X \in R^N$, let the set-valued function $\bar{F}(X)$ be defined as

$$\bar{F}(X) = \bigcap_{\epsilon > 0} \text{cov}\left(\overline{\{F(y) : \|X - y\| \leq \epsilon\}}\right)$$

where the overline indicates the closure and $\text{cov}(A)$ denotes the convex hull of the set A. Then $\bar{F}(X)$ is convex and upper semicontinuous, particularly, $\bar{F}(X) = F(X)$, when F is continuous at X.

For any $z \in R^N, A \subset R^N$, let

$$d(z, A) := \inf_{y \in A} \|z - y\|$$

denote the distance between z and A. Then

$$d(z, A) = \|z - P_A(z)\|,$$

when A is closed and convex.

The conditions for the convergence theorem are now stated.

Assumption C.1

Suppose we fix an initial condition $X^0 \in \mathcal{K}$ and define the sequence $\{X^\tau; \tau = 1, 2, \ldots\}$ by (C.7). We assume the following conditions.

(i) $\sum_{\tau=1}^{\infty} \alpha_\tau = \infty$, $\alpha_\tau > 0$, $\alpha_\tau \to 0$,   as $\tau \to \infty$.

(ii) $d(F_\tau(X), \bar{F}(X)) \to 0$ uniformly on compact subsets of $\mathcal{K}$ as $\tau \to \infty$.

(iii) Define $y(\cdot)$ to be the unique solution to $\dot{X} = \Pi_{\mathcal{K}}(X, -F(X))$ that satisfies $y(0) = y \in \mathcal{K}$. The $w-$limit set

$$w(\mathcal{K}) = \cup_{y \in \mathcal{K}} \cap_{t \geq 0} \overline{\cup_{s \geq t} \{y(s)\}}$$

is contained in the set of stationary points of $\dot{X} = \Pi_{\mathcal{K}}(X, -F(X))$.

(iv) The sequence $\{X^{\tau}; \tau = 1, 2, \ldots\}$ is bounded.

(v) The solutions to $\dot{X} = \Pi_{\mathcal{K}}(X, -F(X))$ are stable in the sense that given any compact set $\mathcal{K}_1$ there exists a compact set $\mathcal{K}_2$ such that $\cup_{y \in \mathcal{K} \cap \mathcal{K}_1} \cup_{t \geq 0} \{y(t)\} \subset \mathcal{K}_2$.

Examples

We now give examples for the vector field $F_{\tau}(X)$. The most obvious example is $F_{\tau}(X) = F(X)$ for $\tau = 1, 2, \ldots$ and $X \in \mathcal{K}$. This would correspond to the basic *Euler scheme* in the numerical approximation of classical ordinary differential equations. We utilize this Euler method to compute solutions to the dynamic models in Chapters 5, 6, and 10. Another example is a Heun-type scheme given by

$$F_{\tau}(X) = \frac{1}{2}[F(X) + F(X + P_{\mathcal{K}}(X - \alpha_{\tau} F(X)))].$$

The convergence result is now stated.

Theorem C.1: Convergence of PDS General Iterative Scheme
Let S denote the solutions to the variational inequality (B.1), and assume Assumption B.1 and Assumption C.1. Suppose $\{X^{\tau}; \tau = 1, 2, \ldots\}$ is the scheme generated by (C.7). Then $d(X^{\tau}, S) \to 0$ as $\tau \to \infty$.

Corollary C.1
Assume the conditions of Theorem C.1, and also that S consists of a finite set of points. Then $\lim_{\tau \to \infty} X^{\tau}$ exists and equals a solution to the variational inequality.

C.3   Algorithms for Network Optimization Problems

Network equilibrium problems, and, in particular, supernetwork problems are variational inequality problems in which the feasible set has a network structure. Hence, such problems are best solved as variational inequality problems in which, typically, at each iteration one applies a network-based algorithm to solve the embedded mathematical programming problems. Indeed, if one applies, for example, either the projection method (cf. (C.1)) (in the case of a strongly monotone and Lipschitz continuous $F(\cdot)$) or the modified projection method (cf. (C.5) and (C.6)) (in the case of a monotone and Lipschitz continuous $F(\cdot)$), then one obtains a sequence of quadratic programming problems (diagonal in the case of the modified projection method and in the case of the projection method if G in (C.1) is selected to be diagonal). These quadratic programming problems are network optimization problems in which the feasible set has a characteristic network structure. Hence, such variational inequality algorithms applied to network equilibrium problems solve a sequence of symmetric network equilibrium problems.

Consequently, the algorithms given in the preceding sections for the solution of finite-dimensional variational inequality problems can, at least in principle, be applied for the computation of network equilibria, provided that the conditions for convergence are satisfied by the problem under study.

However, the overall efficiency of the projection methods and the algorithms induced by the general iterative scheme for the computation of network equilibria depends on the efficiency and effectiveness of the utilized network-based algorithm for the solution of the embedded mathematical programming problems.

Towards that end, we present now an equilibration algorithm for the solution of the network equilibrium problem in the case of linear and separable user link travel cost functions. The algorithm is due to Dafermos and Sparrow (1969). This algorithm is applicable to any network topology. The equilibration algorithm is a path equilibration algorithm for the solution of the symmetric and separable network equilibrium problem in the case of linear user costs on the links. This equilibration algorithm can be embedded in projection methods, for example, for the computation of network equilibria in the case of nonseparable and asymmetric user link costs (see Chapter 3).

C.3.1   An Equilibration Algorithm for Linear and Separable Link Cost Functions

We now present an equilibration algorithm for the solution of problem (3.16)–(3.19), where the user cost on a link (cf. (3.3)) is given by:

$$c_a = g_a f_a + h_a, \quad \forall a \in \mathcal{L},$$

where we assume that g_a and h_a are positive for all links a. Explicitly, the problem that is solved is:

$$\text{Minimize} \quad \sum_{a \in \mathcal{L}} \frac{1}{2} g_a f_a^2 + h_a f_a \qquad (C.8)$$

subject to (3.17), (3.18), and the nonnegativity assumption on the path flows (3.19).

The algorithm is called an equilibration algorithm since it utilizes the network equilibrium conditions (3.15), which in this case are equivalent to the Kuhn-Tucker conditions of problem (3.16)–(3.19), for its motivation. We first present the Single O/D Pair Equilibration Algorithm, and then two alternative Multiple O/D Pair Equilibration Algorithms, which utilize the single/pair equilibration algorithm.

The single pair equilibration algorithm proceeds as follows. One selects the most costly *used* path connecting the O/D pair and the cheapest path. One then distributes the flow from the most expensive used path to the cheapest path using an explicit formula which is actually obtained by solving a minimization problem over a reduced feasible set. One continues in this fashion until the equilibrium conditions (3.15) hold within a prespecified tolerance. For further details, and proof of convergence, see Dafermos and Sparrow (1969).

Single O/D Pair Equilibration

Step 0: Initialization

Construct an initial feasible link flow pattern induced by a feasible path flow pattern and denoted by x^0. Set $k = 1$.

Step 1: Selection and Convergence Verification

Determine:

$$r = \{p|\max_p C_p \quad \text{and} \quad x_p^{k-1} > 0\}$$

$$q = \{p|\min_p C_p\}.$$

If $|C_r - C_q| \le \epsilon$, with $\epsilon > 0$, a prespecified tolerance, then stop; else, go to Step 2.

Step 2: Computation

Compute:

$$\Delta' = \frac{[C_r - C_q]}{\sum_{a \in \mathcal{L}} g_a (\delta_{aq} - \delta_{ar})^2} \tag{C.9}$$

$$\Delta = \min\{\Delta', x_r^{k-1}\}. \tag{C.10}$$

Set:

$$x_r^k = x_r^{k-1} - \Delta \tag{C.11}$$

$$x_q^k = x_q^{k-1} + \Delta$$

$$x_p^k = x_p^{k-1}, \quad \forall p \ne q \cup r.$$

Let $k = k + 1$, and go to Step 1.

In the case that a tie exists for the selection of path r and/or q, then any such selection is appropriate.

On a network in which there are now J O/D pairs, the above single O/D pair equilibration procedure is applicable as well.

We term Step 1 (without the convergence check) and Step 2 of the above equilibration operator E_{w_i}. Now two possibilities for equilibration present themselves. In Equilibration Algorithm I, one equilibrates the costs on the most expensive and cheapest paths for the first O/D pair, then does the same for the second O/D pair, and so on, until the Jth O/D pair. One then verifies convergence; if the algorithm has not converged, one continues in the same manner. In Equilibration Algorithm II, one keeps on equilibrating the most expensive and the cheapest paths for the first O/D pair, until optimality has been reached for this O/D pair. One then does the same for the second O/D pair, and so on through the Jth O/D pair. If convergence has not been reached for all O/D pairs, then one proceeds as above again for all O/D pairs.

Multiple O/D Pair Equilibration Algorithm I

Let $E^1 \equiv E_{\omega_J} \circ \ldots \circ E_{\omega_1}$.

Step 0: Initialization

Construct an initial feasible flow pattern which induces a feasible link load pattern. Set $\mathcal{T} = 1$.

Step 1: Equilibration

Apply E^1.

Step 2: Convergence Verification

If convergence holds, stop; else, set $\mathcal{T} = \mathcal{T} + 1$, and go to Step 1.

Multiple O/D Pair Equilibration Algorithm II

Let $E^2 = (E_{\omega_J} \circ (\ldots \circ (E_{\omega_J}))) \circ \ldots \circ (E_{\omega_1} \circ (\ldots \circ (E_{\omega_1})))$.

Step 0: Initialization (as above).

Step 1: Equilibration

Apply E^2.

Step 2: Convergence Verification (as above).

The difference between E^1 and E^2 is as follows. E^1 equilibrates only one pair of paths for an O/D pair before proceeding to the next O/D pair, and so on, whereas E^2 equilibrates the costs on all the paths connecting an O/D pair using the two-path procedure above, before proceeding to the next O/D pair, and so on.

In the case that the induced network subproblem has even a more specialized structure, such as, for example, when each O/D pair is connected by disjoint paths, that is, paths that share no links, then the path flows can be determined exactly and in closed form using *exact* equilibration (cf. Dafermos and Sparrow (1969) and Nagurney (1999)). This is an algorithm that is guaranteed to converge for such problems in a finite number of steps. For completeness, and easy reference, we now present the exact equilibration algorithm.

Exact Equilibration Algorithm

Consider the network with special structure depicted in Figure C.1. Note that here, for convenience, the links comprising each disjoint path have been aggregated into a single link. There are n paths in the network and a single

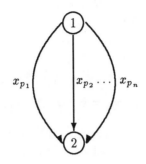

Fig. C.1. Special Network Structure

O/D pair ω consisting of nodes 1 and 2. Hence, we are interested in solving the following problem:

$$\text{Minimize} \quad \frac{1}{2} \sum_{p \in P_\omega} g_p x_p^2 + \sum_{p \in P_\omega} h_p x_p \qquad (C.12)$$

subject to:

$$\sum_{p \in P_\omega} x_p = d_\omega \qquad (C.13)$$

and

$$x_p \geq 0, \quad \forall p \in P_\omega, \qquad (C.14)$$

where $g_p = \sum_{a \in \mathcal{L}} g_a \delta_{ap}$ and $h_p = \sum_{a \in \mathcal{L}} h_a \delta_{ap}$.

The statement of the exact equilibration algorithm is now given. An application of its use is given in Chapter 6.

Step 0: Sort

Sort the fixed cost terms, h_{p_i}, for $i = 1, \ldots, n$, in nondescending order, and relabel the h_{p_i}'s accordingly. Assume, henceforth, that they are relabeled. Set $h_{p_{n+1}} = \infty$. Set $s = 1$.

Step 1: Computation

Compute:

$$\lambda_\omega^s = \frac{\sum_{i=1}^s \frac{h_{p_i}}{g_{p_i}} + d_\omega}{\sum_{i=1}^s \frac{1}{g_{p_i}}}. \qquad (C.15)$$

Step 2: Evaluation

If $h_{p_s} < \lambda_\omega^s \leq h_{p_{s+1}}$, then stop; set $s' = s$, and go to Step 3. Otherwise, let $s := s + 1$, and go to Step 1.

Step 3: Update

Set

$$x_{p_i} = \lambda_\omega^{s'} - h_{p_i}; \quad i = 1, \ldots, s', \qquad (C.16)$$

$$x_{p_i} = 0; \quad i = s' + 1, \ldots, n. \qquad (C.17)$$

These appendices have provided most of the fundamentals for the understanding of the technical contents of this book.

Bibliography

Abello, J., Pardalos, P. M., and Resende, M. G. C. (1999), "On Maximum Clique Problems in Very Large Graphs," in *External Memory Algorithms*, pp. 119-130, J. Abello and J. Vitter, editors, AMS-DIMACS Series on Discrete Mathematics and Theoretical Computer Science **50**.

AboutSchwab.com (2001), "Insights 'Regulatory Cost in the Financial Marketplace of the Future.'"
http://www.aboutschwab.com/proom/crstestimony.html

Ahuja, R. K., Magnanti, T. L., and Orlin, J. B. (1993), *Network Flows: Theory, Algorithms, and Applications*, Prentice-Hall, Upper Saddle River, New Jersey.

Albertson, L. A. (1977), "Telecommunication as a Travel Substitute: Some Psychological, Organizational, and Social Aspects," *Journal of Communication* **27**, 32-43.

Allen, Jr., W. G. (1996), "Model Improvements for Evaluating Pricing Strategies," *Transportation Research Record* **1498**, 75-81.

Amazon.com (2001), "About Amazon.com."
http://www.amazon.com/exec/obidos/subst/misc/ company-info.html/ref =gw_bt_aa/103-9682569-2663803

Anderson, W. P., Kanaroglou, P. S., Miller, E. J., and Buliung, R. N. (1996), "Simulating Automobile Emissions in an Integrated Urban Model," *Transportation Research Record* **1520**, 71-80.

Andersson, A. E., Batten, D. F., Kobayashi, K., and Yoshikawa, K., editors (1993), *The Cosmo-Creative Society: Logistical Networks in a Dynamic Economy*, Springer Verlag, Heidelberg, Germany.

Anderstig, C., and Mattsson, L.-G. (1998), "Modelling Land-Use and Transport Interaction: Policy Analyses Using the IMREL Model," in *Network Infrastructure and the Urban Environment: Advances in Spatial Systems Modelling*, pp. 308-328, L. Lundqvist, L.-G. Mattsson, and T. J. Kim, editors, Springer-Verlag, Heidelberg, Germany.

Apell, D. (2000), "Asian Firms Tempt Investors with No-Risk Funds," *The Wall Street Journal*, November 20, 2000.

Arrow, K. J., and Intrilligator, M., D., editors (1982), *Handbook of Mathematical Economics*, Elsevier Science Publishers, New York.

AT&T (2001a), "AT&T Receives Climate Protection Award from U.S. Environmental Protection Agency."
http://www.att.com/press/item/0,1354,3447,00.html

AT&T (2001b), "Telework Reaches All Time High at AT&T."
http://www.att.com/telework/article_library/alltime_high.html

AT&T (2001c), "The Future of Telework (Part II)."
http://www.att.com/telework/article_library/future_tele_2.html

AT&T (2001d), "In Traffic: Avoiding Internet Rush Hour."
http://www.att.com/telework/article_library/intraffic.html

Balluck, K. (2000), "GE GXS Enables US-Canadian Centralized Product Data Sharing," *Newsbytes News Network*, August 22.
http://www.newsbytes.com/news/00/154019.html

Banister, D., and Button, K. J. (1993), "Environmental Policy and Transport: An Overview," in *Transport, the Environment, and Sustainable Development*, pp. 130-136, D. Banister and K. J. Button, editors, E. & F.N., London, England.

Bar-Gera, H. (1999), "Origin-Based Algorithms for Transportation Network Modeling," National Institute of Statistical Sciences, Technical Report # 103, Research Triangle Park, North Carolina.

Bass, T. (1992), "Road to Ruin," *Discover*, May, 56-61.

Bazaraa, M. S., Jarvis, J. J., and Sherali, H. D. (1990), *Linear Programming and Network Flows*, second edition, John Wiley & Sons, New York.

Bazaraa, M. S., Sherali, H. D., and Shetty, C. M. (1993), *Nonlinear Programming: Theory and Algorithms*, second edition, John Wiley & Sons, New York.

Beckmann, M. J., McGuire, C. B., and Winsten, C. B. (1956), *Studies in the Economics of Transportation*, Yale University Press, New Haven, Connecticut.

Ben-Akiva, M., de Palma, A., and Kaysi, I. (1991), "Dynamic Network Models and Driver Information Systems," *Transportation Research A* **25**, 251-266.

Beniger (1986), *The Control Revolution: Technological and Economic Origins of the Information Society*, Harvard University Press, Cambridge, Massachusetts.

Berhnolz, P. (1990), "The Importance of Reorganizing Money, Credit, and Banking When Decentralizing Economic Decisionmaking," in *Economic Reform in China: Problems and Prospects*, pp. 93-123, J. A. Dorn and W. Xi, editors, University of Chicago Press, Chicago, Illinois.

Bertsekas, D. P., and Gallager, R. (1992), *Data Networks*, second edition, Prentice-Hall, Englewood Cliffs, New Jersey.

Bertsekas, D. P., and Tsitsiklis, J. N. (1989), *Parallel and Distributed Computation*, Prentice-Hall, Englewood Cliffs, New Jersey.

Bertsimas, D., and Odoni, A. (1997), "A Critical Survey of Optimization Models for Tactical and Strategic Aspects of Air Traffic Flow Management," National Aeronautics and Space Administration, NASA report CR-20640, Springfield, Virginia.

Board of Governors (1980), *Introduction to Flow of Funds*, Flow of Funds Section, Division of Research and Statistics, Federal Reserve System, Washington, DC, June.

Bouzaiene-Ayari, B., Gendreau, M., and Nguyen, S. (1998), "Passenger Assignment in Congested Transit Networks: A Historical Perspective," in *Equilibrium and Advanced Transportation Modelling*, pp. 47-71, P. Marcotte and S. Nguyen, editors, Kluwer Academic Publishers, Boston, Massachusetts.

Bovet, D. (2000), *Value Nets: Breaking the Supply Chain to Unlock Hidden Profits*, John Wiley & Sons, New York.

Boyce, D. E. (1980), "A Framework for Constructing Network Equilibrium Models of Urban Location," *Transportation Science* **14**, 77-96.

Boyce, D. E., Chon, K. S., Lee, Y. J., Lin, K. T., and LeBlanc, L. J. (1983), "Implementation and Computational Issues for Combined Models of Location, Destination, Mode, and Route Choice," *Environment and Planning A* **15**, 1219-1230.

Boyce, D. E., and Mattsson, L.-G. (1999), "Modeling Residential Location Choice in Relation to Housing and Road Tolls on Congested Urban Highway Networks," *Transportation Research B* **33**, 581-591.

Boyce, D. E., and Southworth, F. (1979), "Quasi-Dynamic Urban Location Models with Endogenously Determined Travel Costs," *Environment and Planning A* **11**, 575-584.

Bradley, S. P., Hax, A., and Magnanti, T. L. (1977), *Applied Mathematical Programming*, Addison-Wesley, Reading, Massachusetts.

Braess, D. (1968), "Uber ein Paradoxon der Verkehrsplanung," *Unternehmenforschung* **12**, 258-268.

Bramel, J., and Simchi-Levi, D. (1997), *The Logic of Logistics: Theory, Algorithms and Applications for Logistics Management*, Springer-Verlag, New York.

Bryce, R. (2001), "Railroads Make Time, Money on the Web," *Interactive Week*, July 16.
http://www.zdnet.com/zdnn/stories/news/0,4586,2784808,00.html

Button, K. J. (1990), "Environmental Externalities and Transport Policy," *Oxford Review of Economic Policy* **6**, 61-75.

Cascetta, E., and Cantarella, G.E. (1991), "A Day-to-Day and Within-Day Dynamic Stochastic Assignment Model," *Transportation Research A* **25**, 277-291.

Castells, M. (2000), *The Rise of the Network Society*, second edition, Blackwell Publishers, Oxford, England.

Cerf, V. G., and Kahn, R. E. (1974), "A Protocol for Packet Network Interconnection," *IEEE Transactions on Communications Technology*, vol. COM-22 **5**, 627-641.

Chankong, V., and Haimes, Y. Y. (1983), *Multiobjective Decision Making: Theory and Methodology*, North-Holland, New York.

Charnes, A., and Cooper, W. W. (1967), "Some Network Characterizations for Mathematical Programming and Accounting Approaches to Planning and Control," *The Accounting Review* **42**, 24-52.

Chow, G. (1995), "Portfolio Selection Based on Return, Risk, and Relative Performance," *Financial Analysts Journal*, March-April, 54-60.

Cohen, J. (1987), *The Flow of Funds in Theory and Practice, Financial and Monetary Studies* **15**, Kluwer Academic Publishers, Dordrecht, The Netherlands.

Cohen, J. E., and Kelly, F. P. (1990), "A Paradox of Congestion on a Queuing Network," *Journal of Applied Probability* **27**, 730-734.

Colson, G., and De Bruyn, C. (1983), "An Integrated Multiobjective Portfolio Management System," *Mathematical and Computer Modelling* **12**, 1359-1381.

Copeland, M. A. (1952), *A Study of Moneyflows in the United States*, National Bureau of Economic Research, New York.

Cosset, J. C., Siskos, Y., and Zopounidis, C. (1992), "Evaluating Country Risk: A Decision Support Approach," *Global Finance Journal* **3**, 79-95.

Cournot, A. A. (1838), *Researches into the Mathematical Principles of the Theory of Wealth*, English translation, Macmillan, London, England, 1897.

Covisint (2001), "General Facts About Covisint." http://www.covisint.com/faqs/gen_current.shtml

Crainic, T. G. (1999), "Long Haul Freight Transportation," in *Handbook of Transportation Science*, pp. 433-491, R. W. Hall, editor, Kluwer Academic Publishers, Boston, Massachusetts.

Dafermos, S. (1972), "The Traffic Assignment Problem for Multimodal Networks," *Transportation Science* **6**, 73-87.

Dafermos, S. (1976), "Integrated Equilibrium Flow Models for Transportation Planning," in *Traffic Equilibrium Methods, Lecture Notes in Economics and Mathematical Systems* **118**, pp. 106-118, M. A. Florian, editor, Springer-Verlag, New York.

Dafermos, S. (1980), "Traffic Equilibrium and Variational Inequalities," *Transportation Science* **14**, 42-54.

Dafermos, S. (1981), "A Multicriteria Route-Mode Choice Traffic Equilibrium Model," Lefschetz Center for Dynamical Systems, Brown University, Providence, Rhode Island.

Dafermos, S. (1982), "The General Multimodal Network Equilibrium Problem with Elastic Demand," *Networks* **12**, 57-72.

Dafermos, S. (1983), "An Iterative Scheme for Variational Inequalities," *Mathematical Programming* **26**, 40-47.

Dafermos, S. (1986), "Equilibria on Nonlinear Networks," LCDS #86-1, Lefschetz Center for Dynamical Systems, Brown University, Providence, Rhode Island.

Dafermos, S., and Nagurney, A. (1984a), "Sensitivity Analysis for the General Spatial Economic Equilibrium Problem," *Operations Research* **32**, 1069-1086.

Dafermos, S., and Nagurney, A. (1984b), "Stability and Sensitivity Analysis for the General Network Equilibrium - Travel Choice Model," in *Proceedings of the Ninth International Symposium on Transportation and Traffic Theory*, pp. 217-232, J. Volmuller and R. Hamerslag, editors, VNU Press, Utrecht, The Netherlands.

Dafermos, S., and Nagurney, A. (1984c), "On Some Traffic Equilibrium Theory Paradoxes," *Transportation Research B* **18**, 101-110.

Dafermos, S., and Nagurney, A. (1985), "Isomorphism between Spatial Price and Traffic Network Equilibrium Models," LCDS # 85-17, Lefschetz Center for Dynamical Systems, Brown University, Providence, Rhode Island.

Dafermos, S., and Nagurney, A. (1987), "Oligopolistic and Competitive Behavior of Spatially Separated Markets," *Regional Science and Urban Economics* **17**, 245-254.

Dafermos, S. C., and Sparrow, F. T. (1969), "The Traffic Assignment Problem for a General Network," *Journal of Research of the National Bureau of Standards* **73B**, 91-118.

DeCorla-Souza, P., Everett, J., Cosby, J., and Lim, P. (1995), "Trip-Based Approach to Estimate Emissions with Environmental Protection Agency's MOBILE Model," *Transportation Research Record* **1444**, 118-125.

Denning, P. J. (1985), "The Science of Computing: Supernetworks," *American Scientist* **73**, 127-129.

Dertouzos, M. L. (1997), *What Will Be: How the New World of Information Will Change Our Lives*, Harper, San Francisco, California.

De Sola Pool, I., editor (1977), *The Social Impact of the Telephone*, MIT Press, Cambridge, Massachusetts.

Dewar, J. A. (1998), "The Information Age and the Printing Press: Looking Backward to See Ahead," Rand Publication P-8014. http://www.rand.org/publications/P/P8014/

Dhanda, K. K., Nagurney, A., and Ramanujam, P. (1999), *Environmental Networks: A Framework for Economic Decision-Making and Policy Analysis*, Edward Elgar, Cheltenham, United Kingdom.

Dial, R. B. (1967), "Transit Pathfinder Algorithm," *Highway Research Record* **205**, 67-85.

Dial, R. B. (1979), "A Model and Algorithms for Multicriteria Route-Mode Choice," *Transportation Research B* **13**, 311-316.

Dial, R. B. (1996), "Bicriterion Traffic Assignment: Basic Theory and Elementary Algorithms," *Transportation Science* **30**, 93-111.

Dial, R. B. (1999), "Network-Optimized Road Pricing: Part I: A Parable and a Model," *Operations Research* **47**, 54-64.

Dong, J., and Nagurney, A. (2001), "Bicriteria Decision Making and Financial Equilibrium: A Variational Inequality Perspective," *Computational Economics* **17**, 29-42.

Dong, J., Zhang, D., and Nagurney, A. (1996), "A Projected Dynamical Systems Model of General Financial Equilibrium with Stability Analysis," *Mathematical and Computer Modelling* **24**, 35-44.

Dorn, J. A., editor (1997), *The Future of Money*, CATO Institute, Washington, DC.

Drissi-Kaitouni, O., and Hameda-Benchekroun, A. (1992), "A Dynamic Traffic Assignment Model and a Solution Algorithm," *Transportation Science* **26**, 119-128.

Dupuis, P., and Nagurney, A. (1993), "Dynamical Systems and Variational Inequalities," *Annals of Operations Research* **44**, 9-42.

The Economist (1996), "Living with the Car," June 22, 3-18.

The Economist (1997), "Living with the Car," December 26, 21-23.

The Economist (2000a), "Survey: E-Management," November 11, 5-40.

The Economist (2000b), "Define and Sell," February 26, 6-15.

The Economist (2000c), "Going for Brokers," May 20, 9-19.

The Economist (2001a), "Keeping the Customer Satisfied," July 14, 9-10.

The Economist (2001b), "We Have Lift-Off," February 3, 69-71.

Eliasson, J., and Mattsson, L.-G. (2000), "A Model for Integrated Analysis of Household Location and Travel Choices," *Transportation Research A* **34**, 375-394.

Evans, S. P. (1976), "Derivation and Analysis of Some Models for Combining Trip Distribution and Assignment," *Transportation Research* **10**, 37-57.

Evans, P., and Wurster, T. (1999), *Blown to Bits*, Harvard Business School Press, Cambridge, Massachusetts.

Fallows, J. (1996), "The Java Theory," *The Atlantic Online*, The Atlantic Monthly/Digital Edition.
http://www2.theatlantic.com/issues/96mar/java/java.htm

Federal Highway Administration (2000), "E-Commerce Trends in the Market for Freight. Task 3 Freight Trends Scans," Draft, Multimodal Freight Analysis Framework, Office of Freight Management and Operations, Washington, DC.

Federal Reserve Board (1999), "Remarks by Chairman Alan Greenspan; Measuring Financial Risk in the Twenty-First Century," October 14, 1999. http://www.federalreserve.gov/boarddocs/speeches/1999/19991014.htm

Federgruen, A. (1993), "Centralized Planning Models for Multi-Echelon Inventory Systems Under Uncertainty," in *Handbooks in Operations Research and Management Science*, volume on Logistics of Production and Inventory, pp. 133-173, S. C. Graves, A. H. G. Rinooy Kan, and P. Zipkin, editors, Elsevier Science, Amsterdam, The Netherlands.

Fishburn, P. C. (1970), *Utility Theory for Decision Making*, John Wiley & Sons, New York.

Fisk, C. (1979), "More Paradoxes in the Equilibrium Assignment Problem," *Transportation Research B* **1**, 305-309.

Florian, M., and Hearn, D. (1995), "Network Equilibrium Models and Algorithms," in *Network Routing, Handbooks in Operations Research and Management Science* **8**, pp. 485-550, M. O. Ball, T. L. Magnanti, C. L. Monma, and G. L. Nemhauser, editors, Elsevier Science, Amsterdam, The Netherlands.

Florian, M., and Los, M. (1982), "A New Look at Static Spatial Price Equilibrium Models," *Regional Science and Urban Economics* **12**, 579-597.

Florian, M., Nguyen, S., and Ferland, J. (1975), "On the Combined Distribution-Assignment of Traffic," *Transportation Science* **9**, 43-53.

Francis, J. C., and Archer, S. H. (1979), *Portfolio Analysis*, Prentice-Hall, Englewood Cliffs, New Jersey.

Frank, M. (1992), "Obtaining Network Cost(s) From One Link's Output," *Transportation Science* **26**, 27-35.

Friedlander, A. (1995a), *Emerging Infrastructure: The Growth of Railroads*, Corporation for National Research Initiatives, Reston, Virginia.

Friedlander, A. (1995b), *Natural Monopoly and Universal Service: Telephones and Telegraphs in the U.S. Communications Infrastructure 1837-1940*, Corporation for National Research Initiatives, Reston, Virginia.

Friesz, T. L., Bernstein, D., Mehta, J., Tobin, R. L., and Ganjalizadeh, S. (1994), "Day to Day Dynamic Network Disequilibrium and Idealized Traveler Information Systems," *Operations Research* **42**, 1120-1136.

Friesz, T. L., Gottfried, J. A., and Morlok, E. K. (1986), "A Sequential Shipper-Carrier Network Model for Predicting Freight Flows," *Transportation Science* **20**, 80-91.

Gabay, D., and Moulin, H. (1980), "On the Uniqueness and Stability of Nash Equilibria in Noncooperative Games," in *Applied Stochastic Control in Econometrics and Management Science*, pp. 271-294, A. Bensoussan, P. Kleindorfer, and C. S. Tapiero, editors, North-Holland, Amsterdam, The Netherlands.

Gartner, N. H. (1980a), "Optimal Traffic Assignment with Elastic Demands: A Review Part I. Analysis Framework," *Transportation Science* **14**, 174-191.

Gartner, N. H. (1980b), "Optimal Traffic Assignment with Elastic Demands: A Review Part II. Algorithmic Approaches," *Transportation Science* **14**, 192-208.

Gates, B., Myhrvold, N., and Rinearson, P. M. (1995), *The Road Ahead*, Viking Press, New York.

General Electric (2001), "GE's e-Volution of 2000." http://www.ge.com/news/spotlight/evolution.html

Glater J. D. (2001), "Telecommuting's Big Experiment," *New York Times*, Wednesday, May 9, C1.

Glover, E. L., and Brzezinski, D. J. (1989), "MOBILE4 Exhaust Emission Factors and Inspection/Maintenance Benefits for Passenger Cars," Technical Report, EPA-AA-TSS-I/M-89-3.

Gore, A. (1996), "The Technology Challenge: How Can America Spark Private Innovation?" http://www.seas.upenn.edu:80/ museum/goreaddress.html

Gould, J. (1998), "Driven to Shop? Role of Transportation in Future Home Shopping," *Transportation Research Record* **1617**, 149-156.

Graves, S. C., Rinooy Kan, A. H. G., and Zipkin, P., editors (1993), *Handbooks in Operations Research and Management Science*, volume on Logistics of Production and Inventory, Elsevier Science, Amsterdam, The Netherlands.

Hafner K. (2000), "Working at Home Today?" *New York Times*, November 2, 2000, E7-E8.

Hagel, J., and Singer, M. (1999), *Net Worth*, Harvard Business School Press, Cambridge, Massachusetts.

Hallerbach, W., and Spronk, J. (2000), "A Multicriteria Framework for Risk Analysis," in *Research and Practice in Multiple Criteria Decision Making, Lecture Notes in Economics and Mathematical Systems* **487**, pp. 272-283, Y. Y. Haimes and R. Steuer, editors, Springer Verlag, Berlin, Germany.

Hamilton, A. (1949), "Calculating Machines: Brains that Click," *Popular Mechanics* **49**, 162-167.

Handfield, R. B., and Nichols, Jr., E. L. (1999), *Introduction to Supply Chain Management*, Prentice-Hall, Englewood Cliffs, New Jersey.

Harkness, R. C. (1977), *Technology Assessment of Telecommunications / Transportation Interactions*, Stanford Research Institute, Menlo Park, California.

Harlow, A. F. (1936), *Old Wires and New Waves: The History of the Telegraph, Telephone, and Wireless*, D. Appleton-Century Company, New York.

Hartman, P. and Stampacchia, G. (1966), "On Some Nonlinear Elliptic Differential Functional Equations," *Acta Mathematica* **115**, 271-310.

Hensher, D., Button, K., and Brewer, S., editors (2001), *Handbook of Logistics and Supply Chain Management*, Elsevier Science, Oxford, England.

Hu, P. S., and Young, J. (1996), *Summary of Travel Trends: 1995 Nationwide Personal Transportation Survey*, US DOT, FHWA, Washington, DC, December.

Illinois State Bar Association (1997), Advisory Opinion on Professional Conduct, Opinion No. 96-10, Topic: Electronic Communications; Confidentiality of Client Information; Advertising and Solicitation, May 16.
http://www.chicago-law.net/cyberlaw/electric.html

International Telework Association & Council (2000), "Telework America (TWA) 2000 Key Findings."
http://www.telecommute.org/twa2000/research_results_key.shtml

Jacobson, C. (2000), *Ties that Bind*, University of Pittsburgh Press, Pittsburgh, Pennsylvania.

Janson, B. N. (1991), "Dynamic Traffic Assignment for Urban Road Networks," *Transportation Research B* **25**, 143-161.

Johansson, B., and Mattsson, L. G. (1995), "Principles of Road Pricing," in *Road Pricing: Theory, Empirical Assessment and Policy*, pp. 7-33, B. Johansson and L.-G. Mattsson, editors, Kluwer Academic Publishers, Boston, Massachusetts.

Jones, Jr., D. W. (1973), *Must We Travel: The Potential of Communications as a Substitute for Urban Travel*, Report No. PB-227-185/6, Stanford University, Institute for Communications Research, Palo Alto, California.

Kanafani, A., and Parsons, R. (1989), "Program on Advanced Technology for the Highway – Vehicle/Highway Navigation R&D," presented at the Vehicle Navigation and Information Systems Conference sponnsored by IEEE, Toronto, Canada, September 11–13.

Kapner, S. (2001), "Tesco Profits from Online Sales," *International Herald Tribune*, July 21-22, p. 9.

Karush, W. (1939), "Minima of Functions of Several Variables with Inequalities as Side Conditions," M.S. Thesis, Department of Mathematics, University of Chicago, Chicago, Illinois.

Keeney, R. L., and Raiffa, H. (1993), *Decisions with Multiple Objectives: Preferences and Value Tradeoffs*, Cambridge University Press, Cambridge, England.

Kelly, K. (1994), *Out of Control: The Rise of Neo-Biological Civilization*, Addison Wesley Publishing, New York.

Kennedy, R. (2000), "Beaten Track: A Special Report; I-95, a River of Commerce Overflowing with Traffic," *New York Times*, December 29, A1.

Khan, A. M. (1976), "Travel vs. Telecommunications: Current Understanding, Part 1, *Transportation Journal* **10**, 203-216.

Kieve, J. L. (1973), *Electric Telegraph: A Social and Economic History*, David and Charles (Holdings) Ltd., Newton Abbot, England.

Kim, H. (1987), "L. A. is at Center of Cellular War," *Los Angeles Business Journal*, 1, July 27.

Kim, T. J. (1983), "A Combined Land Use-Transportation Model When Zonal Travel Demand is Endogenously Determined," *Transportation Research B* **17**, 449-462.

Kim, T. J. (1989), *Integrated Urban Systems Modeling: Theory and Applications*, Kluwer Academic Publishers, Dordrecht, The Netherlands.

Kinderlehrer, D., and Stampacchia, G. (1980), *An Introduction to Variational Inequalities and Their Applications*, Academic Press, New York.

Kista Science Park (2001), http://www.kistasciencepark.org/kspab.html

Kleinrock, L. (1961), "Information Flow in Large Communication Nets," RLE Quarterly Progress Report, July.

Kleinrock, L. (1964), *Communication Nets: Stochastic Message Flow and Delay*, McGraw-Hill, New York.

Knight, F. H. (1924), "Some Fallacies in the Interpretation of Social Cost," *Quarterly Journal of Economics* **38**, 582-606.

Kobayashi, K. (1994), "Incomplete Information, Rational Expectations and Network Equilibria – An Analytical Perspective for Route Guidance Systems," *Annals of Regional Science* **28**, 369-393.

Kolata, G. (1990), "What if They Closed 42nd Street and Nobody Noticed?" *The New York Times*, December 25, C1.

Korilis, Y. A., Lazar, A. A., and Orda, A. (1999),"Avoiding the Braess Paradox in Non-Cooperative Networks," *Journal of Applied Probability* **36**, 211-222.

Korpelevich, G. M. (1977), "The Extragradient Method for Finding Saddle Points and Other Problems," *Matekon* **13**, 35-49.

Kuglin, F. A., and Rosenbaum, B. A. (2001), *The Supply Chain Network @ Internet Speed*, American Management Association, New York.

Kuhn, H. W., and Tucker A. W. (1951), "Nonlinear Programming," in *Proceedings of Second Berkeley Symposium on Mathematical Statistics and Probability*, pp. 481-492, J. Neyman, editor, University of California Press, Berkeley, California.

Labaton, S. (2000), "F.C.C. to Promote a Trading System to Sell AirWaves," *The New York Times*, March 13, 2000, p. A1.

Lee, S. M., and Chesser, D. L. (1980), "Goal Programming for Portfolio Selection," *The Journal of Portfolio Management*, Spring, 22-26.

Leiner, B. M., Cerf, V. G., Clark, D. D., Kahn, R. E., Kleinrock, L., Lynch, D. C., Postel, J., Roberts, L. G., and Wolff, S. (2000), "A Brief History of the Internet," last revised August 4, 2000.
http://www.isoc.org/internet/history/brief.shtml

Leurent, F. (1993a), "Cost versus Time Equilibrium over a Network," *European Journal of Operations Research* **71**, 205-221.

Leurent, F. (1993b), "Modelling Elastic, Disaggregate Demand," in *Proceedings of the First Meeting of the Euro Working Group on Urban Traffic and Transportation*, J. C. Morenos Banos, B. Friedrich, M. Papageorgiou, and H. Keller, editors, Technical University of Munich, Munich, Germany.

Leurent, F. (1996), "The Theory and Practice of a Dual Criteria Assignment Model with Continuously Distributed Values-of-Times," in *Transportation and Traffic Theory*, pp. 455-477, J. B. Lesort, editor, Pergamon, Exeter, England.

Licklider, J. C. R., and Clark, W. (1962), "On-Line Man Computer Communication," Massachusetts Institute of Technology, Cambridge, Massachusetts, August.

Lintner, J. (1965), "Security Prices, Risk, and Maximal Gains from Diversification, *The Journal of Finance*, December, 587-615.

Los, M. (1979), "Combined Residential Location and Transportation Models," *Environment and Planning A* **11**, 1241-1265.

Los Altos Town Crier (1998), "Professionals Review Silicon Valley Ups, Downs," February 25, 1998.
http://www.losaltosonline.com/latc/arch/1998/08/Business/1review/1review.html

Lundqvist, L. (1996), "Using Combined Network Equilibrium Models for Environmental Assessments of Land-Use/Transportation Scenarios," in *Transport, Land-Use and the Environment*, Y. Hayashi and J. Roy, editors, Kluwer Academic Publishers, Dordrecht, The Netherlands.

Lundqvist, L. (1998) "A Combined Model for Analysing Network Infrastructure and Land-Use/Transportation Interactions," in *Network Infrastructure and the Environment*, pp. 329-343, L. Lundqvist, L.-G. Mattsson, and T. J. Kim, editors, Springer-Verlag, Berlin, Germany.

Lundqvist, L. (1999), "Analysing Transport, Land-Use and the Environment in the Stockholm Region," in *Urban Transport V*, L. J. Sucharov, editor, WIT Press, Southampton, United Kingdom.

Lundqvist, L., and Mattsson, L.-G. (1983), "Transportation Systems and Residential Location," *European Journal of Operational Research* **12**, 279-294.

Lundqvist, L., Mattsson, L.-G., and Kim, T. J., editors (1998), *Network Infrastructure and the Urban Environment: Advances in Spatial Systems Modelling*, Springer-Verlag, Heidelberg. Germany.

Lyne, J. (2000), "Sprint PCS: Locating to Beat the Labor Pinch Blues," *Site Selection Magazine*, July, p. 2.

Mahmassani, H. (1990), "Dynamic Models of Commuter Behavior: Experimental Investigation and Application to the Analysis of Planned Traffic Disruptions," *Transportation Research A* **24**, 465-484.

Mahmassani, H. S., Peeta, S., Hu, T. Y., and Ziliaskopoulos, A. (1993), "Dynamic Traffic Assignment with Multiple User Classes for Real-Time ATIS /ATMS Applications," in *Large Urban Systems, Proceedings of the Advanced Traffic Management Conference*, pp. 91-114, Federal Highway Administration, US Department of Transportation, Washington, DC.

Marcotte, P. (1998), "Reformulations of a Bicriterion Equilibrium Model," in *Reformulation: Nonsmooth, Piecewise Smooth, Semismooth and Smoothing Methods*, pp. 269-292, M. Fukushima and L. Qi, editors, Kluwer Academic Publishers, Dordrecht, The Netherlands.

Marcotte, P., Nguyen, S., and Tanguay, K. (1996), "Implementation of an Efficient Algorithm for the Multiclass Traffic Assignment Problem," in *Proceedings of the 13th International Symposium on Transportation and Traffic Theory*, pp. 217-226, J. B. Lesort, editor, Pergamon Press.

Marcotte, P., and Zhu, D. (1994), "An Efficient Algorithm for a Bicriterion Traffic Assignment Problem," in *Proceedings of TRISTAN II*, pp. 891–897, Capri, Italy.

Marcotte, P., and Zhu, D. (1997), "Equilibria with Infinitely Many Differentiated Classes of Customers," in *Complementarity and Variational Problems. State of the Art*, pp. 234-258, M. C. Ferris and J. S. Pang, editors, SIAM, Philadelphia, Pennsylvania.

Markowitz, H.M. (1952), "Portfolio Selection," *The Journal of Finance* **7**, 77-91.

Markowitz, H. M. (1959), *Portfolio Selection: Efficient Diversification of Investments*, John Wiley & Sons, New York.

Martel, J. M., Khoury, N. T., and Bergeron, M. (1988), "An Application of a Multicriteria Approach to Portfolio Comparisons," *Journal of the Operational Research Society* **19**, 617-628.

Memmott III, F. W. (1963), "The Substitutability of Communications for Transportation," *Traffic Engineering* **33**, 20-25.

Mentzer, J. T., editor (2001), *Supply Chain Management*, Sage Publishers, Thousand Oaks, California.

Miller, T. C. (2001), *Hierarchical Operations and Supply Chain Planning*, Springer-Verlag, London, England.

The Modesto Bee Online (2001), "Report: Traffic, Expense Threats to Silicon Valley," modestobee.com.
http://www.modbee.com/business/story/0,1157,202942,00.html

Mokhtarian, P. L. (1990), "A Typology of Relationships between Telecommunications and Transportation," *Transportation Research A* **24**, 231-242.

Mokhtarian, P. L. (1991), "Telecommuting and Travel: State of the Practice, State of the Art," *Transportation* **18**, 319-342.

Mokhtarian, P. L. (1998), "A Synthetic Approach to Estimating the Impacts of Telecommuting on Travel," *Urban Studies* **35**, 215-241.

Mokhtarian, P. L., Handy, S. L., and Salomon, I. (1995), "Methodological Issues in the Estimation of Travel, Energy, and Air Quality Impacts of Telecommuting," *Transportation Research A* **29**, 283-302.

Mokhtarian, P. L., and Salomon, I. (2002), "Emerging Travel Patterns: Do Telecommunications Make a Difference?" in *In Perpetual Motion: Travel Behaviour Research Opportunities and Application Challenges*, H. S. Mahmassani, editor, Pergamon Press/Elsevier, The Netherlands, in press.

Mossin, J. (1966), "Equilibrium in a Capital Asset Market," *Econometrica* **34**, 768-783.

Muhlemann, A. P., Lockett, A. G., and Gear, A. E. (1978), "Portfolio Modelling in Multiple-Criteria Situations under Uncertainty," *Decision Sciences* **9**, 612-626.

Mulvey, J. M. (1987), "Nonlinear Networks in Finance," *Advances in Mathematical Programming and Financial Planning* **1**, 253-271.

Murchland, J. D. (1970), "Braess's Paradox of Traffic Flow," *Transportation Research* **4**, 391-394.

Nagurney, A. (1989), "Migration Equilibrium and Variational Inequalities," *Economics Letters* **31**, 109-112.

Nagurney, A. (1994), "Variational Inequalities in the Analysis and Computation of Multi-Sector, Multi-Instrument Financial Equilibria," *Journal of Economic Dynamics and Control* **18**, 161-184.

Nagurney, A. (1999), *Network Economics: A Variational Inequality Approach*, second and revised edition, Kluwer Academic Publishers, Dordrecht, The Netherlands.

Nagurney, A. (2000a), "Navigating the Network Economy," *OR/MS Today*, June, pp. 74-75, Lionheart Publishing Company, Atlanta, Georgia.

Nagurney, A. (2000b), "Distinguished Faculty Lecture: Networks for Fun and Profit," April 5, University of Massachusetts, Amherst.
http://intra.som.umass.edu/fomgt/dislec.pdf

Nagurney, A. (2000c), *Sustainable Transportation Networks*, Edward Elgar Publishing Company, Cheltenham, England.

Nagurney, A. (2000d), "A Multiclass, Multicriteria Traffic Network Equilibrium Model," *Mathematical and Computer Modelling* **32**, 393-411.

Nagurney, A. (2000e), "Congested Urban Transportation Networks and Emission Paradoxes," *Transportation Research D* **5**, 145-151.

Nagurney, A. (2001), "Finance and Variational Inequalities," *Quantitative Finance* **1**, 309-317.

Nagurney, A., and Aronson, J. (1989), "A General Dynamic Spatial Price Network Equilibrium Model with Gains and Losses," *Networks* **19**, 751-769.

Nagurney, A., and Dong, J. (1995), "Formulation and Computation of General Financial Equilibrium with Transaction Costs," *Advances in Mathematical Programming and Financial Planning* **4**, 3-24.

Nagurney, A., and Dong, J. (1996a), "General Financial Equilibrium Modeling with Policy Interventions and Transaction Costs," *Computational Economics* **9**, 3-17.

Nagurney, A., and Dong, J. (1996b), "Network Decomposition of General Financial Equilibrium with Transaction Costs," *Networks* **28**, 107-116.

Nagurney, A., and Dong, J. (2000), "A Multiclass, Multicriteria Traffic Network Equilibrium Model with Elastic Demand," to appear in *Transportation Research B*.

Nagurney, A., and Dong, J. (2001), "Paradoxes in Networks with Zero Emission Links: Implications for Telecommunications versus Transportation," *Transportation Research D* **6**, 283-296.

Nagurney, A., and Dong, J. (2002), "Urban Location and Transportation in the Information Age: A Multiclass, Multicriteria Network Equilibrium Perspective," *Environment & Planning B* **29**, 53-74.

Nagurney, A., Dong, J., and Hughes, M. (1992), "Formulation and Computation of General Financial Equilibrium," *Optimization* **26**, 339-354.

Nagurney, A., Dong, J., and Mokhtarian, P. L. (2000), "Integrated Multicriteria Network Equilibrium Models for Commuting Versus Telecommuting," Isenberg School of Management, University of Massachusetts, Amherst, Massachusetts.

Nagurney, A., Dong, J., and Mokhtarian, P. L. (2001a), "Teleshopping versus Shopping: A Multicriteria Network Equilibrium Framework," *Mathematical and Computer Modelling* **34**, 783-798.

Nagurney, A., Dong, J., and Mokhtarian, P. L. (2001b), "Multicriteria Network Equilibrium Modeling with Variable Weights for Decision-Making in the Information Age with Applications to Telecommuting and Teleshopping," to appear in *Journal of Economic Dynamics and Control*.

Nagurney, A., Dong, J., and Mokhtarian, P. L. (2001c), "A Space-Time Network for Telecommuting versus Commuting Decision-Making," to appear in *Papers in Regional Science*.

Nagurney, A., Dong, J., and Zhang, D. (2000), "Multicriteria Spatial Price Networks: Statics and Dynamics," to appear in *Equilibrium Problems and Variational Models*, P. Daniele, A. Maugeri, and F. Giannessi, editors, Kluwer Academic Publishers, Dordrecht, The Netherlands.

Nagurney, A., Dong, J., and Zhang, D. (2001), "A Supply Chain Network Equilibrium Model," to appear in *Transportation Research E*.

Nagurney, A., Dupuis, P., and Zhang, D. (1994), "A Dynamical Systems Approach for Network Oligopolies and Variational Inequalities," *Annals of Regional Science* **28**, 263-283.

Nagurney, A., and Hughes, M. (1992), "Financial Flow of Funds Networks," *Networks* **2**, 145-161.

Nagurney, A., and Ke, K. (2001a), "Financial Networks with Intermediation," *Quantitative Finance* **1**, 441-451.

Nagurney, A., and Ke, K. (2001b), "Dynamics of Financial Networks with Intermediation," Isenberg School of Management, University of Massachusetts, Amherst, Massachusetts.

Nagurney, A., Ke, K., Cruz, J., Hancock, K., and Southworth, F. (2001), "Dynamics of Supply Chains: A Multilevel (Logistical/Informational/Financial) Network Perspective," Isenberg School of Management, University of Massachusetts, Amherst, Massachusetts.

Nagurney, A., and Kim, D. S. (1991), "Parallel Computation of Large-Scale Dynamic Market Network Equilibria via Time Period Decomposition," *Mathematical and Computer Modelling* **15**, 55-67.

Nagurney, A., Loo, J., Dong, J., and Zhang, D. (2001), "Supply Chain Networks and Electronic Commerce: A Theoretical Perspective," Isenberg School of Management, University of Massachusetts, Amherst, Massachusetts.

Nagurney, A., and Siokos, S. (1997), *Financial Networks: Statics and Dynamics*, Springer-Verlag, Berlin, Germany.

Nagurney, A., Takayama, T., and Zhang, D. (1995a), "Massively Parallel Computation of Spatial Price Equilibrium Problems as Dynamical Systems," *Journal of Economic Dynamics and Control* **18**, 3-37.

Nagurney, A., Takayama, T., and Zhang, D. (1995b), "Projected Dynamical Systems and Computation of Spatial Network Equilibria," *Networks* **26**, 69-85.

Nagurney, A., and Zhang, D. (1996), *Projected Dynamical Systems and Variational Inequalities with Applications*, Kluwer Academic Publishers, Boston, Massachusetts.

Nagurney, A., and Zhang, D. (1997), "Projected Dynamical Systems in the Formulation, Stability Analysis, and Computation of Fixed Demand Traffic Network Equilibria," *Transportation Science* **31**, 147-158.

Nagurney, A., and Zhang, D. (2001), "Dynamics of a Transportation Pollution Permit System with Stability Analysis and Computations," *Transportation Research D* **6**, 243-268.

Nagurney, A., Zhang, D., and Dong, J. (2002), "Spatial Economic Networks with Multicriteria Producers and Consumers: Statics and Dynamics," *Annals of Regional Science*, in press.

Nagurney, A., and Zhao, L. (1993), "Networks and Variational Inequalities in the Formulation and Computation of Market Disequilibria: The Case of Direct Demand Functions," *Transportation Science* **27**, 4-15.

Nash, J. F. (1950), "Equilibrium Points in N-Person Games," *Proceedings of the National Academy of Sciences* **36**, 48-49.

Nash, J. F. (1951), "Noncooperative Games," *Annals of Mathematics* **54**, 286-298.

National Research Council (1988), "Towards a National Research Network," Washington, DC.

National Research Council (1994), "Realizing the Information Future: The Internet and Beyond," Washington, DC.

National Research Council (2000), "Surviving Supply Chain Integration: Strategies for Small Manufacturers," Committee on Supply Chain Integration, Board on Manufacturing and Engineering Design, Commission on Engineering and Technical Systems, Washington, DC.

Negroponte, N. (1995), *Being Digital*, Knopf, New York.

Nijkamp, P., Pepping, G., and Banister, D. (1996), *Telematics and Transport Behaviour*, Springer-Verlag, Heidelberg, Germany.

Nilles, J. M. (1988), "Traffic Reduction by Telecommuting: A Status Review and Selected Bibliography," *Transportation Research A* **22**, 301-317.

Nilles, J. M., Carlson, Jr., F. R., Gray, P., and Hanneman, G. J. (1976), *The Telecommunications–Transportation Tradeoff: Options for Tomorrow*, John Wiley & Sons, New York.

Noveen, A., Hartenstein, V., and Chuong, C.-M. (1998), "Gene Networks and Supernetworks: Evolutionarily Conserved Gene Interactions," in *Molecular Basis of Epithelial Appendage Morphogenesis*, pp. 371-391, C.-M. Chuong, editor, Landes Bioscience, Austin, Texas.
http://www.eurekah.com/reports/development/chuong/119/

Papageorgiou, M. (1990), "Dynamic Modelling, Assignment, and Route Guidance in Traffic Networks," *Transportation Research B*, **24**, 471-495.

Pas, E., and Principio, S. I. (1996),"Braess' Paradox: Some New Insights," *Transportation Research B* **31**, 265-276.

Pigou, A. C. (1920), *The Economics of Welfare*, Macmillan, London, England.

Pogue, G.A. (1970), "An Extension of the Markowitz Portfolio Selection Model to Include Variable Transactions' Costs, Short Sales, Leverage Policies and Taxes," *The Journal of Finance* **15**, 1005-1027.

Poirier, C. C. (1996), *Supply Chain Optimization: Building a Total Business Network*, Berrett-Kochler Publishers, San Francisco, California.

Poirier, C. C. (1999), *Advanced Supply Chain Management: How to Build a Sustained Competitive Advantage*, Berrett-Kochler Publishers, San Francisco, California.

Powell, W. B., Odoni, A., and Jaillet, P. (1995), "Stochastic and Dynamic Network Routing," in *Handbooks in Operations Research and Management Science* **4**, pp. 141-295, M. O. Ball, T. L. Magnanti, C. L. Monma, and G. L. Nemhauser, editors, Elsevier Science, Amsterdam, The Netherlands.

PR Newswire (2000), "Small Business E-Commerce Solutions Remove Barriers to Trading in Corporate Supply Chain Networks," June 14.

Purchasing (2000), "Corporate Buyers Spent $517.6 Billion on Telecommunication," **128**, 110.

Quandt, R. E. (1967), "A Probabilistic Abstract Mode Model," in *Studies in Travel Demand VIII*, pp. 127-149, Mathematica, Inc., Princeton, New Jersey.

Quesnay, F. (1758), *Tableau Economique*, reproduced in facsimile with an introduction by H. Higgs by the British Economic Society, 1895.

Ramjerdi, F. (1999), "Transport and Land Use in the Information Society," TRITA-IP FR 99-53, Division of Transport and Location Analysis, Royal Institute of Technology, Stockholm, Sweden.

Ran, B., and Boyce, D. E. (1996), *Modeling Dynamic Transportation Networks*, Springer-Verlag, Berlin, Germany.

Resende, M. G. C. (2000), personal communication.

Rios-Garcia, S., and Rio Insura, S. (1983), "The Portfolio Selection Problem with Multiattributes and Multiple Criteria," in *Essays and Surveys on Multiple Criteria Decision Making, Lecture Notes in Economics and Mathematical Systems* **209**, pp. 317-325, P. Hansen, editor, Springer Verlag, Berlin, Germany.

Roberts, L. (1967), "Multiple Computer Networks and Intercomputer Communication," ACM Gaitlinburg Conference, October.

Roberts, L., and Merrill, T. (1966), "Toward a Cooperative Network of Time-Shared Computers," Fall, AFIPS Conference, October.

Rustem, B. (1998), *Algorithms for Nonlinear Programming and Multiple-Objective Decisions*, John Wiley & Sons, Chichester, England.

Safwat, K. N. A., and Magnanti, T. L. (1988), "A Combined Trip Generation, Trip Distribution, Modal Split, and Trip Assignment Model," *Transportation Science* **18**, 14-30.

Salomon, I. (1986), "Telecommunications and Travel Relationships: A Review," *Transportation Research A* **20**, 223-238.

Samuelson, P. A. (1952), "Spatial Price Equilibrium and Linear Programming," *American Economic Review* **42**, 283-303.

Schneider, M. (1968), "Access and Land Development," in *Urban Development Models*, Highway Research Board Special Report **97**, pp. 164-177.

Shapiro, C. and Varian, H. (1999), *Information Rules: A Strategic Guide to the Network Economy*, Harvard Business School Press, Cambridge, Massachusetts.

Sharpe, W. F. (1964), "Capital Asset Prices: A Theory of Market Equilibrium under Conditions of Risk," *The Journal of Finance* **19**, 425-442.

Sheffi, Y. (1978), "Transportation Network Equilibrium with Discrete Choice Models," Ph.D. thesis, Civil Engineering Department, Massachusetts Institute of Technology, Cambridge, Massachusetts.

Sheffi, Y. (1985), *Urban Transportation Networks – Equilibrium Analysis with Mathematical Programming Methods*, Prentice-Hall, Englewood Cliffs, New Jersey.

Sheffi, Y., and Daganzo, C. F. (1978), "Hypernetworks and Supply-Demand Equilibrium Obtained with Disaggregate Demand Models," *Transportation Research Record* **673**, 113-121.

Sheffi, Y., and Daganzo, C. F. (1980), "Computation of Equilibrium over Transportation Networks: The Case of Disaggregate Demand Models," *Transportation Science* **14**, 155-173.

Shore, J. (2000), "Telework - The Future is Now," Office of Governmentwide Policy, U. S. General Services Administration, October, 2000.
http://www.pueblo.gsa.gov/telework.html

SiliconValley.com (2001), "Commuters Noticing Less Traffic, Smoother Trips." http://www.siliconvalley.com/cgi-bin/printpage/printpage.pl

Silicon Valley/San Jose Business Journal (2001), "Bay Area Traffic Congestion Worsens," May 7, 2001.
http://sanjose.bcentral.com/sanjose/stories/2001/05 /07/daily7.html

Slats, P. A., Bhola, B., Evers, J. J., and Dijkhuizen, G. (1995), "Logistic Chain Modelling," *European Journal of Operations Research* **87**, 1-20.

Slavin, H. (1996), "An Integrated Dynamic Approach to Travel Demand Forecasting," *Transportation* **23**, 313-350.

Smith, M. J. (1979), "Existence, Uniqueness, and Stability of Traffic Equilibria," *Transportation Research B* **13**, 259-304.

Smith, M. J. (1984), "The Stability of a Dynamic Model of Traffic Assignment–An Application of a Method of Lyapunov," *Transportation Science* **18**, 245-252.

Smith, M. J. (1993), "A New Dynamic Traffic Model and the Existence and Calculation of Dynamic User Equilibria on a Congested Capacity Constrained Road Network," *Transportation Research B* **27**, 49-63.

Southworth, F. (2000), "E-Commerce: Implications for Freight," Oak Ridge National Lavoratory, Oak Ridge, Tennessee.

Spronk, J. (1981), *Interactive Multiple Goal Programming Applications to Financial Planning*, Martinus Nijhoff Publishers, Boston, Massachusetts.

Stadtler, H., and Kilger, C., editors (2000), *Supply Chain Management and Advanced Planning*, Springer-Verlag, Berlin, Germany.

Standage, T. (1999), *The Victorian Internet: The Remarkable Story of the Telegraph and Nineteenth Century's On-Line Pioneers*, Berkly Books, New York.

Steinberg, R., and Zangwill, W. (1983), "The Prevalence of Braess' Paradox," *Transportation Science* **17**, 302-318.

Stevens, B. H. (1961), "Linear Programming and Location Rent," *Journal of Regional Science* **3**, 15-26.

Stewart, T. J., and van den Honert, editors (1998), *Trends in Multicriteria Decision Making, Lecture Notes in Economics and Mathematical Systems* **465**, Springer-Verlag, Berlin, Germany.

Stockholm's City Planning Administration (2001).
http://www.sbk.stockholm.se

Storoy, S., Thore, S., and Boyer, M. (1975), "Equilibrium in Linear Capital Market Networks," *The Journal of Finance* **30**, 1197-1211.

Takayama, T., and Judge, G. G. (1971), *Spatial and Temporal Price and Allocation Models*, North-Holland, Amsterdam, The Netherlands.

Tedeschi, B. (2001), "GE Has a Bright Idea," in Ziff Davis Smart Business for the New Economy, June 1, 2001.
http://www.smartbusinessmag.com/print_article/0,3668,a%253D82 35,00.asp

Telecom 95 (1995), "MCI and the Internet: Dr. Vinton G. Cerf, Keynote Address."
http://www.itu.int/TELECOM/wt95/pressdocs/papers/cerf.html

Thore, S. (1969), "Credit Networks," *Economica* **36**, 42-57.

Thore, S. (1980), *Programming the Network of Financial Intermediation*, Universitetsforslaget, Oslo, Norway.

Toffler, A. (1980), *The Third Wave*, William Morrow & Company, New York.

Tzeng, G.-H., and Chen, C.-H. (1993), "Multiobjective Decision Making for Traffic Assignment," *IEEE Transactions on Engineering Management* **40**, 180-187.

United States (2000), Public Law # 106-346, Washington, DC.

United States Department of Commerce (2000), Statistical Abstract of the United States, Bureau of the Census, Washington, DC.

United States Department of Transportation (1992a), "A Summary: Transportation Programs and Provisions of the Clean Air Act Ammendments of 1990," Publication Number: FHWA-PD-92-023.

United States Department of Transportation (1992b), "A Summary: Air Quality Programs and Provisions of the Intermodal Surface Transportation Efficiency Act of 1991, 1992," Publication Number: FHWA-PD-92-022.

United States Department of Transportation (1999), "Guide to Transportation," Bureau of Transportation Statistics, BTS99-06, Washington, DC.

Vickrey, W. S. (1960), "Statement to the Joint Committee on Washington Metropolitan Problems," *Transportation Plan for the National Capital Region*, Hearings, Joint Committee on Washington Metropolitan Problems, November 8-14, 1959, pp. 454-490. Excerpt reprinted in *Journal of Urban Economics* **36** (1994), 42-65.

Vickrey, W. S. (1963), "Pricing in Urban and Suburban Transport," *American Economic Review, Papers and Proceedings* **53**, 452-465.

Vogel, C. M. (1990), "Inheritance Reasoning and Head-Driven Phrase Structure and Grammar," Masters thesis, School of Computing Science, Simon Fraser University, Burnaby, Canada.

Wallich, P. (1995), "The Chilling Wind of Copyright Law?" *Scientific American*, February, 30.

Wardrop, J. G. (1952), "Some Theoretical Aspects of Road Traffic Research," *Proceedings of the Institute of Civil Engineers*, Part II, pp. 325-378.

Watling, D. (1996), "Asymmetric Problems and Stochastic Process Models of Traffic Assignment," *Transportation Research B* **30**, 339-357.

Wegener, M. (1986), "Transport Network Equilibrium and Regional Deconcentration," *Environment and Planning A* **18**, 437-456.

Whinston, A. B., Stahl, D. O., and Choi S.-Y. (1997), *The Economics of Electronic Commerce*, Macmillan Technical Publications, Indianapolis, Indiana.

Wilson, A. G. (1973), "Travel Demand Forecasting: Achievements and Problems," HRB, Special Report **143**.

Wu, J. H., Chen, Y., and Florian, M. (1998), "The Continuous Dynamic Network Loading Problem: A Mathematical Formulation and Solution Method," *Transportation Research B* **32**, 173-187.

Wu, J. H., Florian, M., and He, S. G. (2000), "EMME/2 Implementation of the SCAG-II Model: Data Structure, System Analysis and Computation," submitted to the Southern California Association of Governments, INRO Solutions Internal Report, Montreal, Quebec, Canada.

Yang, H., and Meng, Q. (1998), "An Integrated Network Equilibrium Model of Urban Location and Travel Choices," *Journal of Regional Science* **38**, 575-598.

Yu, P. L. (1985), *Multiple-Criteria Decision Making – Concepts, Techniques, and Extensions*, Plenum Press, New York.

Yu, P. L., and Zhang, D. (1992), "Multicriteria Optimization," in *Handbook of Industrial Engineering*, second edition, pp. 2672-2693, G. Salvendy, editor, John Wiley & Sons, New York.

Zeleny, M. (1982), *Multiple-Criteria Decision Making*, McGraw-Hill, New York.

Zhang, D., and Nagurney, A. (1995), "On the Stability of Projected Dynamical Systems," *Journal of Optimization Theory and Applications* **85**, 97-124.

Zhang, D., and Nagurney, A. (1996), "Stability Analysis of an Adjustment Process for Oligopolistic Market Equilibrium Modeled as a Projected Dynamical System," *Optimization* **36**, 263-285.

Zhang, D., and Nagurney, A. (1997), "Formulation, Stability, and Computation of Traffic Network Equilibria as Projected Dynamical Systems," *Journal of Optimization Theory and Applications* **93**, 417-444.

Zhang, D., Nagurney, A., and Wu, J. H. (2001), "On the Equivalence between Stationary Link Flow Patterns and Traffic Network Equilibria," *Transportation Research B* **35**, 731-748.

Zhao, L. (1989), "Variational Inequalities in General Equilibrium: Analysis and Computation," Ph.D. Thesis, Division of Applied Mathematics, Brown University, Providence, Rhode Island; also appears as: LCDS # 88-24, Lefschetz Center for Dynamical Systems, Brown University, Providence, Rhode Island, 1988.

Zhao, L., and Dafermos, S. (1991), "General Economic Equilibrium and Variational Inequalities," *Operations Research Letters* **10**, 369-376.

Zhao, L., and Nagurney, A. (1993), "A Network Formalism for Pure Exchange Economic Equilibria," in *Network Optimization Problems: Algorithms, Complexity and Applications*, pp. 363-386, D. Z. Du and P. M. Pardalos, editors, World Scientific Press, Singapore.

Zopounidis, C. (2001), "Financial Applications of Multicriteria Analysis," in *Encyclopedia of Optimization* **II**, pp. 114-125, C. A. Floudas and P. M. Pardalos, editors, Kluwer Academic Publishers, Boston, Massachusetts.

Glossary of Notation

This is a glossary of symbols used in this book. Other symbols are defined in the book as needed. A vector is assumed to be a column vector, unless noted otherwise.

$\in$	an element of
$\subset$	subset of
$\cup, \cap$	union, intersection
$\forall$	for all
$\exists$	there exists
R	the real line
R^n	Euclidean n-dimensional space
R^n_+	Euclidean n-dimensional space on the nonnegative orthant
:	such that; also $\mid$
$\equiv$	is equivalent to
$\mapsto$	maps to
$\rightarrow$	tends to
$\circ$	composition
$\|x\| = (\sum_{i=1}^n x_i^2)^{\frac{1}{2}}$	length of $x \in R^n$ with components $(x_1, x_2, \ldots, x_n)$
x^T	transpose of a vector x
$\langle x, x \rangle$	inner product of vector x where $\langle x, x \rangle = x_1^2 + \ldots + x_n^2$
$x^T \cdot x$	also denotes the inner product of x
$\|y\|$	absolute value of y
$[a, b]\,; (a, b)$	a closed interval; an open interval in R
∇f	gradient of $f : R^n \mapsto R$
∇F	the $n \times n$ Jacobian of a mapping $F : R^n \mapsto R^n$
$\frac{\partial f}{\partial x}$	partial derivative of f with respect to x
$\mathrm{argmin}_{x \in K} f(x)$	the set of $x \in K$ attaining the minimum of $f(x)$
A^T	transpose of the matrix A
A^{-1}	the inverse of the matrix A
I	the identity matrix
lim	limit

Index